GW00501305

OFFICIAL HISTORY OF THE AMATEUR ATHLETIC ASSOCIATION

OFFICIAL HISTORY OF THE AMATEUR ATHLETIC ASSOCIATION

Mel Watman

SPORTS
BOOKS

Published in Great Britain by
SportsBooks Limited
1 Evelyn Court
Malvern Road
Cheltenham
GL50 2JR

© Mel Watman and the AAA 2011
First Published June 2011

Most of the photographs have been
supplied by Mark Shearman

The photograph of Her Majesty The Queen is the copyright of
www.royalimages.co.uk

Cover designed by Alan Hunns.

A catalogue record for this book is available from
the British Library.

ISBN 9781907524 01 1

Printed and bound in England by TJI International.

CONTENTS

FOREWORD

by Sir Chris Chataway

NO ORGANISATION HAS played a more central role in the world history of athletics than the AAA and there can be no better person to tell its story than Mel Watman. His working life has been devoted to the sport and anything that he does not know about athletics just cannot be worth knowing.

My qualification for offering this comment is that I must be regarded as the most persistent loser of middle distance races in the history of the AAA Championships. I succeeded in losing the Three Miles by inches on no less than three occasions. Even in 1954 when I broke the world record I was beaten by Freddie Green, who was given the same time. So I can be forgiven, I hope, for still retaining a rather equivocal attitude to the initials AAA. But despite all that I have no hesitation in giving the warmest welcome to this book.

You will find here all the facts and all the figures of the people who have dominated track and field for a century and a half. At the beginning of each decade are listed the prevailing records for each event illustrating the way in which the almost unbelievable for one generation becomes commonplace for the next. But the book is much more than a dry record.

There are the statistics here about Harold Abrahams, 1924 winner of the Olympic 100 metres but there is also the real story behind Chariots of Fire. In the same generation Philip Noel-Baker never got more than a silver medal in the 1500 metres but we learn that later in life he achieved the even greater distinction of a Nobel Peace Prize for his efforts to promote disarmament. The author does not just know about the performance of the people, who flit across the stage. He is interested in them also as human beings.

The story of the AAA is a fascinating part of British social history. It was founded for gentlemen amateurs, who did not wish to mix with professional runners; nor since they were generally faster did the gentlemen wish to compete against them. As social attitudes changed so did the sport and the governing body – usually as a result of fiercely fought controversies.

In due course the gentlemen were prepared to compete against tradesmen and artisans just as long as they gained no material reward from the sport. Geoff Dyson, later the first national coach, had to retire as a high hurdler at his peak because he had taken a job as a sports lecturer at Loughborough College.

It seems extraordinary now that amateurism should have been seen as something grand and noble by otherwise sensible people. Would Shakespeare or Leonardo da Vinci really have been so much better if they had not been paid? But for athletics as for other sports it was a long and bruising struggle before the organisation came to terms with the fact that the first word of its title was no longer operative.

The AAA came into being to serve a new sport. After a while it became its governing body in England and Wales. Over the decades it changed and adapted with the sport. Eventually relieved of its administrative role the AAA has sought new ways of serving athletics. May this great history by Mel Watman be an inspiration in its new role.

INTRODUCTION

SOME THIRTY YEARS ago a splendid book entitled "The Official Centenary History of the Amateur Athletic Association", by Peter Lovesey, was published to mark that special occasion. Much has happened since then and in this volume I have attempted not only to bring the story up to date but reflect also on that first century of the sport's oldest national governing body. I have not gone into the fine detail which was such a feature of Peter Lovesey's work but have provided a broad historical framework, together with highlights of each senior AAA Championships meeting since the start in 1880. As the Centenary History contained a list of all AAA champions from 1880 to 1979 inclusive I have not duplicated that information, but have included all winners in all age groups, indoors as well as outdoors, since 1980. Some of those rolls of champions go back further than 1980 in age groups that were not included in the earlier book, and new championships like those for the Under-23s and Under-15s have been incorporated.

Another new feature is that where a title was won by an overseas athlete then the highest placed British competitor is listed too. Included also is an alphabetical "honours list" featuring the medal and record achievements of British male athletes who have performed with particular international distinction between 1900 and the present day. A section on the historic and valuable AAA trophies has kindly been provided by Jack Miller, with photos by Philip Andrew.

I am particularly gratified and honoured to have been invited by the AAA to write this book as, indirectly, it was the AAA which shaped my life. Until July 1950 when, aged 12, I went with a school party to the AAA Championships my passion had been railways. My trip to the White City changed all that; I was hooked by the sight of men like McDonald Bailey, Arthur Wint, Roger Bannister and Bill Nankeville going through their paces. I discovered *Athletics Weekly* soon afterwards and from that moment on I knew exactly what I wanted to do in life. My burning ambition now was to be an athletics reporter like Joe Binks, Doug Wilson or Roy Moor.

Despite my family and school careers master advising me to go into a "safe" job like banking, insurance or shipping as I prepared to leave school at 16, I was resolute ... journalism was the only career which fired my imagination. I started off in 1954 as a glorified office boy in a Fleet Street newspaper office and then spent three wonderful years learning my trade on a local paper, at the same time contributing articles and reports to *Athletics Weekly*. It seems quaint now, but in those long-distant days I was required to inform Ernest Clynes, the AAA Honorary Secretary, that I was now a professional journalist in order to preserve my amateur status as a very average club runner. At that time I would not have been allowed to continue to compete had I been receiving money for writing on athletics while working in some other field.

Eventually, after National Service in the RAF, I became a full-time employee at "AW", assisting and later succeeding Jimmy as editor of the magazine. It was a dream fulfilled, and all because of that magical school trip to the AAA Championships! Sixty years after that introduction I'm still mad on athletics, and still writing on the sport. How lucky I have been.

I dedicate this book to all who have competed in the AAA Championships, and to the largely unsung band of officials and coaches who have made that participation possible. This book is devoted solely to men's athletics; a history of the Women's AAA and WAAA Championships from 1922 (the WAAA merged with the AAA in 1991) is in the course of preparation.

Mel Watman
May 2011

ACKNOWLEDGEMENTS

IN COLLECTING MATERIAL for this book I have drawn heavily on my own files, collected over a period of 60 years, and such magazine sources as *Athletics Weekly*, *Athletics Today*, *Athletics International*, *Track Stats* and *Athletics World*, newspapers including *The Times* and *The Sporting Life*, British Olympic Association Olympic Reports, AAA Handbooks and programmes, and a multitude of publications by the National Union of Track Statisticians (NUTS), in particular *Progressive British Records (Men's Track Events*, 1994, by Ian Buchanan, Peter Lovesey, Ian Smith & Peter Matthews; and *Men's Field Events*, 1993, by Ian Tempest & Peter Matthews), *The AAA Championships 1880-1939* by Ian Buchanan (2003) and *Who's Who of UK & GB International Athletes 1896-1939* by Ian Buchanan (2000), as well as various NUTS Annuals and ATFS (Association of Track & Field Statisticians) & IAAF publications. The website www.gbrathletics.com has been particularly useful with its lists of champions originally compiled by Martin Rix, and I am also grateful for the immensely helpful co-operation of publisher Randall Northam (SportsBooks Ltd), ace photographer Mark Shearman, Peter Lovesey, Ian Tempest and various AAA officers, particularly George Bunner, Chris Carter, Walter Nicholls and Ken Oakley.

I would also like to express my sincere thanks to Sir Chris Chataway for his generous foreword. Chris was one of my early running heroes and I was fortunate enough to have squeezed into the White City just before the gates were shut that memorable autumnal night in 1954 when he won his epic 5000m duel with Vladimir Kuts. It remains, after all these years, the most enthralling race I've ever witnessed. Despite his modest reference to his defeats in the AAA 3 miles, Chris has always been a winner in life – world record breaker, British Empire Games champion, first recipient of the BBC's coveted Sports Personality of the Year award (in the year in which he helped Roger Bannister to sporting immortality), pioneering TV newscaster, successful politician and businessman. Still indecently fit for an octogenarian, he himself is one of the most remarkable figures in a book which celebrates the highest achievers in our sport's history.

Among other books I have consulted are:
Abrahams, Harold & Kerr, J Bruce – *AAA Championships 1880-1931* (AAA, 1932)
Abrahams, Harold – *Fifty Years of AAA Championships* (Carborundum Co Ltd, 1961)
Buchanan, Ian – *An Encyclopaedia of British Athletics Records* (Stanley Paul, 1961) and *British Olympians* (Guinness Publishing, 1991)
Duncanson, Neil & Collins, Patrick – *Tales of Gold* (Queen Anne Press, 1992)
Huxtable, Andrew – *A Statistical History of UK Track & Field Athletics* (NUTS, 1990)
Hymans, Richard – *Progression of World Best Performances & Official IAAF World Records* (IAAF, 2003)
Lovesey, Peter – *The Official Centenary History of the AAA* (Guinness Superlatives, 1979)
Matthews, Peter & Buchanan, Ian – *All-Time Greats of British & Irish Sport* (Guinness Publishing, 1995)
McWhirter, Norris & Ross – *Get To Your Marks!* (Nicholas Kaye, 1951)

Pash, H F (ed) – *Fifty Years of Progress 1880-1930: AAA Jubilee Souvenir* (AAA, 1930)

Phillips, Bob – *Honour of Empire, Glory of Sport: History of Athletics at the Commonwealth Games* (The Parrs Wood Press, 2000)

Pickering, Ron & Watman, Mel – *Athletics 74, 75, 76* (Queen Anne Press); *Athletics 77, 78, 79* (Macdonald & Jane's) and *Athletics 1980* (Athletics Weekly)

Quercetani, Roberto – *A World History of Track & Field Athletics* (Oxford University Press, 1964)

Rix, Martin & Whittingham, Rob – *British All-Time Lists* (Umbra Software, 1998)

Sheridan, Michael – *British Athletics 1946-1949* (2004), *British Athletics 1950* (2000 & 2004), *British Athletics 1951-1959* (2008) and *Who's Who of British International Athletes 1945-1960* (2010)

Watman, Mel – *The Encyclopaedia of Athletics* (Robert Hale, 1964, 1967, 1973, 1977, 1981); *History of British Athletics* (Robert Hale, 1968), *International Running Guide 1985 & 1986-87* (The Tantivy Press), *Olympic Track & Field History* (Athletics International & Shooting Star Media, 2004) and *All-Time Greats of British Athletics* (SportsBooks, 2006)

Webster, F A M – *Athletics of Today* (Warne, 1929) and *Great Moments in Athletics* (Country Life, 1947)

Whittingham, Rob, Jenes, Paul & Greenberg, Stan – *Athletics at the Commonwealth Games* (Umbra Athletics, 2002)

BIRTH OF THE AAA

THE SEEDS OF modern athletics were sown when the English public schools, recognising the sport's value in bringing out some of the best qualities in a boy, added it to the curriculum. The Crick Run, a tough cross country race, was inaugurated at Rugby in 1837, the year Queen Victoria began her reign; a school sports day was held at Shrewsbury from 1843; annual sprint, hurdle and steeplechase races were staged at Eton from 1845; and the universities' interest originated in 1850 at Exeter College, Oxford, where world record breakers Jack Lovelock and Roger Bannister would study many decades later. The first clash between Oxford and Cambridge, a fixture which survives to this day, was held in 1864.

For a while, organised amateur athletics was confined to public schoolboys, undergraduates and officer cadets, but by the 1860s young men of all backgrounds were finding opportunities to indulge in the sport – although not without opposition from some quarters. The Amateur Athletic Club (AAC), which organised "English Championships" from 1866 to 1879 until superseded by the Amateur Athletic Association (AAA) in 1880, was founded "to supply the want of an established ground upon which competitors in amateur athletic sports might take place, and to afford as completely as possible to all classes of gentlemen amateurs

5

the means of practising and competing against one another, without being compelled to mix with professional runners."

There were three categories of athlete in those times: the 'professional', the 'gentleman amateur' and the 'amateur'. The professionals were completely beyond the pale as far as the clubs and governing bodies were concerned but for several years the AAC and similar organisations would have nothing to do either with amateurs who happened to work for their living.

The AAC's definition of an amateur was: "No person shall be considered an amateur who has ever competed with or against a professional for any prize; who has ever taught, pursued, or assisted in the practice of athletic exercises of any kind as a means of obtaining a livelihood, or who is by trade or employment a mechanic, artisan, or labourer."

Gradually, though, the age-old barriers of class and privilege were broken down. The turning point, perhaps, was when William J. Morgan, the AAC 7 miles walk champion from 1873 to 1875, had his entry accepted for a meeting organised by the influential but traditionally elitist London Athletic Club. Outraged, several of the club's senior and more reactionary members threatened to resign in protest against such heresy (gadzooks, Morgan was a wage earner!) but eventually they were persuaded to accept the situation. It was a victory for democracy and enlightenment and from then on athletics in Britain would not look back.

Growing dissatisfaction with the AAC culminated in members of London Athletic Club boycotting the 1879 English Championships and holding their own version later in the season. The AAC went out of existence the following year when a meeting was held in Oxford to discuss the future of the English Championships and the outcome was the birth of the AAA.

Despite the social restrictions, those AAC Championships did yield a number of world best performances, including a 50.4 440 yards in 1868 by Edward Colbeck even though he collided with a sheep which had wandered on to the track! A report noted that the unfortunate animal stood motionless in Colbeck's path ... "being presumably amazed at the remarkable performance which the runner was accomplishing." The sheep came off the worse in this chance encounter for its leg was broken while Colbeck, despite losing an estimated eight yards (about one second in time), went on to set a record that withstood all assaults for 11 years. Another trail-blazing performance was a 1.80m (5ft 11in) high jump in 1874 by the 19-year-old Hon. Marshall Jones Brooks who would the same year gain an international cap at rugby. In 1876 he jumped an astounding 1.89m (6ft 2^1/2in) from a grass take-off for Oxford against Cambridge. Three weeks later, at the AAC Championships, he ended his brief but brilliant career by taking the title with one disdainful leap over 1.83m (6ft) – complete with top hat, or so the story goes.

With the establishment in 1879 of a Northern Counties Athletic Association (daringly, no mention of amateur in the title) and a Midland Counties AAA due to be formed the following year, athletics was changing fast. The time was ripe for the establishment of a truly national governing body with a more liberal outlook than the AAC.

As Peter Lovesey wrote in his Centenary History: "Athletics had undergone a transformation since the AAC was founded. It was no longer the exclusive pastime of a few enthusiasts in London and the Universities who styled themselves gentlemen. It had become a popular national sport. The upsurge of interest among working men in the North and Midlands now made nonsense of the AAC ban on mechanics, artisans and labourers, which had never been strictly enforced at the Championships. Unless action was taken, the sport would soon be split between regions, each with its own set of rules. There was an obvious need for a governing body everyone would respect."

Step forward three young men from Oxford University. Indian born Clement Jackson (33) was a tutor at Hertford

College and had been an outstanding high hurdler, clocking a time of 16.0 in 1865 which went unbeaten by another Briton for 30 years; Montague Shearman (23), was a graduate of St John's College and 1876 English 100 yards champion in 10.2; and Bernhard Wise (22), born in Australia of English parents, was a scholar at Queen's College, current President of Oxford University AC and winner of the mile in 4:29.0 at the AAC version of the 1879 English Championships.

They booked the banqueting hall of Oxford's celebrated Randolph Hotel for a meeting on 24 April 1880 to which representatives of the NCAA, MCAAA and the leading Southern clubs were invited. Amid a wide measure of agreement among the 28 delegates present, the AAA was set up with three main objectives: (1) To improve the management of athletic meetings, and to promote uniformity of rules for the guidance of local committees; (2) To deal repressively with any abuses of athletic sports; (3) To hold an annual championship meeting. Crucially, the reference to mechanics, artisans and labourers was removed from the amateur definition. The first and most influential national governing body in the world was open for business.

Although the AAA was founded as the governing body for amateur athletics throughout England and Wales, its influence was soon felt worldwide. Other countries modelled their national organisations and laws after the AAA, led by New Zealand in 1887, USA in 1888, Belgium and Canada in 1889, South Africa in 1894, Sweden in 1895. The AAA Rules for Competition, including the weight of throwing implements, number of attempts in field events and height of hurdles, were implemented for the first modern Olympic Games in 1896. From the outset, the AAA Championships were thrown open to the world and until the Olympics started to come into their own the meeting was regarded as the most prestigious of all. In so many ways it was the AAA which set the standard.

THE FIRST FORTY YEARS

Highlights from each of the AAA Championships meetings 1880–1919

1880 (held at Lillie Bridge Athletic Ground, West Brompton, London)

THE INAUGURAL AAA Championships were staged on July 3 with heavy rain falling throughout the meeting, a circumstance which would be repeated all too often over the next century or so! There were 80 entries in total (more than at any AAC Championships), but only one in the mile and shot. The walkover winner of that mile, the opening event and thus the first of thousands of AAA champions to follow, was the brightest athletics star of the Victorian era, Walter George. He sauntered round three laps of the cinder track in 4:28.6 and went on to take the 4 miles title in 20:45.8. One of the AAA's founders and its first Honorary Secretary, Montague Shearman (later to become the Right Hon. Sir Montague Shearman, PC, a distinguished barrister and judge), won the 440 yards in 52.2. The other events contested were 100 yards, 880 yards, 10 miles, steeplechase (1 mile 1440 yards on this occasion), 120 yards hurdles, high jump, pole vault, long jump, hammer and 7 miles walk. The AAA General Committee considered the Championships to be a complete success although they regretted there was a loss of £31 2s 2d on the meeting, which had cost £91 16s 2d to stage.

1881 (Aston Lower Grounds, Birmingham)

THE AAA'S POLICY for the first 20-odd years of its existence was to stage the Championships in rotation between London, the Midlands and the North. On a sunny day in Birmingham a crowd of 12,000 saw the versatile if skeletal American runner Lon Myers, the first man to treat the quarter-mile as a prolonged sprint rather than a middle-distance race and the only challenger to Walter George as the outstanding athlete of the 19th century, become the first overseas entrant to win a AAA title. Myers' time of 48.6 would have broken his own world best of 49.0 but for a drop of over six feet between the start and finish of the race, held on a track bizarrely measuring 501 yards to the lap!

There was a shock in the mile where George, below his best following illness and a severe spiking, was defeated by Bernhard Wise, another of the AAA founders, whose time was 4:24.4. Wise would later become Attorney-General of New South Wales. In the pole vault 19-year-old Tom Ray from the Lake District cleared 3.43m for a world best (the bar could not be raised any higher) and no British athlete would exceed that height in the AAA Championships until Fred Housden – who, decades later, would teach David Hemery how to hurdle – in 1928. Pole vaulting in that era bore little resemblance to the event as we know it today. Utilising a heavy ash, cedar or hickory pole with three iron spikes in the base, the early exponents would thrust the implement into the ground some three feet before the uprights, climb up it and endeavour to cross the bar in a sitting position. Montague Shearman described Ray's technique in these terms: "Grasping the pole about its middle, he takes his leap, and when the pole is perpendicular, poises it almost at a standstill, raises himself clear up it by sheer force of arm, and shoots himself over the bar." Thanks to the large crowd the meeting yielded a handsome profit of £325 17s.

1882 (Stoke-on-Trent)

WALTER GEORGE DEMONSTRATED why he was considered the pre-eminent middle and long distance runner of his era. On one day he won the 880y (1:58.2), mile (4:32.8) and 4 miles (but running only a token lap as there were no challengers), and two days later he added the 10 miles title, over two minutes ahead of the runner-up, in 54:41.0. In addition to setting world bests at the mile, 2 miles, 6 miles and 10 miles he travelled to New York for three races against Lon Myers, winning two and earning the title of the world's greatest runner. William Phillips, a lanky old Etonian, collected his third 100y title, clocking 10.2 each time, and finished second in the 440y to Henry Ball, whose time of 50.2 was a British record. Unhappily, Phillips would die of quinsy the following year, aged 25.

1883 (Lillie Bridge)

THE STAR ATTRACTION was the clash between Walter George and William Snook, the only man capable of giving him a good race. Regrettably, ill health struck George again (he was plagued throughout his career by asthma and hay fever) and he was unable to do himself justice as his Moseley Harriers clubmate beat him in both the mile (4:25.8-4:26.6) and 4 miles (20:37.0-20:44.0). George was defeated also in the 880y the same day, while two days later Snook added a third title by taking the 10 miles in 57:41.0. Snook had the dubious distinction of being the first man to be suspended by the AAA. Holder of the world 2 miles best of 9:33.4, Snook had been banned from racing from August 1881 to the end of 1882 because he had helped a professional enter for an amateur meeting. The very thought of professionals running against amateurs was anathema to the AAA. In September 1882 George had requested permission to race against the leading "pro", William Cummings, offering to donate his share of the gate money – which would have been a tidy sum – to the Worcester Infirmary. Predictably, the governing body refused to sanction such a race.

1884 (Aston Lower Grounds, Birmingham)

THIS WAS WALTER GEORGE'S final year as an amateur, and what a season he enjoyed. After victory in the English Cross Country Championship he set world bests at 2 miles (9:17.4), 3 miles (14:39.0), 4 miles (19:39.8), 6 miles (30:26.0) and 10 miles (51:20.0) prior to the AAA Championships where he notched up a treble with times of 2:02.2 for 880y, a world best of 4:18.4 in the mile with Snook a distant second, and 20:12.8 for 4 miles – again all on the same day – followed by a 10 miles win in 54:02.0 two days later. George went on that year to improve his 6 miles record to 30:21.5 and covered an unprecedented 18,555m in the hour.

Having achieved everything open to him in the amateur field, he turned "pro". He attracted a massive crowd of 30,000 to Lillie Bridge in 1885 for a "mile championship of the world" against William Cummings, which George won by a distance, and the next year he ran a stunning 4:12.75 (not an electrical time but 4 min 12¾ sec). Just how far ahead of his time he was could be gauged by the fact that no miler ran faster until 1915 and no Briton bettered his time until Sydney Wooderson crept past with 4:12.7 in 1935! A contemporary described George as "a tall thin man with a prodigious stride, which arises from his bringing his hips into play more than any distance runner we have ever seen, and years of practice and training cultivated his staying power to an extraordinary degree."

1885 (Southport)

WITH WALTER GEORGE now out of the picture, William Snook had it all to himself at the AAA Championships. He bagged the mile, 4 miles and steeplechase titles in slow times, in each case against only one other competitor, but had to push himself in the 10 miles against William Coad for a championship best of 53:25.2. That would prove to be his swansong, for the following year he was banned for life from amateur athletics, accused of what was termed "roping" after finishing second in the 1886 English Cross Country Championship, a race he had been a strong favourite to win. There were allegations that, because of betting considerations, he had deliberately lost. Snook explained that he was underweight that day and was hampered by sore feet, but his appeal was rejected and another star performer (and by no means the last) was evicted by an uncompromising governing body.

1886 (Stamford Bridge, London)

HELD FOR THE first time at what would be the venue of the Championships from 1909 to 1931 and is now the home of Chelsea Football Club, it was appropriate that the star of the meeting should be a man who shone also as a soccer player. Arthur Wharton, who hailed from the Gold Coast (now Ghana) and was the first black man to win a AAA title, played in goal for Preston North End and as a professional in another sport was fortunate that the AAA did not rule him ineligible. Born of a half-Scottish half Grenadian father and a half Scottish half Ghanaian mother, he moved to England in 1882 and, aged 20, equalled the world 100y best of 10.0 in heat and final.

As Montague Shearman commented: "At last, after years of struggling and disputing, a genuine level time performance [10 sec] has been achieved." He described Wharton's action thus: "At the crack of the pistol he is off like lightning, running in a wondrous fashion ... with body bent forward and running almost on the flat of his foot." Another significant performance was achieved by Charles Wood, who became the first Briton to break 50 sec for the quarter-mile with 49.8 while Charles Daft tied the British 120y hurdles record of 16.0.

1887 (Stourbridge)

DESTINED THE FOLLOWING season to smash Lon Myers' world 880y best of 1:55.4 with 1:54.6, the sturdily built Francis Cross completed an 880y (1:59.0) and mile (4:25.4) double. Unplaced in the mile was the Irish-born Tommy Conneff, who won the title the following season but would really flower several years later as an American citizen with world amateur records of 4:17.8 in 1893 and 4:15.6 in 1895. His finest performance was probably his 3:02.8 three-quarter mile in 1895, which stood as a world record until 1931. As a sergeant in the 7th US Cavalry he met his death in 1912, drowned in Manila Bay. Arthur Wharton retained the 100y title in 10.1 on the loose, newly laid cinder track half a yard ahead of the quarter-mile champion Charles Wood, who had the previous week become the first man in the world officially to break 22 sec for 220 yards with 21.8 on a straight track. The furlong did not become a AAA Championships event until 1902.

1888 (Crewe)

STILL ONLY 26, Tom Ray – the most celebrated of the climbing-style pole vaulters from the Lake District – collected a record seventh title, sharing first place on this occasion with his Ulverston clubmate Ernest Latimer Stones who had earlier beaten him in the Northern Championships with a world's best height of 3.53m. Stones would win the following year while Ray would go on to finish second in 1889 and 1890, third in 1891. The US-resident Canadian George Gray put the shot 13.28m from a 7ft square, a championship record which would survive until 1895. Later in the season he would set the first of eight world bests from a 7ft circle, finishing up with 14.75m in 1898 when aged 33.

1889 (Stamford Bridge)

ONE OF THE most outstanding performances from the early years of the AAA Championships came in the 440y when the Rev Henry Charles Lenox Tindall, a Kent county cricketer, produced a world best of 48.5, breaking Lon Myers' mark of 48.8. Admittedly, the shape of the Stamford Bridge track as it was then was advantageous – only one bend following a straight of 280 yards – but there can be no belittling Tindall's achievement. It was not bettered by another amateur until 1900, stood as a British record until 1908 and only in 1937 was it removed as the championship record! For good measure, he returned the same afternoon to win the 880y in a highly respectable 1:56.4. *The Sporting Life* reporter enthused: "Come, tell us where to find Tindall's fellow beyond the white cliffs of 'perfide Albion'". The 100y was won in a slow 10.4 but was notable for the fact that the winner, Ernest Pelling, was the first in AAA Championships history to use a crouch start.

1890 (Aston Lower Grounds, Birmingham)

WHAT A DIFFERENCE a year can make in an athlete's life. Harry Curtis had finished a distant second in the 7 miles walk in 1889 in 57:00.2, yet 12 months later he literally walked away with the title, by a two minute margin, in a world best of 52:28.4. It would be the first of four consecutive championship victories – a feat no other walker in this event would emulate until Roland Hardy (1950-1953). The sequence could have been longer had the 7 miles walk not been dropped from 1894 to 1900 in favour of a 4 miles event, Curtis winning the inaugural race.

1891 (Old Trafford, Manchester)

AN EARLY EXAMPLE of American sprinters with their fancy clockings back home being brought down to earth by English conditions and timekeepers was provided by

Luther Cary. Credited with a world best equalling 9.8 100y in New Jersey earlier in the month, he enjoyed a three-yard margin of victory in Manchester but the time, against a light breeze, was an ordinary looking 10.2. With the first AAA President, The Earl of Jersey, having resigned in 1890 on being appointed Governor-General of New South Wales, his successor was Viscount Alverstone, who from 1900 to 1913 was England's Lord Chief Justice.

1892 (Stamford Bridge)

WITH A TIME of 4:19.2 on what was now a standard 440 yards track, Harold Wade produced the fastest mile in the world since Walter George's heyday. Charles Bradley (10.2) won the first of four successive 100y titles, while the busiest athlete on show was Ireland's Daniel Bulger who won the 120y hurdles in 16.0, equalling the fastest by an athlete from the British Isles, placed first also in the long jump and finished third in the 100y.

1893 (Northampton)

HAVING BEEN WARNED that the slightly downhill grass track on the county cricket ground and wind assistance would rule out any records, Charles Bradley persuaded the officials to reverse the direction of the 100y. The Yorkshireman told them: "I'll run oop hill and againt t'wind, and then nobody can say nowt against it." That was true, for he equalled the British record of 10.0, winning by four yards against his only opponent. Three years later Bradley would be one of several leading athletes banned for life by the AAA for receiving cash to compete. The meeting saw the start of a remarkable sequence of shot putting victories by the 5ft 10in (1.78m) Denis Horgan from County Cork.

The boisterous, fun loving Irishman chalked up no fewer than 13 AAA titles over a 19-year period and the total might have been higher still had he not temporarily lost his amateur status in 1901-1902. As his weight increased (he was 11st 11lb or 75kg in 1893) so did his distances. He became unofficial world record holder in 1894 and improved to 14.88m by 1904. Not only his athletic career, but his very life, nearly came to an end in 1907. A New York policeman, Horgan had his skull broken by a shovel while he was trying to stop a brawl. The doctors did not hold out much hope of recovery, yet such was his resilience that the very next year, aged 37, he made his Olympic debut in London, taking the silver medal for the Great Britain & Ireland team. He then weighed in at 17st (108kg). His records outlived him, for he died in 1922 but it wasn't until 1949 that anyone else from the British Isles put the shot farther.

1894 (Huddersfield)

THE 4 MILES RACE, then the classic distance event, resulted in future world mile record holder Fred Bacon defeating George Crossland, shortly to break the world 20 miles record, by less than a yard in a championship record of 19:48.8. Two of the world's finest runners, they too would be disqualified for life in 1896 for accepting appearance money. Charles Bradley again equalled the 100y record of 10.0 and Edgar Bredin scored a 440y (50.0) and 880y (1:56.8) double although that wasn't as outstanding as in 1893 when he ran 49.2 and 1:55.3. The 10 miles championship, held in April, went to Sid Thomas – holder of world bests at 3 miles (14:24.0), 6 miles (30:17.8) and 15 miles (1:22:15.4). Thomas won the title for the fourth time, clocking 51:37.0 as compared to his 51:31.4 in 1889 (a time that would remain the championship record until 1933), but he was yet another to fall foul of the amateur rules.

1895 (Stamford Bridge)

HIS TIME WAS still far inferior to Walter George's "pro" record but Fred Bacon set a world amateur best of 4:17.0

when winning the mile, his lap times being wildly uneven at 60.0, 65.0, 68.8 and 63.2. It was his third consecutive mile title and earlier, in April, he had become 10 miles champion in 52:43.8. Bacon's mile record didn't last long as Tommy Conneff ran 4:15.6 in New York the following month. However, in the professional ranks, he would achieve such outstanding performances as 3:02.4 for three-quarters of a mile and covering 18,743m in the hour. Charles Bradley took his fourth 100y title, again equalling the British record of 10.0 when defeating Alf Downer, who had himself twice been timed at 10.0 that season.

Exactly a month later, at Stoke-on-Trent, the pair dead-heated in a sensational 9.8 which would have tied the world best, but it was rejected as a record by the AAA as there was only one timekeeper. Downer, born in Jamaica of Scottish parents, would the following year join Bradley and the others in the AAA's purge of athletes who had flouted the amateur laws. Edgar Bredin (1:55.8) won his third 880y title but surprisingly was beaten in the 440y by William Fitzherbert in 49.6.

On the same track only two weeks earlier Bredin had equalled Henry Charles Lenox Tindall's world best of 48.5. Bredin produced an even greater shock in 1897 when he decided to turn professional. It was, in the revealing words of Montague Shearman, "a step which was received with great surprise, as he was a gentleman by birth and education." However, Bredin was never a conventional figure; during his time he was a tea planter in Ceylon and a 'Mountie' in Canada, and he was never averse to a cigarette between races. There was a landmark performance in the high hurdles when Godfrey Shaw (15.8) became the first Briton to break 16 sec. Later, in New York, Shaw ran estimated times of 15.6 and 15.5 behind world bests of 15.4 by the American, Stephen Chase, but place times were rarely taken in those days and so 15.8 remained his official best.

1896 (Northampton)

NONE OF THE handful of British athletes who took part in the first Modern Olympic Games in Athens two months earlier competed in these Championships, but a future multiple Olympic champion (in 1900, 1904 and 1908), Irish-American John Flanagan, won the hammer with 40.21m. Steeplechase titlist Sidney Robinson, only 19, would go on to win gold (5000m team race), silver (2500m steeplechase) and bronze (4000m steeplechase) at the 1900 Games in Paris, while shot put champion Denis Horgan was destined to take the silver medal at the 1908 Games in London. Performances in all the events which could be compared were far superior at the AAA meeting to those registered in Athens except for the high jump and pole vault. The best mark in Northampton was a 15.6 120y hurdles by Godfrey Shaw but that was ruled out as a British record because of a strong following wind. At the AAA AGM the amateur definition was altered to read: "An amateur is one who has never competed for a money prize or monetary consideration, or for any declared wager or staked bet, who has never engaged in, assisted in or taught any athletic exercise as a means of pecuniary gain, and who has never taken part in any competition with anyone who is not an amateur." The AAA also ruled that "every competitor shall wear a sleeved jersey, and loose drawers to the knees, and any competitor shall be excluded unless properly attired."

1897 (Fallowfield, Manchester)

ALFRED TYSOE, WHO would be crowned Olympic 800m champion three years later, competed in the AAA Championships for the first time and came away as a double champion, winning by a narrow margin in each race in a slow time. In April he took the 10 miles in 55:59.6 and in July the mile in 4:27.0. On a day which was described as "very cold, dull and windy", the meeting's most meritorious performance came in the 4 miles walk in which Bill Sturgess claimed the third of his six consecutive titles in the British record time of 28:24.8, an improvement of over half a minute despite a potentially suicidal opening mile of 6:46. Later in the year, at a committee meeting, a momentous decision was reached … according to the minute book it was agreed that egg and spoon races do not come under the jurisdiction of the AAA!

1898 (Stamford Bridge)

IRISH ATHLETES HAD, ever since the second edition in 1881, won numerous titles – particularly in the field events – and with four more successes they brought the number of AAA victories to 50. Denis Horgan, of course, won the shot; the astonishingly versatile Tom Kiely (who would become the 1904 Olympic "all-around champion") the hammer; Patrick Leahy (the 1900 Olympic silver medallist) the high jump; and Walter Newburn – who would make history two weeks later in Dublin by becoming the world's first 24ft long jumper with 7.33m – took that event with a championship record leap of 7.19m. Another visitor to carry off a title was the impressively named steeplechaser George Washington Orton, from Canada, who in Paris two years later would beat Sidney Robinson for Olympic gold. The best performances by home athletes were a British record equalling 10.0 100y by Reg Wadsley (heat) and Fred Cooper (final) and a 4:17.2 mile by the Scot, Hugh Welsh, just a fifth of a second outside Fred Bacon's British record.

1899 (Wolverhampton)

DENIS HORGAN WON his seemingly obligatory shot title, the seventh of 13, with a distance (14.03m) which would remain as the championship record until 1913. Nothing else in the meeting measured up to that although Charles Bennett, an engine driver who would steam to Britain's first Olympic gold medal (in the 1500m) the following year, made his mark by winning his third 4 miles title as well as finishing a close second to Hugh Welsh in the mile, having already succeeded in the 10 miles held in Derby in April.

BRITISH AMATEUR RECORDS AT 1 JANUARY 1900
100y: 10.0 Arthur Wharton 1886, Charles Bradley 1892, 1893 & 1895, Alf Downer 1895, Reg Wadsley 1898, Fred Cooper 1898 & Charles Thomas 1899; 220y (turn): 22.2 James Cowie 1885 & Charles Wood 1886; 440y: 48.5 Henry Charles Lenox Tindall 1889 & Edgar Bredin 1895; 880y: 1:54.6 Francis Cross 1888; Mile: 4:17.0 Fred Bacon 1895; 2M: 9:17.4 Walter George 1884; 3M: 14:24.0 Sid Thomas 1893; 4M: 19:39.8 George 1884; 6M: 30:17.8 Thomas 1892; 10M: 51:20.0 George 1884; 120yH: 15.8 Godfrey Shaw 1895; 440yH: 59.4 Shaw 1896 (57.8 Thomas Donovan IRL 1896); HJ: 1.90 George Rowden 1889 (1.95 Patrick Leahy IRL 1898); PV: 3.58 Richard Dickinson 1891; LJ: 7.17 Charles (C.B.) Fry 1893 (7.33 Walter Newburn IRL 1898); TJ: 13.56 John Hargreaves 1877 (14.70 John Purcell IRL 1887); SP: 13.18 James Macintosh 1896 (14.68 Denis Horgan IRL 1897); DT: not contested; HT: 38.78 Nelson Robbie 1891 (46.30 Tom Kiely IRL 1898); JT: not contested.

Note: the inaugural list of British records officially ratified by the AAA was issued in April 1887, but they were marks made in the UK by any athlete, not necessarily British. Records referred to above and in the text are for reportedly authentic performances by UK athletes. Godfrey Shaw was timed at 57.2 for 442y (sic) hurdles in 1891 but the mark was not ratified.

1900 (Stamford Bridge)

THERE WAS A foreign invasion as the American Olympic team, on its way to Paris, scooped up eight of the 13 titles on offer. Writing in the AAA Jubilee Souvenir (1930), H.F. Pash reminisced: "They introduced many new ideas, some of them of a very amusing character, according to English views, such as wearing coloured dressing-gowns in the centre of the ground, and joining in College yells." Leading the way for the Americans was Alvin Kraenzlein, who would become the star of those Games by becoming the only athlete to this day to claim four individual Olympic titles at one celebration. In Paris he would win the 110m hurdles, long jump and two events which were only briefly in the Olympic programme, the 60m and 200m low hurdles.

At Stamford Bridge, on the grass infield, he took the 120y hurdles in a strongly wind aided 15.4 (he ran the same time for a world best in Paris) and long jumped 6.97m. A distant second in the hurdles was the Indian-born Briton, Norman Pritchard, who would pick up Olympic silver medals in the 200m and 200m hurdles. He later made his way to Hollywood in the mid-1920s where as Norman Trevor he acted in silent films starring Ronald Colman and Clara Bow. Other Americans who won AAA titles prior to victory in Paris were Maxie Long (49.8 440y), Irving Baxter (1.88m high jump), Richard Sheldon (13.98m shot) and John Flanagan (49.78m hammer).

However, Walter Tewksbury – who went on to take Olympic gold at 200m and 400m hurdles, silver at 60m and 100m and bronze at 200m hurdles – had to settle for third place in the AAA 100y, won by his team-mate Arthur Duffey in 10.0 ahead of Frank Jarvis, the Olympic 100m champion in waiting. Embarrassingly, no Briton made the final. However, it wasn't all one-way traffic, for 880y winner Alfred Tysoe went on to lift the Olympic 800m title (tragically he died from pleurisy the following year, aged 27); mile champion Charles Bennett took the 1500m gold medal and John Rimmer, winner of the 4 miles, became Olympic 4000m steeplechase champion. Oddly, the AAA did not refer to Olympic Games as such. A General Committee meeting in December 1899 talked of sending a team to the Paris Exhibition Athletic Festival, while at the AGM in April 1900 a sum of £100 was allotted for sending a team to the 1900 International Championships in Paris. Thanks to a crowd of 6,800 and the sale of 4000 programmes, the AAA meeting showed a profit of £353, the largest since 1881.

1901 (Huddersfield)

THE AMERICAN PRESENCE was less marked this time in these first post-Victorian Championships but Arthur Duffey (10.0 100y), Alvin Kraenzlein (15.6 120y hurdles) and Irving Baxter (1.85m high jump) retained their titles although Maxie Long, who had set a world quarter-mile record of 47.8 in New York the previous September, lost his speciality by two yards to Reg Wadsley, the 100 and 440 yards champion in 1899. The name of Coe was inscribed in the AAA's archives for the first time as William Wesley Coe Jr of the USA won the shot title, he being the sole entrant; 19 years later, aged 41, he would win the 56 pound weight the one and only time it was ever held. Another event with only one contestant was the long jump, in which Ireland's Peter O'Connor won the first of six consecutive titles and was sufficiently motivated to set a championship record of 7.22m. That was on July 6. Later in the month he twice jumped a world best of 7.60m and in Dublin on August 5 he established what was later accepted by the IAAF as the first official world record of 7.61m, which went unbeaten for almost 20 years.

It wasn't until Lynn Davies jumped 7.72m at the 1962 Commonwealth Games that anyone from the British Isles bettered that mark! Field events were certainly the poor relation in these early days of the AAA Championships; the three jumping and two throwing events drew a grand total of nine entrants. Alf Shrubb, who would develop into the world's greatest distance runner, won his first AAA titles, taking the 10 miles (in Crewe) in 53:32.0 and the 4 miles in 20:01.8 as well as placing second in the mile and third in the steeplechase. One new event was added to the programme: the 2 miles walk.

1902 (Stamford Bridge)

THE SPECTATORS WERE treated to a great mile race. Content to follow while the first three laps were covered in 60.2, 66.2 and 67.6, Joe Binks saved his finish until the final straight and sailed past Lt. Henry Hawtrey (destined to win the 5 miles race at the interim Olympics of 1906) to win by a couple of yards in 4:16.8 to break Fred Bacon's British record. No British amateur would run faster until 1921. Binks went on to become the highly respected, long serving and ever enthusiastic athletics correspondent of the *News of the World*, covering every Olympics from 1908 to 1956 and retiring at age 82. He was also an astute athletics meeting organiser and the popular British Games, sponsored by his newspaper, were a brainchild of his. Alf Shrubb failed to finish in the mile after leading at halfway but did retain his 4 miles (20:01.4) and 10 miles (52:25.4) titles. The 220 yards (on a straightaway) was added to the schedule and the inaugural champion was Reg Wadsley in 22.4. He thus became the first to win AAA titles at 100, 220 and 440 yards, a feat which would not be emulated until Harry Edward won all three on one day in 1922. The American, Sam Jones, who would become Olympic champion two years later in St Louis, high jumped 1.90m (6ft 3in), which remained the championship record until 1920 and he went close at a world record 1.97m (6ft 5³/4in). A winning pole vault height of 3.25m was nothing to write home about but history was made when Jakab Kauser of Hungary became the first continental European to win any AAA title. A proposal at the AAA AGM that the hammer be dropped from the Championships programme was lost only narrowly, 19-16.

1903 (Northampton)

ARTHUR DUFFEY, CONSIDERED the "world's fastest human" of his era after running a world's best time of 9.6 in New York in 1902, captured the 100y title for a fourth consecutive year but as on the three previous occasions he had to settle for a relatively modest 10.0 clocking. After winning the 10 miles title in April by over five minutes in 51:55.8, Alf Shrubb defeated Joe Binks in the mile (4:24.0) and took the 4 miles also in 20:06.0.

1904 (Rochdale)

ALF SHRUBB ENDED his AAA Championship career in some style (he was declared a professional the following year) by retaining all three of his titles: 10 miles in 54:30.4, mile in 4:22.0 (his first and last laps totalling 2:01.4) and, 75 minutes later, the 4 miles in 19:56.8. It was an incredible year for him as he also won the English and International cross country championships and set several world bests including 9:09.6 for 2 miles (which survived until 1926), 14:17.2 for 3 miles, 19:23.4 for 4 miles, 29:59.4 for 6 miles (a British record until 1936), 31:02.4 for 10,000m, 50:40.6 for 10 miles (which stood until 1928) and 18,742m in the hour, which remained the British record until 1953, the year in which the AAA made a pleasant, if somewhat belated, gesture by reinstating him! Arthur Duffey's reign as 100y champion came to a conclusion when Jack Morton beat him by inches in 10.0 (again), the first of four such titles for him. Morton and Shrubb might well have challenged for Olympic honours in St Louis that summer but Britain was not represented because of the expense that would be incurred. Also starting an impressive sequence of AAA titles was George Larner, who took both the 2 miles (13:57.6) and 7 miles (52:57.4) walks. Although 29, this Brighton policeman was in only his second season as a walker. Tom Nicolson from Scotland retained his hammer title with a British record throw of 47.99m.

1905 (Stamford Bridge)

THE NEWLY LAID track at the remodelled stadium was described by *The Sporting Life* as "a long way from being fit for championship running" and times suffered accordingly. Indeed, the inside lane became so loose that many competitors avoided it and ran or walked well beyond the proper distance. The outstanding performer was George Larner, whose 2 miles walk time of 13:50.0 was a championship record which lasted until 1932 and who also won the 7 miles in 52:34.0. He had much faster world best times to his credit with 13:11.4 (unsurpassed by a Briton until 1960) and 50:50.8 and it came as a shock when he announced his retirement. Happily he came back in 1908 bound for further glory. Spectators were pleasantly entertained, for The London Victoria Military Band played 14 pieces, finishing with "Entry of the Gladiators" and "God Save The King" [Edward VII]; the meeting started at 3 pm with heats of the 100y and ended with the 440y final at 6 pm (won by Wyndham Halswelle in 50.8), followed by the presentation of prizes. Fans were well informed, too, by the 48 page programme, price sixpence [2.5p], which in addition to listing all previous champions, including those under AAC auspices from 1866, printed "Scotch", Irish, French, Hungarian, American and Australasian records as well as records passed by the General Committee of the AAA. That last list, which represented the best marks set in Great Britain and Ireland by any athlete and thus included foreigners like Arthur Duffey and Alvin Kraenzlein, was split into four categories: "running" (100y to 50 miles), "walking" (1 to 100 miles), "time records" (1 hour run, 12 hours walk etc) and – reflecting the low status of field events at that time – "odd events" (i.e. high jump, pole jump as it was referred to, long jump, shot and hammer).

1906 (Stamford Bridge)

FOR THE FIRST time not a single championship record was set, although Wyndham Halswelle – two years before finding lasting fame as Olympic champion – went close to Henry Charles Lenox Tindall's long standing British 440y record with 48.8 despite being thrown off his stride in the scramble at the first turn (the race was not run in lanes in those days), and George Butterfield took the mile in a fastish 4:18.4. Tom Kirkwood from Scotland set a British shot record of 13.83m, Ireland's world record holder Peter O'Connor annexed his sixth straight long jump title with 7.15m and Freddie Hulford, who 42 years later would be firing the gun as Chief Starter at the London Olympics, won the 4 miles in 20:27.4.

1907 (Fallowfield, Manchester)

FOR THE LAST time for 81 years the AAA Championships were held outside London and it would be 97 years before Manchester would again host the meeting. Again, in wet and windy conditions, there were no championship records but Scottish farmer Tom Nicolson went very close to his British hammer record of 48.44m with a throw of 48.39m. He would go on to win a total of six titles and end his championship career with second place in 1924, aged 44! He continued as one of Britain's foremost throwers until he was 50 and held the Scottish native record until 1947. Jack Morton collected his fourth consecutive 100y title, defeating Nate Cartmell (USA), the 1904 Olympic 100m and 200m silver medallist, but such was the strength of the headwind that the winning time was merely 10.8, a full second outside his best. Morton, who was also second in the 220y, and Alexander Duncan, first at 4 miles and second at 10 miles, were announced as the inaugural joint holders of the Harvey Memorial Gold Cup, awarded to the competitor who is adjudged to be the best AAA champion of the year. It was presented by Gordon C. Harvey, MP, in memory of his brother, Charles Harvey, a former President of the Northern Counties AA.

1908 (White City, London)

WITH THE LONDON Olympics just a week or so away the Championships were staged at the newly opened White

City, then known as the Great Olympic Stadium and claimed to be "the largest, most costly and best appointed the world has yet known." Several of the competitors would go on to taste Olympic glory. Irish-born Bobbie Kerr of Canada, who scored a sprint double in 10.0 and 22.4, would emerge as Olympic 200m champion and South Africa's Reggie Walker, second in the 100y, became the 100m champion of the world. A London-born Scot by the name of Wyndham Halswelle, destined to win the Olympic 400m crown in a sensational walkover after his American opponents refused to take part in a re-run of the original, controversial race, warmed up with a gentle 49.4 440y. He had just recently set a world 300 yards best of 31.2 and a British quarter-mile record of 48.4 that would survive for 26 years. Other British gold medallists in waiting seen in action were Emil Voigt (the 5 miles champion), who won the AAA 4 miles in a championship record 19:47.4; Arthur Russell, second in the steeplechase but an Olympic winner; and George Larner (13:58.4 2 miles walk) who was successful at the Games in both the 3500m and 10 miles walk events. Britain also won the Olympic 3 miles team race with Joe Deakin the individual winner, and his preparation included finishing second in the mile to Harold Wilson, the first man to break 4 min for 1500m and a close second in the Olympic 1500m. Deakin, 29 at the time and like Halswelle a veteran of the Boer War, remained an active athlete for another 60 years despite having been gassed during the First World War! He died in 1972, aged 93, whereas Halswelle was destined to be killed by a sniper's bullet while serving in France in 1915. Among the spectators at the White City was Prince Albert of Wales, the future King Edward VIII – a royal first for the AAA.

1909 (Stamford Bridge)

FROM THIS YEAR through to 1931 the Championships would always be staged at Stamford Bridge. Reggie Walker, the diminutive South African who won the 1908 Olympic

100m at the age of 19 thanks largely to the coaching of Sam Mussabini, added his name to the long list of co-holders of the 100y championship record of 10.0. Two new championship records were set in the 220y by Nate Cartmell (USA) with 22.0 and in the hammer by Tom Nicolson with 50.19m. Tim Ahearne, the Irishman who won the Olympic triple jump (hop step and jump in those days) title with a world record 14.92m, had to make do with winning the long jump and placing second in the high jump as his speciality did not become a AAA Championships event until 1914. The attendance was a healthy 16,000, and *The Sporting Life* enthused: "The character of the performances generally uphold the claims of Britishers that the AAA Championships may be regarded as the world's premier contests when the Olympic Games are not on the tapis."

1910 (Stamford Bridge)

IT WOULD BE ten years and a World War away before he would make Olympic history at 800m and 1500m but, as a 21-year-old distance runner, Albert Hill won his first AAA title, taking the 4 miles on a very heavy track in 20:00.6. Held separately in April, the 7 miles walk was won for the third successive year by Olympic silver medallist Ernest Webb, whose time of 51:37.0 stood as the championship record until 1932. Webb had an adventurous past. He ran away to sea at 12, later enlisted in the Army and in the Boer War was in charge of the horses in the retreat to Ladysmith. He did not take up race walking until 1906, aged 34. A notable honour for the Association was the news in November 1910 that King George V, who had only recently come to the throne, would become Patron of the AAA.

1911 (Stamford Bridge)

ALBERT HILL'S SUCCESSOR as 4 miles champion, in 20:03.6, was the first of the Flying Finns – Hannes

Kolehmainen. He only just beat William Scott, the 10 miles champion, but became the star of the 1912 Olympics in Stockholm by winning the 5000m, 10,000m and cross country, followed in 1920 by the Olympic marathon title. Philip Baker, an unobtrusive fourth in the mile after finishing fifth the previous year (his only AAA appearances), would finish second to Albert Hill in the 1920 Olympic 1500m and much later, in 1959, as the Right Hon. Philip Noel-Baker, who served as Minister of Fuel and Power in Clement Attlee's Government, he was awarded the Nobel Peace Prize for his campaigning for an international arms control treaty. It was Baker, then President of Cambridge University AC, who suggested the AAA should select a team to take on Cambridge University. It was agreed, a match took place at Cambridge in December and for nearly a century meetings involving AAA teams were among the domestic highlights of the season. Roger Bannister's first four minute mile in 1954 occurred in a match between the AAA (which he represented) and Oxford University AC. Recognising the growing popularity of relay races, which had been taking place since 1895, a mile medley was added to the AAA Championships programme. Championships at 4x110y and 4x440y would be instituted in 1927.

1912 (Stamford Bridge)

AT LONG LAST "evens" was broken in the 100y, 10.0 having stood as the oft-equalled championship record since Arthur Wharton set the ball rolling back in 1886. The man responsible was South Africa's George Patching, his time of 9.8 giving him a yard and a half margin over Willie Applegarth, who would fare better than his rival in that year's Stockholm Olympics. Patching finished fourth behind an American trio in the 100m, while Applegarth (the AAA 220y champion in 22.0) took the 200m bronze medal and anchored Britain to victory in the 4x100m relay. Curiously, Britain's only individual gold medallist in

Stockholm, Arnold Strode-Jackson of Oxford University in the 1500m, never competed in the AAA Championships. Gerard Anderson, who had recently set a British record of 15.2, tied Alvin Kraenzlein's championship record of 15.6 in the high hurdles. He was one of the favourites for the Olympic title but fell in his semi-final. Far more tragically, he would be killed in action in France just two years later. Denis Horgan, now 41, signed off with a 13th shot title since 1893 – a tally for a single event which may never be matched. He was also second on one occasion and was runner-up in the hammer seven times between 1896 and 1909. The year saw the creation of a pioneering but severely limited AAA Coaching Scheme with Frederick W. Parker, the Secretary of London AC, appointed Chief Athletic Adviser charged with visiting training centres and supervising the training of competitors throughout England, with Alec Nelson as Chief Trainer. Over in Stockholm at the time of the Olympics the International Amateur Athletic Federation (IAAF) was founded, its rules largely based on the AAA's.

1913 (Stamford Bridge)

UNUSUALLY, THERE WERE no Irish winners at this edition but there was a highly successful Swedish invasion as five titles went to that nation, including a championship record in the shot of 14.44m by Einar Nilsson. John Zander, winner of the mile in a slow 4:25.8, would later blossom into a world record breaker at 1500m (3:54.7 in 1917) and 3000m (8:33.2 in 1918). Willie Applegarth scored a neat sprint double in 10.0 and 21.6 (a British record), while the ill-fated George Hutson smashed the 4 miles championship record with 19:32.0. Sidney Abrahams, who had been the top British placer in the long jump when finishing second in 1909 and third in 1911, won on this occasion to open the family's AAA title account; brother Harold was just 13 at the time and his first victory would be ten years hence. On the programme since the start in 1880, the steeplechase had not previously been contested at a standardised distance but from here on (until it switched in 1954 to 3000m) it was run over 2 miles, although the number of obstacles to be negotiated did not become regulated until 1932.

1914 (Stamford Bridge)

THERE WERE SEVERAL innovations at these Championships, staged just one month before Britain and Germany were at war. Owing to the large entry, the meeting was held, for the first time, over two days (yielding a record profit of around £600) and as part of a campaign to popularise field events in Britain the triple jump, discus and javelin were added to the programme as well as 440y hurdles. The initial results were disappointing: only one of the four men entered for the triple jump was British and he came last with 12.66m while the few home competitors in the two new throwing events were outclassed by their foreign opposition, who included Finland's Olympic discus champion Armas Taipale, whose throw of 44.05m would not be bettered by a British athlete in the AAA Championships until 1950. The javelin was even worse as the 59.71m throw of Olympic bronze medallist Mor Kóczán of Hungary also went unbeaten by any UK athlete until 1938 and at the Championships until 1951. However, it wasn't all gloom as Willie Applegarth not only completed another sprint double but this time followed his 10.0 100y with a fantastic 21.2 220y which was ratified by the IAAF as the first official world record. It stood as the fastest time around a bend until 1932 and a British record until as late as 1958! Attending his first AAA Championships, a 14-year-old Harold Abrahams was profoundly impressed. As he wrote many years later: "I well remember the thrill of seeing Willie Applegarth in the inside string [lane] tearing round the [banked] bend in the 220 yards race with his strides following one another with incredible rapidity." Placing 15th in the mile, won by George Hutson in 4:22.0, was the Irish champion, the Hon. Harold Alexander, who as Earl Alexander of Tunis became one of Britain's most famous soldiers. During the First World War his "conspicuous gallantry in action" earned him the Military Cross, Distinguished Service Order and *Légion d'honneur*. In 1937 he became the youngest General in the British Army; during the Second World War he was Commander-in-Chief in various campaigns and was promoted to the highest rank of Field Marshal in 1944 and elevated to the peerage in 1946.

The AAA formally joined the IAAF in June although it would not be until 1921 that international matches involving Britain (styled, though, as England) would commence. However, in July, there was a clash between England, Scotland and Ireland at Hampden Park, Glasgow. Another important development was the appointment in February for three years at a salary of £400 per annum of the AAA Olympic Committee's first professional Chief Coach. He was a dynamic 36-year-old Scots-Canadian by the name of Walter Knox, a former "pro" who had been credited with a 9.6 100y and 7.36m long jump. He was particularly keen to improve the woeful field event standards but at the AGM in April it was stated that "the Olympic Committee in view of the European crisis and the present state of affairs considered it desirable to terminate Mr Knox's engagement as Chief Coach in view of there being no chance of the Olympic Games being held in 1916." The Olympic Committee was disbanded, Knox was paid £400 to cancel the agreement and he returned to Canada. Not until 1947 would the AAA appoint another full-time Chief Coach.

1915-1918

NO CHAMPIONSHIPS WERE staged although in 1915 an Emergency Committee was appointed to carry on the business of the AAA for the duration.

Among those killed during the First World War were 1908 Olympic 400m champion Wyndham Halswelle (AAA 440y champion in 1905, 1906 & 1908) aged 32; 1912 Olympic 5000m bronze medallist George Hutson (winner of the 4 miles in 1912, 1913 and 1914 and mile champion in 1914) aged 24; Douglas McNicol (1911 mile champion); Gerard Anderson (120yH champion in 1910 & 1912) aged 25; Alfred Flaxman (pole vault champion in 1909 and hammer winner in 1910) aged 36; and Henry Leeke (hammer champion in 1906) aged 35. On the German side, the 1908 Olympic 800m bronze medallist Hanns Braun – a popular AAA half mile winner in 1909, 1911 and 1912 – met his death at 31. The first two Presidents of the AAA, The Earl of Jersey (who held the office from 1880 to 1890) and Viscount Alverstone (who had presided since 1891), both died in 1915. Sir Montague Shearman, one of the Association's founders 36 years earlier, took over as President in 1916.

1919 (Stamford Bridge)

REVERTING ONE LAST time to a one day meeting and with the three "new" field events not on the programme, the Championships were revived after five years. One athlete dominated the proceedings: 30-year-old Albert Hill, the 4 miles champion from 1910 and 880y runner-up in 1914. Miraculously, after serving amid the horrors of France for three years as a wireless operator with the Royal Flying Corps, he managed to regain full physical fitness and within a three hour span he ran a heat of the 880y, won the final in 1:55.2, followed up with a mile victory in 4:21.2 and contributed the half mile leg to Polytechnic Harriers' victorious mile medley relay team! If you thought that was good, wait a year to see what he achieved in Antwerp. That was one veteran bound for Olympic glory but the meeting also saw the AAA debuts of two youthful talents. Guy Butler (19), a cousin of the future Home Secretary Rab Butler, hadn't yet received his Blue at Cambridge but emerged as the national 440y champion in 49.8 with Oxford's Bevil Rudd of South Africa fourth. It was the start of an intense rivalry which would lift them into the forefront of world 400m running. Somewhat less conspicuous was another lad of 19, one Harold Abrahams. He was eliminated in his 220y heat in outside 23 sec and placed fifth in the long jump with the rather embarrassing distance of 6.30m. From small beginnings .... Just one pre-war champion succeeded in retaining a title. That was the one-armed dentist Bobby Bridge, winner of the 2 miles walk for the fourth time in succession.

BRITISH RECORDS AT 1 JANUARY 1920
100y: 9.8 Jack Morton 1904 & 1905, Vic d'Arcy 1911, Henry Macintosh 1913 & Willie Applegarth 1913 & 1914; 100m: 10.7 Macintosh 1913; 220y (turn): 21.2 Applegarth 1914; 440y: 48.4 Wyndham Halswelle 1908; 880y: 1:54.6 Francis Cross 1888 & Herbert Workman 1901; 1500m: 3:56.8 Arnold Strode-Jackson 1912; Mile: 4:16.8 Joe Binks 1902 & Albert Hill 1919; 2M: 9:09.6 Alf Shrubb 1904; 3M: 14:17.6 Shrubb 1904; 4M: 19:23.4 Shrubb 1904; 6M: 29:59.4 Shrubb 1904; 10M: 50:40.6 Shrubb 1904; Marathon: 2:38:17 Harry Green 1913; 2M Steeplechase: 10:58.0 Sidney Robinson 1903; 120yH: 15.2 Gerard Anderson 1912; 440yH: 56.8 Anderson 1910; HJ: 1.90 George Rowden 1889 (1.95 Patrick Leahy IRL 1898 & Tim Carroll IRL 1913); PV: 3.58 Richard Dickinson 1891; LJ: 7.17 Charles (C.B.) Fry 1893 (7.61 Peter O'Connor IRL 1901); TJ: 13.58 Philip Kingsford 1912 (14.92 Tim Ahearne IRL 1908); SP: 13.93 Tom Kirkwood 1906 (14.88 Denis Horgan IRL 1904); DT: 39.13 Walter Henderson 1912; HT: 50.84 Tom Nicolson 1908; JT: 43.66 Frederick Kitching 1914; 2M Walk: 13:11.4 George Larner 1904; 7M Walk: 50:50.8 Larner 1905.

THE TWENTIES
AND THIRTIES

THE FIRST WORLD WAR led to profound changes in the country's social structure and the AAA reflected that. The full General Committee reconvened in January 1919 and various measures to modernise and popularise the sport were set in motion. A new generation of fitter young men, drawn from all classes, was developing and athletics needed to make changes to cater for them. For a start, the AAA AGM of 1919 encouraged the formation of county associations and the promotion of county championships, which led to the foundation in 1926 of the Counties Athletic Union, whose annual Inter-Counties Championships became one of the most prestigious fixtures on the calendar.

The public schools had an athletics tradition stretching back to Victorian days and, thanks to the pioneering London Athletic Club, there had effectively been a national Public Schools Championships since 1897. Such schools also benefited from matches against the Achilles Club,. founded in 1920 and open to past and present Oxford and Cambridge University athletes. With physical education being added to the curriculum, athletics competition was growing increasingly popular in state schools too and in response to that the Schools' Athletic Association was formed in 1925.

Oxford and Cambridge continued to be a hotbed of athletic talent, producing a remarkable number of Olympic gold medallists throughout the inter-war period. From Oxford came Bevil Rudd (representing South Africa; 1920 400m), Tom Hampson (1932 800m) and New Zealander Jack Lovelock (1936 1500m); while Cambridge contributed Guy Butler (1920 4x400m), John Ainsworth-Davis (1920 4x400m), Harold Abrahams (1924 100m), Douglas Lowe (1924 & 1928 800m), Lord Burghley (1928 400m hurdles), Ireland's Bob Tisdall (1932 400m hurdles) and Godfrey Brown (1936 4x400m). It was an amazing record, particularly when one considers how many silver and bronze medals were involved also. One third of the British Olympic team in 1928 were members of the Achilles Club. Athletics was also being taken more seriously than before at other seats of learning, the Universities' Athletic Union being founded in 1919 to cater for their needs, and in 1928 a team was sent for the first time to the International University Games.

The twenties saw the birth of true dual international matches. There had been an Ireland v England encounter in Dublin as long ago as 1876 but it wasn't until 1921 that the first of a long series of clashes between England and France commenced. That was a three-a-side match at Stade Colombes in Paris, won by the visitors by 123 points to 118. The first match on home soil was staged at Stamford Bridge in 1922 before a crowd of 12,000 with England beating France 57-42. The Anglo-French confrontations continued on virtually an annual basis throughout the 1920s and 1930s, and other opponents were Germany (every other year between 1929 and 1939), Italy (1931 and 1933), Finland (1935 and 1937) and Norway (1937 and 1938). From 1933 the teams competed as Britain instead of England, for in 1932 the International Board (known as the British Amateur Athletic Board from 1937) was formed, consisting of representatives from the AAA, Scottish AAA and Northern Irish AAA, and it replaced the AAA as Britain's affiliated body to the IAAF.

In addition to the Olympics (1920 Antwerp, 1924 Paris, 1928 Amsterdam, 1932 Los Angeles, 1936 Berlin) and international matches, further opportunities for international competition arose with the founding in 1930 of the British Empire Games, staged in Hamilton (Canada). Subsequent editions were held in 1934 at London's White City Stadium (which had become the home for the AAA Championships from 1932) and in 1938 in Sydney. European Championships were inaugurated in 1934, in Turin, but Britain did not send a team. That was rectified for the second edition in Paris in 1938, where Godfrey Brown (400m), Sydney Wooderson (1500m), Don Finlay (110m hurdles) and Harold Whitlock (50km walk) were victorious.

During the 1920s the AAA was less than enchanted by the make-up and work of the International Olympic Committee. A few months after the 1920 Games in Antwerp, where British athletes won four titles and eight other medals, the AAA General Committee declared "the IOC is not composed of men with a sufficient general knowledge of sport and further they have not taken proper steps to carry out regulations and decisions previously agreed upon. It is therefore thought necessary that the IOC should be re-organised and composed of men who have a practical knowledge of sport and that this body should have absolute control of the Games in the country holding the Olympiad with full powers to enforce their rulings and regulations." The resolution continued: "The financial position must definitely be assured if the AAA is to participate in future Games." Equally disgruntled was Sir Theodore Cook, a member of the British Olympic Council, who wrote to *The Times* complaining that the Olympic movement had "become entirely alien to English thought and character" and suggesting that Britain should withdraw.

That letter prompted an indignant reply from athletics team captain Philip Baker, a future Nobel Peace Prize winner who finished second to Albert Hill in the 1500m, and co-signed by over 40 members of his team. "We can only suppose that Sir Theodore Cook shares the views of the numerous but ill-informed critics of the Games who for so many years have spread the belief that the Olympic Games are not carried out in a sporting spirit, that they lead to 'bad blood' among the nations who take part in them, and that they lead also inevitably to professionalism. But we wish as emphatically as we can to deny that they are in any way correct. On the contrary, these contests have without exception been run in a spirit of fairness and good sportsmanship which we believe to be equal to the highest standards of British tradition."

Seven years later the AAA General Committee voiced its concern over a resolution passed by the IOC recognising "broken time" payments [compensation paid to athletes who lost income from their employers in order to compete in the Olympics], stressing it was "emphatically of opinion that it will seriously affect the success of not only the Olympic Games at Amsterdam in 1928, but also of future Olympiads." A few weeks later, at a special meeting, the General Committee confirmed it was "directly opposed to the fundamental principles laid down by the IOC" but agreed to a resolution that "so long as the rules of the IAAF maintain the strict definition of amateurism to which the AAA has always adhered, the AAA is justified in sending a team of athletes to compete at Amsterdam."

Although he was later widely perceived to be an establishment figure, Harold Abrahams opposed the views of the AAA and British Olympic Association in this matter. Writing in *The Sunday Times* in 1929, he stated: "In truth the attempt to draw a clear-cut line between amateurs and professionals grows more and more complicated every day, and the sooner we admit that there is but little place for the old time casual amateur in this modern world of specialisation and international encounter, the better we will be able to face in a logical manner the bogy of 'broken time'."

Various rule changes were implemented during this period, including a dress code for athletes which was a little less restricting than previously. From 1922, instead of the "sleeved jersey and loose drawers to the knees", competitors could now brazenly wear "a half-sleeved vest and loose drawers, reaching at least halfway to the knees, with slips." That same year saw the first written definition of race walking: "Walking is progression by steps so taken that the heel of the foremost foot must reach the ground before the toe of the other foot leaves it." That, in line with some other rules, was amended to comply with IAAF regulations and in 1928 the definition became: "Walking is progression by steps so taken that unbroken contact with the ground is maintained."

Also in 1928 the AAA instituted what were known as English native records for performances made in England or Wales by athletes born in England or Wales. This gave rise to numerous anomalies as, for example, Godfrey Brown – having been born in India – was never credited with the English 440y record, while many of the best marks by eligible athletes could not be ratified as they were posted abroad, like Dick Webster's 4.00m pole vault at the 1936 Olympics in Berlin. Official British records remained a puzzle from their start in 1887 to their demise in 1948 as they were awarded for performances made in the UK by athletes from anywhere in the world; in effect British all-comers' records. As a result, many British records were never held by British athletes!

Those inter-war years saw a dramatic rise both in athletics performance and participation. In contrast to Walter George's walkover at the inaugural Championships in 1880, there were 48 entries for the AAA mile in 1924 (and no heats!). Crowds of 30,000 at Stamford Bridge were not unusual.

Writing in the *News of the World* in December 1930, the former British mile record holder Joe Binks was upbeat in his assessment of British athletics. "In my opinion, the physique, performances and general standard of British athletes have never been so good. This despite the loss of thousands of our best men in the Great War. Britain, the acknowledged schoolmaster of the athletic world, now has to contend with thousands of foreign competitors who specialise, but we are still able to conquer all comers in races on the track, and, so far from being a decadent nation, I believe the class to be higher than ever." He went on to state: "That old time bugbear in sport, 'class distinction', has been thoroughly stamped out. We old-timers can appreciate what a grand thing it is for the sport to see the Burghleys, Lowes, Butlers and Stallards rubbing shoulders as one happy international team with Cyril Ellis, Cecil Griffiths, Ernest Harper and Harry Payne, to mention only four famous athletes who have come from the mines and the workshops."

One AAA initiative which did not succeed at the time was the introduction of an English Championship Meeting in Northampton, open only to athletes of English or Welsh birth or parentage as distinct from the "open to the world" format of the AAA Championships. They were staged in 1923, 1924 and 1925 but then discontinued as area championships took hold. Of more lasting benefit was the institution of AAA Junior Championships in 1931, although one famous figure who expressed disapproval was Harold Abrahams. Writing in *Athletic News*, he commented: "The first Junior AAA Championships have come and gone. Before the meeting was held I expressed the opinion that such a venture was undesirable, and I hope the AAA will take the views of prominent ex-athletes on this point before deciding to repeat the experiment." Fortunately, the AAA persevered and among the early winners was William Loader (1935 100y in 10.1), who wrote the highly esteemed *Testament of a Runner* 25 years later. Another far-sighted move was the introduction in 1934 of annual AAA Summer Schools at Loughborough, run by Captain F.A.M. Webster (many of whose books became classics of athletics literature), 1924 Olympic steeplechaser Evelyn Montague and Britain's most successful ever hammer thrower, 1924 Olympic bronze medallist Malcolm Nokes. Many an athlete and coach would bear witness to the value of those residential courses, including a young high jumper and future coach and European AA President by the name of Arthur Gold. AAA Indoor Championships were first held at Wembley's Empire Pool in 1935, on which occasion the 70y sprint and long jump were won by Sandy Duncan, who would serve for 26 years as General Secretary of the British Olympic Association from 1949.

Intriguingly, the Indoor Championships incorporated women's events under the auspices of the Women's AAA, but it would not be until 1988 that the two organisations would hold a combined Championship meeting outdoors. General Committee had decided in 1922 to turn down an application by the newly formed Women's AAA to be affiliated to the AAA like the Race Walking Association and English Cross-Country Union were. They thought that it would be advisable for women's athletics to be governed by a separate body. In other words, it wanted no part of an activity that many AAA members deemed unfeminine. Consequently, the WAAA remained an autonomous organisation for some 70 years. However, the men and women did work together within the framework of the BAAB from 1937.

Highlights from each of the
AAA Championships meetings 1920–1939

1920 (Stamford Bridge)

THE CHAMPIONSHIPS SERVED as a selection trial for the following month's Antwerp Olympics and, after finishing second to Bevil Rudd in the 880y (1:56.6 to the South African's 1:55.8) and not contesting the mile, Albert Hill was chosen only for the 800m. As he recalled many years later: "I well remember the strong argument I had with Sir Harry Barclay, the secretary of the AAA [who was knighted in 1930 for services to athletics], when the teams were being selected, for the committee were opposed to my attempting the 800m and 1500m. But I was adamant on tackling the double and in the end Sir Harry bowed to my arguments. Most of the critics, too, were against my decision – the more so because I had been defeated by Bevil Rudd. But when he beat me at Stamford Bridge my leg was still troubling me. Shortly afterwards, with the aid of a bandage above the ankle, it improved 100 per cent and I was determined to show the critics that I was not the has-been they thought I was." Show them he did, for at the Olympics he took the 800m in the British record time of 1:53.4, with Rudd (who later won the 400m ahead of Guy Butler) third, and two days later he (4:01.8) and Philip Baker finished first and second in the 1500m. It was a double that would not be replicated until Peter Snell in 1964, and at 31 Hill remains the oldest man to have won either title. The other Briton to win an individual gold medal in Antwerp was Percy Hodge in the 3000m steeplechase with a British record of 10:00.4; he had earlier retained his AAA title over 2 miles in a very slow 11:22.8. There was a reason for that. Badly spiked on the second lap, he stopped to remove his shoe and inspect the damage. By the time he rejoined the race he was 100y behind but went on to win comfortably. Howard Baker, who had served as a lieutenant in the Royal Navy during the war and was equally celebrated as an Everton, Chelsea and England international goalkeeper as well as being a top class tennis and water polo player, collected the fifth of six AAA high jump titles with a British record of 1.91m (6ft 3^{1}/4in) – a height that would have gained the Olympic silver medal. Unfortunately, on that occasion he could manage only 1.85m for sixth place.

Harry Edward, destined to win two Olympic bronze medals, scored a AAA sprint double in 10.0 and 21.6, with Harold Abrahams placing fifth and fourth respectively (plus fourth in the triple jump and ninth and last in the long jump with dinky marks of 11.64m and 6.18m!). Four years later Abrahams would become an Olympic champion. However, an even more unlikely candidate for future Olympic honours was hammer thrower Malcolm

Nokes. Holder of the Military Cross, he finished last of five with just 30.78m ... but he would throw 52.76m in 1923, which stood as a British record for 24 years, and in Paris the following year he excelled by taking the bronze medal.

1921 (Stamford Bridge)

ALBERT HILL'S AAA farewell proved frustrating in that he planned with coach Sam Mussabini to run four laps in 62 sec apiece in a bid to smash the world mile record of 4:12.6 held by the American, Norman Taber. Leading throughout, in a field of 22, he did reach halfway spot on in 2:04.0 with uneven quarters of 59.6 and 64.4 but a third lap of 67.2 put paid to any chance of a world record. However, he did cover the final circuit in 62.2 to smash the British record with 4:13.8. He was closely pressed by Hyla Stallard (4:14.2), 12 years Hill's junior, as both finished way inside the previous mark established by Joe Binks in 1902 and equalled by Hill in 1919, and the pair were carried shoulder high from the track.

A delightfully mischievous touch was lent to the proceedings by a section of the crowd who, having sensed the British record was doomed, chanted for the 'benefit' of Joe Binks in the press box: "It's going, it's going; His head is falling low; I hear those unkind voices calling; Poor Old Joe!"

Despite a sluggish start in both races, Harry Edward scored another sprint double (10.2/22.2) with Harold Abrahams second in both races, while Olympic champion Percy Hodge only just missed the British record in the 2 miles steeplechase with 10:57.2 despite running with "a sprained stomach muscle bandaged up". He "ran with wonderful gameness," declared one reporter. One week after raising his British high jump record to 1.95m (6ft 5in), barely two inches below the world record, Howard Baker contented himself with a clearance of 1.90m for his sixth and final AAA title.

1922 (Stamford Bridge)

GRACED BY THE presence of the AAA's Patron, King George V, and attended by a record crowd of more than 25,000, this proved to be one of the most memorable of Championship meetings. It featured the English debut of the great Finnish runner, Paavo Nurmi, who won both the 4 miles (19:52.2) and steeplechase (11:11.2), but the undoubted star of the show was Polytechnic Harriers' Harry Edward. A tall and stylish sprinter from British Guiana, he thrilled the spectators with a unique treble, winning the 100y (10.0), 220y (22.0) and 440y (50.4) all within the space of one hour on a heavy track! As one besotted observer put it: "For smoothness, pace and poetry of motion it can never have been equalled, surely." Harold Abrahams was smitten too. "He was one of the most impressive sprinters I have ever seen," he remarked ... and later took the highly practical and productive step of inviting Edward's coach, the ubiquitous Sam Mussabini, to advise him. Good as he was, Edward may have lost his best sprinting years as he was studying in Germany at the outbreak of the First World War, when he was 19, and was interned for the duration.

Another notable visitor was Norway's 20-year-old Charles Hoff, winner of the pole vault (3.66m) and long jump (7.08m) and runner-up in the triple jump with 14.04m. Hoff's versatility was breathtaking, for later that year he became pole vault world record holder with 4.12m (improving to 4.25m in 1925 and 4.32m as a professional in 1931) and yet he was also a highly talented runner, setting a 500m world best of 65.0 in 1923 while at the 1924 Olympics, unable to contest the pole vault because of injury, he entered the 800m instead and made the final. That race, by the way, was won by Britain's Douglas Lowe who, as a 19-year-old, placed an inconspicuous fifth in the 880y at Stamford Bridge.

1923 (Stamford Bridge)

CONTRARY TO WHAT was portrayed in *Chariots of Fire*, Harold Abrahams and Eric Liddell never did clash over the short sprint. The opportunity presented itself at these Championships, but a septic throat led to Abrahams being eliminated in his heat of the 100y (although he did set a British long jump record of 7.23m that afternoon), whereas Liddell equalled the British record of 9.8 in his semi and set new figures of 9.7 in the final, only one-tenth outside the world record. The watches read 9.67, 9.65 and 9.65 and that time was not bettered by a Briton until McDonald Bailey in 1947. No English-born athlete ran faster until Peter Radford in 1958! Although the Scottish divinity student's time was received in some quarters with scepticism, mainly because two Englishmen (William Nichol and Tom Matthewman) who were considered even-timers at best finished within a yard of the winner, everything was according to the rules and the time was officially ratified. Liddell went on to win the 220y in 21.6.

Another British record was equalled in the 120y hurdles where Fred Gaby – yet another of Sam Mussabini's pupils – won the second of his five titles in 15.2. Two distinguished military men with the same initials were among the competitors. Frederick A.M. Browning, representing South London Harriers and the Grenadier Guards, placed third in the 440y hurdles and F.A. Michael Webster was fourth in the javelin. Captain Webster, as he was best known, was an influential figure in the world of coaching, particularly of field events, and wrote several classic books on athletics and its history, while "Boy" Browning, who rose to the rank of Lieutenant General, was awarded the DSO and *Croix de Guerre* in 1917 and during the Second World War was appointed by Winston Churchill to command the 1st Airborne Division. In 1928 he was a member of the British bobsleigh team at the Winter Olympics; he married the celebrated writer Daphne du Maurier ("Rebecca") in 1932 and was knighted in 1946.

1924 (Stamford Bridge)

BRITISH ATHLETES WON three gold medals at the Paris Olympics a fortnight or so later but one would hardly have expected those successes judging from the results at the AAA Championships. The two *Chariots of Fire* heroes won their events at Stamford Bridge but their times were modest indeed compared to prevailing world standards. Harold Abrahams clocked a personal best 100y time of 9.9 in heat and final, whereas the 1920 Olympic champion Charles Paddock (USA) was co-holder of the world record at 9.6, while Eric Liddell equalled his fastest 440y time of 49.6, a far cry from the cluster of opponents he would face who could boast times of around the 48 sec mark. Yet in Paris both were in inspired form, Abrahams winning the 100m in 10.6 (worth 9.7 for 100y) and Liddell the 400m in a European record of 47.6– both being Olympic records.

The third Olympic champion in waiting, Douglas Lowe, didn't even win his AAA race. Running 1:54.8 behind Hyla Stallard's 1:54.6, which tied a British record which had stood since 1888, Lowe travelled to Paris as second string in the 800m. There Stallard set a hot pace for 700m before fading and it was Lowe who triumphed with a British record of 1:52.4. Field events in Britain were not measured in metric in those days, so he wouldn't have been aware of it, but Jack Higginson's new British triple jump record translated to a retrospectively frustrating 13.99m although he did get beyond 14m two years later.

1925 (Stamford Bridge)

HYLA STALLARD, WINNER of the mile title in 1922 and 1923 and the 880y champion in 1924, completed an unique triple by taking the 440y in 50-flat. Such versatility was overshadowed by Harold Osborn (USA), the Olympic high jump and decathlon champion and the world record holder for both events. He was everywhere, winning the high jump at a relatively modest 1.93m (his record was

2.03m), but only after two failures at 1.75m, and placing second in the triple jump, fourth in the pole vault and shot, and sixth in the discus. An obscure competitor from Haiti of all places finished an unnoticed sixth in the long jump with 6.79m. His name was Silvio Cator, and in 1928 – following an Olympic silver medal – he would make history by becoming the first man to leap over 26ft with 7.93m. The marathon was added to the roster of AAA Championships and the winner of the race from Windsor to Stamford Bridge, held in conjunction with the celebrated Polytechnic Harriers event, was Ulsterman Sam Ferris whose time of 2:35:59 was a British record.

1926 (Stamford Bridge)

FOR THE FIRST time since the end of the war, German athletes were permitted to enter, and one of them – Dr Otto Peltzer – was responsible for the first world record at the Championships since 1914. The huge crowd (35,000 according to *The Times*) got their money's worth from the half mile clash between him and Douglas Lowe. Peltzer had clocked 1:52.8 for 800m in 1925, fastest in the world that year, while Olympic champion Lowe had sharpened up with a world record of 1:10.4 for 600y seven days before this eagerly awaited meeting. Lowe led at halfway in a sizzling 54.6, repelled Peltzer's persistent challenges along the back straight but found himself unable to counter his rival's final sprint for home. Peltzer stormed home three yards ahead in 1:51.6, with Lowe's time untaken but estimated at 1:52.0 – both inside the world record of 1:52.2 by Ted Meredith (USA) in 1916. A more official British record fell in the 440y hurdles where Lord Burghley ran 55.6 in his heat and 55.0 in the final. Among many other future distinctions he would serve as IAAF President from 1946 to 1976, to be succeeded by the Dutchman, Adriaan Paulen, a world record breaker at 500m who at these Championships placed third in the 440y, which was won by Dutch-born British international John Rinkel in 49.8.

1927 (Stamford Bridge)

FAST FINISHING LORD BURGHLEY reduced his 440y
hurdles time to 54.2, which not only smashed his British
record but, thanks to the difference in time zones, stood
equal to the world record for a few hours ... until John
Gibson reeled off a remarkable 52.6 for the American title
in Nebraska the same afternoon. Third in the London race
after starting too fast was Italy's Luigi Facelli and he and
Burghley would fight it out for this title many times over
the coming years, the final score being 3-3. Douglas Lowe
completed a neat 880y/440y double in 1:54.6 and 48.8, and
Fred Gaby accumulated his fifth and final 120y hurdles title
in the British record time of 14.9 in conditions described as
"against a fitful breeze and on a wet and treacherous turf."
Second in 1924, Gaby would later finish runner-up also in
1928 and 1930. Another durable AAA champion was triple
jumper Wim Peters from the Netherlands. He won on this
occasion with a UK all-comers record of 15.47m, just 5cm
shy of a world record which had stood since 1911, and he
would go on to take five more titles and two second places
between then and 1939.

1928 (Stamford Bridge)

ACCORDING TO *THE TIMES* no fewer than 40,000 spectators were on hand for the final day, although another
source refers to over 29,000. The crowd – whatever its true
size – went home happy as two firm favourites, Douglas
Lowe (1:56.6 880y) and Lord Burghley (British 440y hurdles record of 54.0), won their events in preparation for the
Amsterdam Olympics a few weeks later where both men
struck gold with new British records: Lowe with 1:51.8 in
the 800m and Burghley with 53.4 in the 400m hurdles.
Another Olympic champion-to-be on view was South Africa's Syd Atkinson, winner of the 120y hurdles in London in 14.7. New Zealander Stanley Lay threw the javelin
67.89m, which stood as the championship record for 29

years. That distance would have won him the Olympic title but at the Games he threw five metres less and failed to reach the final. Three AAA medallists who made their mark other than as athletes were Fred Housden, equal second in the pole vault (holder of the Military Cross from the First World War, he would help coach David Hemery to Olympic 400m hurdles gold 40 years later), Evelyn Montague, second in the steeplechase (he would become the respected athletics correspondent of the *Manchester Guardian* from 1928 to 1947) and Vernon Morgan, third in the steeplechase (who also became a distinguished journalist, long-time sports editor of Reuters). The pole vault winner, with a championship record of 3.83m, was Franklin Kelley, an American representing Southampton AC; in fact he was the US Vice-Consul in that city. The decathlon was added to the programme, but was then not held again until 1936. The runner-up to South Africa's Harry Hart was Howard Ford, of the RAF, who rose to the rank of Air Vice Marshal in 1960. Another innovation: the stadium announcer, the ubiquitous Harold Abrahams, addressed the crowd via a loudspeaker system instead of a megaphone as previously.

1929 (Stamford Bridge)

HARRY PAYNE, AGED 36, left Sam Ferris (who would win the Olympic silver medal three years later) over eight minutes behind in the Windsor to Stamford Bridge marathon, and in the process broke Ferris's British record of 2:33:00 with a magnificent 2:30:58, fastest in the world that year. No Briton ever ran faster until Jim Peters in 1951. Two future marathon greats finished first and second in the 10 miles, held earlier in the season in Birmingham. Ernie Harper, who had first won this title in 1923 but whose finest moment would come at the Berlin Olympics of 1936 when he took the marathon silver medal, clocked 52:15.8 ahead of a youthful Jack Holden (52:35.0). Holden would go on to win the International Cross Country Championship four times between 1933 and 1939, while in 1950 he proved himself the world's top marathoner, winning all five of his races. Those included the Empire Games and, having turned 43, the European Championship! Don Finlay, who would enjoy a similarly long and fruitful career, made his AAA debut with a distant third place in the 120y hurdles, won by Lord Burghley in 15.4. Finlay would win the first of seven consecutive titles in 1932 ... and then again in 1949, aged 40. Burghley hardly had time to recover from that race before it was time for the 440y hurdles and was well beaten by his Italian rival, Luigi Facelli (53.4). Fred Housden again tied for second in the pole vault, joined by Jack Longland who clearly had a head for heights as he was a member of the Mount Everest expedition in 1933, setting up camp at 27,400ft. A man of many parts, he was knighted for services to education and for 20 years, from 1957, was the urbane chairman of the popular BBC radio quiz "My Word!".

Another runner-up was Robert "Bonzo" Howland, in the shot with 12.85m. The field events at the AAA Championships were such a happy hunting ground for foreigners that although he was the highest placed British competitor ten times between 1929 and 1939 Howland never managed to win the title, placing second nine times. The first Briton to use starting blocks was Jack London, the 1928 Olympic 100m silver medallist who was brought over from British Guiana (Guyana) when he was three months old. He won his only AAA title with a 10.0 100y. London admitted that he broke all the rules of good sprinting technique. Even Sam Mussabini failed to cure him of his bad starting, over-striding and too upright carriage. One day after Mussabini died, London was practising starts when Albert Hill, the great middle distance runner turned coach, came over and made a few comments. "Believe it or not," London stated, "in that one lesson he gained me three-quarters of a yard on my start alone!" Hill became his coach and London attributed all his chief successes to Hill's guidance. He later made a name for himself in show business circles.

1930 (Stamford Bridge)

THESE WERE THE Jubilee Championships, celebrating 50 years since the AAA was founded, and it was poignant that Sir Montague Shearrnan, so intricately linked to the Association since its inception and its President since 1916, should die just before the golden anniversary. His successor was the remarkable all-round sportsman Lord Desborough. It was somehow appropriate that the star performer of the meeting should be Lord Burghley, who only six years later would take over the AAA presidency from Lord Desborough. The fans were thrilled to see him complete an unique double by winning both hurdles events, the highs in a routine 15.2 and the intermediates with a British (and newly introduced English native) record of 53.8 in a nail-biting finish with Luigi Facelli, given the same time. The Italian was clearly ahead for most of the race but the Olympic champion produced a dynamic finish on the run-in from the final hurdle to snatch victory. As Douglas Lowe's estimated 880y time of 1:52.0 behind Otto Peltzer in 1926 was never officially recognised, Tom Hampson's winning time of 1:53.2 at this meeting was ratified as an English native record. He left Séra Martin, the French holder of the world 800m record (1:50.6), a dozen yards behind. Both Hampson and Burghley (in both hurdles) would become inaugural British Empire Games champions in Canada later in the summer, as would Stanley Engelhart in the 220y (he won the AAA title in 22.0), Reg Thomas in the mile (AAA champion in 4:15.2), Stan Tomlin (a future AAA Championships Secretary and athletics magazine editor) in the 3 miles, Scotland's Dunky Wright in the marathon (AAA winner in 2:38:30), George Bailey in the steeplechase (AAA champion in 10:55.4) and Malcolm Nokes (third but first Briton at the AAA with 45.62m) in the hammer. Oh, and "Bonzo" Howland, second of course in the AAA shot, was – you guessed it – second again in the British Empire Games.

1931 (Stamford Bridge)

THESE WERE THE last Championships to be staged at Stamford Bridge, which had been the home of British athletics as well as Chelsea Football Club for so many years. The craze for speedway motor cycle racing from 1929 was increasingly damaging the cinder track and it was time to move on. The AAA now had a new Honorary Secretary as well as a new President: none other than the 28-year-old barrister, Douglas Lowe, who served until 1938 when he handed over to Ernest (Billy) Holt. The double Olympic gold medallist had retired from racing shortly after the 1928 Games but now Britain had another half miler of the highest standard in the even-pace exponent Tom Hampson, who on this occasion defended his title in 1:54.8, with Lowe's great German rival of old, Otto Peltzer, in third place after being badly spiked early in the race. Lord Burghley was hard pressed by Don Finlay to win the 120y hurdles – run on the grass infield for the last time – in a fast 14.8 but was beaten into third place in the longer hurdles event won in 54.4 by Luigi Facelli. Godfrey Rampling, later to make his mark as a particularly brilliant relay runner, took the flat 440y in 48.6. Seven of the eight field events were won by foreigners, including Jan Blankers in the triple jump with 14.22m. The Dutchman, who won also in 1933, would later become better known as the husband of 1948 Olympic star Fanny Blankers-Koen.

1932 (White City)

WHEN THE 1908 Olympics were held at the stadium the cinder track measured three laps to a mile and was set inside a banked concrete cycle track, while the grass infield contained a 100m long swimming pool! The stadium had changed radically over the intervening years. The pool had gone, the cycle track had been replaced by a greyhound racing track and the athletes were provided with a standard quarter mile circuit. There was another major change for the first AAA Championships to be staged at the White City since 1908. The traditional 4 miles race was replaced by 3 miles and 6 miles to fall more in line with the Olympic distances of 5000m and 10,000m. Fifth in that inaugural 3 miles, won by Walter Beavers in 14:23.2, was Les Cohen who would many years later become one of the most recognisable and industrious of officials, his posts including that of AAA Championships Secretary. The event at last being held on cinders, Don Finlay (14.9) won the first of seven consecutive 120y hurdles titles while Lord Burghley, in Luigi Facelli's absence, regained the 440y hurdles crown in 54.6, his runner-up being Joe Simpson (later Sir Joseph Simpson), who was Commissioner of the Metropolitan Police from 1958 until his early death ten years later.

There was a British record in the 2 miles steeplechase where Tom Evenson (10:13.8) was hard pressed by his Salford clubmate George Bailey (10:14.8), and another in the shot where the luckless Cambridge don, "Bonzo" Howland, found 14.54m insufficient for victory. Both walks produced championship records with Bert Cooper (winning the first of seven consecutive titles) clocking 13:44.6 for 2 miles and Alf Pope 51:25.4 for 7 miles. Two Oxonians fought out the mile with Jerry Cornes edging New Zealand's Jack Lovelock, 4:14.2 to 4:14.4.

The closest race of all was the marathon. Two Scots, both from Maryhill Harriers, entered the stadium level and there was just one second between them at the finish with Donald McNab Robertson (who would win five more AAA titles) prevailing over the holder, Dunky Wright, in 2:34:33. The high jump produced a youthful champion in Bill Land (1.85m). The previous year, at 16, he had become Britain's youngest international, winning against Italy (1.86m) and Germany (1.87m), and such was his versatility that he went on to set British records in the javelin (58.40m) and discus (43.08m) in 1935. In six years of war service with the Royal Engineers, reaching the rank of captain, he was a "Desert Rat" who fought at El Alamein, took part in the Sicily and

D-Day invasions and made his way through Germany to link up with the Red Army.

Less than two weeks after the AAA Championships, the British Olympic team, captained by Lord Burghley, set off for Los Angeles. Sailing from Southampton to Quebec and then by train across North America, the journey took 12 days! The British heroes there were Tom Hampson (who had won the AAA 880y in a pedestrian 1:56.4), gold medallist in the 800m in an even-paced world record 1:49.8, and Tommy, who took the 50km walk in 4:50:10. Silver medals were won by Jerry Cornes in the 1500m, Sam Ferris in the marathon, Tom Evenson in the steeplechase and by the 4x400m team of Crew Stoneley, Hampson, Burghley and Godfrey Rampling, while Don Finlay took a bronze. Burghley just missed out on a medal in the 400m hurdles but displayed the form of his life by setting a British record of 52.2, which would last until 1954, and in the relay he contributed a leg timed at 46.7, second fastest of the race.

1933 (White City)

THE MEMORABLE SERIES of 440y hurdling duels continued. As in 1929 and 1931 it was the turn of 35-year-old Luigi Facelli to win in 53.6 but it was close as a fast finishing Lord Burghley, now an MP and making his final championship appearance, ran 53.8. Don Finlay won his second title in 15.0, followed home by Roly Harper – who as Lt Col Roland Harper would in 1946 propose the adoption of the AAA Coaching Scheme and become the Honorary Secretary of the new AAA Coaching Committee.

Finland's Olympic 5000m champion Lauri Lehtinen ran the fastest 3 miles ever seen in Britain with 14:09.2 and his compatriot, Olympic steeplechase champion Volmari Iso-Hollo, left George Bailey and Tom Evenson half a minute and more behind as he set a championship record of 10:06.6 which would survive until 1950. That was the year of Jack Holden's momentous marathon triumphs but it was in 1933 that he won his first AAA title (30:32.2 6 miles).

Bert Cooper lowered his 2 miles walk championship record to 13:39.8, while the oldest championship record on the books – Syd Thomas's 51:31.4 10 miles back in 1889 – fell at last when George Bailey ran 50:51.0 in Sheffield in April. However, the track was found to be 4ft 4in short of 440y and thus the distance covered was about 58 yards (or about 10 sec in time) short of 10 miles. Third in the 440y, won by future Olympic relay gold medallist Freddie Wolff in 49.0, was Roy Moor, who became an ever enthusiastic and highly popular athletics correspondent, principally for the *News Chronicle*.

1934 (White City)

THE MAIN ATTRACTION was the mile, bringing together the former world record holder (at 4:07.6) Jack Lovelock, promising 19-year-old Sydney Wooderson and Olympic silver medallist Jerry Cornes. However, the winning time turned out to be the second slowest since 1900 at 4:26.6! No one was prepared to cut out a decent pace and halfway was reached in 2:22.5. Covering the last lap in 58.5, Lovelock left Wooderson 1.2 sec behind. With Lord Burghley retired and Luigi Facelli not seeking to defend, the 440y hurdles champion – the first new name since 1925 – was a future Judge, Ralph Kilner Brown, in 55.2. Brown, who was knighted in 1970, was the eldest of three remarkable siblings; Godfrey would win gold (4x400m relay) and silver (400m) medals at the 1936 Olympics and Audrey would strike silver in the 4x100m relay.

The athletics programme of the 2nd British Empire Games, held three weeks later at the White City, was organised by the AAA and English athletes were dominant. Victories were gained by Irish-born Arthur Sweeney (100y and 220y), Godfrey Rampling (440y), Walter Beavers (3 miles), Arthur Penny (6 miles), Stanley Scarsbrook (steeplechase), Don Finlay (120y hurdles), 37-year-old Malcolm Nokes (hammer) and both relay teams. Lovelock, representing his native New Zealand although for his entire international running career he studied and worked in England, gained revenge over Wooderson in the mile but the latter had the consolation of equalling Reg Thomas's British record of 4:13.4 in second place .

1935 (White City)

EARLIER IN THE year the AAA introduced its Indoor Championships at the Empire Pool, Wembley, giving "Bonzo" Howland the opportunity to win a national shot put title at last. Outdoors it was business as usual: second for a fifth time, with four more to come. The mile, watched by an enthralled crowd of 40,000, was notable for Sydney Wooderson's revenge over a self-confessed "stale" Jack Lovelock, who had just recently won a 'mile of the century' in the USA against Bill Bonthron and Glenn Cunningham, respectively world record holders at 1500m and mile. Lovelock led at the bell in 3:16.0 but Wooderson took charge along the back straight to win comfortably, 4:17.2 to 4:18.4. Three weeks later, before 50,000 spectators at the Glasgow Rangers Sports, he beat Lovelock again, this time with a British record of 4:12.7.

Arthur Sweeney, who along with Cyril Holmes would dominate British sprinting for the rest of the 1930s, won his first AAA title. His 100y time of 10.2 may have been the slowest for many years but he beat two fine runners in Martinus Osendarp of Holland (a 10.5 100m performer who would finish third in the next year's Olympics) and the Hungarian holder of the title, József Sir, who had run 10.4 for 100m in 1934. Osendarp, who won the 220y and then the 100y in 1936 and 1938, would be found guilty of war crimes. He became a member of the German SS and in 1948 was sentenced to 12 years imprisonment for collaboration with the enemy, although he was released after four years and died in 2002. You won't find his name among the finalists but the man who would revolutionise coaching in British athletics after the Second World War did pick up a AAA standard medal for beating 16 sec in his heat of the 120y hurdles ... 21-year-old Geoff Dyson.

1936 (White City)

BEFORE ANOTHER 40,000 crowd, Sydney Wooderson, who three weeks earlier had set a British record of 4:10.8, again got the better of Jack Lovelock, 4:15.0 to 4:15.2 in wet and windy conditions – but at a price. He finished the race limping with an ankle injury which would cause him to drop out in his Olympic 1500m heat in Berlin. By way of contrast, Lovelock planned his season perfectly and ran the race of his life when it mattered most: in the Olympic final, which he won in the world record time of 3:47.8. Although Lovelock was regarded almost as a British athlete (his father was born in England), the only members of the British team to strike gold in Berlin were Harold Whitlock in the 50km walk (he had used the AAA 7 miles walk as a speed session, placing fifth) and the 4x400m relay team, who upset the more fancied Americans in the European record time of 3:09.0.

The squad was picked on the basis of the AAA 440y, won by Godfrey Brown in 48.6 ahead of Godfrey Rampling, Bill Roberts and Freddie Wolff. The first three all excelled themselves in the individual 400m in Berlin. Brown came so close to winning the gold medal with his European record of 46.7 (on electrical timing he was just 2/100ths behind the USA's Archie Williams) with Roberts timed at 46.8 in fourth place, 3/100ths away from a bronze medal. Rampling, the father of acclaimed film actress Charlotte Rampling and who lived to celebrate his 100th birthday in 2009, lowered his personal best to 47.5, narrowly missing a place in the final. There were silver medals also for Don Finlay in the 110m hurdles with a British record of 14.4 and Ernie Harper in the marathon (2:31:24), just four weeks after finishing one second behind Donald McNab Robertson (2:35:03) in a gripping AAA championship staged on an out and back course from the White City. Speaking of Olympic heroes, Lord Burghley succeeded Lord Desborough as AAA President this year.

Dick Webster, the son of Capt (later Lt.Col.) F.A.M. Webster, set a British pole vault record of 3.88m, and two of Alf Shrubb's long standing national records fell at last. The 10 miles title, contested in April, went to Bill Eaton in 50:30.8, and Peter Ward ran 3 miles in 14:15.8. Shrubb's 6 miles record had been broken by Eaton earlier in the year with 29:51.4 and Alec Burns lowered that to 29:45.0 at the White City behind Poland's Jozef Noji. Tragically, Eaton would die from pneumonia in April 1938, aged only 28, while British discus record holder Douglas Bell – third in that event – died aged 35 of wounds sustained when his Army Company attempted to cross the Antwerp-Turnhout Canal in 1944. Laurence Reavell-Carter, second in the discus, did survive the war as an RAF Flight Lieutenant but was lucky to avoid being executed. As a prisoner of war in 1944 he took part in The Great Escape, of movie fame, and actually got away from the Stalag Luft III camp, only to be recaptured soon afterwards. Fifty of his comrades were murdered by the Gestapo in an act of revenge.

1937 (White City)

SYDNEY WOODERSON RAN away with his third AAA mile title in 4:12.2 to lower the championship record of 4:13.8 set by his coach, Albert Hill, in 1921. The following month this diminutive, bespectacled athlete would make an indelible mark on miling history by setting a world record of 4:06.4. Don Finlay improved his year-old 120y hurdles championship record to 14.5, two yards ahead of John Thornton (who would die during the Normandy landings in 1944), while the 440y saw the demise of the oldest of all championship records. The time of 48.5 by the Rev Henry Charles Lenox Tindall, a world best at the time, had withstood all assaults since 1889, with Godfrey Rampling in 1931 and Godfrey Brown in 1936 falling just short with 48.6. At last, with no opposition to speak of, Bill Roberts demolished the mark with 48.2.

However, the top performance of the meeting was a world record in the 7 miles walk of 50:19.2 by John Mikaelsson. The Swede would enjoy a glittering career, for he won the Olympic 10,000m walk in 1948 and 1952. Another competitor at those 1952 Games would be a young Gordon Pirie, the connection with 1937 being that his father, Alick Pirie, placed tenth in the AAA marathon (2:54:46), won for a fifth time by Donald McNab Robertson (2:37:20). Luz Long, the German who befriended and finished second to Jesse Owens in the previous year's Olympic long jump, set a championship record of 7.47m. Both Long and Hans Wöllke (the Olympic shot champion and AAA winner with 15.39m) were destined to die on the Eastern Front in 1943. Of the previous 18 javelin championships held, the title went overseas on 15 occasions, but this time there was a home winner in Stanley Wilson whose throw of 59.18m was a British record. Placing equal third in the high jump was Arthur Gold, who rose to become one of the most influential of all British athletics officials and in 1984 would be knighted for his services to the sport.

1938 (White City)

Don Finlay, with a wind assisted 14.4 hurdles, and Bert Cooper, who walked 2 miles in 14:02.2, matched the record of Irish shot putter Denis Horgan (1893-1899) by notching up a seventh consecutive AAA title. There was another link with the distant past in the decathlon victory (at Loughborough) of Tom Lockton, grandson of Charles Lockton, who was not only the very first AAA long jump champion back in 1880 but had won the AAC title in 1873 at age 16. Early in the year, in Sydney, only three UK male athletes won gold medals at the British Empire Games: Cyril Holmes in the 100y and 220y, Bill Roberts in the 440y and Jim Alford of Wales (a future coach of note) in the mile. Holmes, who would play rugby union for England in 1947/48, pulled a muscle in his 220y heat at the AAA Championships, while Roberts and Alford placed third in their events, won by Godfrey Brown (49.2) and Sydney Wooderson (4:13.4). Later in the season, Britain was represented for the first time in the European Championships, held in Paris. There were four British winners: Brown (400m), Wooderson (1500m), Finlay (in a British record of 14.3) and Harold Whitlock (50km walk).

1939 (White City)

Don Finlay was a non-starter due to injury but Bert Cooper attempted a record eighth successive title in the 2 miles walk, only to settle for second place to Harry Churcher (13:50.0), a man who would set world records at 5 miles in 1948 and 1949. Sydney Wooderson, who in August 1938 had added world records at 800m (1:48.4) and 880y (1:49.2) to his mile record, ran out the mile winner for a fifth consecutive year, improving his championship record to 4:11.8 with a 57.2 last lap, but only just from Denis Pell (4:12.0), who would die at 26 in an RAF flying accident during the war which was only weeks away. Donald McNab Robertson (2:35:37) gained his sixth marathon title, followed in by Squire Yarrow, the 1938 European silver medallist who would become President of the AAA in 1978. Stan Cox, who in 1952 became the second fastest ever marathoner with 2:21:42 behind Jim Peters' revolutionary 2:20:43, finished fourth in the 3 miles (14:13.6), a race won by Jack Emery in a British all-comers record of 14:08.0.

The versatile Godfrey Brown, who once beat Arthur Sweeney over 100y and was timed at 9.7 on a slightly downhill track, signed off as 880y champion in 1:55.1.The aforementioned Sweeney (who like Pell would perish in a wartime flying accident) won a close 100y against Cyril Holmes in 9.9, with placings reversed in the 220y (21.9). Unremarked at the time was an 18-year-old from Trinidad who progressed no further than the heats of the 100y and semi-finals of the 220y. He would, after the war, occupy an honoured place in AAA Championships history ... McDonald Bailey.

BRITISH RECORDS AT 1 JANUARY 1940

100y: 9.7 Eric Liddell 1923 & Cyril Holmes 1938; 100m: 10.4 Arthur Sweeney 1937; 220y (turn): 21.2 Willie Applegarth 1914 & Holmes 1938; 400m: 46.7 Godfrey Brown 1936; 800m/880y: 1:48.4/1:49.2 Sydney Wooderson 1938; 1500m: 3:48.7 Wooderson 1938; Mile: 4:06.4 Wooderson 1937; 2M: 9:03.4 Jack Emery 1939; 3M/5000m: 14:02.0/14:31.6 Peter Ward 1937; 6M: 29:45.0 Alec Burns 1936; 10,000m: 30:58.2 Burns 1936; 10M: 50:30.8 Bill Eaton 1936; Marathon: 2:30:58 Harry Payne 1929; 3000mSC: 9:18.8 Tom Evenson 1932 (9:16.0 estimated George Bailey 1932); 2M SC: 10:13.8 Evenson 1932; 110mH: 14.3 Don Finlay 1938; 400mH: 52.2 Lord Burghley 1932; HJ: 1.95 Howard Baker 1921; PV: 4.00 Dick Webster 1936; LJ: 7.38 Harold Abrahams 1924; TJ: 14.77 Edward Boyce 1934; SP: 14.86 Robert Howland 1935; DT: 46.83 David Young 1938; HT: 52.76 Malcolm Nokes 1923; JT: 61.63 James McKillop 1939; Decathlon: (re-scored on 1985 tables) 5466 Tom Lockton 1938; 2M Walk: 13:11.4 George Larner 1904; 7M Walk: 50:28.8 Alfred Pope 1932; 50km Walk: 4:30:08 Harold Whitlock 1936.

THE FORTIES AND FIFTIES

THE AAA CONTINUED to operate, albeit in a restricted capacity, throughout the Second World War. Of particular value were the matches organised by the AAA against various teams which raised considerable sums for war charities.

Despite poor health, Sydney Wooderson managed to fit in some races every year. He ran the mile in 4:11.0, a Scottish all-comers record, at the Glasgow Rangers Sports in 1940; 4:12.8 at the British Games at the White City, 4:11.5 at Fallowfield, Manchester, and 4:11.8 again at the White City in an Allied Forces meeting in 1943; and 4:12.8 in the "Stalin Mile" at an "Aid to Russia" meeting at Fallowfield in 1944. Later that summer he developed such severe rheumatism that he was in hospital for nearly four months, followed by two months' convalescence, and was told by doctors he could never run again. They bargained without Wooderson's iron will. Physically frail he might have looked but he was a real fighter. Within six months of leaving hospital he was racing again.

In July 1945 he won the Army championship in 4:14.8; in August he ran the world record breaking Swede, Arne Andersson, close at a packed out White City (with well over 50,000 fans, including a 16-year-old Roger Bannister, inside) in 4:09.2; while – even more amazingly – in September he produced the fastest mile of his life, a British record of 4:04.2! Wooderson reckoned that race in Gothenburg, in which he again finished just behind Andersson, was the best of his career. "I got through the war without proper training and racing, and yet finished only a couple of yards behind." He added: "It was most gratifying after spending the war years running times of between 4:11 and 4:16 on bumpy grass tracks to improve over two seconds so long after I'd set my record." En route he set a British 1500m record of 3:48.4. Wooderson was then 31 and one has to wonder what he might have achieved had he not lost his best running years to the war. He could have become the world's first four minute miler, a decade or so before Bannister, and he would surely have been a strong medal contender at the Olympic Games which were originally scheduled for 1940 and 1944.

By the time of the 1948 Olympics in London, Wooderson's track racing career was over – although it remains a scandal that Britain's greatest and most popular athlete was passed over for the honour of carrying the Olympic torch around the track at Wembley Stadium in favour of a virtually unknown but handsome quarter-miler named John Mark. Although that Gothenburg race was his last major mile event, Wooderson had other worlds to conquer. At the first post-war AAA Championships in 1946 he smashed the British 3 miles record with 13:53.2 and then captured the European 5000m title in Oslo in what was then the world's second fastest ever time of 14:08.6, his defeated rivals including Emil Zátopek and Gaston Reiff, both of whom would strike gold at the Olympics two years later. Even that wasn't quite the end for in March 1948 Wooderson became English cross country champion over a gruelling 10 miles course! No one since could claim to have been at one time or another the world's best runner at 800m, the mile and 5000m.

Two other pre-war champions who returned to add further lustre to their careers were Jack Holden, who developed into the world's leading marathon runner, and evergreen sprint hurdler Don Finlay. Holden, the International Cross Country champion four times between 1933 and 1939 and three times AAA 6 miles champion, won the AAA marathon four times running between 1947 and 1950 and in the latter year – when he turned 43 – also became Empire Games and European champion. Finlay, an Olympic 110m hurdles medallist in 1932 and 1936 and winner of seven consecutive AAA titles between 1932 and 1938, served with distinction during the war. A Wing Commander in the RAF, he was a fighter pilot and was decorated with the DFC and AFC. He began an astonishing comeback in 1947, made the Olympic team (and was given the honour of pronouncing the Olympic Oath at Wembley Stadium on behalf of all the competitors), reclaimed the AAA title in 1949 and was the second fastest European in 1950, aged 41!

The AAA played a vital role in the organisation of those 1948 Olympics. The Games were awarded to London in March 1946 and, with only two years to prepare, the organising committee – chaired by AAA President Lord Burghley – faced a formidable task, particularly in view of the austerity of immediate post-war Britain. But although there weren't too many frills (the male competitors were housed in military camps, the women in colleges) the Games were a great success. 'Billy' Holt, who was AAA Hon. Treasurer from 1932 to 1938 and Hon. Secretary between 1938 and 1947 before becoming Hon. Secretary-Treasurer of the IAAF, was given the demanding task of being the professional overall Director of the Games, while an army of unpaid AAA officials, including such former champions as Tom Hampson, Malcolm Nokes, Harry Payne, Cyril Holmes, Stan Tomlin, Sam Ferris, Harold Whitlock and Sandy Duncan, ensured the smooth running of the athletics programme. The committee responsible for that was headed by Donald Pain, who was also Arena Manager. He succeeded Billy Holt as Hon. Secretary-Treasurer of the IAAF in 1952, the world governing body of which Lord Burghley (the Marquess of Exeter from 1956) was President from 1946 to 1976.

The biggest crowds ever to watch athletics in Britain, often in excess of 80,000, flocked to Wembley each day. Although, unsurprisingly, Germany and Japan were not invited, and the Soviet Union would not make its Olympic debut until 1952, a record 59 nations (52 in athletics) participated in the Games, which were declared open by King George VI. For the first time in the 20th century no Olympic titles were won by representatives from Great Britain or Ireland, although the home fans did witness six silver medals by the British team, four of them in the women's events. The men who stood on the medal dais were Welshman Tom Richards from the marathon (the Welsh AAA had been created as a fourth Area Association that year) and the 4x100m relay squad of Jack Archer, England rugby international Jack Gregory, Alistair McCorquodale and Welsh rugby legend Ken Jones. Although he represented Jamaica, Arthur Wint – who won the 400m and finished second in the 800m – was also regarded as a home athlete. He arrived in Britain in 1944 as an RAF officer, won his first AAA titles in 1946 and ran for Britain in international matches. He and fellow West Indian and Polytechnic Harrier, sprinter McDonald Bailey from Trinidad, were Britain's most popular athletes in the late 1940s and early 1950s.

Sigfrid Edström, the Swedish President of the International Olympic Committee, summed up London's achievement in a message printed in the British Olympic Association's Official Report.

"The staging of the Olympic Games in London this year was recognised as the most crucial occasion in the history of sport. How could such a project in the Grand Manner be accomplished in the threadbare and impoverished world of 1948? It was a challenge to the British genius for improvisation, for Britain had to hold the Games in a city afflicted with an unparalleled housing shortage – yet homes had to be found for tens of thousands of foreign visitors, not to mention some 6,000 athletes. The great test was taken; and the organisation rose gloriously to the supreme challenge. The visitors were housed and fed; the athletes were made at home in camps where every care was taken of their waking and sleeping hours. Wembley Stadium itself, where day after day huge crowds assembled, surpassed in magnificence and convenience any previous homes of the Games. The first Olympic Games for 12 years have come and gone – an unqualified success."

Alongside the Olympic preparations, the other key development shortly after the war ended was the implementation of the AAA Coaching Scheme and the appointment of a professional Head Coach. Three full-time professional coaches were to have been appointed in 1939 only for the outbreak of war to put paid to that initiative, but at a General Committee meeting in October 1946 Lt Col "Roly" Harper, an Olympic 110m hurdles semi-finalist in 1932, proposed the adoption of the Coaching Scheme. The main objects were to provide a comprehensive national scheme of coaching co-ordinated by the AAA and create a body of professional and amateur coaches conforming to standards to be laid down by the AAA; to establish a chain of communication between the AAA and clubs and schools so that assistance could be provided to all and the most made of the country's athletic talent; and to issue bulletins to coaches and county organisations, and later it was hoped to clubs and schools, in order to keep them abreast of latest developments. The scheme would be operated by the AAA Coaching Committee, comprising Malcolm Nokes as Chairman, Harper as Hon. Secretary and Sandy Duncan as Assistant Hon. Secretary.

The charismatic 32-year-old Geoff Dyson, who had been Britain's third fastest high hurdler in 1938 with a time of 14.9, was the man appointed as Chief Coach in February 1947. He had been obliged to retire from competition when at his peak as he forfeited his amateur status by becoming a lecturer in athletics at Loughborough College. Returning for war service with the Army, which he had first joined at 16, he rose to the rank of Major, commanding Army schools of physical training in East Africa and Italy. After his demob he returned to Loughborough prior to his AAA appointment. His main function was to coach honorary coaches to a higher standard and establish a network of qualified coaches throughout the country. He lectured extensively with the aid of loop films and personally coached a small squad of athletes in what were then considered "Cinderella" events: John Disley in the steeplechase, Geoff Elliott in the pole vault and decathlon, the gigantic John Savidge in the shot, Shirley Cawley in the long jump and Maureen Gardner (who he later married) in the 80m hurdles. All five went on to set British records and three of them won Olympic medals. A later pupil was Arthur Rowe, who became European record holder in the shot.

An outstanding innovator and well versed in sports science, Dyson wrote the definitive coaching book, *The Mechanics of Athletics*, in 1962 and his coaching disciples – men like Denis Watts, John Le Masurier and Ron Pickering – went on to produce such Olympic champions as Ann Packer, Mary Rand and Lynn Davies. Norris and Ross McWhirter described him as "probably the greatest all-round coach in the world", while the American coaching authority and former star miler Fred Wilt called him "one of the greatest coaches who has ever lived and a legend in his own life." Roly Harper wrote of him in 1949: "Whatever developments occur in the future, and however big our scheme becomes, there will be no question as to who deserves the credit for laying its foundations, and all athletes throughout the country for generations to come will owe a debt of gratitude to Geoffrey Dyson." The plaudits were well merited, but unfortunately some of the most influential amateur officials of the day failed to appreciate his qualities and professionalism, there was a clash of personalities and disputes over his status, salary and coaching budget, and Dyson resigned in September 1961.

Helped by funding by the Ministry of Education as well as sponsorship from the *News of the World*, the AAA appointed 42m-plus discus thrower Tony Chapman later in 1947 as a National Coach, while three more started in

1948: Denis Watts, who in 1946 scored a AAA long and triple jump double, was made responsible for the North, Allan Malcolm for the Midlands (succeeded by former Welsh javelin champion Lionel Pugh in 1952) and the 1938 Empire Games mile champion Jim Alford for Wales. John Le Masurier, who succeeded Chapman in 1949, was allocated the South. They all worked hard and in the first five years of the scheme the number of honorary coaches rose from 160 to 1,000. By 1965 that total had risen to 2500. Thanks to the efforts of the AAA Development Committee, who worked in close liaison with the National Playing Fields' Association, the number of cinder tracks in England rose from 106 in 1952 to 184 in 1959 and 326 by 1966.

Although during the 1930s Capt F.A.M. Webster had edited a AAA official monthly magazine it wasn't until the early post-war years that the Association was able to disseminate information on a wide basis. *Athletics*, a monthly founded and edited by Jimmy Green at the end of 1945, carried regular notices of AAA activities, as did its successor (from January 1950) *Athletics Weekly*. The *AAA Coaching Bulletin* began publication in 1949 and that was incorporated in *The Athlete* (1950-1952), which in turn became *The Modern Athlete* (1953-1957) and *Modern Athletics* (1957-1964), publications edited by Stan Tomlin, a prominent official as well as journalist and former Empire Games 3 miles champion.

Between them, the National Coaches produced a widely admired series of AAA Instructional Booklets, the first of which was on high jump by Geoff Dyson in 1949, while starting in the 1950s – with the Hammer Circle first to swing into action in 1952 – specialist clubs sprang up to cater for each of the field events plus milers, steeplechasers and road runners. A Specialist Clubs Committee was formed in 1956 under the chairmanship of Malcolm Nokes. The first major indoor meeting since 1939 was staged at Harringay Arena in London in 1952, although national championships would not be revived until 1962. Another welcome innovation was the setting up in 1959 of a standards scheme for seniors, juniors and youths, with one of the sport's most industrious officials, Les Golding, acting as Hon. Secretary of the relevant committee.

Understandably, so soon after such a devastating war and with the country still in the throes of food rationing and general austerity, British athletics was initially at a fairly low ebb. The number of affiliated clubs and associations in 1946 was 326, a drop of 157 from 1939. As AAA Team Manager (from 1937 to 1952) Jack Crump wrote in the first ever issue of *Athletics* in December 1945: "I think it will save a lot of disappointment, and perhaps some ill-judged adverse criticism later, if we face up to the fact that we are likely to be in for a pretty thin time for a season or so. Our losses during the war have been grievous. We must also recognise that many of our best athletes will still be on service duties, at any rate for the 1946 season, and the choice for international teams will be restricted in consequence. A further blow has been the lack of first-class athletes at our premier universities. In short, it will take us several years before we can hope to reach our pre-war standard."

However, the 1950s proved to be a golden era. There may have been only one Olympic winner (Chris Brasher in the 1956 steeplechase) but there were many European and Empire Games victories to savour and British male athletes produced a wonderful collection of world records: McDonald Bailey at 100m, Roger Bannister and Derek Ibbotson at the mile, Gordon Pirie at 3000m, 5000m and 6 miles, Chris Chataway and Freddie Green at 3 miles (and Chataway also at 5000m), Jim Peters in the marathon, Roland Hardy at 5 miles walk and relay records at 4x880y, 4x1500m and 4x1 mile with Bill Nankeville featuring in all three.

Highlights from each of the AAA Championships meetings 1946–1959

1946 (White City)

SYDNEY WOODERSON TOOK over from where he left off in 1939: as AAA champion. The little man with the long stride and big heart contested his first serious 3 miles race before an adoring crowd of over 25,000 and, outkicking the formidable Dutchman Wim Slykhuis with a 59.2 last lap, he pulverised Peter Ward's 1938 British record of 14:05.6 with a time of 13:53.2. He had covered the final mile in 4:29.8, exactly the same time as when 13 years earlier he had become the first schoolboy to break 4:30. A few other pre-war champions put in an appearance. The 1936 Olympic 4x400m gold medallist Bill Roberts finished a close second in 48.6 to Jamaica's Arthur Wint (48.4) in the 440y; 1938 Empire Games mile champion Jim Alford placed fourth in the 880y, also won by the very tall, long striding Wint (1:54.8); Harry Churcher was second in the 2 miles walk and third over 7 miles with Bert Cooper fourth, the races being won by Sweden's Lars Hindmar in 13:59.0 and 52:30.0. Other doubles were achieved by McDonald Bailey in the 100y (9.8) and 220y (22.3) and by Denis Watts – like Alford soon to become a National Coach – with a 7.11m long jump and 14.29m triple jump. Doug Wilson, Wooderson's closest rival in wartime races and a future athletics correspondent alongside Joe Binks at the *News of the World*, won a close mile in 4:17.4.

Another tight finish occurred in the marathon. Due to a scheduling mix-up the leaders entered the stadium while the steeplechase was still being run and chaos reigned as they tried to avoid the barriers around the track, but it didn't stop Squire Yarrow and Donald McNab Robertson (both aged 40) fighting it out to the last stride with Yarrow prevailing by 0.2 sec in 2:43:14.4. Tom Richards, destined to win an Olympic silver medal two years later, was third.

More significantly for the future of the marathon, Jim Peters became the 6 miles champion in an unexceptional 30:50.4 ... but several years later he would astound the world of road running. The brightest young star on show was the 6ft 6in tall Scottish high jumper Alan Paterson (18), whose winning leap of 1.88m was well below the British record of 2.00m he had set a fortnight earlier. Paterson went on to take the silver medal at the European Championships in Oslo, where Jack Archer won the 100m in 10.6 and Wooderson obliterated the British 5000m record with a time (14:08.6) which was the world's second fastest ever. In view of his appointment in Oslo as Hon. Secretary of the IAAF, 'Billy' Holt gave notice of his intention to resign as Hon. Secretary of the AAA. Ernest Clynes, who had been a middle distance runner with Polytechnic Harriers, took over in 1947 and would serve until 1965.

1947 (White City)

AFTER AN ABSENCE of nine years, a silver-haired 38-year-old RAF war hero made a remarkable return to the AAA Championships. Wing Commander Don Finlay led for half the race in the 120y hurdles before being edged by Belgium's Pol Braekman as both were timed at 14.9. Another champion of old, Harry Churcher, was second again to Lars Hindmar (13:54.4) in the 2 miles walk but triumphed over 7 miles in 52:48.4. McDonald Bailey, with times of 9.7 (equalling Eric Liddell's 1923 championship record) and 21.7, gained the second of what would prove to be a record seven sprint doubles, while Harry Whittle not only won the first of seven consecutive 440y hurdles titles (55.0) but captured the long jump also with 7.25m. Overseas athletes were prominent in many events, filling first three places in the pole vault and javelin, which was not surprising, but also in the 440y where British athletes had a proud tradition. The first home finisher in an estimated 49.9 was John Mark, who would carry the Olympic torch at the opening ceremony a year later.

The most exotic new champion was Nigeria's Prince Adegboyega Adedoyin, a medical student at Belfast's Queens University who won the high jump at 1.93m in Alan Paterson's absence, placed a close second in the long jump and fourth in the 120y hurdles. The following year he represented Britain at the Olympics. Jack Holden, who had been controversially omitted from the team for the European Championships, won the first of his four successive AAA marathon titles. The race was held at Loughborough and his time was 2:33:21 ahead of Tom Richards and Donald McNab Robertson, the last named destined to die from thrombosis only two years later. Fifth in 2:46:03 was Alan Turing, who was named by *Time Magazine* as one of the 100 most important people of the 20th century for his role in the creation of the modern computer and ranked 21st in a BBC poll to determine the 100 greatest Britons. His vital work as a code-breaker at Bletchley Park was said to have shortened the war considerably.

1948 (White City)

JOHN PARLETT WAS one of the most impressive winners, finishing very fast to pip the highly rated New Zealander Doug Harris in the 880y in 1:52.2, with Arthur Wint a distant third, but at the London Olympics a month later he was badly bumped in the final and finished eighth while Wint took the silver medal prior to winning the 400m. McDonald Bailey, hampered by an injury which would ruin his Olympic chances, finished third in the 100y behind Australia's John Treloar (9.8) and the extraordinary Alistair McCorquodale of the Coldstream Guards, who had come from nowhere the previous year to run 9.9 for 100y and, in this his only season of international competition, would wind up finishing fourth in the Olympic 100m final in 10.4 and win a silver medal in the relay. Coached by four-time Olympic medallist Guy Butler (the official photographer to the AAA), the Scot slipped away from the sport after the Games, being more interested in his first love, cricket.

Bailey, who had run 21.8 in his heat and semi-final, was unable to start in the 220y final, won by McCorquodale in a modest 22.2.

Two of the Olympic 4x400m heroes of 1936 took part in the 440y. Bill Roberts, now 36, finished a commendable third in 48.8, the first Briton home, but Godfrey Brown failed to survive his heat. Two pre-war champions added further titles: Harry Churcher, who scored a walks double in 13:49.3 and 52:23.8, and pole vaulter Dick Webster (3.73m). Don Finlay had to withdraw from the 120y hurdles with a pulled muscle but there was compensation for the spectators as that event threw up the Championships' most unexpected winner in 18-year-old schoolboy Joe Birrell, who clocked 15.1 in his first meeting ever on a cinder track. He never did run faster than 15.0 but he coached his younger brother Bob to a British record of 14.2 in 1961. The mile, won by Bill Nankeville in 4:14.2, threw up a couple of interesting names in his wake. Runner-up in 4:15.4 was Josy Barthel of Luxembourg, who would become an unexpected Olympic 1500m champion in 1952, while in fifth place came 19-year-old Roger Bannister in 4:17.2.

1949 (White City)

THE STARS OF the first AAA Championships to be televised by the BBC were McDonald Bailey with his 9.7/21.7 sprint double; Bill Nankeville, whose championship record in the mile of 4:08.8 was the fourth fastest ever by a Briton after Sydney Wooderson's 4:04.2, 4:06.4 and 4:07.4; and Don Finlay, champion again after an interval of 11 years and in the remarkable time of 14.6. Bailey, now fully recovered from the injury which had cost him possible Olympic glory, had earlier in the season in Iceland been credited with a 9.5 100y, the fastest yet by a European although it was never ratified as a record. Nankeville (father of comedian Bobby Davro) uncorked a 58.8 last lap for what may have been the best run of his distinguished career in view of the fact that the track was flooded after a thunderstorm and downpour.

The Forties and Fifties

Conditions were so bad that Jimmy Green, editor of *Athletics* (forerunner of *Athletics Weekly*), commented in his report: "One felt sorry for the walkers, who went round lap after lap on what resembled a duck pond more than a track." The winner of that 7 miles race in 52:41.8 was 38-year-old Harry Churcher. Finlay, two years older, won by the huge margin of six-tenths and two weeks later closed his international match career with victory against France on the same track in 14.4, which was ratified as a British national and English native record for 120y hurdles. In 16 dual internationals between 1931 and 1949 he won 14 times and was second in the other two to team-mates Lord Burghley and John Thornton. What a record.

1950 (White City)

IT WASN'T QUITE the end of Don Finlay's international career as 16 years after his Empire Games victory in 1934 he participated in the 1950 edition, held in Auckland in February, and only just missed a medal, placing fourth in 14.7. Relatively few of Britain's top athletes made the lengthy sea trip and England's only winners were John Parlett in the 880y, Len Eyre in the 3 miles, 42-year-old Jack Holden in the marathon (a race in which Arthur Lydiard, later to become one of the world's most celebrated coaches, finished 11th) and Tim Anderson in the pole vault, while Scotland's Duncan Clark won the hammer. Parlett won a second medal, silver, in the 4x440y relay, his team-mates including Terry Higgins (third in the 1949 AAA 440y) who would serve as a Conservative MP from 1964 to 1997 when he was created Baron Higgins of Worthing. Five British records were set at the White City.

In good conditions on the first day McDonald Bailey tied his official 100y mark of 9.6, a new championship record after 27 years, but wind and rain on the second day slowed him to 9.9 in the final. Dr Frank Aaron sparked a revival in British long distance track racing with a 6 miles time of 29:33.6, Roland Hardy walked 7 miles in 50:11.6 with

75

Lol Allen also inside the old British record with 50:22.6, Duncan Clark threw the hammer 54.36m which counted as a British national record although he had reached 56.02m in New Zealand in March, and Welshman John Disley was timed at 10:05.4 in the 2 miles steeplechase behind a world best of 10:02.4 by Petar Segedin of Yugoslavia. One of the most spectacular performances for the 30,000 crowd to relish came from the hugely popular Arthur Wint, who led all the way in the 880y to equal Otto Peltzer's 1926 championship record of 1:51.6. Trailing in the wake of his giant stride were Roger Bannister (1:52.1) and John Parlett (1:53.1). Other championship records to be tied came in the 440y where Les Lewis ran 48.2 ahead of Derek Pugh (48.5) and in the high jump where Alan Paterson cleared 1.93m. Bailey completed his customary double in 21.8 after a 21.3 heat on the first day. Fourth in that final in a modest 22.4 was Brian Shenton ... but in Brussels the following month he was crowned European 200m champion in 21.5 after coming into the team only as a reserve! Those European Championships proved that British athletics was progressing satisfactorily despite the handicap of there being only 66 cinder tracks in the whole of England and Wales, 37 of them privately owned.

The other UK winners were Pugh in the 400m (47.3), Parlett in the 800m (1:50.5) with Bannister third in 1:50.7, Holden in the marathon in 2:32:14, Paterson in the high jump at 1.96m and the 4x400m team in 3:10.2 with Pugh anchoring in 46.2. The ever astonishing Holden, by now 43, had in July won his fourth AAA marathon title in a lifetime best of 2:31:04 and when in Brussels he was presented to the 19-year-old Prince Baudouin of Belgium he was able to remark "Glad to meet you, sir. Met your father and grandfather before you." There were British records by Bill Nankeville (AAA mile winner in 4:12.2) with 3:48.0 for third place in the 1500m, Frank Aaron with 30:31.6 for fourth in the 10,000m and Geoff Elliott with a decathlon score of 6116 (5900 on 1985 tables) in 11th place. Two bronze medals came Britain's way in the hurdling events: Peter Hildreth, who would go on to earn a record number of British international vests, in the 110m and Harry Whittle in the 400m.

1951 (White City)

THE *ATHLETICS WEEKLY* report was headlined "Best Ever Meeting?" and certainly the 1951 edition produced a flurry of championship records, including a world's best 2 miles steeplechase time of 9:58.6 by Petar Segedin with John Disley lowering his British record to 10:04.0. There were two other British records with 20-year-old Gordon Pirie announcing his entry on the big stage with a 6 miles record of 29:32.0 and 'Mac' Bailey equalling his 100y mark of 9.6 in semi-final and final. Bailey went on to take the 220y in 21.4 with fourth place being filled by Norris McWhirter, who would become world famous after he and twin brother Ross launched the *Guinness Book of Records* in 1955. Later in the summer, in a match against Yugoslavia in Belgrade, Bailey equalled the world 100m record of 10.2 first accomplished by the legendary Jesse Owens in 1936. European champion Derek Pugh broke the 440y championship record with 47.9, which was accepted as an English native record although Godfrey Brown, a quintessential Englishman, had run 47.6 at the White City in 1938 (itself greatly inferior to his 400m time of 46.7 at the 1936 Olympics) ... but Brown happened to be born in India. It was no great loss when English native records were scrapped in 1960, to be replaced by AAA national records which included marks by athletes whose fathers were born in England or Wales.

There was a majestic half mile victory by Arthur Wint, who passed 440y in 53.4 and won by 3.6 sec in a championship record of 1:49.6, only 0.4 sec outside the world record set by Sydney Wooderson and equalled by Mal Whitfield (USA). Other championship records fell in the mile, with Roger Bannister clocking 4:07.8 ahead of Bill Nankeville (4:08.6), high jump with Ron Pavitt clearing 1.95m, shot with Gunnar Huseby of Iceland putting 15.87m and discus where Italy's Giuseppe Tosi threw 53.58m. The most thrilling event, though, produced no records; just a great 3 miles duel in which Roy Beckett edged Chris Chataway after a last lap of close to 57 sec, both timed at 14:02.6.

1952 (White City)

HER MAJESTY THE QUEEN, who had succeeded her late father King George VI as Patron of the AAA, attended the Championships, which attracted the largest crowd in its long history – something in excess of 46,000. British hopes of success in the Helsinki Olympics the following month were boosted by a world best of 9:44.0 in the soon to be defunct 2 miles steeplechase by John Disley, with Chris Brasher second in 10:03.6 ahead of defending champion Petar Segedin; and a new British record of 28:55.6 for 6 miles by Gordon Pirie. McDonald Bailey tied his 100y record of 9.6 yet again as well as taking the 220y in 21.4; Peter Hildreth equalled Don Finlay's British national record of 14.4 in the 120y hurdles behind the same winning time by Australia's Ray Weinberg; Harry Whittle's 53.3 440y hurdles was not only a British record but surpassed Luigi Facelli's 1929 championship record although intrinsically it was far inferior to Lord Burghley's metric 52.2 (worth 52.5/52.6) at the 1932 Olympics. Other noteworthy victories were gained by Roger Bannister in the 880y (1:51.5), Bill Nankeville in the mile in 4:09.8 with a 57.6 last lap which left a then little known Australian by the name of John Landy second in a personal best of 4:11.0, Chris Chataway in the 3 miles (13:59.6), Roland Hardy (who had recently set a world record of 35:15.0 for 5 miles) with a pair of walking championship bests of 13:27.8 and 50:05.6, and John Savidge in the shot with a championship record of 16.50m.

Better than anything at the White City, though, was the astonishing AAA marathon held in conjunction with the famous Polytechnic event from Windsor to Chiswick the previous Saturday. Until then the world best stood at 2:25:39 and the fastest by a Briton was 2:29:24 by Jim Peters in the previous year's "Poly". This time Peters ran 2:20:43, followed by Stan Cox in 2:21:42 and Geoff Iden in 2:26:54! As another marathon great Sam Ferris reported in *Athletics Weekly*: "I have had the privilege of witnessing the most amazing marathon of all time, and I doubt if we shall again witness the like in our time. It is unbelievable and reads more like a chapter from an H.G.Wells novel! These three Britishers made the rest of the world's marathon runners look second raters even by Olympic standards." Those times were rendered even more phenomenal when re-measurement of the course found it to be 260 yards long. Peters and Cox, both coached by 'Johnny" Johnston (second in the 1924 AAA mile and an Olympic 5000m finalist in 1928), travelled to Helsinki as favourites for gold and silver but both collapsed during the Olympic marathon, won by the incomparable Emil Zátopek in 2:23:04 after having triumphed also in the 10,000m and 5000m.

Their demise was all too symbolic of the British team overall with the only male medallists being McDonald Bailey in the 100m and John Disley, with a British record of 8:51.8 in the steeplechase, both finishing third. Frustrating fourth places were gained by Bailey in the 200m, Bannister in the 1500m with a British record of 3:46.0, Pirie in the 5000m, Rex Whitlock (Harold's younger brother) in the 50km walk and the 4x100m relay team. Arthur Wint, the AAA 440y winner in 48.1, finished second in the 800m and helped Jamaica win the 4x400m relay in world record time. A few weeks later this former RAF pilot, who qualified as a doctor from London's St Bartholomew's Hospital and would become Jamaica's High Commissioner in London from 1974 to 1978, bowed out of international athletics with an emotional and well merited lap of honour at a White City floodlit meeting.

1953 (White City)

ALREADY HOLDER OF British records at 6 miles (28:55.6) and 3 miles (13:41.8), Gordon Pirie produced what Harold Abrahams described as "one of the most magnificent doubles ever achieved in the Championships". On the Friday evening he smashed the world 6 miles record of 28:30.8 by Finland's Viljo Heino with 28:19.4, setting world bests *en route* at 4 miles (18:45.2) and 5 miles (23:34.2), and ignored blisters on his left foot to return next afternoon for the 3 miles, where he lowered Sydney Wooderson's championship record to 13:43.4. His front running pulled several of his opponents to personal bests also. Frank Sando (28:47.2) and Ian Binnie with a Scottish record of 28:53.4 finished inside the previous British record, while Freddie Green – a year away from becoming a world record breaker himself – ran Pirie close with 13:46.0. The "English Zátopek", Pirie at age 22 enjoyed a fantastic year, his achievements ranging from the first of three consecutive English cross country titles to outkicking the American star Wes Santee in the inaugural Emsley Carr Mile. He won 27 of his 32 individual track races between 800 and 10,000m and his British records included 8:11.0 for 3000m, 13:34.0 for 3 miles, 14:02.6 for 5000m and 29:17.2 for 10,000m, plus contributing to a world record in the 4x1500m relay. Not since the days of Walter George and Alf Shrubb had there been such a prolific record breaker.

The other athlete whose appearances, though much rarer, most excited the public was Roger Bannister, by now considered the man most likely to become the first sub-four minute miler. He had broken Wooderson's British record with 4:03.6 in May and two weeks before the Championships he had run an unratified 4:02.0 in what was essentially a paced time trial. At the White City he contented himself with a championship record of 4:05.2. The meeting marked the farewell of two of the most durable of champions. McDonald Bailey signed off with his seventh sprint double (9.8/21.4) and two weeks later signed on as a Rugby League professional, while 1952 Olympic team captain Harry Whittle chalked up his seventh consecutive 440y hurdles title, his time of 52.7 equalling the British record. In third place was Amadeo Francis of Puerto Rico, who would later become a prominent IAAF official.

That winning streak of seven equalled the most in AAA history, by Denis Horgan (shot, 1893-1899), Don Finlay (120y hurdles, 1932-1938) and Bert Cooper (2 miles walk, 1932-1938). Having also won the 220y hurdles in 1953, the long jump in 1947 and 1949 and the decathlon in 1950, Whittle's total of of AAA titles was 11 as against Bailey's 14 and Horgan's 13. As Harold Abrahams observed: "For a man who was, to say the least of it, an indifferent hurdler, and looked upon as only a moderate quarter-miler, he had had a phenomenal innings." Jim Peters bounced back from his Olympic disappointment with four brilliant marathon victories: the Polytechnic race in a world's best of 2:18:41, the AAA Championship in 2:22:29, Enschede (Netherlands) in 2:19:22 and Turku (Finland) in another world's best of 2:18:35. He also substantially improved his 6 miles time and, on a blazing hot afternoon, surpassed Walter George's 69-year-old English one hour record.

1954 (White City)

THIS WAS AN amazingly long and memorable season. Wearing a AAA vest in the match against Oxford University at Iffley Road on May 6, Roger Bannister won the race to the first sub-4 minute mile with 3:59.4, unofficially equalling the world 1500m record of 3:43.0 on the way, and one of his pacemakers, Chris Chataway, prevailed in one of the most thrilling races of all time in the London v Moscow match at the White City on October 13 when he set a world 5000m record of 13:51.6 inches ahead of Vladimir Kuts. Such was the impact of that epic duel, televised live, that it was Chataway and not Bannister who was voted by the public as the first BBC Sports Personality of the Year. In the summer months in between came the AAA

Championships, British Empire & Commonwealth Games and European Championships.

Bannister and Chataway were involved in all of those major events. Bannister produced what was at the time the quickest ever final quarter of 53.8 in winning the AAA mile in 4:07.6 while Chataway set a world record of 13:32.2 for 3 miles ... only he didn't win the race! Freddie Green, second to Gordon Pirie the previous year, ran out of his skin to hold off his rival in the same time, the previous record having been 13:32.4 by Sweden's miling ace Gunder Hägg in 1942. More significant in historical terms was the performance by the distant third finisher in 13:54.8, Nyandika Maiyoro of Kenya, the first East African runner to make a mark in international competition. He held a lead of some 45 yards after a seemingly suicidal first mile of 4:23.4 and was still on world record pace as he traded strides with Chataway and Green at 2 miles in 9:01.6 before dropping away.

Jimmy Green enthused about Maiyoro in *Athletics Weekly*: "His action was the nearest to the ideal I have yet seen for a track distance runner, so effortless, so economical, yet so effective." He added: "Never again shall we nurse the idea that the coloured races are no good at anything beyond a mile." What for many years we have taken for granted with the endless line of great runners from Kenya and Ethiopia was a blinding revelation then. Pirie, hampered by a foot injury, was a non-finisher in the 6 miles won by Peter Driver in 28:34.8, with Jim Peters fourth in a personal best of 28:57.8. Peters had, just a fortnight earlier, lowered his world best to 2:17:40 in the AAA/ Polytechnic Marathon from Windsor to Chiswick. In other action, Ken Johnson became the inaugural 3000m steeplechase champion in 9:00.8; George Ellis, who would run 1:53.2 for 880y eight years later, won the 100y in 9.9 and Olympic hammer champion József Csermák of Hungary set a UK all-comers record of 59.42m.

English winners at the Commonwealth Games in Vancouver were Derek Johnson in the 880y (1:50.7), Chataway in the 3 miles (13:35.2) with Green second, Driver in the

6 miles (29:09.4), Geoff Elliott in the pole vault (4.26m), Ken Wilmshurst in the long jump (7.54m) and triple jump (15.28m), John Savidge in the shot (16.77m), the 4x440y relay team (3:11.2) ... and, of course, Bannister (British record of 3:58.8) ahead of Australia's world record holder John Landy in what was truly "the mile of the century". Unhappily, Peters – running at an uncompromising pace in the searing heat and becoming seriously dehydrated – collapsed just before the finish of the marathon, won by Scotland's Joe McGhee in 2:39:36. The only Briton crowned European champion in Bern was Bannister, who uncorked an unprecedented 25.0 last 200m to take the 1500m in 3:43.8. That was his final race as his work as a doctor left him insufficient time to train seriously. He went on to have an illustrious career as a neurologist and was knighted in 1975 for services to medicine.

Lesser medals gained were silver by Chataway in the 5000m, ahead of Emil Zátopek but a long way behind a world record 13:56.6 by Kuts, Jack Parker in the 110m hurdles and by the 4x100m team, and there was bronze for Ellis in the 100 and 200m and Elliott in the pole vault where he set a British record of 4.30m. Another British record fell in the 800m where Johnson smashed Sydney Wooderson's 1938 figures with 1:47.4 but such was the quality of the race that he had to settle for fourth. There was a further blow for Johnson in the 4x400m relay for after running an outstanding 46.2 to anchor Britain to victory in a British record of 3:08.2 the team was disqualified.

1955 (White City)

ALTHOUGH THERE were no international championships that year, the AAA Championships continued to draw big crowds and 35,000 witnessed victories by the world's newest sub-4 minute milers, Chris Chataway and Brian Hewson, both of whom had run 3:59.8 behind Hungary's László Tábori at the White City earlier in the season. Hewson, winner of the 880y the two previous years, produced a

54.0 last lap to take the mile in 4:05.4 ahead of Ken Wood (4:06.2). Wood had placed 24th out of 27 in the AAA 3 miles two years earlier and fifth in 1954 but had now found his event, although his best distance was 2 miles at which he had recently set a British record of 8:34.8. Despite the very hot weather, the charismatic Chataway produced a good 3 miles time of 13:33.6, with a 56.4 last lap, followed in by an up and coming Derek Ibbotson (13:37.0).

Two weeks later, on the same track and assisted by Ibbotson, Chataway would reclaim the world record he had lost to Vladimir Kuts by clocking 13:23.2. He never ran as well again, for in September 1955 he became ITV's first newscaster and short of training retired after the 1956 Olympics. He went on to be a high achiever off the track; he became an MP in 1959, served as a Minister in Edward Heath's Conservative Government between 1970 and 1974 and was made a Privy Counsellor, then left politics for merchant banking and while chairman of the Civil Aviation Authority was knighted in 1995 for services to the aviation industry. While Kuts died at 48 and Pirie at 60, Chataway – who trained far more sparingly and was a smoker – ran a 5:36 mile when he was 64 and at 79 completed the 2010 Great North Run half marathon in a remarkable 1:52. For the second year running Pirie failed to complete the 6 miles. This time he was the victim of dehydration and he collapsed just before the bell, leaving Ken Norris the winner in 29:00.6. The 220y low hurdles, which was a championship event only from 1952 to 1962, threw up a British record of 23.7 by Paul Vine.

1956 (White City)

THE QUEEN, AS Patron of the AAA, attended the first day of the Championships, accompanied by the Duke of Edinburgh, President of the BAAB. They were treated to a battle royal in the 6 miles with Ken Norris (28:13.6) and Frank Sando (28:14.2) both inside Gordon Pirie's British record. Pirie, who had set world records of 13:36.8

for 5000m and 7:55.6 for 3000m the previous month, did not compete. Next day, before a near capacity crowd of 45,000, the highlight was the 3 miles, where Chris Chataway – as in 1951 and 1954 – shared the winning time but finished second. In a great finish Derek Ibbotson inched ahead on a quagmire of a track in 13:32.6. The conditions spoiled all the times with 9.9 sufficing for a 100y victory by 18-year-old schoolboy John Young, who later played for the England rugger team. In the mile Ken Wood stole a march on the field by moving away before the bell and a 55.3 last lap carried him to victory in 4:06.8 ahead of Brian Hewson (4:07.4) with the versatile Derek Johnson placing fifth in 4:10.8.

At the Melbourne Olympics in late November, Johnson would go so close to becoming Olympic 800m champion, clocking 1:47.88 to Tom Courtney's 1:47.75 with Mike Farrell – who would in time become General Secretary of the AAA and BAAB – excelling to place fifth. Pirie and Ibbotson took the silver and bronze medals in the 5000m well behind Vladimir Kuts and the 4x400m team of John Salisbury, Mike Wheeler, Peter Higgins and Johnson were third. Just out of the medals in fourth place with a British record of 54.27m was four-time AAA champion Mark Pharaoh – still by far the finest showing in a global championship by a British discus thrower.

One English-born athlete did strike gold. No, not Chris Brasher (born in what is now Guyana) but Sussex-born Norman Read, the AAA junior mile walk champion in 1950. However, having emigrated in the meantime, he won the 50km walk in New Zealand's colours. Brasher's steeplechase triumph came as a delightful surprise. Ironically, whereas his more exalted training companions Roger Bannister and Chris Chataway never won an Olympic medal, Brasher became Britain's first Olympic athletics champion since 1936. He went to Melbourne as only Britain's third string for whereas Eric Shirley outsprinted John Disley for the AAA title, 8:51.6 to 8:53.4, Brasher finished far behind in 9:02.6 and it was only later when he ran Disley close with a personal best of 8:47.2 that he clinched his place in the team. At the Games he was in peak form and ran the race of his life, breaking Disley's British record with his Olympic record time of 8:41.2. He was at first disqualified "for interference in the last lap" but an appeal was upheld.

As Chataway remarked of him: "He is 5 per cent ability and 95 per cent guts." It was Brasher's last track race but in 1981 he masterminded, along with Disley, the first London Marathon. A man of many talents, he also became a prize winning journalist and television broadcaster as well as popularising the sport of orienteering in Britain and being a successful businessman. Brasher, considered something of a plodder – relatively speaking – for much of his running career eventually reaped the rewards for perseverance, and so on a more modest level did long jumper Roy Cruttenden. Five times since 1950 he had finished second in the AAA Championships but, at 31, he finally won that coveted title with 7.25m. At the end of the year he broke the British record in the British Empire v USA match in Sydney with 7.59m.

The Melbourne Olympics were notable also for a highly publicised rift between athletes and management over various issues. As a consequence an Athletes' Advisory Committee, chaired by Roly Harper, was set up in 1957 to give active athletes, for the first time, the opportunity of taking part in the deliberations of the AAA, Women's AAA and BAAB alongside officials and national coaches. In October 1958 the International Athletes' Club was formed, a dynamic organisation which pressed for reforms in the sport.

1957 (White City)

DEREK IBBOTSON CAPTURED all the headlines. Having succeeded Roger Bannister as the British mile record holder with 3:58.4 in Glasgow a month previously, "Ibbo" created a sensation by being knocked out in the mile heats on the Friday night. He had arrived at the stadium too late

Her Majesty The Queen, Patron of the Amateur Athletic Association
(c) www.royalimages.co.uk

The three founders of the AAA (top left) MONTAGUE SHEARMAN, (top right) CLEMENT JACKSON and (bottom left) BERNHARD WISE, together with CHARLES HERBERT, Hon. Secretary of the AAA 1883-1906

WALTER GEORGE
Greatest runner of the 19th century

ALF SHRUBB
Another multi-world record breaker

Action from the 1898 AAA Championships at Stamford Bridge. Note that athletes in those days ran in a clockwise direction

BILL STURGESS

GEORGE LARNER

GEORGE PATCHING (S Africa)

WILLIE APPLEGARTH

ALBERT HILL

GUY BUTLER

HAROLD ABRAHAMS

PAAVO NURMI (Finland)

*Clockwise from top left: LORD BURGHLEY,
ERIC LIDDELL, LORD BURGHLEY with
LORD DESBOROUGH (AAA President
1930–1936), DOUGLAS LOWE*

Capt. F.A.M. WEBSTER (right), the celebrated coach and author, in a training session with New Zealand javelin star STANLEY LAY, the 1928 AAA champion

TOM HAMPSON
Winning 1932 Olympic 800m

ROBERT 'BONZO' HOWLAND
AAA shot runner-up nine times!

SYDNEY WOODERSON
Versatile world record breaker

GODFREY RAMPLING
Relay runner par excellence

HAROLD WHITLOCK
1936 Olympic 50km walk champion

BERT COOPER
Seven successive AAA 2 mile walk titles

JACK LOVELOCK   DON FINLAY

Britain's victorious 1936 Olympic 4x400m relay team. From left: GODFREY BROWN, FREDDIE WOLFF, GODFREY RAMPLING, BILL ROBERTS

ARTHUR WINT
A giant of the 400 and 800 metres

McDONALD BAILEY
Won seven AAA sprint doubles

ALAN PATERSON, the 1950 European high jump champion who was world number one the previous year

CHRIS BRASHER
On his way to 1956 Olympic victory

JIM PETERS
World record breaking marathoner

JOHN PARLETT wins the 1950 European 800m title ahead of France's MARCEL HANSENNE (206) and ROGER BANNISTER

One of the most iconic moments in athletics history: ROGER BANNISTER breaks through the four minute mile barrier at Oxford on 6 May 1954

*DEREK IBBOTSON (left) just gets the better of CHRIS CHATAWAY in the 1956 AAA
3 miles at the White City – long before the days of all-weather tracks!*

*GORDON PIRIE during his world record equalling 7:55.6 3000m
in Trondheim in 1956*

DEREK JOHNSON (right) finishes a close second to TOM COURTNEY (USA) in the 1956 Olympic 800m

An elated BRIAN HEWSON wins the 1958 AAA half mile from MIKE RAWSON (35), with Australia's HERB ELLIOTT (14) third

Clockwise from top left: JOHN PENNEL (USA), who set a world pole vault record at the 1963 AAA Championships; MENZIES 'MING' CAMPBELL, a UK 100m record holder who became a prominent politician; DAVID JONES, four times the AAA 220 yards champion

to warm up properly and found himself unable either to win the heat or qualify for the final as one of the six fastest losers, his time of 4:15.5 missing out by one-tenth of a second. In his absence, Brian Hewson won untroubled in 4:06.7 ... but the immensely popular Yorkshireman lined up instead for the 3 miles and despite heavy rain he broke Chris Chataway's British record with 13:20.8, winning by over 20 seconds. Better still was to come on the same track just six days later when "The Four Minute Smiler" beat a formidable international field to become world record holder with 3:57.2. It was an astonishing transformation by this international cross country runner, whose fastest mile before 1957 was 4:07.0. Among the men Ibbotson beat was Ireland's Olympic 1500m champion Ron Delany, who had equalled Arthur Wint's AAA championship record of 1:49.6 in the 880y.

New championship records were Peter Higgins' 47.6 440y, Tom Farrell's 52.1 440y hurdles, Mike Ellis' British hammer record of 60.27m at age 20 and Peter Cullen's 72.11m javelin throw trumping Colin Smith's British record of 71.00m minutes earlier. This was a most promising period for British throwers as Arthur Rowe (20) won the first of his five AAA titles and Mike Lindsay won the discus while aged only 18. Ken Wilmshurst landed his fifth consecutive triple jump title, Roy Cruttenden defended successfully in the long jump and Ian Ward, later to become a National Coach, won the second of his pole vault titles.

1958 (White City)

THANKS PARTLY TO a strong influx of athletes tuning up for the Commonwealth Games in Cardiff no fewer than 13 championship records were broken or equalled, among them the oldest in the books: Willie Applegarth's 21.2 220y dating from 1914. That was tied by Dave Segal in his semi-final prior to taking the final in 21.4. British as well as championship records were posted in the 440y by John Salisbury (47.2), 6 miles by Stan Eldon (28:05.0), that race being staged at Chiswick during the Kinnaird Trophy a fortnight earlier, and the shot by Arthur Rowe (17.30m). The most eagerly awaited appearance was that of Australia's Herb Elliott – who would set world records of 3:36.0 for 1500m and 3:54.5 for the mile a few weeks later – but he went away empty handed from the half mile, clocking 1:49.0 behind Brian Hewson's championship record of 1:48.3 and Mike Rawson's 1:48.6.

However, in Cardiff, Elliott turned the tables on the two Englishmen thanks to an unprecedented 50.5 last lap. Fred Norris set a British record of 49:39.0 in the 10 miles, an event revived after an 11-year gap and held at Hurlingham in April. Among other championship records were an 8:51.0 steeplechase by Eric Shirley narrowly ahead of John Disley (8:51.2) with David Shaw, a future General Secretary of the BAAB, third in 9:02.4 and future great Maurice Herriott seventh in a world junior best of 9:11.8; and a hammer throw of 61.92m by Mike Ellis. The 3 miles proved a disastrous race for two of Britain's most celebrated runners as Derek Ibbotson failed to finish and Gordon Pirie trailed in 12th in 14:11.0 over half a lap behind Eldon (13:32.4) and Kenya's Nyandika Maiyoro (13:34.8). Stan Vickers, with times of 13:33.4 and 51:10.2, joined the illustrious list of walkers to defend successfully both track titles in the same year: George Larner in 1905, Ernest Webb in 1910, Bobby Bridge in 1913 and Roland Hardy in 1951.

Athletes from England fared well in the field events at the Commonwealth Games with wins for Geoff Elliott (4.16m pole vault), Rowe (British shot record of 17.57m), Ellis (62.90m hammer) and Colin Smith (71.29m javelin) but not one individual title was gained on the track. Compensation came later in the season at the European Championships in Stockholm. John Wrighton won the 400m in a British record of 46.3, Rawson the 800m in 1:47.8 and Hewson the 1500m in 3:41.9 (British record of 3:41.1 in his heat!), while Rowe took the shot with another British record of 17.78m and Vickers the 20km walk in 1:33:09. Stan Eldon set a British 10,000m record of

29:02.8 in fourth place. There were relay gold medals for the England 4x110y team in Cardiff (40.7) and the British 4x400m squad in Stockholm (3:07.9).

1959 (White City)

THE TOP PERFORMANCE came not at the White City in July, which drew a crowd of only 17,000, but at Hurlingham in April when coal miner Fred Norris, with a British record of 48:32.4, and Basil Heatley (48:58.4) became the world's second and third fastest ever at 10 miles, the world record of 48:12.0 belonging to the legendary Czech runner, Emil Zátopek. The only other championship records fell to Arthur Rowe in the shot with 17.95m and Ken Matthews in the 2 miles walk with 13:19.4, the closest approach yet to George Larner's venerable British record of 13:11.4. Matthews, destined to become Olympic 20km champion in 1964, had earlier won the 7 miles title in 50:28.8. It was a great year for him, as he also set world bests at 5 miles on the track (34:26.6) and 7 miles on the road (48:14). The much anticipated clash between Britain's top three half milers proved a disappointment in terms of time as the first lap took an agonisingly slow 59.4. Brian Hewson dashed ahead early on the second lap to open up a 15-yard lead and held on for victory in 1:52.0 ahead of Mike Rawson (1:52.3) and Derek Johnson (1:52.5). Derek Ibbotson finished a distant seventh in the 3 miles, won by the barefooted Bruce Tulloh in 13:31.2. Three titles went to immensely promising teenagers: Peter Radford, credited with an unratified 9.4 in the Staffordshire Championships, took the 100y in 9.7, David Jones the 220y in 21.7 and Maurice Herriott the steeplechase (the first of his eight titles) in 8:52.8.

BRITISH RECORDS AT 1 JANUARY 1960
100y: 9.5 Peter Radford 1959; 100m: 10.2 McDonald Bailey 1951; 200m: 20.8 Radford 1958; 220y: 21.0 Radford 1958; 400m: 46.3 John Wrighton 1958; 440y:

46.8 Ted Sampson 1958; 800m: 1:46.6 Derek Johnson 1957; 880y: 1:47.8 Brian Hewson 1958; 1500m: 3:41.1 Hewson 1958; Mile: 3:57.2 Derek Ibbotson 1957; 3000m: 7:52.7 Gordon Pirie 1956; 2M: 8:34.8 Ken Wood 1955; 3M: 13:20.8 Ibbotson 1957; 5000m: 13:36.8 Pirie 1956; 6M: 28:05.0 Stan Eldon 1958; 10,000m: 29:02.8 Eldon 1958; 10M: 48:32.4 Fred Norris 1959; Marathon: 2:17:40 Jim Peters 1954; 3000mSC: 8:41.2 Chris Brasher 1956; 110mH/120yH: 14.3 Don Finlay 1938, Jack Parker 1955, Peter Hildreth 1957 &1958; 400mH: 51.1 Tom Farrell 1957; 440yH: 51.6 Chris Goudge 1958; HJ: 2.05 Crawford Fairbrother 1959; PV: 4.30 Geoff Elliott 1954, 1957, 1958 & 1959; LJ: 7.59 Roy Cruttenden 1956; TJ: 15.60 Ken Wilmshurst 1956; SP: 18.59 Arthur Rowe 1959; DT: 54.54 Gerry Carr 1958; HT: 64.95 Mike Ellis 1959; JT: 75.16 Colin Smith 1957; Decathlon: (re-scored on 1985 tables) 6398 Geoff Elliott 1952; 2M Walk: 13:11.4 George Larner 1904; 7M Walk: 49:28.6 Roland Hardy 1952; 20km Walk: 1:30:08 Ken Matthews 1959; 50km Walk: 4:12:19 Don Thompson 1959.

THE SIXTIES

JUST AS PROFOUND sociological and cultural changes occurred in Britain during this tumultuous decade, so athletics evolved in many ways although those who sought to set up a single governing body for the UK were frustrated. As for the past 80-90 years the AAA continued to be responsible for the men's side of the sport in England and Wales.

As early as the 1960 AGM of the Association, Hon. Treasurer Phil Gale argued for the formation of a United Kingdom AAA and his proposal that the possibilities of such a body be investigated was carried almost unanimously. Two years later a motion at the AGM that "our title be changed to the AAA of Great Britain & Northern Ireland" was also overwhelmingly approved. Groups like the International Athletes' Club and the British Athletics Union kept up the pressure for change, but the other parties involved opposed such a move. At the 1963 AGM it was announced that AAA General Committee had decided it was not practicable at that time to explore the possibility of forming a UK AAA as the Women's AAA, Scottish AAA and N Irish AAA had stated they were fully satisfied with the present BAAB constitution. A proposal at that meeting by the BAU for a British AAA was defeated by 297 votes to 111, as was a similar motion by the BAU and IAC the following year (289-186).

Meanwhile, the AAA's financial situation was becoming increasingly parlous and the Annual Report for 1966/67 stated "bankruptcy is a very real threat." As attendance at the AAA Championships plummeted, from over 46,000 in 1952 to a low of 8000 on the Saturday in 1963, so income was lost and from 1961 the Championships were commercially sponsored: in 1961 by the Carborundum Company, in 1962 by Wall's Meat Company and from 1963 by Pepsi-Cola. Previously the sport's main benefactor over a period of many years had been the *News of the World*. However, despite that injection of sponsors' cash, television fees and Government funding (mainly to pay the National Coaches' salaries), the situation was such that in 1967 Hon. Treasurer Frank Read revealed a loss for the year of £6000. More state aid, as in most European countries, was required but first the administration of the sport needed to be analysed.

In March 1967 the AAA and BAAB commissioned a Committee of Inquiry, chaired by Lord (Frank) Byers, the Liberal Party leader in the House of Lords and a former British Universities 440y hurdles record holder. The Committee included 1962 European 5000m champion Bruce Tulloh (an Athletes' Representative on the BAAB) and three members of the legal profession with good athletic pedigrees in Judge (Ralph) Kilner Brown, AAA champion and Empire Games bronze medallist at 440y hurdles in 1934, Thomas Curry QC, the 1948 AAA steeplechase champion and Olympian, and Sir Geoffrey de Freitas, MP, a pre-war Cambridge high jump Blue. Its terms of reference were "to examine the problems of development of athletics under the jurisdiction of the AAA and BAAB, including matters of organisation, administration, finance, coaching services and competition, and to make recommendations thereon."

Conclusions of The Byers Report, published in May 1968, included: "Firstly, we find the case for one governing body for athletics in the UK to be proved beyond doubt, and secondly, we recommend that a new administrative organisation headed by a 'Director of British Athletics' should be established. ... The 'British Athletic Federation' would represent England and Wales, Scotland and Northern Ireland, the Women's Associations, the Cross Country Unions, the Race Walking Association, the Tug of War Association and the Schools. It would affiliate to the IAAF as the governing body for athletics in the UK." Other recommendations included an annual registration scheme for all athletes, reorganisation of the coaching scheme, more league competitions and improvement of facilities, particularly for field events. The Report received a mixed reception. Although there was broad agreement over much of what was recommended, the Women's AAA made no secret of its reluctance to give up its independence, while the AAA and BAAB were annoyed that they had not been given the opportunity for further discussions with the Committee before the Report was published, and pointed out that several of the suggestions were already being carried out.

The Report concluded: "We do not believe that there is anything so fundamentally wrong with British amateur athletics which cannot be put right with common sense, goodwill and patience. There could be a bright future for the sport at every level in the coming years." That sentiment was similar to the view put forward by British 100m record holder and future politician Menzies (Ming) Campbell four years earlier when he told *Athletics Weekly* that he disliked "the attitude that suggests there is no solution to problems except by an athletes v officials contest. Both should have the intelligence to appreciate that they require each other and that co-operation and understanding will go a long way."

Speaking of a future British Athletic Federation at the 1969 AGM, Barry Willis, a former Berkshire 440y and shot put champion who succeeded Ernest Clynes as AAA Hon. Secretary in 1965, said: "It will be evident that the role of the AAA will thus be greatly reduced and it may well be that the need for its existence will disappear altogether." He added that the BAAB had appointed Cyril Sinfield, Secretary of the AAA's Rules Revision & Records Committee, to examine the rules and constitutions of the various existing governing bodies and "put forward recommendations on the steps we should take to bring into being this new Federation with a constitution acceptable to all."

A national registration scheme had been the subject of much controversy ever since the AAA General Committee proposed it be introduced from January 1967 in a bid to raise much needed extra income. The idea was for every male athlete aged 17 or over to pay a maximum of 10 shillings (50p) per year. That scheme was approved by 164 votes to 140 at the 1966 AGM, despite considerable opposition from some of the club delegates present, but a couple of months later the AAA announced it would not implement the scheme after all and instead would investigate other means of raising revenue. The issue came up again at the AAA AGM in 1968, with a view to starting the scheme in April 1969, but after lively discussion it was agreed to defer any further action until a referendum could be conducted by General Committee. That poll spelt the end of a registration scheme for the foreseeable future as only 415 athletes voted in favour while 1172 preferred the option of increased club affiliation fees, 255 didn't mind either, 91 wanted a levy on entry fees and 127 submitted either invalid forms or were against any money raising scheme.

Another thorny subject was whether the AAA and Women's AAA Championships should be combined into one meeting. A poll of International Athletes' Club members in 1961 voted 57-23 in favour of a mixed meeting and at their AGM proposed combined Championships be staged in 1962. That led nowhere as the WAAA was implacably against the idea (although the Indoor Championships had been a mixed affair ever since 1935), and it wasn't until as late as 1988 that the women were persuaded to share the outdoor stage with the men.

The amateur code continued to be applied, although "shamateurism" was rife among some leading athletes whose appearance at a meeting was guaranteed to boost gate money. However, for the vast majority of club athletes the sport remained totally amateur and the most they could win as a prize were goods with a value not exceeding 7 guineas (£7.35), raised to 10 guineas (£10.50) in 1963. In 1968 Tony Ward, Secretary of the National Athletics League and a former Southern Counties AAA Administrator, wrote: "Britain took the lead in legitimising the 'shamateur' state which shamed tennis for so long; have we the guts and foresight to do so in track and field?" The answer was yes ... but not for another ten years.

In today's world, where athletes can earn whatever they can and with the blessing of the IAAF and national governing bodies, it might seem incredible that a man who won a paltry £17 as a teenage boxer could be banned from competition as a runner. But that's what happened to John Tarrant, "The Ghost Runner". Under the strict AAA laws then in operation, Tarrant had forfeited his amateur status. In 1952 he applied for reinstatement for the first of many times but as that was denied he started gate-crashing road races. He was a good runner and his predicament was widely reported. *Athletics Weekly* and various newspapers campaigned on his behalf but it wasn't until 1958 that he was informed by the Hon. Secretary of the Northern Counties AA that he had indeed been reinstated and could now race officially. In 1960 Tarrant finished second to Brian Kilby in the AAA Marathon in 2:25:17, won his next marathon in his fastest time of 2:22:35 and went on to become a world record breaker at 40 and 100 miles. But he remained frustrated as because of IAAF rules, to which the BAAB was subject, he was never permitted to fulfil his dearest wish of representing Britain. Tragically, he died from cancer aged 42.

Other areas of the sport in the fifties which would puzzle today's younger generation concerned tracks and Sunday competition. Cinder and grass tracks at the mercy of our damp climate remained the norm and it wasn't until 1967 that the first En-Tout-Cas all-weather track, made of plastic and rubber crumbs, opened at the Leicester Sports Centre, the manager of which was marathon star Brian Kilby. At the inaugural meeting, despite almost incessant rain, the track held firm and athletes flocked to use it. The first Tartan track in Europe was laid at Crystal Palace the following year and quickly became a world record surface when Australia's great Ron Clarke set new 2 miles figures of 8:19.6 at an international meeting organised by the IAC with sponsorship from Coca-Cola. The AAA Championships switched to "The Palace" in 1971. Holding meetings on a Sunday was only allowed with special permission granted by the appropriate Area Association on condition that no admission or programme money was charged and that remained the case until the 1970s. The first major meeting to be staged, but free, on a Sunday was the first day of the British Games and Inter-Counties Championships at Crystal Palace in 1968 and it wasn't until 1982 that the AAA Championships began to be held on a Saturday/Sunday.

The issue that would cast a shadow over the sport right through to the present day, the use of performance enhancing drugs, began to rear its ugly head. The practice wasn't new but it was clearly becoming more widespread as the decade progressed. Dr Martyn Lucking, the Commonwealth shot champion in 1962, said in 1968 that circumstantial evidence pointed to a number of current British throwers taking anabolic steroids and that year the AAA National Coaches issued this statement: "We deplore the increasing incidence in the taking of steroid drugs by athletes throughout the world, because it is in direct contravention of the IAAF's rules and detrimental to their future health and well being."

Speaking of National Coaches, the sixties got off to a calamitous start when within the space of a few months in 1961 Head Coach Geoff Dyson, Jim Alford and Lionel Pugh resigned. Denis Watts and John Le Masurier became the Senior National Coaches and men of the calibre of Bill Marlow, Ron Pickering, Tom McNab, Wilf Paish, John Anderson and others were appointed during the decade to uphold the Coaching Scheme's prestige. Among Arthur Gold's first actions after he succeeded Jack Crump as Hon. Secretary of the BAAB in 1965 was to invite the Senior National Coaches to attend selection meetings and two active internationals to be co-opted by the Board, a move welcomed by the International Athletes' Club. In 1969 the BAAB signalled the advent of a UK Coaching Scheme in which the two Senior National Coaches would spend more of their time on British team development while Regional Coaches (AAA National Coaches and some leading honorary coaches) would take responsibility for an event or group of events throughout the UK, for men and women.

Barry Willis explained to the 1969 AAA AGM that "if progress should seem slow to some of you, I would stress that it can only be made with the assent of the representatives of all the existing bodies and ultimately of the clubs they represent, and that they have to be persuaded by the merits of the proposed changes." The UK Coaching Scheme eventually came into effect in 1972.

One of the most successful and imaginative of initiatives, the Five Star Award Scheme (sponsored by Wall's Ice Cream), was Tom McNab's brainchild. A former top class triple jumper who became a National Coach in 1963, McNab's idea was to encourage children from 10 to 17 of all levels of ability to try three events, one of which must be a jump or throw. Their performances would be scored on decathlon-style tables and certificates, from one to five stars, awarded free. In the first full year, 1968, some 25,000 certificates were issued, and that rose to more than 100,000 in 1969.

By the late 1970s that figure ran to over a million a year and income from badges which could be bought provided valuable revenue for the Area Associations who then helped fund schools' athletics. As Lynn Davies remarked: "I only wish that something like this had existed when I was at school. To run, jump and throw are activities to be enjoyed by all children."

Progress was made in many areas during this decade. Metrication came in, so tracks were converted to 400m and it was out with the 100 yards, 220 yards etc, although the mile retained its mystique and status. Metric distances were introduced into the Indoor Championships (revived in 1962) in 1968 and outdoors a year later. Electronic timing became widespread at big meetings with sprinting and hurdling records determined by hundredths rather than tenths of a second. Some events changed their nature, due to the advent of the Fosbury Flop in the high jump and fibre glass vaulting poles. The hop step and jump was renamed the triple jump. A National (later British) League, which revolutionised club competition, began in earnest in 1969. AAA 12-Stage Relay Championships began in 1967, 6-Stage Relay two years later. AAA Youth Championships were inaugurated in 1967, as were junior international matches. There was more senior international competition than ever with the introduction of the European Cup in 1965 and European Indoor Games or Championships from 1966.

Practically every British record dating from before 1960 was broken and there was a world record bonanza: by Peter Radford (20.5 200m/220y in 1960), Basil Heatley (47:47.0 10 miles in 1961, 2:13:55 marathon in 1964), Mel Batty (47:26.8 10 miles in 1964), Ron Hill (47:02.2 and 46:44.0 10 miles in 1968, 1:12:48.2 15 miles and 1:15:22.6 25,000m in 1965), Jim Alder (1:34:01.8 30,000m, 1:40:58.4 20 miles and 37,994m in two hours in 1964), Tim Johnston (1:32:34.6 30,000m in 1965), Jim Hogan (1:32:25.4 30,000m in 1966), David Hemery (48.12 400m hurdles in 1968), Ken Matthews (34:21.2 5 miles walk in 1960, 69:40.6 10 miles walk in 1964) and the British 4x110y relay team (40.0 in 1963).

Four gold medals were obtained by British men from the three editions of the Olympic Games staged during the decade: by Don Thompson (1960 50km walk), Lynn Davies

(1964 long jump), Ken Matthews (1964 20km walk) and David Hemery (1968 400m hurdles). Other medals were silver for Basil Heatley (1964 marathon), Maurice Herriott (1964 steeplechase), John Cooper (1964 400m hurdles), Paul Nihill (1964 50km walk) and the 4x400m relay team in 1964, while bronze awards were gained by Peter Radford (1960 100m), Stan Vickers (1960 20km walk), John Sherwood (1968 400m hurdles) and the 4x100m team in 1960.

There were three editions of the European Championships between 1962 and 1969, producing ten British gold medals from Robbie Brightwell (400m), Bruce Tulloh (5000m), Brian Kilby (marathon) and Matthews (20km walk) in 1962, Jim Hogan (marathon) and Davies (long jump) in 1966, and John Whetton (1500m), Ian Stewart (5000m), Ron Hill (marathon) and Nihill (20km walk) in 1969. At the Commonwealth Games there were titles for Kilby (marathon), Martyn Lucking (shot), Howard Payne (hammer) and the England 4x110y relay team in 1962, and Hemery (120y hurdles), Payne again, John FitzSimons (javelin) and Ron Wallwork (20 miles walk) for England, Davies (long jump) for Wales and Jim Alder (marathon) for Scotland in 1966. England continued to dominate the International Cross Country Championship, including an undefeated stretch in the team race between 1964 and 1972. British walkers dominated in the early editions of the Lugano Cup, winning the trophy on the first two occasions in 1961 and 1963.

Sadly, it was a decade which robbed British athletics of many prominent athletes and officials – among them Alf Shrubb, Joe Binks, Albert Hill, Percy Hodge, Harry Payne, Stan Tomlin, Tom Hampson, Jack Crump (AAA Team Manager 1936-1948, BAAB Team Manager 1936-1964 and Hon. Secretary 1946-1964), John Willie Turner (Chairman of AAA General Committee from 1948 to 1964) and no fewer than three AAA Hon. Treasurers in Walter Jewell (1947-57), Phil Gale (1960-66) and George Cooper (1966-67).

Highlights from each of the AAA Championships meetings 1960-1969

1960 (White City)

CHAMPIONSHIP RECORDS WERE achieved in no fewer than 13 events, two of them at Hurlingham in April when despite the strong chilly wind Ken Matthews walked 7 miles in 49:42.6 and Basil Heatley smashed Fred Norris' British 10 miles record with 48:18.4. Heatley was in front from the second lap and but for the conditions might have broken Emil Zátopek's world record. As it was he missed it by only 6.4 sec. In sixth place (51:54.2) was Harry Wilson, who would many years later coach Steve Ovett to world records and an Olympic 800m title. Colin Andrews set a British decathlon record of 6481 (as rescored on 1985 tables) at Welwyn Garden City in July a week before the main meeting, which drew a crowd of more than 26,000. Matthews bettered the British record in the 2 miles walk with 13:09.6 but after a great race he had to settle for second to Stan Vickers, whose spectacular 91.6 sec final lap carried him to a time of 13:02.4, breaking George Larner's 56-year-old figures at last.

Crawford Fairbrother's British high jump record of 2.05m was equalled by Gordon Miller although the title went to Ghana's Richard Kotei at 2.08m. That was the best ever at the AAA Championships, as were Dave Segal's 220y semi-final time of 21.1 (but he lost to David Jones' 21.3 in the final), a 46.5 440y by the smooth striding Indian Milkha Singh (whose son, Jeev Milkha Singh, is a world ranking golfer), an 8:51.0 steeplechase, equalling his own record, by Eric Shirley, 18.04m shot by Arthur Rowe, 64.18m hammer by Mike Ellis and 76.38m javelin by Mohammed Nawaz of Pakistan.

The 100y championship record of 9.6 by McDonald Bailey in 1950, 1951 and 1952 fell to 20-year-old Peter Radford. A few weeks earlier he had registered a British record of 9.4 at

The Sixties

the Staffordshire Championships in Wolverhampton and an even more sensational world record of 20.5 for 200m/220y around a turn. In the final he ran 9.7 ahead of 9.8 by David Jones and Nick Whitehead, the latter becoming a British team manager some years later. Radford himself served as Executive Chairman of the British Athletics Federation from 1994 to 1997 and wrote a well received biography of the famed 19th century long distance walker, Captain Barclay, in 2001. He was elected President of the National Union of Track Statisticians (NUTS) in 2009, a position previously held by Harold Abrahams, Norris McWhirter and Sir Eddie Kulukundis. The mile threw up three records for the 80-year-old meeting as Hungary's László Tábori, history's third sub-4 min miler, and France's Michel Jazy (destined a few weeks later to finish second to Herb Elliott in the Rome Olympic 1500m) both ran 4:03.8 in their heat to better Roger Bannister's mark, with Tábori taking a thrilling final in 4:01.0 just ahead of Mike Wiggs (4:01.2) and Jazy (4:01.3). In other action, Gordon Pirie returned to form with a 6 miles victory, nine years after his first title at that distance, in a personal best of 28:09.6 and Frank Salvat left the likes of Bruce Tulloh and Derek Ibbotson well behind as he sprinted to a 3 miles win in 13:33.0. Two weeks earlier Tulloh had set a British record of 13:17.2. Another big name to suffer defeat was Brian Hewson, third in the 880y won in 1:49.3 by Tom Farrell, previously better known as British record holder for 400m hurdles at 51.0.

The Rome Olympics featured disappointing showings by such prospective medallists as Gordon Pirie and Arthur Rowe but as veteran reporter Armour Milne put it, "for every flop by a British athlete in Rome there was a balancing high-level performance." Don Thompson, who had learned the hard way at the previous Olympics what dehydration and heat exhaustion can do to someone who has not prepared for a 50km walk in high temperatures, acclimatised himself brilliantly this time to win the gold medal in 4:25:30, thus following in the footsteps of Tommy Green (1932) and his own adviser Harold Whitlock (1936). Stan Vickers gained a bronze medal in the 20km walk (1:34:57), as did Peter Radford in the 100m (10.3), and the 4x100m relay team of Radford, David Jones, Segal and Whitehead who tied the British record of 40.1 in their heat. New British records were set by Robbie Brightwell with 46.2 in his 400m heat and 46.1 in his semi-final, John Merriman with 28:52.6 for eighth in the 10,000m and Fred Alsop with 15.65m in the triple jump qualifying round.

1961 (White City)

THE TOP PERFORMANCE came not at the White City but at Hurlingham in April when Basil Heatley took all of 25 sec off Emil Zátopek's world 10 miles record with 47:47.0. Heatley, who would win an Olympic silver medal in the marathon three years later, also shone at the main meeting. He broke the championship record for 6 miles with 28:03.0 although the title went to Australia's Dave Power in 27:57.8. With the meeting being commercially sponsored for the first time, by the Carborundum Company to mark its Golden Jubilee, efforts were made to invite a host of overseas athletes and the outcome was that 12 of the 20 titles at stake at the White City left these shores.

Disappointingly, there were only 15,000 spectators on the Saturday and the atrocious weather didn't help. Canada's Harry Jerome, co-holder of the world records of 9.3 for 100y and 10.0 for 100m, was slowed to 9.6 on what was described as "a pudding of a track" yet won by a massive three-yard margin. A 440y victory in 47.6 on a flooded track by a sensational new star, Adrian Metcalfe (19), who had the previous week broken the British 400m record with 45.8, was also commendable running in the circumstances and later in the season he improved to 45.7, the fastest 400m time in the world that year. In his farewell AAA appearance, Gordon Pirie won the 3 miles again after a gap of eight years in 13:31.2, but his chief opponent, the shoeless Bruce Tulloh, found the underfoot going too difficult and quit early in the race. The following weekend the pair fought a great duel in Britain's match against the USA on the same track, Pirie setting a British record of 13:16.4 to win by 0.2, but Tulloh had the last laugh as in Southampton a month later he regained the record with 13:12.0, only 2 sec outside the world record.

As for Pirie, he won at 5000m in the England v Russian Federal Republic encounter at the White City and ran a lap of honour. He turned professional shortly afterwards. The Scot, Crawford Fairbrother, high jumped 2.06m for a British record, while Arthur Rowe won his fifth and last AAA shot title with a championship record of 18.58m. That was quite a modest distance for him as a few weeks later he improved his European record to 19.56m for third place on the world all-time list. In July 1962, still only 24, he signed professional Rugby League forms for Oldham .... a great loss to British athletics. Even the greatest of champions have to start somewhere and, in his AAA senior debut, Lynn Davies (19) representing Ogmore Grammar School in Wales, placed sixth in both the long jump with 6.83m and the triple jump, his stronger event then, with 14.43m.

1962 (White City)

IT WAS A pity that the attendance was so small for these Championships as there were so many outstanding performances to appreciate. On the Friday night the true *aficionados* thrilled to an epic 6 miles in which the diminutive Roy Fowler just got the better of his lanky rival Mike Bullivant as both were timed at 27:49.8. That was a British record, only Hungary's Sándor Iharos with 27:43.8 having ever run faster. Martin Hyman, holder of the previous record of 27:54.4, clocked 27:52.0 and Mel Batty chopped nearly a minute off his best with 27:56.6. Other championship records on that first day were achieved by Maurice Herriott (8:43.8 steeplechase), Jorma Valkama of Finland in the long jump (7.65m) with Lynn Davies only ninth at 6.88m – although before the year was over he would set a British record of 7.72m – and Jay Silvester, the

American who would eventually unofficially throw beyond 70m, and here despatched the discus 60.84m. The 220y hurdles was staged as a championship for the last time "in view of lack of support."

Highlight of day two was Robbie Brightwell's splendid 440y. Despite a heavy track, he won with so little strain that he thought his time would be around 47 sec; instead it was a European record of 45.9 (worth 45.6 for 400m), just 0.2 sec outside the world record! Other championship records fell to Bruce Tulloh in the 3 miles with 13:16.0, pressed hard by the 18-year-old Canadian prodigy Bruce Kidd (13:17.0), American Russ Rogers in the 440y hurdles with 51.0, Kuniyoshi Sugioka of Japan in the high jump (2.09m), his compatriot Tomio Ota in the triple jump (15.66m), Finland's Pentti Nikula with a vault of 4.42m with one of the newly developed fibre glass poles which were revolutionising the event, and a UK record of 79.26m (exactly 260 feet) by the 20-year-old left hander John McSorley, who thus became Britain's first world class male javelin thrower. Seraphino Antao, a Kenyan originally from Goa, scored a sprint double, his 220y time of 21.1 equalling the meeting record, and in all 13 of the 17 titles contested by visitors went abroad.

Earlier in the year, at Wembley's Empire Pool, the AAA Indoor Championships were revived after 23 years with Derek Ibbotson the star performer with his 8:52.2 2 miles victory. Fourth and last in the junior 440y was one Andy Norman, destined to become the most powerful not to mention controversial individual in British athletics administration. The European Championships in Belgrade produced gold medals for Brightwell (45.9 400m), Tulloh (14:00.6 5000m), Brian Kilby (2:23:19 marathon) and Ken Matthews (1:35:55 20km walk), while the Commonwealth Games in Perth, Australia yielded victories for Kilby again (2:21:17), Martyn Lucking (18.08m shot), Howard Payne (61.65m hammer) and the England 4x110y relay team (40.6).

1963 (White City)

ATTENDANCE AT THE White City reached a new low as only 8,000 enthusiasts were in the vast stadium on the Saturday to see John Pennel soar over 5.10m (16ft 8³/₄in) for a new world pole vault record. The American only made 4.57m at the third attempt but then had first time clearances at 4.72m, 4.87m and 5.10m before three unsuccessful tries at becoming the first 17ft performer. As the 3 miles (won by Bruce Tulloh in 13:23.8) was in progress, he twice had to wait for the runners to pass before he could attempt 5.10m because he started his approach run out on the track. Oddly, it was never ratified by the IAAF as a world record, probably overtaken by events as Pennel went on to register 5.13m back at the White City three weeks later at the Britain v USA match (which drew a 35,000 crowd on the Bank Holiday Monday) and 5.20m (17ft 0³/₄in) in Florida later in August. The dawn of the fibre glass era transformed performance levels, the world record moving from 4.83m to 5.28m in the space of three seasons (1962-1964). During that period the British best went from 4.30m to 4.61m. David Jones captured his fourth 220y title (21.3), second only to McDonald Bailey's seven.

The 120y hurdles saw the first appearance of David Hemery (18), who excelled to reach the final won by Laurie Taitt in a British record 14.1, equalling the championship record. Mike Parker, second in 14.2, later in the season became the first Briton under 14 sec with 13.9 for the metric event. Taitt's time equalled the championship record, as did Ron Hill's in the 6 miles. He tied the British record of 27:49.8 after a good scrap with Irish-born Jim Hogan (27:54.2). No one was more astonished than Hill, who had been anticipating a time of between 28:30 and 28:40. On the morning of the race (Friday) he went for a four mile run around the streets of Manchester before a six hour drive down to London! In tenth place Brian Kilby smashed his personal best with 28:26.4 just six days after winning the Welsh Open Marathon in a European record of 2:14:43

that would have been a world record had Buddy Edelen, an American living and teaching in Essex, not won the Polytechnic race the previous month in 2:14:28. Kilby later won the fourth of five consecutive AAA titles in 2:16:45, breaking Jim Peters' championship record. The season ended on a high note late in September when the British men's team unexpectedly defeated Russia in Volgograd, a welcome boost as preparations began for Olympic year.

1964 (White City)

WITH THE TOKYO OLYMPICS on the horizon, a much bigger crowd of 22,000 assembled this year although once again the choice event, the 6 miles, took place before the faithful few on the Friday night. It was a classic race as seven Britons dipped under 28 minutes, and the last lap – run in close to 59 sec – was a thriller as Mike Bullivant prevailed in a European record of 27:26.6, just 0.4 sec ahead of Ron Hill, who like third placed Jim Hogan (27:35.0) was running barefoot. Bullivant and Hill became the second and third fastest of all time behind Ron Clarke's 27:17.6. There were two other British records: John Cooper clocked 51.1 to win the 440y hurdles and Trevor Burton pole vaulted 4.57m (15 ft), the same as winner Fred Hansen, the American holder of the world record with 5.23m and Olympic champion in waiting.

Among the new championship records was a wind assisted 7.95m long jump by Lynn Davies, who was also the first British finisher in the 100y (9.7) although a long way behind Cuba's stocky little Enrique Figuerola, who was timed at 9.4 for a championship best. The 220y had only four starters in the final as past (20.5) and present (20.2) holders of the world record, Peter Radford and Henry Carr (USA), withdrew with leg injuries. Menzies (Ming) Campbell seized his opportunity and won in a championship record equalling but wind aided 21.1. The Scot, at the time an apprentice solicitor, would become a QC in 1982, be knighted in 2004 for services to Parliament and lead the Liberal Democrats in 2006/07. As an athlete he reached his peak in 1967 when, within one week in California, he twice equalled McDonald Bailey's British 100m record of 10.2.

Earlier in the year, at Easter, the Indoor Championships drew a record attendance of 7200 for the second day at Wembley's Empire Pool. One athlete, who would hardly have been noticed as he placed fifth in the 600 yards representing Loughborough Colleges, went on to become one of the key figures in the sport ... Frank Dick, Director of Coaching during British athletics' most successful period. That same weekend Ken Matthews broke the British record when capturing his fifth AAA title in the 7 miles walk (48:23.0) and two weeks later, on the same Hurlingham track, national cross country champion Mel Batty smashed Basil Heatley's world 10 miles record with 47:26.8. Batty was coached by the outstanding ultra long distance walker Colin Young, and Batty in turn eventually became coach to London Marathon winner Eamonn Martin. Heatley, however, was recompensed for the loss of one record by the claiming of another as he won the Polytechnic Marathon in a world best of 2:13:55 with Ron Hill also inside Buddy Edelen's old figures with 2:14:12. Brian Kilby, meanwhile, notched up a record fifth consecutive AAA marathon title in 2:23:01.

Tokyo in October proved a happy hunting ground for the British team. Mary Rand in the long jump became the nation's first female Olympic athletics champion, swiftly followed by Ann Packer in the 800m, both setting world records, and there were gold medals for Ken Matthews in the 20km walk (1:29:34) and Welshman Lynn Davies in the long jump with a British record of 8.07m despite the appalling conditions. Only the USA (14) and the USSR (5) gained more victories. Silver medals in the men's events came from Heatley in the marathon (2:16:20 behind a world record 2:12:12 by Ethiopia's Abebe Bikila), Maurice Herriott in the steeplechase (British record of 8:32.4), John Cooper in the 400m hurdles (British record of 50.1), Paul

Nihill in the 50km walk (British record of 4:11:32) and the 4x400m squad of Tim Graham, Adrian Metcalfe, Cooper and team captain Robbie Brightwell whose heroic 44.8 anchor leg carried the team to a European record of 3:01.6 and helped make up for Brightwell's disappointment at finishing fourth in the individual 400m (British record of 45.7), a race he had expected to win. Other fourth places, often described as the worst of all positions in a major championship, were filled by Alan Simpson in the 1500m (3:39.7), Kilby in the marathon (2:17:03) and Fred Alsop in the triple jump, who at the Games improved his British record from 16.13m to 16.46m.

1965 (White City)

WHAT HAS BEEN the greatest single performance ever witnessed at the AAA Championships? Anyone in the 16,000 crowd that day, or among the millions of televiewers, would probably nominate Ron Clarke's 3 miles on July 10. The author, reporting for *Athletics Weekly*, wrote: "Clarke's achievement in covering 3 miles in 12:52.4 is, I submit, the most prodigious in the long history of track running. It is his third improvement on the world record, having clocked 13:07.6 in December 1964 and 13:00.4 in June 1965. Thus, in seven months, he has cut no less than 17.6 sec from Murray Halberg's 1961 figures of 13:10.0. Perhaps the full enormity of Clarke's feat can best be brought home by noting that his 2 miles time of 8:36.4 on the way would have constituted a world record prior to May 1955, and yet he went on to cover another mile at even faster speed." On a rainsoaked track and after seven weeks of globe-trotting, racing hard two or three times a week, the 28-year-old Australian reeled off lap after lap at unheard of speeds – head and trunk erect, arms held low and relaxed, his magnificently fluent stride never faltering. Astonishingly, the 19-year-old Gerry Lindgren clung to him for as long as 2 miles and was rewarded by smashing the American record with 13:04.2. A wildly applauded joint lap of honour by the pair was richly deserved. Clarke had been favourite to win the Olympic 10,000m in Tokyo the previous year but after a sensational last lap the victory had gone to the unconsidered American Billy Mills with Mohamed Gammoudi of Tunisia second and Clarke third. Mills never did compete in the AAA Championships but Gammoudi did and won the 6 miles in fine style in 27:38.2, a 4:20.4 final mile carrying him ahead of Ron Hill (27:40.8) and Mike Bullivant (27:43.8). Two American Olympic champions won their events: Mike Larrabee the 440y, but only just, in a mediocre 47.6 and Rex Cawley the 440y hurdles in a championship record of 50.9. Olympic hero John Cooper, second in 51.5, never recovered his 1964 form and, sadly, perished in an air crash over Paris when only 33.

The Indoor Championships transferred from Wembley to the vastly superior AAA-owned 220y banked board track at RAF Cosford, the winners including a rejuvenated Derek Ibbotson (32) in the 2 miles (8:42.6). The pole vault title went to British record holder David Stevenson, who as the son of the founder of the clothing retailer, Edinburgh Woollen Mill, became one of the richest men in Britain. The decathlon, traditionally a weak event in Britain, received a boost when the first three in the AAA Championship staged at Loughborough exceeded the previous national record with Norman Foster the winner with a score that equates to 6662 on the current tables, just ahead of Derek Clarke and Dave Travis, the latter having recently won the first of seven AAA javelin titles.

Noteworthy too was that runners from Coventry Godiva Harriers filled first three places in the AAA Marathon, Bill Adcocks (2:16:50) deposing Brian Kilby with Juan Taylor third ... and the club's biggest star, Basil Heatley, didn't compete. Placing 29th in 2:40:21 was the New Zealander Norman Harris, author of several outstanding athlete biographies. Speaking of authors, the best-selling novelist Jeffrey Archer finished last in his 100y heat and reached the 220y semis at the White City, but would fare better the next year when finishing fourth in the semis of both events in 9.9w and 21.5.

1966 (White City)

IT WAS A pity they didn't race each other but Ron Clarke and Mohamed Gammoudi returned to retain their titles. For Clarke it was virtually an exhibition run as he clocked 12:58.2 for 3 miles, some 120 yards in front of his nearest opponent, but the Tunisian found himself in a red hot competition as a devilish pace set by Jim Hogan ensured fast times all round in the 6 miles. No fewer than 12 men passed halfway inside 13:40 and there were still six clustered together with two laps remaining. A 58.2 last quarter took Gammoudi clear in a championship record of 27:23.4 but in close attendance were Bruce Tulloh and Hungary's Lajos Mecser, who shared a European record of 27:23.8, while Roy Fowler (27:24.8) and Ron Hill (27:26.0) weren't far back.

There was one other British record as John Sherwood equalled John Cooper's 440y hurdles time of 51.1 although that was considerably inferior to Cooper's metric mark of 50.1. Future National Coach Peter Warden was second in 51.5 with David Hemery fifth in 52.6. At this point in his career Hemery was more adept at the high hurdles, which he won in a championship record of 14.0. There were other new championship bests by Ireland's Noel Carroll in the 880y with 1:48.0, Maurice Herriott in the steeplechase (8:37.0) with Ernie Pomfret (8:39.0) also inside the old mark and Lachie Stewart (whose golden moment would come over 10,000m at the 1970 Commonwealth Games) setting a Scottish record of 8:44.8, Lynn Davies in the long jump with 8.06m, the world's first 17m triple jumper Józef Schmidt of Poland (15.99m) and Finland's future world javelin record holder Jorma Kinnunen (83.22m). There was an outstanding run also by Trinidad's Wendell Mottley, a graceful winner of the 440y by nearly ten yards in 45.9, equalling Robbie Brightwell's meeting record. With South

Africa's Paul Nash (19) taking a sprint double in 9.6/21.2 and John Camien (USA) the mile in 4:01.1 it meant that all seven flat running titles went overseas for the first time.

Chris Carter, first Briton home in the 880y for the third year running, went on in Budapest in September to set a British 800m record of 1:46.3 for fourth place in the European Championships, missing the bronze medal by inches after leading for almost the entire race, but his connection with the AAA Championships was not at an end. His son Richard became AAA Junior 5000m champion in 1983 and Chris is the current Chairman of the AAA. Another prominent official of the future, John Lister (who held office at AAA, British and European levels), placed second in the AAA Indoor 60y hurdles.

Those European Championships proved a disappointment after the four gold medals obtained in 1962. This time there were just two – for Davies (7.98m) and marathoner Hogan (2:20:05) – and no other medals. Earlier, at the Commonwealth Games in Kingston, Jamaica, English victories were obtained by Hemery (14.1 120y hurdles), Howard Payne (61.98m to retain his hammer title), John FitzSimons (79.79m for a British javelin record) and Ron Wallwork (2:44:43 20 miles walk), by Welshman Davies (7.99m) and Scotland's Jim Alder (2:22:08 marathon). Allan Rushmer, third in the 3 miles, set a British record of 13:08.6 behind Kip Keino and Ron Clarke; Mike Bull of N Ireland broke David Stevenson's UK pole vault record of 4.67m with 4.72m for the silver medal; and a silver medal and British decathlon record went to Wales' Clive Longe with 6950 on the present tables – a mark he improved to 6996 for ninth place in Budapest.

Davies made history that year by becoming the first athlete ever to win the "grand slam" of Olympic, European and Commonwealth titles. Although Hogan and Alder went on to win international championships that year and both competed in the AAA Marathon, held in conjunction with the Polytechnic race in June, the title winner was Graham Taylor, who had become eligible to run the distance only 38 days earlier when he celebrated his 21st birthday. Up against the finest field ever assembled in Britain, he uncorked a spectacular 30.5 final furlong to win in 2:19:04, followed in by Hogan (2:19:27), Hill (2:20:55), Bill Adcocks (2:24:09), Brian Kilby (2:24:48) and Alder (2:25:07), with Scotsman Alastair Wood ninth in 2:28:29. Just a month later, in a wind aided Inverness to Forres race (11 starters!), Wood broke Basil Heatley's British record with a startling 2:13:45.

1967 (White City)

MAURICE HERRIOTT NOT only trimmed his championship record in the steeplechase to 8:33.8 but by winning for a seventh consecutive year he equalled the record sequence of titles in any event shared by Denis Horgan, Bert Cooper, Don Finlay and Harry Whittle. The crowd of 20,000 also enjoyed UK records by John Boulter (1:47.3 880y) and John Sherwood (50.9 440y hurdles), while there were championship records also by Andy Green in the mile (4:00.6) over five-time indoor champion John Whetton (4:00.8) and British record holder at 3:55.7, Alan Simpson (4:01.0), and in the 120y hurdles by Italy's Eddy Ottoz, whose 14.0 tied the existing mark. Despite being troubled by a groin strain, Ron Clarke returned for his third 3 miles title, a 4:13.6 final mile carrying him to another sub-13 (12:59.6), ahead of Lajos Mecser who set a Hungarian record of 13:03.4 only 20 hours after finishing second in the 6 miles in 27:36.0. Ian McCafferty clocked 13:09.8 for a Scottish record – and just two days later, in Dublin, he broke the British record with 13:06.4 behind Clarke's 12:59.0. The 6 miles title fell to East Germany's European 10,000m champion Jürgen Haase in 27:33.2, graced by a last lap of 55.8. Lynn Davies long jumped 7.93m against strong foreign opposition, while Fred Alsop – like Herriott one of the quiet unsung heroes of British athletics – notched up his fifth triple jump title (15.67m) to add to three previous long jump victories.

Earlier in the year, the star of the Indoor Championships at Cosford had been McCafferty with a European 2 miles best of 8:36.4. Alan Pascoe, at 19, gained his first senior title, taking the 60y hurdles in 7.5, followed by Stuart Storey (7.6), who would for so many years sit alongside David Coleman and Ron Pickering in the BBC television commentary team. Another celebrated figure of the future placed tenth in the triple jump. He was Malcolm Arnold, the fourth ranked performer in Britain in 1963 with 14.94m, who would guide four athletes to Olympic or world championships in John Akii-Bua, Colin Jackson, Mark McKoy and Jason Gardener, while in 2010 another of his charges, David Greene, became European 400m hurdles champion. There was another superb race for the 10 miles championship at Hurlingham as Ron Hill (47:38.6) and Fergus Murray with a Scottish record of 47:45.2 moved to second and third on the UK all-time list, while Mike Turner, more of a cross country specialist who later became British Team Manager, took third in 47:51.4. The marathon championship at Baddesley Colliery in August had a field of only 29 but in hot and humid conditions Jim Alder held off Alastair Wood by 13 sec in a championship record of 2:16:08.

1968 (White City)

WHITE CITY HAD been at the heart of British athletics since 1932 but it was never an ideal situation for the sport to hire a stadium owned by the Greyhound Racing Association, and what occurred in the pole vault at this meeting, attended by the Queen for the first time since 1956, made it clear that a new home was necessary. The problem was that the pole vault, which started at 2 pm, dragged on far beyond its contracted finishing time of 5.30. "The dogs" were due to start at 7.45 and preparations had to be made. Spectators were asked to leave the stadium, a request that was ignored, and although the announcer's microphone was cut off the vaulters continued. Eventually, after 7 pm, Italy's Renato Dionisi was obliged to call it a day after one abortive attempt at a championship record of 5.15m.

David Hemery, who had been chipping away at the British 440y hurdles record all season in the USA, improved the mark again with 50.2 (49.8 at 400m) ... but that was only the tip of the iceberg, for three months later in high altitude Mexico City he would set a phenomenal metric world record of 48.12 when running away with the Olympic title. John Sherwood, second at White City in 50.8, also ran the race of his life to take Olympic bronze in 49.03. The last time Britain collected two medals in the same event was the 400m in 1924, and it was appropriate that the medals should be presented by AAA President, the Marquess of Exeter, who as Lord Burghley won this very title in 1928. Another link with the past: Hemery's British coach was Fred Housden, AAA pole vault runner-up in 1928 and 1929. Disappointingly, these were Britain's only medals in the Olympic men's events. Lynn Davies (7.94m in the AAA) had visions of retaining his long jump title after extending the British record to 8.23m, a mark which stood until 2002, but the shock of Bob Beamon's incredible opening leap of 8.90m left him shell-shocked and he could only go through the motions to place ninth with 7.94m.

The AAA 6 miles again provided a memorable race as 12 men, ten of them British, broke 28 minutes. Former world 30,000m record holder Tim Johnston turned in an impressive 59.8 last lap to win in the European record time of 27:22.2, followed in by Mike Tagg (27:26.4), Jim Alder (Scottish record of 27:28.6) and Ron Hill (27:30.6). The thin air of Mexico City was too much of a handicap for the Britons and Hill did well to place seventh in the 10,000m, as did Bill Adcocks with fifth in the marathon. Johnston, who had won the AAA marathon in July in a championship best of 2:15:26 ahead of Adcocks' 2:15:41, was reduced to 2:28:05 in eighth place at the Games. In a remarkable year for British distance running Hill had in April smashed Ron Clarke's world record with 47:02.2

for the AAA 10 miles title on the new all-weather track at Leicester and returned there in November to clock 46:44.0 on the way to a British one hour record of 12 miles 1268 yards (20,472m). Adcocks set European marathon records of 2:12:17 in May and 2:10:48 in December.

Back at the White City another great name in distance running was starting to draw attention to himself as Dave Bedford (18) front ran to an 8:59.4 victory in the AAA Junior 2 miles held in conjunction. Here was the man who, when the big meetings transferred to Crystal Palace, drew the crowds back to athletics. Buried in the shot result was one Geoff Capes, also 18, seventh with 15.19m in his AAA senior debut, while his coach Stuart Storey booked his Olympic berth by placing third in the 120y hurdles (14.2), won by Alan Pascoe in 14.1. Among the competitors in the 440y hurdles, placing fourth in his heat, was David Clementi – a future Deputy Governor of the Bank of England. London-born South African Paul Nash, who in April had equalled the world 100m record of 10.0 at altitude, scored a sprint double but was brought down to earth by his 100 yards time of 9.9, worth 10.8 for 100m! After winning seven AAA indoor titles, one at 1000y, five at the mile and one at 1500m, not to mention three victories at 1500m in the European Indoor Championships, John Whetton finally added his name to the roll of outdoor mile champions in a time of 4:06.0.

1969 (White City)

MERELY 8,000 SPECTATORS were in place to watch the first edition of the Championships to be staged at metric distances. The classiest performance came from one of the few visitors, Poland's Wladyslaw Nikiciuk, who dethroned defending javelin champion Dave Travis (80.04m) with a final throw of 85.08m, a championship record which survived until 1985. There was a rare occurrence in the discus when brothers filled the first two places: Bill Tancred throwing 53.08m and Peter 52.14m.

A fiery last lap of 53.3 carried Frank Murphy to victory in an Irish record of 3:40.9 in the 1500m, with John Whetton second in 3:41.8, but it was Whetton who would go on to win the European crown in Athens later in the season in 3:39.4 just ahead of Murphy. Making his AAA debut, Brendan Foster was seventh in his heat in 3:51.0. Ian Stewart, only 20 and already European Indoor 3000m champion (7:55.4), ran a mature race to take the 5000m in a personal best of 13:39.8 and would run five seconds slower in Athens for the European title. Dave Bedford (19), the early leader, faded to 12th in that race and fared even worse in the 10,000m, placing 13th about a minute behind Dick Taylor's winning 28:27.6. Both men broke the British record that season: Bedford with 28:24.4 for the Southern title at Crystal Palace in April and Taylor with 28:06.6 on the same track in June, beating Ron Clarke no less. Taylor also set British records at 3000m, 2 miles, 3 miles, 5000m and 6 miles that summer but had the misfortune in Athens to suffer from dehydration and finished near the back of the 10,000m field. Dave Cropper won his only AAA 800m title in a modest 1:49.0; he would serve as AAA Chairman from 1991 to 2004.

Ron Hill enjoyed another brilliant year. He went one better than Alf Shrubb by winning a fifth consecutive AAA 10 miles title with 47:27.0, finished almost two minutes clear of the Lancashire-born Australian Derek Clayton (world record holder at 2:08:34) in the AAA/Maxol Marathon in 2:13:42, captured the European title in 2:16:48 and ended the year with a personal best of 2:11:55 in Japan.

The other gold medallist in Athens was Paul Nihill in the 20km walk (1:30:41). Twelve days earlier, in a training session at Crystal Palace, Britain's finest all-round walker had clocked an unofficial world best of 6:06 for the mile, paced by (a running) David Hemery! There were silver medals in Athens for Mike Tagg in the 10,000m, Hemery in the 110m hurdles, John Sherwood in the 400m hurdles and Lynn Davies in the long jump, with bronze going to Alan Blinston (5000m), Jim Alder (marathon), Alan Pascoe (the European Indoor 50m hurdles champion) in the 110m hurdles and Andy Todd in the 400m hurdles. The tally of 12 medallists in the men's events equalled Britain's best ever showing, in 1958, although 15 would be obtained in Barcelona in 2010. It was an upbeat ending to a decade during which every pre-1960 British record was broken except for the 100m, where McDonald Bailey's former world record of 10.2 was equalled by Ming Campbell.

BRITISH RECORDS AT 1 JANUARY 1970

100y: 9.4 Peter Radford 1960; 100m: 10.2 McDonald Bailey 1951 & Menzies Campbell 1967; 200m/220y: 20.5 Radford 1960; 400m: 45.7 Adrian Metcalfe 1961 & Robbie Brightwell 1964; 440y: 45.9 Brightwell 1962; 800m: 1:46.3 Chris Carter 1966; 880y: 1:47.2 Carter 1968; 1500m: 3:39.1 Alan Simpson 1964 & Ian Stewart 1969; Mile: 3:55.7 Simpson 1965; 3000m: 7:47.6 Dick Taylor 1969; 2M: 8:30.2 Taylor 1967; 3M: 13:04.6 Taylor 1969; 5000m: 13:29.0 Taylor 1969; 6M: 27:10.2 Taylor 1969; 10,000m: 28:06.6 Taylor 1969; 10M: 46:44.0 Ron Hill 1968; Marathon: 2:10:48 Bill Adcocks 1968; 3000mSC: 8:30.8 Gerry Stevens 1969; 110mH/120yH: 13.6 David Hemery 1969; 400mH: 48.1 Hemery 1968; HJ: 2.08 Gordon Miller 1964; PV: 5.06 Mike Bull 1968; LJ: 8.23 Lynn Davies 1968; TJ: 16.46 Fred Alsop 1964; SP: 19.56 Arthur Rowe 1961; DT: 57.78 John Watts 1968; HT: 68.06 Howard Payne 1968; JT: 81.92 John FitzSimons 1969; Decathlon: (re-scored on 1985 tables) 7308 Clive Longe 1969; 2M Walk: 13:02.4 Stan Vickers 1960; 7M Walk: 48:22.2 Ken Matthews 1964; 20km Walk: 1:28:15 Ken Matthews 1960; 50km Walk: 4:11:31 Paul Nihill 1964.

THE SEVENTIES

THE 1970 AAA Championships, the last to be staged at the White City, proved a sombre affair with the lowest attendance in living memory, but a renaissance occurred in 1971. The move to fresh new surroundings at Crystal Palace and the capturing of the public's imagination by the flamboyant young Dave Bedford (like Gordon Pirie before him you either loved him or hated him; you couldn't ignore him) drew a then capacity crowd of 14,000 for the Championships that year and the sport was in the process of being rejuvenated. During the next few seasons, thanks to saturation coverage of the major events by television, the triumphs of men like Brendan Foster, David Jenkins, Ian Stewart, Alan Pascoe, Geoff Capes, Steve Ovett and Seb Coe built on the foundations laid by Bedford. An unprecedented rapport developed between athletes and spectators; the world's top stars attracted big crowds to meetings at Gateshead and Meadowbank as well as Crystal Palace; and with all the publicity generated athletics became a major spectator sport again. Athletics was big business, too, with commercial sponsorship and television fees augmenting the gate money to provide the major sources of finance.

A new breed of athlete emerged as the amateur rules were made more liberal to allow substantial sponsorship

JOHN COOPER
1964 Olympic 400m hurdles silver
medallist who died tragically young
in an air crash

ROBBIE BRIGHTWELL
1962 European 400m champion who,
with Cooper, won 1964 Olympic silver
in 4x400m relay

Several of Britain's finest distance runners pictured during the 1964 Inter-Counties
6 miles. MIKE BULLIVANT leads from RON HILL, MARTIN HYMAN (13) and JIM
HOGAN (20). MEL BATTY (10) is just to the outside of BASIL HEATLEY

LYNN DAVIES
The Welsh long jumper held three major international titles simultaneously after winning at the Olympics in 1964 (pictured here) and the Commonwealth Games and European Championships in 1966. His British record of 8.23m (27 feet) in 1968 stood as the British record until 2002

RON CLARKE (Australia)
Here he is on the way to one of the greatest performances in the long history of the
AAA Championships. The year is 1965, the venue is the White City and Clarke
clocked what was then regarded as the phenomenal 3 miles time of 12:52.4,
smashing his own world record by eight seconds

Clockwise from top: CHRIS CARTER (366), the current Chairman of the AAA, and JOHN BOULTER (362) battle for the lead in the 1966 European 800m championship; BRUCE TULLOH (4); eight-time AAA steeplechase champion MAURICE HERRIOTT

DON THOMPSON

He made up for his collapse in the 1956 Olympic 50km walk by taking the gold medal in Rome four years later, having acclimatised himself in an improvised steam room at his parents' house. Known affectionately in Italy as 'il topolino' (the little mouse) he had only expected to finish fifth or sixth. He won the 53 mile race from London to Brighton for eight consecutive years and in 1991, aged 58, he became Britain's oldest international representative

KEN MATTHEWS
Britain's most successful walker, winner of four major international titles at 20 kilometres. He was European champion in 1962, led Britain to victory in the first two finals of the Lugano Trophy (effectively the world team championship) in 1961 and 1963, and crowned his career with victory at the 1964 Olympics in Tokyo. He set British records at all events from 5 miles to two hours, including world bests for 5 and 10 miles

PAUL NIHILL
His range as a world class walker was extraordinary. At the 1964 Olympics he finished a close second at 50km in the British record time of 4:11:32; in 1969 he became European 20km champion; in 1970 he broke George Larner's 1904 British mile record with 6:17.0; and in 1972 he set a world 20km best of 1:24:50. He was the first British male athlete to compete in four Olympics (1964-1976) and he amassed a record total of 27 national titles

Right: TIM JOHNSTON, a world record breaker at 30km in 1965 and AAA champion in 1968 at both 6 miles (in the British record time of 27:22.2) and marathon. Below: British medallists at the 1969 European Championships in Athens. Standing, from left: John Whetton. Ron Hill (and son), Rosemary Stirling, Mike Tagg, Lillian Board, David Hemery, Alan Pascoe, Andy Todd, Ian Stewart, Jim Alder, Pat Lowe, John Sherwood, Janet Simpson, Alan Blinston & Paul Nihill. Seated: Lynn Davies and officials Marea Hartman, Arthur Gold, Cecil Dale & Brenda Bedford. On ground: Anita Neil, Denise Ramsden, Sheila Cooper & Val Peat

FRED ALSOP

Long before Keith Connor, Jonathan Edwards and Phillips Idowu achieved the highest honours in the event, Fred Alsop was Britain's most successful triple jumper. He set the first of eight British records with 15.65m at the 1960 Olympics and the last when he reached 16.46m for fourth place at the Tokyo Olympics of 1964, only 11cm away from a medal. That stood as the British record until Aston Moore jumped 16.52m in 1976. Between 1960 and 1967 Alsop collected five AAA triple jump titles, plus three in the long jump

DAVID HEMERY
Pictured at the 1968 Olympics in Mexico City where he astounded everyone by smashing the world record for 400m hurdles with a time of 48.12, becoming the first British man since Tom Hampson 36 years earlier to achieve the ultimate in athletics: an Olympic gold medal with a world record performance. Although he was Commonwealth 120 yards hurdles champion in 1966, Hemery was practically a novice at 400m hurdles prior to 1968 – his personal best for 440 yards hurdles was the equivalent of 51.5. He travelled to the Games as British record holder with 49.6, ranking fourth in the world behind three Americans. In his Olympic semi-final he progressed to 49.37 but that hardly was an indication of what was to come in the final, which he won by a margin of at least seven metres with a time which broke the world record by 0.7 sec. One American track nut proclaimed it as 'the greatest performance in track history.' Team-mate John Sherwood finished third, the first time since 1924 that Britain had won two Olympic medals in the same event, and it was appropriate that the awards were presented by the AAA President, the Marquess of Exeter, who as Lord Burghley won this very title in 1928

Top: DICK TAYLOR, the 1969 AAA 10,000m champion who set British records at 3000m (7:47.6), 2 miles (8:30.2), 5000m (13:29.0 and 13:26.2) and 10,000m (28:06.6); and HOWARD PAYNE, three times Commonwealth Games hammer champion and winner of five AAA titles between 1964 and 1973. Middle: JOHN WHETTON, the 1968 AAA mile and 1969 European 1500m champion whose greatest successes came indoors. He was European champion on the boards in 1966, 1967 and 1968 and picked up seven AAA indoor titles. Bottom: BILL TANCRED, seven times AAA discus champion between 1966 and 1973 and Britain's first 60m and 200ft thrower, pictured with his coach JOHN Le MASURIER

IAN STEWART & IAN McCAFFERTY
A memorable moment for Scottish athletics as Ian Stewart, born in Birmingham of a Scottish father, wins the 5000m at the 1970 Commonwealth Games in Edinburgh in a European record 13:22.8 ahead of team-mate Ian McCafferty (13:23.4). Those times propelled them to second and third on the world all-time list behind Ron Clarke, who finished fifth in this race

ALAN PASCOE
As well as his 1972 Olympic 4x400m relay silver medal and 1974 Commonwealth Games and European 400m hurdles titles, he was a prolific winner of AAA championships: 200m in 1971 and 1972; 120y/110m hurdles in 1968, 1971 and 1972; 400m hurdles in 1973, 1976 and 1978

MIKE BULL
Representing N Ireland, he was Commonwealth Games champion at pole vault in 1970 and decathlon in 1974. He won five AAA vault titles between 1966 and 1972

ANDY CARTER
Seen here winning his third AAA 800m title at Crystal Palace in 1973, setting a British record of 1:45.12 in the process of defeating South Africa's Danie Malan (37)

GEOFF CAPES
Winner of seven AAA shot titles and UK record holder from 1972 to 2003

DAVE BEDFORD
World record at 1973 AAA Championships! Bedford takes the 10,000m title in 27:30.80,
breaking Lasse Viren's mark by 7.6 sec, after reaching halfway in an unprecedented 13:39.4

STEVE OVETT
*Celebrating after defeating the favourite Seb Coe, for the
Olympic 800m title in Moscow in 1980*

and broken-time payments, although closely scrutinised and administered by the governing bodies. Thanks to organisations like the Sports Aid Foundation, the BAAB was able to channel four-figure sums annually to several top athletes to enable them to compete on equal terms with heavily state-sponsored or athletic scholarship supported opponents from abroad. By this means they were able, if thought advantageous, to take prolonged leave from work without financial handicap, travel abroad for training and competition, obtain the best coaching, equipment and so on. For an Olympic medal contender it was possible to be – quite legally – a full time athlete. For example, Foster took a year's leave of absence from his post as recreation officer for Gateshead, while Daley Thompson spent so many hours a day training and recuperating it would have been impossible for him to hold down a job as well.

Sponsorship was officially sanctioned, but appearance money was not, and so "shamateurism" continued to flourish. In 1972 the AAA raised the maximum value of prizes to £40 exclusive of tax and in 1977 to the IAAF approved figure of the equivalent of 100 US dollars, but that was of concern only to the good club athlete. World class performers wanted an end to the hypocrisy of shamateurism by which some athletes received illicit payments to compete and governing bodies usually chose to turn a blind eye to the practice.

In 1973, following comments by Harold Abrahams and the Marquess of Exeter upholding the code of amateurism, the International Athletes' Club, under the chairmanship of John Whetton, stated: "In any democracy it is the duty of the governing body to legislate for the effective fulfilment of the wishes of the people they represent, rather than to insist on trying to perpetuate what they believed to be right in the good old days. Is it too much to hope that they will see the need and desire for a change in the amateur laws so as to enable all athletes to compete openly and honourably at all levels without being inhibited by the prejudices of the 19th century?"

A poll among IAC members had resulted in almost unanimous support (by 49 votes to 3) for completely open athletics.

In 1973 there was a perceived threat to the established order when a series of professional meetings was organised in the USA by the International Track Association. Several big names of the recent past signed up, including such American stars as Bob Hayes, Lee Evans, Jim Ryun, Bob Beamon and Randy Matson, and Kenya's Kip Keino and Ben Jipcho, and in 1975 the troupe moved to Britain with meetings at Meadowbank and Crystal Palace where the competitors included David Hemery and Bruce Tulloh. AAA General Committee requested amateur officials not to carry out any duties at those meetings. The authorities need not have worried. In 1976 ITA announced it was ceasing operations because it was unable to recruit famous new names to its ranks. Why? Because top "amateur" athletes could earn more in under-the-counter payments than openly as professionals!

Slowly but steadily the climate of opinion changed and at the AGM of the AAA in November 1979 a resolution proposed by Hastings AC "that this meeting urges the General Committee to make an urgent revision of the amateur rules" was approved by an overwhelming majority. Squire Yarrow, the 1938 European marathon silver medallist who had succeeded the late Harold Abrahams as AAA President in 1978, said: "We set the lead one hundred years ago, and there is no reason why we shouldn't – indeed it's our duty to – set the lead again." Within weeks General Committee had set up an internal committee of enquiry, chaired by Welsh AAA Hon. Secretary Dr Bill Evans, to consider the urgent revision of the amateur rules as agreed at the AGM. The days of amateurism and shamateurism were numbered.

Another topic endlessly debated during the decade was the Byers Report recommendation that a British Athletic Federation be created, headed by a professional Director of British Athletics. An *Athletics Weekly* referendum conducted in 1972 and involving more than 700 readers resulted in 90% voting in favour of such a Director being appointed, with 81% wanting a combined men's and women's national championships. At about the same time the IAC at its AGM voted for Arthur Gold's resignation as BAAB Hon. Secretary in order that a professional Director take his place. Others in the sport preferred that Mr Gold should himself occupy that post but he declined, as he had in 1970 when he was invited by the Board to accept a salaried appointment. In 1977 Mr Gold (later Sir Arthur), on being elected President of the European Athletic Association, was succeeded as BAAB Hon. Secretary by Robert Stinson, while in 1978 former international steeplechaser David Shaw was appointed the BAAB's first professional General Secretary.

The issue of replacing the strictly separate AAA and Women's AAA Championships with a mixed UK National Championships was also a controversial topic. Mr Gold's annual report in 1972 stated that such a meeting, to be organised by the BAAB, "is being extensively examined and has already received qualified approval from some of our Constituent Members." If run as a closed event it would still be possible to continue with the AAA and WAAA Championships as open international events. Although the AAA – the major Constituent Member of the BAAB – was opposed to UK Championships, which it saw as a potential threat to its own long established Championships and financial security, they were inaugurated at Cwmbran in 1977. Entrants were restricted to men and women eligible to represent Great Britain & N Ireland. Although initially welcomed by most of Britain's top athletes, the UK Championships as a separate meeting lasted only until 1993.

After 40 years in office, the Marquess of Exeter (Lord Burghley) stepped down as AAA President in 1976, with his Olympic contemporary Douglas Lowe making a presentation at the AGM. A third Olympic champion, Harold Abrahams, was elected, fulfilling a lifetime ambition, but he died only two years later. Other prominent figures in the sport who passed away during the seventies included two more Olympic champions in Arnold Strode-Jackson and Tommy Green, legendary hurdler Don Finlay and long serving officials 'Billy' Holt and Ernest Clynes. The saddest death of all was that of Lillian Board, who had succeeded Mary Rand as the "golden girl" of British athletics. She died of cancer at 22.

Some progress was made towards a marriage between the AAA and its female counterpart. A proposal at the AAA AGM of 1974, by journalist and coach Cliff Temple on behalf of Folkestone AC, that the WAAA be approached "with a view to the amalgamation of the two Associations at the earliest possible moment" was approved by a large majority. However, the redoubtable WAAA Chairperson, Vera Searle, remarked that half a century ago "the then officers of the AAA told us we would be better off on our own, and so it has proved." She added that the WAAA was not, at the present time, kindly disposed towards amalgamation but as soon as the WAAA became convinced that their athletes would benefit from such a move they would approach the men. Ron Goodman, Chairman of AAA General Committee, pointed out that there was nothing to prevent clubs, counties and areas amalgamating. The following year a WAAA Special General Meeting rejected by 50 votes to 10 a proposal which sought "an eventual amalgamation between the two Associations" but voted 69-0 for setting up a joint committee which would discuss and encourage as much amalgamation as was practicable. In the years that followed men's and women's athletics did become increasingly entwined, combined AAA and WAAA Championships being staged from 1988, but not until 1991 did the two governing bodies actually amalgamate to become the AAA of England.

The decade had opened with a warning from retiring Hon. Treasurer Frank Read. He told the 1970 AGM that the AAA faced a deficit of £8000 in the current financial year and a special finance committee had been set up with the task of saving some £11,000 in annual expenditure, a 20% reduction. "To my mind, the future is very grim," he said. Economy measures followed swiftly: two area administrators were axed, as were three members of the central administrative staff. Under the new Hon. Treasurer, John Martell, the financial situation improved. A £3000 loss in the year ending in March 1971 was followed by a surplus of £14,000 the following year. One of the main reasons for the change in fortunes was that the expensive AAA Coaching Scheme transferred to the BAAB's responsibility as the UK Coaching Scheme in 1972, a significant step – as recommended by the Byers Report – towards organising the sport on a UK-wide basis for men and women combined. The knock-on effect was to render the BAAB almost bankrupt as the annual costs of the Coaching Scheme soared throughout the decade, from around £30,000 under the AAA in 1970 to £114,000 in 1978. After some 30 years' distinguished service with first the AAA and then the BAAB, the two Principal National Coaches, Denis Watts and John Le Masurier, retired in 1979, leading to Frank Dick, the 38-year-old National Coach for Scotland and the AAA Junior 200y hurdles champion in 1960, to be appointed the BAAB's first Director of Coaching.

One of the AAA's money spinning successes as well as encouraging schoolchildren to test their athletic ability was the Five Star Award Scheme, sponsored by Wall's Ice Cream until 1980 when Esso Petroleum took over. More than half a million certificates were issued in 1970 and that figure rose to over 1,200,000 in 1978. By 1979, Ray Stroud – who had taken over as Hon. Treasurer when John Martell became the AAA's professional National Administrator in 1974 – was able to announce assets in excess of £100,000, thanks in part to Nationwide Building Society sponsoring the AAA Championships each year from 1972 to 1980.

The performance enhancing drugs problem intensified during the seventies. The use of anabolic steroids was expressly forbidden under the IAAF's new doping rule in 1970 but despite persistent warnings of potentially dire side effects an increasing number of athletes and their coaches and medical advisers chose to cheat. The development of reliable testing procedures, used for the first time at the 1974 European Championships, led many athletes to stop taking the drugs a few weeks before a major event to avoid detection. Two female throwers were the first to be found guilty of taking anabolic steroids in 1975 and East Europeans (particularly women) built up an increasingly bad record as the decade progressed. The IAAF hesitated to apply swingeing punishments in those early days and who knows how widespread the practice was in the USA, for they didn't even hold tests there. To his credit, from the moment he was elected President of the European AA in 1976, Arthur Gold was unwaveringly firm in his opposition to doping and he welcomed a BAAB resolution, presented at the 1979 EAA Congress held ironically in East Berlin, that athletes be tested out of competition as well as at meetings.

Mary Peters, of course, struck gold but for Britain's men the two Olympic Games of 1972 (Munich) and 1976 (Montreal) proved a disappointment with just three individual bronze medals (Ian Stewart at 5000m, David Hemery at 400m hurdles and Brendan Foster at 10,000m) plus silver for the 4x400m team.

Britain made little impact on the European Cup with a highest placing of fourth and all too many AAA titles went abroad – 13 out of 19 at the 1979 Championships. From the three editions of the European Championships staged in 1971, 1974 and 1978 there were gold medals for David Jenkins (400m), Steve Ovett (1500m), Foster (5000m), Ian Thompson (marathon), Alan Pascoe (400m hurdles) and the 4x400m team. The Commonwealth Games of 1970, 1974 and 1978 produced wins for England's Dave Moorcroft (1500m), Foster (10,000m), Ron Hill and Ian Thompson (marathon), Hemery (110m hurdles), John Sherwood and Alan Pascoe (400m hurdles), Alan Lerwill and Roy Mitchell (long jump), Keith Connor (triple jump), Geoff Capes (shot, twice), Howard Payne and Ian Chipchase (hammer), Dave Travis and Charles Clover (javelin), Daley Thompson (decathlon), John Warhurst and Olly Flynn (road walk).

Allan Wells (200m), Ian Stewart (5000m), Lachie Stewart (10,000m) and the 4x100m relay team of Scotland also won golds, as did Berwyn Price (110m hurdles) and Lynn Davies (long jump) of Wales and Mike Bull (pole vault & decathlon) of N Ireland.

The only British records in standard events which survived from the sixties were Hemery's 400m hurdles and Davies' long jump. World records or bests were established by Seb Coe (1:42.33 800m, 3:32.03 1500m, 3:48.95 mile), Foster (7:35.1 3000m, 8:13.68 2 miles), Ovett (8:13.51 2 miles), Dave Bedford (27:30.80 10,000m), Jim Alder (1:31:30.4 30,000m) and Paul Nihill (1:24:50 20km road walk).

Highlights from each of the AAA Championships meetings 1970-1979

1970 (White City)

THE FINAL GATHERING at the White City was a somewhat melancholy occasion as just 4,721 enthusiasts – the lowest attendance anyone could remember – assembled on the Saturday in the echoing old stadium. It was farewell to an historic venue, and goodbye also to one of its heroes in Ron Clarke, who ran a valedictory lap of honour (timed at 80.5 sec) to mark his impending retirement. The Australian, creator of 17 world records but holder of no major titles, shared with Emil Zátopek the distinction of attracting not just respect and admiration from the fans but also deep affection for his human qualities. Meanwhile, another front running record setter was getting into his stride. Returning from injury, Dave Bedford led from the start of the 10,000m and gradually wore down the opposition, finishing some 70m clear of Trevor Wright (the 10 miles champion in 47:20.2) in 28:26.4, barely 2 sec outside his best but in view of the state of the cinder track worth well inside his former British record at Crystal Palace. The very next day the indefatigable Bedford won the Shaftesbury 10 miles road race in 47:55! The best performances otherwise came from Martin Reynolds, winner of the 200m in 21.0 after a 20.9 semi, a 13.9 110m hurdles by David Hemery and a 12:13.8 3000m walk by a metronomic Paul Nihill, whose kilometre splits were 4:04.8, 4:04.8 and 4:04.2! Bill Tancred notched up his fifth discus title with 53.88m.

The Championships were rather an anti-climax after the excitement of the Commonwealth Games in Edinburgh the previous month. Englishmen claimed five titles there courtesy of Ron Hill with a European marathon best of 2:09:28 (passing halfway in a futuristic 62:36), Hemery with a windy 13.6 hurdles, John Sherwood with 50.0 400m hurdles, Howard Payne with a 67.80m hammer throw to become the first man to win three successive titles in any event, and Dave Travis with a javelin throw of 79.50m.

Scottish fans revelled in the victories of Birmingham-born Ian Stewart, whose European 5000m record of 13:22.8 made him the second fastest in history behind Clarke, and Lachie Stewart, who outkicked Clarke in a 28:11.8 10,000m. Lynn Davies of Wales collected another long jump title (wind assisted 8.06m) and Northern Ireland's Mike Bull cleared a British record of 5.10m to take the pole vault. Brendan Foster opened his medal count with a bronze in the 1500m, improving his pb by over two seconds with 3:40.6, while AAA marathon champion Don Faircloth clocked the fastest ever time by a 21-year-old of 2:12:19 for third place behind Scotland's Jim Alder (2:12:04). Alder, a freelance journalist at the time, created his own headlines later in the year with a world 30,000m record of 1:31:30.4. It was altogether a vintage year for British distance running, for Ricky Wilde won the European Indoor 3000m in a world indoor best of 7:47.0, Mike Tagg won the International cross country title, and Hill had in April become the world's second fastest marathoner with his 2:10:30 victory in Boston.

1971 (Crystal Palace)

THANKS LARGELY TO publicity surrounding Dave Bedford's bid to break Ron Clarke's world 5000m record of 13:16.6, the first AAA Championships to be staged at Crystal Palace and its highly praised all-weather track and field event surfaces were a sell-out with some 14,000 fans – many of them new to big time athletics – packing the arena. Bedford had been in fantastic form, following up the coveted International cross country title with a European 5000m record of 13:22.2 which would have been several seconds faster but for gale force winds in Edinburgh and another European record of 27:47.0 when winning the AAA 10,000m title on a hot day in Portsmouth, a race which was memorable also for the times of the opening two laps: 70.0 and 59.0! With his Mexican bandit appearance and swashbuckling attitude he brought a new public appeal to the rather staid world of British athletics. Bedford went out very fast and was ahead of Clarke's schedule at 2000m but unfortunately his record attempt came to an abrupt and painful end when cramp in the right hamstring forced him out of the race shortly after the 3000m mark, the title going in an unremarkable 13:39.6 to Mike Baxter. Bedford's luck wasn't much better in the 10,000m at the European Championships in Helsinki, the climax of the season. After setting a fast pace for most of the race he had nothing left for a furious last lap which saw him drop back to sixth, the title going to Finland's Juha Vaatainen in 27:52.8.

Britain's only European winner was David Jenkins (19) who in the closing stages of the 400m was drowning in lactic acid after zipping through the first 200m in 21.1 but he held on gallantly for a British record of 45.5 as against a disappointing 47.1 for the AAA title. There were silver medals for Alan Pascoe (14.1 110m hurdles), who had completed an unique AAA double by taking the sprint hurdles (14.5) and 200m (21.1), both into strong winds, and for Trevor Wright (2:14:00 marathon), who earlier in the season had won the AAA 10 miles in a championship best of 46:51.6

and in his first ever race beyond 10 miles had finished second in the AAA/Maxol Marathon in 2:13:27 behind Ron Hill's 2:12:39. Hill (2:14:35) was a bronze medallist in Helsinki, as were Andy Carter, whose 1:46.2 800m shaved a tenth off his namesake Chris Carter's British record, Paul Nihill in the 20km walk with a national record of 1:27:35, and Brendan Foster, again rising to the big occasion with a 1500m pb of 3:39.2. At the AAA meeting Foster had finished third behind New Zealander Tony Polhill (3:40.0) and Peter Stewart (3:40.4) in 3:40.7. Stewart had become European Indoor 3000m champion earlier in the year, two years after his younger brother Ian ... while their sister Mary would win the 1500m title in 1977 with a world indoor record for good measure. And that's not all, for Mary's son Adam Cotton won the junior 800m at the 2009 national indoor championships. What a family! Meanwhile, other stars of the future were on the rise: Dave Moorcroft (18) won the AAA Junior 1500m, a powerfully built 15-year-old by the name of Steve Ovett took the AAA Youth 400m title in 49.8, and a diminutive 14-year-old (weighing all of six and a half stones) was beginning to be noticed up in Yorkshire after winning the county's Colts cross country title. Although his best 1500m time was only 4:31.8, his father and coach had already drawn up a projection of progress designed to take him to a world record shattering 3:30 by 1980. Absurd? Not when you're talking about Peter Coe and his son Sebastian!

1972 (Crystal Palace)

THE REPORT IN *Athletics Weekly* could not have been more enthusiastic. "From every standpoint the 1972 AAA Championships must be judged the greatest in the meeting's 92-year history. Competition was at its keenest with Olympic team places at stake, scintillating performances abounded, the stadium was filled to capacity on the Saturday and the weather was gorgeous." Championship bests were broken or equalled in no fewer than 12 of the

18 events, including British records in the 1500m by Peter Stewart (3:38.2) and pole vault by Ulsterman Mike Bull (5.21m). Topping the bill, though, was – almost inevitably – the man who had attracted so many of the fans in the first place ... Dave Bedford. No less an authority than Ron Clarke described Bedford's double as "the greatest in athletics history". The 5000m came first on the Friday evening and Bedford showed his intention of chasing Clarke's world record of 13:16.6 from the outset. By 3000m (7:53.6) he was nearly 40m clear of Ian Stewart and he stayed ahead of Clarke's corresponding lap times until 4400m. Passing 3 miles in 12:52.0, smashing his own European record of 12:58.2 and so close to Clarke's world record of 12:50.4, he finished in 13:17.2 to pulverise his previous European record of 13:22.2. Ian McCafferty was also inside the old figures with 13:19.8, with Stewart third in 13:24.2. Barely 19 hours later, in hot weather, Bedford returned to win the 10,000m by a 300m margin over Lachie Stewart in 27:52.8, a time only he and Clarke had ever surpassed, and it would have been even quicker had he not cruised the last circuit, seemingly incorporating his victory lap as he veered over to the fifth lane along the finishing straight as the crowd of nearly 20,000 cheered him home. It was a spine tingling occasion.

The other eight British athletes who achieved championship records were Brian Green (the new UK record holder at 10.1) with 10.3 in his 100m semi (he was second in the final, won by Greece's Vassilios Papageorgopoulos – a commentator's nightmare – in a windy 10.2), Alan Pascoe with a personal best of 20.9 in the 200m and 13.9 in the 110m hurdles, David Jenkins with an unstraining 45.5 400m semi and a much more difficult looking 45.4 in the final to miss his British record by a tenth, Steve Hollings with an 8:31.2 steeplechase, David Hemery (in his first 400m hurdles competition in Britain for almost four years) with 49.7 just inches ahead of Uganda's John Akii-Bua, Alan Lerwill with a wind aided long jump of 8.15m, Geoff Capes with 19.47m in the shot (the first of his seven titles) and

Bill Tancred with 61.06m in the discus for his sixth title. A welcome innovation was that the highest placed athlete in each event eligible to represent Great Britain & N Ireland was designated UK champion and received a special gold medal from the BAAB.

Unhappily, all these fine performances, and there were others, did not translate into great success for the men at the ill-fated Munich Olympics. Just two individual bronze medals were gained: by Ian Stewart (13:27.61) and Hemery (48.52, with Akii-Bua taking the gold medal and Hemery's world record with 47.82). The 4x400m squad of Martin Reynolds 46.3, Pascoe 45.1, Hemery 45.0 and Jenkins 44.1 took silver in a European record 3:00.46, while Brendan Foster placed fifth in the 1500m after clocking a British record of 3:38.20 in his semi. As for Bedford, after a casual looking 27:53.64 10,000m heat, he over-stretched himself in the final, leading through 5000m in 13:44.0 for the fastest ever halfway split before dropping back to sixth in 28:05.44 while Finland's Lasse Viren – despite a fall – won in a world record 27:38.35! Viren went on to take the 5000m in 13:26.42 with a played-out Bedford 12th in 13:43.22. Like Ron Clarke, Bedford was never to do himself justice in the major track championships ... but what memories he left behind.

1973 (Crystal Palace)

THE ONLY PREDICTABLE feature about Dave Bedford was his unpredictability. Only those closest to him had any inkling of his intentions at these Championships. He had been out of the public eye for a long period while he recovered from a hamstring injury, but he sensed he was ready for a great run. Normally he, the best showman in British athletics, would have announced his plan – an attempt on Lasse Viren's world 10,000m record, no less – and the fans would have flocked to "The Palace", creating high expectations and unwanted pressure. This time he played it cool and so only the faithful few, some 3500 in number, were privileged to witness a momentous run on the evening of Friday the 13th of July. The pace set was prodigious with Bedford reaching just inside his 13:40 target at halfway with 13:39.4, although Welsh-born Tony Simmons wasn't that far behind in 13:41.6 – the two fastest 5000m splits on record at that time. Amazingly, Bedford reeled off five consecutive laps of exactly 67 sec and pushed hard all the way for a glittering final time of 27:30.80 to become the first Briton since Alf Shrubb in 1904 to set a world record in this event. Simmons finished a gallant second in 28:19.19. Bedford returned next day for the 5000m but it was really a token appearance for the crowd's benefit. Drained emotionally if not physically, he came home a distant sixth while Brendan Foster romped away with the title in his first serious race at the distance, clocking a splendid 13:23.71 to finish a full seven seconds ahead of runner-up Ian Stewart.

In addition to Bedford's 10,000m there were two other British records. Geoff Capes put the shot 20.27m and Andy Carter beat a high class international field in the 800m in 1:45.12, also an all-comers record, with Steve Ovett placing sixth in 1:47.34, a world best by a 17-year-old. Third was Australia's Bill Hooker in 1:45.36 ... his son Steve (born nine years later) would become Olympic pole vault champion in 2008! Both Steve Hollings (8:30.81 steeplechase) and Bill Tancred (61.22m discus) improved on their-year-old championship records, Tancred winning his seventh AAA title. Howard Payne, at 42, landed his fifth hammer title (67.98) but even more impressive is that between 1961 and 1974 he was the highest placed UK competitor on 13 occasions.

A few days after his 800m, Ovett went on to run exactly four minutes for the mile and later collected the European Junior 800m title. He was well on his way to greatness. Seb Coe (16) was at an earlier stage of his journey but was also progressing nicely, winning the AAA Youth 1500m in 3:55.0 and the English Schools Intermediate 3000m in 8:40.2. There were two other exciting developments later in the season as athletes began to gear up for the Commonwealth Games to be held in New Zealand in January 1974. Foster broke Viren's world 2 miles record at Crystal Palace with 8:13.68 and the AAA marathon at Harlow was won by Ian Thompson in 2:12:40, then the fastest debut on record. He had never raced beyond 10 miles before, only took part to help his club in the team race and had set himself a target of 2:20! And that proved to be only the start of a remarkable sequence, to be continued in 1974.

1974 (Crystal Palace)

IT HAD LONG been a controversial issue as to whether the AAA Championships, in effect Britain's national championships, should continue to be thrown open to the world. Those in favour of the traditional format argued that the presence of top-line stars from abroad enhanced the meeting's crowd appeal and afforded valuable international competition for Britain's leading athletes. Others felt that true national championships should be restricted to UK competitors and that the influx of foreigners deprived many home athletes of the chance of reaching finals. The 1974 edition added fuel to the fire. Despite the presence of a strong American squad, including three world record holders, merely 7000 fans turned up on a damp, cold Saturday. Meanwhile, only nine of the 19 titles at stake stayed at home, Americans claiming eight of the 11 events they contested; there were five visitors among ten runners in one heat of the 1500m and 11 out of 29 in the 5000m. Particularly impressive were Steve Williams, whose seemingly effortless though gigantic strides carried him to a casual 100m victory in a wind-aided 10.16, and his two USA colleagues Jim Bolding and Al Feuerbach, who set UK all-comers records of 49.1 in the 400m hurdles and 21.37m in the shot respectively. Geoff Capes did well to edge out world indoor record holder George Woods for second place, 20.77m to 20.69m. The most eye-catching British victories came in the middle and long distance running department. Steve Ovett, still only 18, moved from seventh to first in the final 200m of the 800m (1:46.84) – and a few days later would become Britain's youngest sub-4 minute miler with a Bannisterish 3:59.4 – while Brendan Foster tossed in a murderous 59.2 eighth lap to destroy the 5000m field in 13:27.4. John Davies set a championship record of 8:26.8 in the steeplechase and Dave Bedford ran an atypical race in the 10,000m, sitting in for once and kicking home in 28:14.80 to win for a fifth consecutive year. With a throw of 75.20m Dave Travis notched up his seventh javelin title since 1965.

It was a long year for Britain's top athletes as the Commonwealth Games were in Christchurch in January, the AAA Championships in July and the European Championships in Rome in September. Seven gold medals went to English representatives in New Zealand: Ian Thompson created a second sensation in his two-marathon career to date by setting a European record of 2:09:12, winning by over two minutes; 18-year-old Charles Clover was another to make an astonishing breakthrough as he threw the javelin a Commonwealth senior and world junior record 84.92m; Geoff Capes raised the Commonwealth shot record to 20.74m; Alan Pascoe improved vastly to clock 48.83 in his "new" event, the 400m hurdles; Alan Lerwill long jumped 7.94m, Ian Chipchase threw the hammer 69.56m and John Warhurst took the 20 miles walk in 2:35:23. Mike Bull of N Ireland scored 7417 for decathlon victory. John Davies, wearing the Welsh vest, set a British record of 8:24.8 for second place in the steeplechase behind Kenya's Ben Jipcho. Brendan Foster also saw the Kenyan's back in an epic 5000m, finishing 0.2 sec behind in 13:14.6 to break Bedford's British record. Four days later Foster lowered his British 1500m record to 3:37.64 ... for seventh place in a fantastic race in which Filbert Bayi of Tanzania front-ran to a world record 3:32.16.

As for Bedford, he was unfortunate to be spiked in brushes with some Kenyan runners in the 10,000m, lost his cool as well as his concentration, and wound up fourth in 28:14.8. It was a doubly unlucky situation as Bedford reckoned he was in the form of his life and capable of lowering his world record to around 27:10. New Zealander Dick Tayler won in 27:46.4 with England's 21-year-old Dave Black a brilliant second in 27:48.6. Four days later Black placed third in the 5000m in another personal best of 13:23.6.

In other early season action Capes won the European indoor title with a European record of 20.95m and Foster ran a phenomenal long leg in the AAA Road Relay at Sutton Coldfield, clocking 24:28 for 5 miles 900 yards – sub-27:40 10,000m pace. It was quite a year for Foster as at the meeting he organised to inaugurate Gateshead's new Tartan track, in front of a worshipping full to overflowing crowd of over 10,000, he set a superb world 3000m record of 7:35.1 and then went on to run away with the European 5000m title in hot, humid conditions in 13:17.2, having been 80m clear at the bell after breaking away with a courageous 60.2 eighth lap. Also crowned European champions were Ian Thompson (2:13:19), Pascoe (48.82) and the 4x400m team (3:03.3) of Glen Cohen, Bill Hartley, Pascoe and David Jenkins, who produced a magnificent anchor leg of 44.3 to hold off West Germany's Karl Honz, who had earlier well beaten him in the individual 400m, 45.04 to 45.67. Other medals won were silver for Steve Ovett (unhappy at losing despite his outstanding European junior 800m record of 1:45.76) and Tony Simmons (given the same time as the winner of the 10,000m at 28:25.8 after a sub-55 last lap), and bronze for Geoff Capes (20.21m) and Roger Mills (1:32:34 20km walk).

1975 (Crystal Palace)

THESE WERE THE 100th Championships since the AAA's predecessor, the Amateur Athletic Club, held its inaugural meeting in 1866. As in 1974 ten of the 19 titles at stake left these shores, with South Africans accounting for half that total. They included the massive world discus record breaker John van Reenen (2.02m tall, weighing 135kg) whose final throw of 62.26m agonisingly deprived Bill Tancred of an eighth title ... by just 4cm or two inches! It was the ninth occasion on which Tancred was the highest placed Briton in the event, his brother Peter carrying on the family tradition with four "UK champion" successes, including the AAA title in 1977 and 1978. Home victories included a fifth consecutive 400m victory (45.87) by David Jenkins, still high from winning the American title in a brilliant UK record of 44.93, while English junior 6 miles cross country champion Steve Ovett – still all of 19 – successfully defended his 800m title in 1:46.1.

Dave Black won the 10,000m in a brisk 27:54.2, but hopes that Ian Stewart would take the 5000m were dashed when he dropped out on the seventh lap. A medical examination showed he was run down and suffering from gastric flu, and the USA's crack miler Marty Liquori won the race in 13:32.6. It was a sad end to Stewart's season as earlier, returning to the sport after a spell as a racing cyclist, he had won the European Indoor 3000m and International 12km cross country championship on successive weekends. Seb Coe and Daley Thompson, who would ultimately become arguably Britain's two most successful athletes ever, continued their climb up the ladder. Coe (18) won the AAA Junior 1500m in 3:47.1 and placed third in the European Junior Championships in 3:45.2, and Thompson (17), the Junior 100m champion, took the Junior decathlon title with a score that was higher than that which won the senior championship!

1976 (Crystal Palace)

COMING A COUPLE of weeks after a deeply disappointing Olympics in Montreal, where the only British medallist was Brendan Foster with bronze in the 10,000m, the AAA Championships were conducted in a somewhat sombre atmosphere, not helped by the high number of withdrawals.

Jamaican sprinters of today such as Usain Bolt and Asafa Powell attract immense media and public acclaim, but an earlier sprinting superstar from that Caribbean island was the elegant Don Quarrie who in Montreal had won the 200m and finished second at 100m. He took the AAA 100m in an unexceptional 10.42, although that afforded him a two metre margin over an up and coming Scot named Allan Wells (10.62), but in the 200m he cut loose with an outstanding championship record of 20.35, winning by six metres. David Jenkins (45.86) extended his sequence of 400m titles to six, while Steve Ovett – fifth in the Olympic final – won his third straight 800m in 1:47.3, outkicking newly crowned Olympic 1500m champion John Walker.

Walker's New Zealand team-mate Rod Dixon was more successful in the 1500m, uncorking a 51.9 last lap to win in 3:41.2 ahead of National cross country runner-up Dave Moorcroft (3:41.6) with Seb Coe fourth in his best time yet of 3:42.7. Foster won the 5000m in 13:33.0 and there were championship records by Berwyn Price (13.80w 110m hurdles), Mike Tully of the USA (5.33m pole vault), European junior champion Aston Moore (16.30m triple jump) and John Powell of the USA (65.52m discus). Geoff Capes put the shot 20.92m, while Milton Palmer at 17 became one of the youngest ever national champions by high jumping 2.06m, although even more precocious was the 14-year-old Scot, Ross Hepburn, who placed fourth with a world age best of 2.03m. Daley Thompson, who in his Olympic baptism had impressed the American gold medallist and world record smasher Bruce Jenner as a likely successor to himself, set a world age-17 best in the AAA decathlon and later improved to a Commonwealth senior and world junior record score of 7941 on today's tables.

1977 (Crystal Palace)

A CROWD OF 14,000, the largest attendance for several years, watched The Queen's Silver Jubilee Championships on the Saturday, but it was the smaller band of enthusiasts on the Friday evening who witnessed the meeting's outstanding performance. The bare result of the 10,000m showed Brendan Foster the winner in 27:45.7, a world class time but no sort of a record. However, it ranked among the finest of distance runs of that era, taking into account the humid conditions and the fact that Foster was alone against the clock for the last 15 laps. Shooting for the world record of 27:30.5 by Kenya's Samson Kimobwa, Foster reached 5000m way ahead of schedule in 13:38.9, the fastest halfway split yet, but from 7000m onwards his pace slipped although a gritty 60.3 last lap took him to the finish half a lap ahead. Runner-up Dave Black had his moment of glory next day when he unexpectedly captured the 5000m in 13:33.2 with Kimobwa and another world record breaker in New Zealand's Dick Quax among the vanquished.

Of the seven titles which went abroad the one that gave rise to the most frustration was the 400m win of Tom Andrews (USA), who passed David Jenkins in the finishing straight, 46.00 to 46.34, thus depriving the Scot of a record-equalling seventh straight title. Also having to settle for second was Seb Coe in the 800m, running an outdoor personal best of 1:46.8 just ahead of John Walker but a few metres adrift of Yugoslavia's Milovan Savic (1:46.3). Earlier, during the indoor season, Coe had not only picked up his first senior AAA title (1:49.1) but had gone on to win the European title, leading all the way, in the UK record time of 1:46.5 which was only 0.1 sec outside the world indoor record. Berwyn Price collected his fifth consecutive 110m hurdles title in 14.17, while Roger Mills chalked up his sixth in a row in the 3000m walk, equalling Paul Nihill's championship record of 12:08.4 in the process. Another meeting record was tied when Alan Dainton high jumped 2.14m to match the 1974 figures of the American former world record holder Dwight Stones. Geoff Capes continued on his merry way with a shot put of 20.70m and Daley Thompson, who raised his Commonwealth senior and world junior decathlon record three times during the summer with a best of 8082 (current tables), won the AAA long jump with a modest 7.52m. An interesting name tucked away in the results: Welshman Steve Jones, who seven years later would break the world marathon record, placed fifth in his steeplechase heat in 8:54.5. A message from The Queen, the AAA's Patron, sending her best wishes for a successful meeting, was read out over the loudspeakers by AAA President Harold Abrahams in what proved to be among his last public appearances. He died in January 1978.

Despite opposition from the AAA, the BAAB inaugurated UK Championships the previous month in Cwmbran, a mixed meeting restricted to athletes eligible to represent Great Britain & N Ireland. Another innovation was that the second day of the meeting was staged on a Sunday, a move the AAA would not make until 1982. Two of the best performances came from athletes who did not compete in the AAA Championships, which was another bone of contention: Steve Ovett missed Frank Clement's British 1500m record by a tenth with 3:37.5 and would have broken it but for waving to the crowd along the finishing straight, and Ian Stewart – who had recently clocked an extraordinary 45:13 for 10 miles on the road – set a personal best of 27:51.3 in the 10,000m.

Later in the season, at the first edition of the IAAF World Cup in Düsseldorf, Ovett ran his first truly memorable 1500m, covering the final 200m in 25.1 to destroy a star-studded field in a UK record 3:34.45. The season came to a resounding end with the International Athletes' Club Coca-Cola Invitational, which drew a capacity crowd to Crystal Palace, and among the treats were a British 800m record of 1:44.95 by Coe and the world's third fastest ever 10,000m of 27:36.62 by Foster for a splendid finish to a year which had started for him with the fulfilment of a long standing ambition by winning the English cross country title. Coe and Ovett were by now well on their way to becoming middle distance legends ... and 1977 saw another taking his first steps as Steve Cram ran 1500m in 3:47.7 for a British age-16 best. Lightning was about to strike for a third time.

1978 (Crystal Palace)

IT WAS A chilly evening, the rain was teeming down and there were puddles on the track. It was not, on the face of it, an occasion for record breaking, yet Brendan Foster overcame the conditions and the lack of opposition to produce arguably the greatest run of his distinguished career. In the lead after only four of the 25 laps, he was 60m up at halfway in 13:45.1 and a second 5000m in just one tenth of a second slower carried him to the finish half a lap ahead of Mike McLeod in the European record time of 27:30.3. But for a mark of 27:22.4 by Kenya's Henry Rono just 12 days earlier it would have been a world record. That was the sixth 10,000m final of his career and his fifth victory, his only defeat having been third place in the 1976 Olympics when he was suffering from a stomach upset.

The other British record to fall also occurred on that wet night. Until then in second place to Keith Connor's 16.39m, Aston Moore (who these days coaches Phillips Idowu) triple jumped 16.68m in the final round to obliterate both his own official record of 16.52m and Connor's indoor best of 16.54m as well as setting a championship record. Contesting his last AAA Championships, Alan Pascoe won the 400m hurdles in 50.39 to bring his title tally, including indoors, to 13 while in the 110m hurdles Berwyn Price (14.14) brought his run of titles to six in a row.

David Jenkins lost again in the 400m to an American visitor, this time Maurice Peoples (45.78 to 46.33), but it marked the eighth year in a row that he had been the first British finisher. The African domination of distance running, so prevalent today, was beginning to take hold then as evident in the 5000m, won by Rono in 13:20.8 with Africans filling four of the top five places. Among new championship records was 12:05.8 for the 3000m walk with Roger Mills registering his seventh title win.

An unwelcome first was the disqualification of discus winner Colin Sutherland, just returned from California and making a late bid for inclusion in Scotland's Commonwealth Games team. He refused to take a doping test and forfeited the title in accordance with the rules.

The year midway between Olympic celebrations was again a hectic one for British athletes with the finish of the Commonwealth Games in Edmonton, Alberta and the start of the European Championships in Prague separated by only 17 days. There were seven English successes in Canada: Roy Mitchell long jumped a wind-aided 8.06m, 20-year-old Connor triple jumped a windy 17.21m (his series including a legal British record of 16.76m), Geoff Capes put the shot 19.77m, Olly Flynn walked 30km in 2:22:04 and Daley Thompson easily surpassed his British decathlon record of 8226 (current scoring tables) with 8470 but that couldn't count for record purposes as his 8.11m long jump was too heavily wind assisted.

Foster ran his slowest ever 10,000m time of 28:13.7 but in very hot weather and at an altitude of 2500ft that was admirable running and good enough for the gold medal after taking bronze at 1500m in 1970 and silver at 5000m in 1974. England's other track champion was Dave Moorcroft. He was a revelation in the 1500m, improving on his personal best by over three seconds to defeat world record holder Filbert Bayi of Tanzania in 3:35.48, the fastest time in the world in 1978. Price of Wales won the 110m hurdles in 13.70w while Allan Wells took the 200m in 20.12w and helped Scotland win the 4x100m relay in the UK record time of 39.24.

Seb Coe and Steve Ovett preferred to concentrate on the European Championships, where they played a prominent role in an astonishing 800m. Coe attempted to run the legs off his rivals by sweeping through the first 200m in 24.3 and reached 400m in an heroic but suicidal 49.32. He went by 600m in 76.2 and was still in the lead entering the final straight but by then he was a spent force and powerless to prevent first Ovett and then the unheralded East German

Olaf Beyer going past. Beyer won in 1:43.84, never to show such form again, with Ovett second in a British record of 1:44.09 and Coe a commendable but dejected third in 1:44.76.

Three days later Ovett won Britain's only gold medal, a 53.2 last lap bringing him victory in the 1500m in 3:35.6 ahead of Ireland's Eamonn Coghlan and Moorcroft. The only other British medallist was Thompson in the decathlon but his new record of 8258 on today's tables did little to compensate for his acute disappointment at finishing second, particularly as he had led by nearly 300 points after the first day. He resolved never to lose again and he didn't until injury laid him low in 1987. Fatigue caught up with Foster in the 10,000m and although he was only just outside his best time with 27:32.65 it sufficed only for fourth place. Coe and Ovett wouldn't clash again until the 1980 Olympics but went their separate record breaking ways. Coe relieved his rival of the British 800m record with a late season 1:43.97 at Crystal Palace while Ovett set a world 2 miles best of 8:13.51 at the same meeting, followed by a British mile record of 3:52.8 a few days later.

Steve Cram, meanwhile, was progressing nicely: in his first ever mile race he ran 3:57.43 to break Jim Ryun's world age-17 best, and he always expressed his appreciation of the AAA for selecting him for the Commonwealth Games. The experience gained stood him in good stead for the future. And another future middle distance great was just starting to attract attention: Peter Elliott set a UK age-15 best of 1:52.1 when finishing second in the AAA Junior 800m.

1979 (Crystal Palace)

ALL EYES WERE on Sebastian Coe, making his first appearance in Britain since clocking the phenomenal time of 1:42.33 in Oslo eight days earlier to become the first Briton to set a world 800m record since Sydney Wooderson in 1938. Opting for the 400m, he improved his personal best from 47.6 to 46.95, easing up, and in the final next day

– watched by a capacity crowd of 17,000, the highest figure for the Championships since 1967 – he finished strongly to finish second to Sudan's Kasheef Hassan (45.82) in 46.87. Third in 47.01, representing Barclays Bank, came Roger Jenkins (David's younger brother), who had been AAA Junior champion in 1974 and is better known these days, thanks to his work as an investment banker, as one of the wealthiest men in Britain!

What a range Coe had. Early in the year, racing at 3000m for the first time since he was 18, he won the AAA Indoor title in 7:59.8 and now here he was the first Briton to finish at 400m. It proved a good sharpener for him, for three days after that final it was back to Oslo and another earth-shattering exploit, this time a world mile record of 3:48.95 although on paper he was the slowest man in the field with a previous best of 3:57.67. Coe went on to run a 45.5 400m relay leg at the European Cup Final and in Zürich picked up his third world record in the space of 41 days when he covered 1500m in 3:32.03 (ratified as 3:32.1). Steve Ovett, now dispossessed of his British records at 1500m and mile, was content to take his first AAA 1500m title in a relatively pedestrian 3:39.1. However, previously unconcerned with breaking records, he now felt he had to respond to Coe's challenge and he went close with 3:49.57 for the mile and 3:32.11 for 1500m. Not yet in their class but progressing steadily was Steve Cram, who at 18 became AAA and European Junior 3000m champion, improved his 800m time from 1:53.5 to 1:48.5 and ran a 3:57.03 mile; while Peter Elliott won the AAA Youth 800m title and set a UK age-16 best of 1:50.7.

Such was the strength of the overseas invasion of Crystal Palace that athletes from five continents became champions and merely six of the 19 titles stayed at home, including a seventh shot title by Geoff Capes (19.39m), an eighth success at 3000m walk by Roger Mills (12:09.1) and a wind-aided championship record in the 110m hurdles of 13.78 by Mark Holtom. In a much too large field of 31 runners, Brendan Foster tripped and fell on the tenth lap of the 5000m, leaving Ireland's Eamonn Coghlan the winner in 13:23.6 ahead of English cross country champion Mike McLeod (13:24.3), and another Irish victory came in the 10,000m where International cross country champion John Treacy won a close race against American marathon star Alberto Salazar in 28:12.1. So many of the world's most distinguished athletes have graced the AAA Championships with their presence and none greater than four time Olympic discus champion Al Oerter. The 42-year-old American, still a world class performer, had last competed at Crystal Palace at its opening (with a London v New York match) back in 1964, but although he threw 59.64m way ahead of all British opposition he had to settle for second place to his compatriot John Powell (61.50m). Another legendary American athlete, Ed Moses, was in a class apart in the 400m hurdles, setting a championship record of 48.58 that stands to this day.

BRITISH RECORDS AT 1 JANUARY 1980
100m: 10.15 Allan Wells 1978; 200m: 20.42 Allan Wells & Ainsley Bennett 1979; 400m: 44.93 David Jenkins 1975; 800m: 1:42.33 Seb Coe 1979; 1000m: 2:15.91 Steve Ovett 1979; 1500m: 3:32.03 Coe 1979; Mile: 3:48.95 Coe 1979; 2000m: 4:57.82 Ovett 1978; 3000m: 7:35.1 Brendan Foster 1974; 2M: 8:13.51 Ovett 1978; 5000m: 13:14.6 Foster 1974; 10,000m: 27:30.3 Foster 1978; Marathon: 2:09:12 Ian Thompson 1974; 3000mSC: 8:18.95 Dennis Coates 1976; 110mH: 13.69 Berwyn Price 1973; 400mH: 48.12 David Hemery 1968; HJ: 2.20 Brian Burgess 1978 (2.22 indoors Mark Naylor 1979); PV: 5.42 Brian Hooper 1978; LJ: 8.23 Lynn Davies 1968; TJ: 16.76 Keith Connor 1978; SP: 21.55 Geoff Capes 1976; DT: 64.32 Bill Tancred 1974; HT: 74.98 Chris Black 1976; JT: 84.92 Charles Clover 1974; Decathlon: (re-scored on 1985 tables) 8258 Daley Thompson 1978; 3000m Walk: 11:51.1 Paul Nihill 1971; 10,000m Walk: 41:55.6 Phil Embleton 1971; 20km Walk: 1:24:50 Nihill 1972; 50km Walk: 4:07:22 Bob Dobson 1979.

THE EIGHTIES

Despite all the infighting which went on for control of the sport, these were boom years for British athletics. The rivalry between Seb Coe and Steve Ovett made headline news throughout the world, while Steve Cram and Daley Thompson also achieved legendary status, and the London Marathon – the brainchild of Chris Brasher aided and abetted by another outstanding former steeplechaser in John Disley – developed into the world's greatest road race with Brendan Foster's Great North Run becoming pre-eminent among half marathons.

The move towards a single governing body for British athletics, as advocated by the Byers Report, continued in fits and starts throughout the 1980s, generating much heated debate, but as the 1990s dawned the AAA, Women's AAA and BAAB all remained in place as separate organisations as they had for decades. However, a major breakthrough occurred in 1988 when the AAA and WAAA held joint championships outdoors for the first time. That meeting, incorporating the Olympic Trials, was staged in Birmingham – the first time the AAA Championships had been held outside London since 1907. The amount of money invested in British athletics through sponsorship, television fees and state aid increased enormously during the 1980s and although the sport wasn't yet completely

144

"open" it was now possible, via trust funds scrupulously administered by the BAAB, for top athletes to earn large sums as a result of their sporting prowess.

The international drive towards ending "shamateurism" and legitimising payments to athletes was originated by British officials, many of whom served with the AAA. Early in 1980 the BAAB Council unanimously approved recommendations by the Board's IAAF Rules Working Party, chaired jointly by Robert Stinson and Charles Rice. They favoured a change to the IAAF rule, which limited the value of prizes to US $250 or equivalent to permit the payment of prize money at certain international meetings and also allow athletes (and their governing body) to benefit from advertising contracts. The Board's General Secretary, former steeplechaser David Shaw, stated that "instead of jumping headlong into a system of open athletics ... we recognise that the rules have got to change because many of them are incapable of effective working at the moment. The point about prize money and encouragement to be able to participate in advertising and endorsements is an attempt to get away from the over-emphasis at the moment, illegally, of appearance money."

At the same time the newly formed AAA Amateur Status Sub-Committee, chaired by Welsh AAA Secretary Dr Bill Evans and including international athletes Lynn Davies, David Cropper and Mike Turner, invited the views of organisations and individuals regarding such topics as open athletics, the upper limit in value for prizes, cash or otherwise, and sponsorship. Their report later in the year to AAA General Committee stated that athletes should be permitted to receive cash prizes and appearance money, and to benefit from advertising and promotion. "Within the sport," said the report, "there would undoubtedly be a small number who might gain appreciable financial reward from open athletics but the vast majority would continue to participate as they do today in a truly amateur tradition."

Meanwhile, the IAAF Council's Working Group – whose members included former Cambridge 220 yards hurdler Robert Stinson (who became the IAAF's Hon. Treasurer in 1984) and the 1957 AAA Junior 440y champion and 1:50.0 half miler John Holt (the IAAF General Secretary) – was engaged in proposing "a set of recommendations that would guide the development of athletics on a practical and sound basis for the future". The Group argued that the word "amateur" should be deleted from the rules (the International Olympic Committee had not used this term since 1974), but the IAAF Council at its meeting in March 1981 did not agree and the majority view was that a new definition – "an amateur is one who abides by the eligibility rules of the IAAF" – should supplant the existing definition that an amateur "is one who competes for the love of sport and as a means of recreation, without any motive of securing any material gain from such competition".

The first Briton to take advantage of the new international rules which permitted athletes to advertise and endorse products without prejudicing their eligibility – or what used to be known as amateur status – was Seb Coe. In February 1982 he appeared in TV commercials thanks to a contract drawn up between the manufacturers and the BAAB with Coe able to draw expenses against what was described as a substantial fee. The rest, after commission had been retained by the Board to plough back into the sport, would be held in a trust fund for Coe. This was the blueprint for other deals; it was an interim arrangement until complete professionalism was permitted. Later that year Steve Ovett announced a lucrative sponsorship deal and both these world renowned runners became wealthy young men during the 1980s, as did others like marathon record breaker Steve Jones, who earned $194,000 in prize money and record bonuses between 1985 and 1987, not including appearance fees. The prize money he pocketed for winning the Chicago Marathon in 1984 represented about five years pay as the RAF aircraft technician he remained until 1988! Some in the sport may have resented

146

the concept of certain star athletes being richly and openly rewarded but to reach and stay at the top required huge commitment as well as talent and there was a widespread feeling that those athletes should benefit financially from their status as public entertainers and crowd pullers in the same way as professional footballers, boxers, opera singers, show business personalities and the like.

The IAAF, under the presidency of Dr Primo Nebiolo, launched a Grand Prix circuit in 1985, including two meetings in London. A total of $542,000 in prize money was available with the overall Grand Prix winner receiving $25,000, to be paid into the athlete's trust fund administered by his governing body. Even this was small beer for some athletes. It was estimated that Carl Lewis earned $783,000 in 1984 and fellow American Olympic hero Ed Moses $617,000, while in 1985 the ever controversial Zola Budd received no less than $125,000 from television sources for a race at Crystal Palace in which she finished fourth! IAAF General Secretary John Holt commented on Budd's fee: "This is not what we intended when we opened up the rules for a new era."

In 1986 eight categories of subventions were drawn up for British athletes competing in any of seven televised meetings at Crystal Palace (including the AAA Championships), Gateshead and Birmingham. The sums per appearance ranged from Category 1 (Steve Cram) at £12,000 to Category 8 (£100). In 1987 there were ten categories, from £100 to £15,000 (Cram again) with a total of £852,000 awarded, but the subventions budget was cut drastically in 1988 with £10,000 the top rate and that remained the case in 1989 during which £534,000 was paid out.

The AAA's financial situation improved out of all recognition during the decade. An exclusive TV contract between the BBC and the AAA/BAAB for four years from 1981 to 1985 was worth £1.6 million, several times the value of the previous agreement. However it was ITV who won the next contract, for five years from April 1985, for a figure of £10.5 million, making the AAA – which had been close to bankruptcy some years earlier – one of the wealthiest sports bodies in the country. ITV's commentators included two prominent ex-athletes in Adrian Metcalfe and Alan Pascoe, the latter's company (Alan Pascoe Associates Ltd) being appointed late in 1984 to handle the marketing of all AAA and BAAB televised events and guaranteeing at least £3 million over five years (in fact is raised far more). During the 18 months from 1 April 1985 to 30 September 1986 a total of almost £2.2 million was received from ITV and APA, out of which over £650,000 was paid to athletes in the form of subventions. The picture was less rosy the following year for although £3.8 million accrued from TV and sponsorship more than £1.26 million was paid out in subventions and the AAA finished up with a deficit for the year ending 30 September 1987 of £74,182. The following year, though, as a result of a severe cut in subventions, Hon Treasurer John Lister was able to announce a surplus of £558,712 and for the year ending 30 September 1989 it reached a whopping £1,303,966 with reserves of over a million pounds.

As well as television fees and commercial sponsorship, athletics in the UK was reliant on government funding in the shape of grants from the Sports Council and in 1982 an inquiry, led by Sports Council chairman Dick Jeeps, was set up by Neil Macfarlane, the Minister of Sport, "to determine whether he [Jeeps] is satisfied that the public money spent on athletics is used in the most beneficial way for the sport." The report, published in July 1983, pointed out that there were 19 organisations with controlling interests in athletics in the UK and in the financial year ended 31 March 1982 they received Sports Council grants totalling £330,000, of which £223,000 went to the BAAB, much of that for the UK Coaching Scheme. The AAA did not receive anything. The current overlapping structure was not being utilised to make the best use of people or resources and the report highlighted the anomalous situation whereby the AAA was declaring taxable surpluses while the BAAB was declaring losses. A more unified and cohesive strategy for the development of athletics in the UK was called for. Mike Farrell, the AAA General Secretary, announced that the AAA was contributing about £60,000 towards the BAAB's international commitments in 1986. "We felt it right as the strongest domestic association, with 80% of the clubs and probably 90% of the athletes, to lend this extra support to the British Board."

The move towards one governing body trundled on, the end at last in sight as the decade neared its completion. There was overwhelming support at the 1982 AAA AGM for Cardiff AAC's motion "that athletics in the UK be administered by a single governing body" (only four out of more than 100 delegates at the meeting voted against), and a Working Party, chaired by former cross country star Mike Turner, was appointed by General Committee to find ways and means of implementing the resolution. In December 1983 it recommended that a UKAAA be formed as "the only national governing body for all amateur athletics in the UK", dissolving the BAAB and transferring the right of affiliation to the IAAF from the Board to the UKAAA. It proposed that the AAA should amend its constitution so as to redefine its area of responsibility as extending exclusively to England, that it changed its name to English AAA and that the men's and women's Associations in each of the four home countries should be encouraged to amalgamate. The recommendations were not dissimilar to those of the Byers Report of 1968.

With its finances in a parlous state, the BAAB virtually signed its own death warrant at an Extraordinary General Meeting in October 1987. The Board voted overwhelmingly (180-30) in favour of a motion which read: "This meeting agrees that in order to rationalise the financial arrangement of the BAAB, it recommends that one governing body for British Athletics be established not later than 1 January 1989. Meantime, the AAA functions as the Caretaker Association for the affairs of the BAAB and, in order for the AAA to exercise its responsibilities, this meeting recommends that the AAA voting powers on the BAAB Council be increased by six votes at meetings of the Council." At the BAAB's AGM in December 1988 it was agreed that the AAA's caretaker status continue until 1991 when a British Athletic Federation (BAF) should be in place.

Earlier, at an EGM of the AAA in July 1988 to decide on the structure of the proposed BAF and following an unprecedented war of words in the form of ads in *Athletics Weekly* from the AAA, Southern Counties AAA, Women's AAA and other interested parties, the AAA plan put forward by President Arthur McAllister was defeated. His proposal, in which an English AA would represent the Southern, Northern and Midland Counties and would negotiate all major TV, marketing and sponsorship contracts, received 583 votes as against 783 by the Southern Counties plan where the area associations would be represented in their own right and could organise their own deals. The AAA set up a Working Party under the chairmanship of Welsh AAA Hon Secretary Dr Bill Evans to come up with an acceptable compromise. Dr Evans, who became Chairman of AAA General Committee in January 1989, stated he would aim to bring cohesion and harmony into the sport and would work hard for the formation of the BAF. In April 1989 General Committee unanimously accepted his draft constitution for a British Athletic Federation ... and, as will be seen in the next section, a short-lived BAF finally came into existence in October 1991.

Mike Farrell, the 1956 Olympic 800m finalist and one of the sport's most prominent officials, became the AAA's first professional General Secretary in August 1982. Another significant appointment by the AAA was that Andy Norman, who placed third in the 1960 Southern Youths 440 yards and as a junior in 1952 clocked 1:55.7 for 880 yards, became England team manager at the end of 1981. The then police sergeant quickly rose to become the most powerful (not to mention controversial) figure in British athletics and in 1985 was appointed the AAA/BAAB's Promotions Officer, a

BRENDAN FOSTER
World record breaker at 3000m and 2 miles, he set a European 10,000m record, won European 5000m and Commonwealth Games 10,000m titles and was Britain's only medallist at the 1976 Olympics

Clockwise from top left: DAVE TRAVIS, seven times AAA javelin champion; DAVID JENKINS, winner of six consecutive AAA 400m titles; DON QUARRIE (Jamaica), winner of AAA sprint double in 1976 shortly after becoming Olympic 200m champion; KEITH CONNOR, Britain's greatest triple jumper prior to Jonathan Edwards

DALEY THOMPSON
Contesting the eighth event, the pole vault, en route to his first Olympic decathlon victory in Moscow in 1980. He scored 8522 points on the present tables, comprising 10.62 for 100m, 8.00m long jump, 15.18m shot put, 2.08m high jump, 48.01 for 400m, 14.47 for 110m hurdles, 42.24m discus throw, 4.70m pole vault, 64.16m javelin throw and 4:39.9 for 1500m

DAVE MOORCROFT
His greatest achievement was smashing the world 5000m record in Oslo in 1982 with 13:00.41, which remained the British record until 2010. He won Commonwealth Games titles at 1500m in 1978 and at 5000m in 1982, and also in 1982 set a European 3000m record of 7:32.79 and ran a 3:49.34 mile

Three of Britain's greatest marathon runners: BRIAN KILBY (56), the 1962 European and Commonwealth Games champion and AAA title winner five times running; BILL ADCOCKS (57), rated as the world's top marathoner in 1968, the year he set European records of 2:12:17 and 2:10:48; and RON HILL, the 1969 European and 1970 Commonwealth Games champion who clocked a European record of 2:09:28 in the latter race

More of Britain's most distinguished marathoners. Clockwise from top left: `
JIM HOGAN, 1966 European champion; IAN THOMPSON, Commonwealth `
Games and European champion in 1974; CHARLIE SPEDDING, here winning the
1984 London Marathon prior to gaining an Olympic bronze medal; and `
STEVE JONES, who set a world best of 2:08:05 in 1984 and still holds the `
UK record with 2:07:13 the next year

Top: SEB COE (third in 1:44.76 after a 49.32 first lap) and STEVE OVETT (second in a British record of 1:44.09) after a sensational 1978 European Championships 800m final in Prague. Bottom: EAMONN COGHLAN wins the 1979 AAA 5000m in an Irish record of 13:23.6 ahead of MIKE McLEOD (22) and New Zealand's ROD DIXON

Clockwise from top left: BERWYN PRICE, who won six consecutive AAA 110m hurdles titles; BRIAN HOOPER, who vaulted a British record 5.59m to win an epic 1980 AAA duel with Keith Stock; Australia's DARREN CLARK, winner of four successive AAA 400m titles, the first (in 1983) with a world age-17 best; PETER ELLIOTT, aged 19, winning the 1982 AAA 800m ahead of New Zealand's JOHN WALKER with DAVE MOORCROFT (28) fifth

ALLAN WELLS
At Moscow in 1980 he became the second Briton, 56 years after Harold Abrahams,
to capture the Olympic 100m title … and went on to finish second, just 2/100ths
behind Italy's Pietro Mennea, in the 200m

Agony and ecstasy as STEVE OVETT unexpectedly wins the 1980 Olympic 800m title in Moscow in 1:45.40 ahead of world record holder SEB COE (1:45.85)

SEB COE, here seen leading from STEVE CRAM and STEVE OVETT, compensated for that shock 800m defeat by winning the Moscow 1500m in 3:38.40 with a 52.2 last lap. Ovett finished third and 19-year-old Cram was eighth

DALEY THOMPSON
Here seen finishing the 1500m to clinch the gold medal in Moscow, he successfully
defended his Olympic title four years later in Los Angeles – as did Seb Coe

Clockwise from top left: RENALDO NEHEMIAH (USA), then the world record holder, was AAA 110m hurdles champion in 1981; TODD BENNETT, world indoor 400m record breaker; DAVE OTTLEY, 1984 Olympic javelin silver medallist; DAVE SMITH, 1986 Commonwealth Games hammer champion and AAA winner five years running

STEVE CRAM
*Already the reigning Commonwealth Games and European champion, Cram captures
the inaugural world 1500m title in Helsinki in 1983. He clocked 3:41.59 with a
final lap of 52.0 to win from Steve Scott (USA), not in picture, and Morocco's SAÏD
AOUITA (549) with STEVE OVETT (341) fourth*

Top (left): JON SOLLY wins 1986 AAA 10,000m; JACK BUCKNER takes the 1986 European 5000m title; (below): A British clean sweep in the 1986 European 800m : SEB COE (326) won in 1:44.50 from TOM McKEAN (351) and STEVE CRAM

Clockwise from top left: JOHN REGIS, six times AAA 200m champion between 1986 and 1996 and still the British record holder; KRISS AKABUSI, AAA 400m winner in 44.93 in 1988 and holder of the UK 400m hurdles record; MICK HILL, 1993 World Championships bronze medallist and seven times AAA javelin champion between 1987 and 2003; and MARK ROWLAND, UK steeplechase record holder and 1988 Olympic bronze medallist

professional post which involved organising international events and liaising with sponsors. Early in 1986 the AAA appointed British Athletics League founder Tony Ward as its Public Relations Consultant, fronting press conferences, acting as a spokesman and editing the AAA Newsletter that was the Association's link to the clubs. Later that year the first full-time AAA Development Officers were appointed.

On 24 April 1980, 100 years to the day since the foundation of the AAA, the Marquess of Exeter unveiled a plaque recording the events of 1880 at the Randolph Hotel in Oxford. In September an exhibition of programmes and photos was staged at The Guildhall in London and the AAA Centenary Championships were celebrated at the Crystal Palace. Tom McNab presented a reconstruction of what the sport was like at the time of the first Championships with various athletes, suitably attired in the racy knee-length shorts of the day, demonstrating the sprinting, hurdling, high jumping and pole vaulting techniques of the era. Brian Hooper, complete with twirly moustache, even re-enacted an amusing little piece of AAA Championships history. He played the part of Irving Baxter (USA), the 1900 Olympic champion, who in 1901 arrived at the stadium minus his pole. None of his fellow competitors was gracious enough to lend him one, so he uprooted a nearby flagpole and vaulted with that ... tying for the title! However, President Squire Yarrow voiced disappointment at the AAA AGM in November 1980 over "a lack of appreciation in certain quarters" of the significance of the Centenary – a reference, possibly, to the absence of royalty from the Centenary Championships and the fact that no AAA officers appeared in the Birthday Honours List.

After more than 20 years of argument over its merits or otherwise, a voluntary AAA Registration Scheme came into existence in 1983 for a trial period. Club members of 18 or over paid £2.50 per year, of which 50p went back to the club, and a number of benefits were offered, including personal accident insurance and various discounts. Steve Ovett was awarded the first membership number in recognition of his help towards the scheme's formation, and in 1984 the scheme had 45,000 members. But by 1986 membership was down to around 26,000, the scheme lost nearly £60,000 between 1 April 1985 and 30 September 1986, and it was discontinued. Overall, the number of clubs affiliated to the AAA continued to grow and in 1986 there were 1357, of which 95 were affiliated to the Welsh AAA.

Among the AAA's responsibilities was attracting youngsters to the sport and the great success story continued to be the Esso AAA Five Star Award Scheme, providing opportunities for boys and girls to assess their performance within their age groups and administered by the AAA through schools and clubs. In 1982 some one and a half million certificates were issued. Another important contribution by the AAA was saving the Young Athletes League from extinction in 1982 by providing annual sponsorship and renaming it the AAA Young Athletes League, while Sportshall Athletics – the brainchild of George Bunner (AAA Junior half mile champion in 1950) – continued to attract youngsters into athletic activity by stressing the fun element.

The inaugural London Marathon in 1981 proved an outstanding success and has never looked back, developing into one of the capital's most popular annual happenings and ranking as the world's leading one-day charity fund raising event. Of the 20,000 who applied to run, 7747 were accepted, 7055 actually started and 6255 finished. The race proved such an inspiration that more than 90,000 applied for the 1982 edition, of whom 18,059 were accepted, 16,350 started and 15,116 finished. The race, which incorporated the AAA Championship from 1983, grew year by year. There were over 20,000 finishers for the first time in 1988, in excess of 25,000 in 1994 and 30,000 in 1999. The largest field was in 2010 when, from 51,000 applicants, 36,984 toed the start line and 36,549 finished. The Great North Run from Newcastle to South Shields has enjoyed similar success. It also began in 1981 and that year, with over 12,500 starters and 10,681 official finishers, it became Britain's biggest ever race although at the height of the jogging boom in 1984 the *Sunday Times* National Fun Run in London's Hyde Park attracted 33,000 entrants divided among numerous age groups. Another important road racing initiative was the launching of a series of 10km races in 1983 and half marathons in 1984. AAA road race championships at 10 miles started in 1983 and at 10km and half marathon in 1984.

Three men held the prestigious office of AAA President during the decade. Squire Yarrow, who succeeded the late Harold Abrahams in 1978, died in 1984, while Ron Goodman served from 1984 to 1986, in which year Arthur McAllister took over. The long-time AAA President, the Marquess of Exeter (1928 Olympic 400m hurdles champion Lord Burghley), died in 1981 and other notable athletes, coaches and officials who passed away during the 1980s included quadruple Olympic medallist Guy Butler, double Olympic 800m champion and former AAA Hon. Secretary Douglas Lowe, Olympic 50km walk winner Harold Whitlock, Les Truelove (AAA Life Vice-President and former GB team manager), the coaching genius that was Geoff Dyson, Nobel Peace Prize winner and Olympic 1500m medallist Philip (Lord) Noel-Baker, Norman Cobb (Hon. Secretary of the British Coaching Scheme for over 15 years), Don Pain (the 1948 Olympics technical manager and IAAF Hon. Secretary/Treasurer from 1953 to 1970), former AAA administrator Leslie Higdon, Southern Counties AAA stalwart Arthur Kendall, Lord (Frank) Byers and Les Cohen (for many years the AAA Championships Secretary).

Although Prime Minister Margaret Thatcher was in favour of following the Americans in boycotting the Moscow Games of 1980, the British Olympic Association decreed otherwise and British athletes competed in all three Olympics staged during the 1980s. Gold medals were won in Moscow by Allan Wells (100m), Ovett (800m), Coe (1500m) and Thompson (decathlon) and by Coe and Thompson again plus Tessa Sanderson (javelin) in Los

Angeles in 1984. Olympic runners-up in men's events were Wells (200m) and Coe (800m) in 1980, Coe (800m), Cram (1500m), Mike McLeod (10,000m), Dave Ottley (javelin) and the 4x400m team in 1984, and Linford Christie (100m), Peter Elliott (1500m), Colin Jackson (110m hurdles) and the 4x100m team in Seoul in 1988. World Championships were introduced by the IAAF in 1983, the British winners in Helsinki being Cram and Thompson, while javelin thrower Fatima Whitbread was triumphant in the second edition in Rome in 1987.

On the men's side European champions in Athens in 1982 were Cram (1500m), Keith Connor (triple jump) and Thompson (decathlon) and in Stuttgart in 1986 were Christie (100m), Roger Black (400m), Coe (800m, followed in by Tom McKean and Cram), Cram (1500m with Coe second), Jack Buckner (5000m), Thompson (decathlon) and the 4x400m team. The Commonwealth Games in Brisbane in 1982 provided victories by Scotland's Wells (100m & 200m, dead-heating with Mike McFarlane in the latter), Cram (1500m), Dave Moorcroft (5000m), Connor (triple jump), Robert Weir (hammer), Thompson (decathlon), Steve Barry of Wales (30km walk) and England in the 4x400m; winners in Edinburgh in 1986 were Black (400m), Cram (800m & 1500m), Ovett (5000m), Jon Solly (10,000m), Northern Ireland's Phil Beattie (400m hurdles), Andy Ashurst (pole vault), John Herbert (triple jump), Billy Cole (shot), Dave Smith (hammer), Dave Ottley (javelin), Thompson (decathlon) and the England 4x400m team. There was also a world record bonanza featuring Coe (1:41.73 800m, 2:13.40 and 2:12.18 1000m, 3:48.53 and 3:47.33 mile), Ovett (3:32.1, 3:31.36 and 3:30.77 1500m, 3:48.8 and 3:48.40 mile), Cram (3:29.67 1500m, 3:46.32 mile, 4:51.39 2000m), Moorcroft (13:00.41 5000m), Steve Jones (2:08:05 marathon), Thompson (8648, 8730, 8774 and 8847 decathlon) and the 4x800m team of Peter Elliott, Garry Cook, Cram and Coe (7:03.89). And as if all that were not enough, the British men lifted the prestigious European Cup for the first time in 1989.

Highlights from each of the AAA Championships meetings 1980-1989

1980 (Crystal Palace)

IT WAS A proud occasion: the Nationwide Building Society AAA Centenary Championships. They came after the Moscow Olympics, too late in the season for the best turn-out of athletes or a really large crowd, but for the AAA – at the time playing a more influential role in national and international affairs than for many a year – the proceedings were more than a track and field meeting. They were a celebration of 100 years of history.

Brian Hooper, who had earlier impersonated 1900 Olympic champion Irving Baxter and completed his flagpole vault to the manner born, later used his fibre glass model to stunning effect and it was he, along with Keith Stock, who provided the highlight of these Championships. There have been odd occasions when a British record has been broken more than once in the same competition but in this wonderful, crazy contest the record was raised SEVEN times in the space of about three-quarters of an hour! The record had stood at 5.51m by Hooper, with Stock's best 5.40m. After Hooper cleared 5.50m at the second attempt and his rival faced elimination after two failures, Stock opted to take his remaining try at 5.52m and he made it to become British record holder. The bar went up to 5.54m, a Commonwealth record. Stock elected to pass, Hooper cleared at the second attempt. At 5.55m the advantage swung back to Stock; he made it at the final attempt and Hooper, after two misses, decided to save his remaining try for 5.56m – and over he went. The cat and mouse game continued as the bar was raised a centimetre at a time. Stock slid over 5.57m at the first attempt for his third British record and an improvement of 17cm over his pre-Championship best. Now it was Hooper who was fighting for survival but his initial try at 5.58m was successful. Stock came back in at 5.59m and missed at his first attempt while Hooper cleared. Stock could still retrieve the advantage if he made 5.60m but he failed his two remaining attempts and victory went to Hooper: 5.59m to 5.57m. Two years later Hooper would find wider fame by becoming the British and World Superstars champion.

Nothing else compared for prolonged excitement but a 37.5 final 300m by newly crowned Olympic 800m champion Steve Ovett proved too much for John Walker in a 4:04.4 mile (held instead of 1500m to mark the historic occasion). Another Moscow gold medallist, Scotsman Allan Wells, won his first 100m title in 10.36; Miklos Németh of Hungary, whose father Imre was AAA hammer champion in 1947 and 1949, threw 83.34m for the javelin title, while two Americans – deprived of their Olympic chance by the US boycott – were particularly impressive. Rod Milburn, the 1972 Olympic champion, took the 110m hurdles in a championship record of 13.69 although only narrowly from Mark Holtom, whose 13.71 broke David Hemery's AAA national record; and Brian Oldfield, a reinstated professional who had once put the shot an extraordinary 22.86m in 1975, reached 21.25m with Geoff Capes – in his farewell AAA appearance – second at 20.10m, the tenth year running he had either won or finished as top Briton. Capes, who won more British international vests than any other man with 67, went on to turn professional and twice won the World's Strongest Man title

It was altogether a memorable year for British athletics. The American-led boycott of the Moscow Games may have devalued certain events but there was no disputing the quality of Britain's four Olympic winners: Wells (10.25 100m after setting a UK record of 10.11 in his quarter-final), Ovett (1:45.40 800m), Seb Coe (3:38.40 1500m with a 52.2 last lap) and Daley Thompson (8522 decathlon). There were silver medals also for Wells in the 200m, beaten by just 2/100ths in a British record 20.21, and Coe (1:45.85 800m), while bronze awards went to Ovett (3:38.99 1500m) and Gary Oakes (49.11 400m hurdles). It was all a far cry from the solitary bronze in Montreal 1976.

Apart from their epic confrontations in Moscow, with both winning the "wrong" event, Coe and Ovett came up with four world records between them. Coe ran 1000m in 2:13.40, while Ovett – now a record seeker with the best of them – set new mile figures of 3:48.8 before equalling Coe's ratified 1500m mark of 3:32.1 (although his electrically timed 3:32.09 was slightly inferior to Coe's 3:32.03 of the previous year) and then clarifying the issue with a run of 3:31.36. Not to be outdone, Thompson set a world record score of 8648 points. Other British records included a 2.24m high jump by Mark Naylor, 17.16m triple jump by Keith Connor, 21.68m shot put by Capes and 85.52m javelin throw by Dave Ottley. Steve Cram, in his first year as a senior, set a world teenage best of 3:34.74 for 1500m, ran a 3:53.8 mile and reached the Olympic 1500m final; Peter Elliott (17) won the English National Youths cross country title. Also just beginning to be noticed was a sprinter by the name of Linford Christie, at 19 a close third in the AAA Indoor 200m in 22.2, although it would be many years before he knuckled down to serious training and burst into world class.

1981 (Crystal Palace)

IT WAS EXACTLY 100 years earlier, in the second edition of the Championships, that for the first time an American – the great Lon Myers in the 440y – carried off a AAA title. Uncle Sam's representatives were particularly dominant at the Championships of 1900 and 1974, with eight victories on each occasion, but it was the 1981 meeting (sponsored for the first time by Robinson's Barley Water) that could be remembered as the supreme American celebration, for of the 15 events they contested they won nine, together with seven seconds and seven thirds. In the discus they occupied first four places, John Powell (62.46m) again getting the better of 44-year-old Al Oerter (61.88m).

Particularly outstanding were Renaldo Nehemiah who clocked 13.17 for 110m hurdles, the fourth fastest legal time in history, and Larry Myricks who long jumped 8.38m, a distance only he and four others had ever exceeded. Both marks were UK all-comers records and there were other championship records by Tony Darden (USA) with a 45.11 400m, Steve Cram with 3:36.82 for 1500m and Roger Mills, whose 3000m walk time of 11:44.68 was also a British record.

The huge global star of 1981 was Seb Coe. For the third year running he produced breathtaking world record performances, starting with 800m in 1:41.73 in June and 1000m in 2:12.18 in July, two marks that went unbeaten for 16 and 18 years respectively and remain British records to this day. On August 19 he clocked 3:48.53 for the mile, only to lose the record to Steve Ovett's 3:48.40 on August 26 and then reclaim it with 3:47.33 on August 28! At the AAA Championships he gained his first senior title outdoors, sauntering through 800m in 1:45.41. That made him one of the select few to collect AAA titles in all three age groups; in his case the 1973 Youth 1500m, 1975 Junior 1500m and 1981 Senior 800m. Much earlier in the year he had won the indoor 3000m title in a personal best of 7:55.2.

The indoor 200m champion in 21.9, Linford Christie hardly set the track alight in his first outdoor AAA Championships. While Americans Mel Lattany and Stanley Floyd captured the sprint titles in 10.24 and 20.51, he failed to survive the heats with 10.85 and 21.85. Olympic glory was fully 11 years away. The pole vault proved a disappointment after the previous year's excitement. Although Keith Stock had broken Brian Hooper's British record with 5.60m, followed by 5.65m, he could manage only 5.20m for third behind two Americans while Hooper bowed out with fifth place at 5.00m. The year's other record breaker, Keith Connor, who had set a world indoor triple jump best of 17.31m in March, did not compete.

1982 (Crystal Palace)

ALTHOUGH ONLY THREE championship records were set, this edition of the Championships – the first to be staged over a Saturday and Sunday – underlined the healthy state of British athletics. The meeting also served as unofficial selection trials for England's Commonwealth Games team and the British squad for the European Championships, and several athletes rose to the challenge. Steve Cram in particular shaped up as not only a likely winner in Brisbane and Athens but as a potential world record breaker as, in the absence of Seb Coe and Steve Ovett, he dominated the 1500m, winning by over 20m in a championship record of 3:36.14. Peter Elliott (19), another precocious talent well on the way to stardom, had the nerve and ability to lead all the way in the 800m, claiming his first senior title in 1:45.61, which supplanted Ovett's UK "teenage best" of 1:45.77 from 1974. His non-selection for Brisbane was controversial to say the least.

The year's sensation, Dave Moorcroft, dropped down to the 800m just a fortnight after his fabulous 5000m world record of 13:00.41 and reduced his personal best to 1:48.29 in his heat and 1:46.64 for fifth in the final. He was in the midst of a magical few weeks during which he couldn't put a foot wrong, also running 3:49.34 for the mile, setting a European 3000m record of 7:32.79 which was only just outside the world record, and other bests of 3:33.79 for 1500m and 8:16.75 for 2 miles. He had made a notable start to this momentous year by placing fourth in the National cross country and breaking Brendan Foster's esteemed 1974 long stage record in the AAA 12-Stage Road Relay with 24:27.

Also shining at the 3000m distance, but in his case in a scrupulously fair race walking mode, was Roger Mills. He clocked 11:58.18 to notch up his TENTH AAA title in this event since 1969, the most up to that date in any one event by a Briton. The outright record of 13 titles belongs to Irish shot putter Denis Horgan between 1893 and 1912, while

Colin Jackson would amass 11 in the 110m hurdles between 1986 and 2002. Another athlete with a long sequence of AAA successes was David Jenkins, although his reputation was blotted by his admission of drug taking during the later stages of his career. Aged 30, 11 years after winning the European title, he ran 45.93 for second place in the 400m to Trinidad's Mike Paul (45.74), making it nine times that he finished as the top Briton in this event.

An encouraging feature of British athletics has been the number of distinguished athletes who later made their mark also as coaches and the 1982 Championships included quite a number. Linford Christie, the indoor 200m champion in 21.75, clocked a 100m personal best of 10.50 in his semi but pulled a muscle in the final. Mike Whittingham was first Briton home in the 400m hurdles, fourth in 51.13. John Herbert improved massively on his previous best of 16.44m to set a AAA national record of 16.91m for second in the triple jump to Australia's Ken Lorraway (championship record with a wind-aided 17.19m), while Aston Moore placed fifth; Mike Winch retained his shot title with 18.90m, Robert Weir won the hammer with 71.92m and John Trower was second in the javelin with 76.90m.

Winners of European titles were Cram in the 1500m (3:36.49), Connor in the triple jump (17.29m) and Daley Thompson in the decathlon with his second world record score of the year: 8774 after 8730 in Götzis. Silvers went to Cameron Sharp in the 200m in 20.47, Coe in the 800m in 1:46.68 (it later transpired that he was suffering from low level glandular fever) and the 4x400m team (3:00.68), while Moorcroft, by then physically and mentally depleted, had to settle for bronze in the 5000m (13:30.42) although he did manage to emerge victorious in the Commonwealth Games in 13:33.00. There in Brisbane the other English winners were Mike McFarlane (another future coach of note), who dead-heated in the 200m in 20.43 with Scotland's Allan Wells (the 100m champion in 10.02w), Cram in the 1500m (3:42.37), Connor in the triple jump with the exceptional if wind-aided distance of 17.81m, Weir in the hammer with a British record of 75.08m, Thompson in the decathlon with 8424 and the 4x400m team in 3:05.45. Steve Barry, representing Wales, won the 30km walk in 2:10:16.

Among England's other medallists was Mark Holtom, second in the 110m hurdles with a British record of 13.43. Other British records during the year included 4:57.71 for 2000m by Ovett before injury ended his season prematurely, 8:18.80 steeplechase by Colin Reitz and a triple jump of 17.57m at altitude by Connor. One other highlight was a world record in the 4x800m relay of 7:03.89, which stood until 2006, by Elliott (1:49.14, having lost fitness after not being selected for the Commonwealth Games), Garry Cook (1:46.20), Cram (1:44.54) and Coe (1:44.01 after an exciting 49.1 first lap!).

1983 (Crystal Palace)

STEVE CRAM WON his third AAA 1500m title, content to run a pedestrian 3:41.69 against a modest field from which Eamonn Martin (who would win the London Marathon ten years later) emerged as a distant runner-up. The other two British miling superstars were less fortunate. After clocking an easy looking 1:46.29 heat, Steve Ovett believed he was in sub-1:44 800m form but he was badly spiked on the first lap of an exceedingly physical race and eventually pulled up in pain, although several weeks later he had recovered sufficiently to regain the world record for 1500m with 3:30.77. The AAA title went, for the first time, to a Venezuelan – William Wuycke – in 1:45.44 with Peter Elliott close behind in 1:45.64. Seb Coe did finish his race, the AAA for the first time staging an invitation mile at the Championships (held at 10.15 pm mainly for the benefit of American TV viewers), but for the first time since 1976 he lost at that distance, clocking 3:52.93 behind the 3:51.56 by Steve Scott of the USA. Coe had begun the year in storming fashion, setting world indoor records of

1:44.91 for 800m and 2:18.58 for 1000m followed by an early season 1:43.80 800m, but again illness took its toll and, debilitated by glandular toxoplasmosis which led to a number of unexpected defeats, he withdrew from the inaugural World Championships in Helsinki on medical advice.

At that great universally supported event, a timely IAAF innovation when both the 1980 and 1984 Olympics were devalued by politically inspired boycotts, Cram took his chances superbly to become the first world 1500m champion, producing a 52.0 last 400m for victory in 3:41.59 – practically the same time as at the AAA, although he had run 3:35.77 in his semi-final. Ovett placed fourth, as did Elliott in the 800m with a personal best of 1:44.87. Britain's other world champion was the incomparable Daley Thompson, who despite missing 14 weeks of training through injury and making a late decision to compete, demoralised the opposition and scored 8714. Bronze medals in Helsinki went to Colin Reitz (the AAA champion in 8:28.42) with a British steeplechase record of 8:17.75 and the 4x400m team. Reitz's record lasted only five days as Graeme Fell, who would later represent Canada, clocked 8:15.16 and other British records during the year were a 2:09:08 marathon by Geoff Smith in an epic race against New Zealand's Rod Dixon in New York, a 2.25m high jump by the towering and precocious Geoff Parsons at the English Schools Championships and, one of the highlights of the AAA Championships, a 75.40m hammer throw (also a championship record) by Scotland's Chris Black.

There were three other championship records: Australian prodigy Darren Clark set a world age-17 best of 45.05 in the 400m, a final in which the highest placed Briton finished seventh; the high jump where the American pair of Leo Williams and James Howard cleared 2.29m; and the 3000m walk with Australia's Dave Smith timed at 11:36.04. Overseas visitors again cleaned up, winning 12 of the 19 titles with eight of those going to Americans. They included Mike Conley, who completed the first long/triple jump double (7.82m/16.49m) since Fred Alsop in 1965, and Mike Carter who put the shot 20.80m for the widest winning margin of victory since 1899. Calvin Smith, who had recently set a world 100m record of 9.93 at altitude, found 10.30 sufficed for victory although he was pressed hard by Allan Wells (10.34). Again, Linford Christie made little impression, eliminated in the heats of both sprints in 10.88 and 22.18. In other AAA title events that year, Mike Gratton won the London Marathon in 2:09:43 with 93 men finishing inside 2:20 as against 18 in 2009 and 2010, Richard Carter (son of former UK 800m record holder and current AAA Chairman Chris Carter) the Under-20 5000m in 14:12.61, and the Youths 100m hurdles saw Jon Ridgeon beat Colin Jackson, 13.12 to 13.23, after setting a championship best of 13.07 in his heat.

1984 (Crystal Palace)

IT ALL TURNED out marvellously in the end but Seb Coe was a very worried man after losing to Peter Elliott over 1500m at the first Championships to be sponsored by U-Bix Copiers. It was not officially a trial for the forthcoming Los Angeles Olympics but both men were under the impression that victory would ensure filling the one vacancy as Steve Cram and Steve Ovett had been pre-selected. These were troubled times for Coe. After illness had ruined his last two seasons he appeared to be well on his way back to top form until an injury in training halted his progress. To safeguard against the risk of further injury he would have preferred not to race as soon as the AAA Championships in late June, but he felt obliged to as the Olympic team selection date was looming and the selectors required evidence of his fitness at 1500m. And so he lined up for a 'shoot-out' with Elliott, already picked like himself for the 800m and equally keen to go for the double in LA.

Prior to 1984 it would have appeared an unlikely match, for Elliott's best stood at 3:49.1 – some 17 seconds slower than the Olympic champion's fastest time. But in January

Elliott had improved drastically to 3:38.13 and his vow to be a thorn in Coe's side was no empty threat. The race could hardly have been more dramatic. They entered the last lap practically abreast and when Coe kicked away at the start of the final straight it looked all over. However, Elliott never lost heart; he stuck in and, as Coe ran out of steam in the closing stages, he inched past to snatch victory, 3:39.66 to 3:39.79, to become the first Briton to beat Coe at this distance for eight years. Nonetheless, provoking great controversy, it was Coe who was awarded the team place. As Frank Dick, the BAAB's Technical Director of Coaching, explained: "The selectors looked at the past and present records of both athletes and at the conclusion voted that Sebastian Coe was the athlete to go." Their faith in Coe proved fully justified as at the Olympics he followed up another silver medal in the 800m (1:43.64) with a successful defence of his 1500m title, his 53.25 last lap carrying him to a six-metre victory over Steve Cram, 3:32.53 to 3:33.40.

After walking across the line in last place in the 800m final and ignoring medical advice to withdraw from the 1500m, having in the meantime been admitted to hospital suffering from bronchial problems, dehydration and hyperventilation, Ovett miraculously fought his way to another final but further chest discomfort forced him to drop out on the third lap. Elliott suffered misfortune also, for after running a season's best of 1:45.49 in the second round of the 800m he had to scratch from the semis because of a stress fracture of the foot. Britain's other male gold medallist (Tessa Sanderson won the javelin) was Daley Thompson, who had no need to compete in the AAA Championships. He not only retained his decathlon title but for good measure compiled a world record score of 8847! He opened up an enormous lead over his German arch-rival Jürgen Hingsen in the first two events with a 10.44 100m and 8.01m long jump, and after overcoming a crisis in the discus and despite using the 1500m as a prolonged lap of honour he finished 152 points clear.

Mike McLeod timed his peak well for at the Games he took the 10,000m silver medal in 28:06.22, whereas at Crystal Palace he had finished second to former steeplechaser Steve Jones (28:09.97) in 28:16.87. RAF Corporal Jones placed eighth in LA in 28:28.08 ... and then found his true event when, in October, he won the Chicago Marathon in the world record time of 2:08:05. With athletics at the elite level now openly professional, Jones pocketed £30,000 in prize money. The 1983 AAA 10,000m champion Charlie Spedding also found the marathon to be his forte and followed up his London/AAA victory in 2:09:57 with the Olympic bronze medal in 2:09:58. Another bronze went to triple jumper Keith Connor (16.87m), while Dave Ottley, the AAA javelin winner with 81.34m, advanced to 85.74m for the Olympic silver medal.

Another excellent performance came from the 4x400m team of Kriss Akabusi (45.87), Garry Cook (44.74), Todd Bennett (44.17) and Phil Brown (44.35) who finished second to the Americans with a barrier-breaking European record of 2:59.13. Todd Bennett had an extraordinary background in the sport as he was a steeplechaser as a schoolboy before finding he was really a sprinter. At the 1984 UK Championships he shocked everyone by setting an English 200m record of 20.36 and went on to win the AAA title in a windy 20.79. His best distance, though, was 400m and the following year he would set a world indoor record of 45.56 when capturing the European title.

Back to the AAA Championships and the biggest shock was the elimination of the legendary Cuban, Alberto Juantorena, in the heats of the 800m, the final of which was won by Cram in 1:46.84. Another, future, Cuban world record breaker in Javier Sotomayor (then only 17) high jumped 2.30m but the title went on countback to his compatriot Francisco Centelles, a championship record for both. There was a championship record also for Domingo Ramon of Spain with 8:23.12 for the steeplechase, while Phil Vesty set a UK record of 11:42.94 in the 3000m walk with Tim Berrett second with a UK junior record of

11:54.23. Berrett later emigrated to Canada and, at 50km walk, competed in five Olympics. Another youngster to make his mark in the senior ranks was Jon Ridgeon, fourth in the 110m hurdles in 14.18 for a British age-17 best. At this stage he had the beating of Colin Jackson, winning the AAA Junior title over 3ft 3in hurdles in a UK junior record of 13.92 to his rival's 13.95. Incidentally, three of today's most familiar TV commentators made the Olympic team: Cram of the BBC, of course, and Eurosport's Tim Hutchings (fourth in the Olympic 5000m in 13:11.50) and Martin Gillingham, AAA 400m hurdles winner in 50.24.

1985 (Crystal Palace)

NEVER BEFORE, IN the 105-year history of the Championships, had so many titles gone abroad – which was ironic considering this edition, sponsored by Kodak, was the first in which specific leading British athletes were paid (via subventions) to take part. Of the 18 events contested by overseas athletes, no fewer than 13 were won by visitors. Americans claimed six titles, with one apiece for Australia, Bahrain, Brazil, Canada, Cuba, Ghana and Ireland. The only home winners were 18-year-old Ade Mafe in the 200m (20.99), Dave Lewis in the 5000m (13:42.82), Billy Cole in the shot (17.88m), Dave Smith in the hammer with a championship and English record of 77.30m, Dave Ottley in the javelin, improving in the final round from 82.12m to a championship record of 88.32m, and Ian McCombie who set a UK record of 11:41.73 in an all-domestic 3000m walk. Smith's throw was second only to Martin Girvan's 1984 UK record of 77.54m, while Ottley – the Olympic silver medallist and with a best of 90.70m – confirmed his standing as UK no 1 although earlier in the season Roald Bradstock had set a British record of 91.40m in Texas. Astonishingly, Bradstock – who later took US citizenship – is not only still active (71.22m in 2010) but plans at age 50 to compete in the 2012 British Olympic Trials! Another athlete still setting records as a veteran or master is Dalton Grant, who as a junior was the highest placed British high jumper at these Championships, fourth equal at 2.20m. He cleared 2.15m in 2008 and 2.08m indoors in 2009, aged 42!

Field event athletes stole the show for in addition to Smith and Ottley's exploits there were championship records by the charismatic American world record holder at 17.97m, Willie Banks, with 17.22m in the triple jump and by Cuba's Juan Martínez with a discus throw of 65.72m. Track highlights included a third consecutive 400m title for Australia's Darren Clark, by now all of 19, in 45.45. Hopes were high for a home victory in the 110m hurdles after Jon Ridgeon (18) posted the fastest heat time of 13.87 but in the final he fell at the eighth hurdle. Colin Jackson, just four days younger, placed fifth in 14.14 in his first senior AAA outing. The following month, at the European Junior Championships, they finished first and second with Ridgeon timed at a European junior record of 13.46 (only 0.03 outside Mark Holtom's UK senior record) and Jackson 13.69. The list of all-time greats who competed for but never won AAA titles, which already featured such legends as Al Oerter, Alberto Juantorena and Javier Sotomayor, could now include world pole vault record holder Sergey Bubka of the Ukraine and USSR. He cleared 5.40m for second place in the Indoor Championships at Cosford, the winner being his elder brother Vasiliy at 5.60m. That summer Sergey achieved the landmark height of six metres.

British records were set during 1985 by Derek Redmond with 44.82 for 400m, Colin Reitz with an 8:13.50 steeplechase and Steve Jones, who followed up a London/AAA win in 2:08:16 with new record figures of 2:07:13 in Chicago. But far and away the brightest star in athletics that year was Steve Cram. Despite continuing calf problems, which had caused him to scratch from the AAA 800m final, he put together one of the greatest series of races in middle distance history. In Oslo on June 27 he ran the third fastest ever 1500m with 3:31.34 and, three days after his AAA 800m heat on July 13, he achieved athletic immortality in Nice by becoming the first to duck under 3:30, holding off Morocco's Saïd Aouita with a 53.4 last lap for a time of 3:29.67.

That was just the start of a world record blitz. Back in Oslo on July 27 he not only defeated Seb Coe but took 1.01 sec off his mile record with 3:46.32, covering the final 200m in a sizzling 25.39. When Coe broke three world records in the space of 41 days in 1979 we doubted whether we would ever see the like again. Well, Cram surpassed that by setting three world records in just 19 days! In Budapest on August 4 he set new 2000m figures of 4:51.39. Indeed but for cold and windy weather in Gateshead on August 9 he might have made it four world records in 24 days; as it was he ran 2:12.85 compared to Coe's 2:12.18 set in near perfect conditions. He even finished a momentous season by defeating Brazil's Olympic champion Joaquim Cruz over 800m in Zürich in a personal best of 1:42.88, for fourth spot on the world all-time list.

1986 (Crystal Palace)

IN CONTRAST TO the wave of overseas victories the previous year, these Championships proved a celebration of British and predominantly English athletics talent. They were among the very best ever for all-round quality of performance by home athletes, and it was a pity the attendance was not greater. Perhaps the most exciting feature was the standard of sprinting. On a high after winning the European Indoor 200m title in Madrid and then breaking Allan Wells' UK 100m record with a startling 10.04 in the same city, Linford Christie won the AAA final in 10.22 ahead of Mike McFarlane's 10.26 and Daley Thompson's 10.34 and had hopes of becoming the first Briton to complete the sprint double since McDonald Bailey over 30 years earlier. However he weakened in the closing stages of the 200m and despite a personal best of 20.51 he finished third behind 19-year-old John Regis (20.41) and Todd Bennett (20.50). The 400m brought together two of the most prodigiously talented young exponents of this event.

Australia's Darren Clark, still only 20, captured his fourth AAA title with a superbly controlled championship record of 44.94, while European Junior champion Roger Black – also 20 – improved his best to 45.16, moving him to third on the UK all-time list behind Derek Redmond and David Jenkins. Another athlete of immense promise who would go on to fulfil his potential was Colin Jackson, still a junior, who ran out a dynamic winner of the 110m hurdles in 13.51. It wasn't surprising that Jackson would in time become a world beater ... but who could have predicted such an outcome for the 20-year-old who made the 12-man triple jump final with a modest wind assisted 15.33m and then proceeded to foul twice and pass up his remaining attempt to record a zero. His name? Jonathan Edwards. Jackson would later win the World Junior title in 13.44 by a margin of nearly five metres over Jon Ridgeon, and another gold medallist was David Sharpe in the 800m, having finished a fighting third in the AAA final in 1:46.81 behind Steve Cram (1:46.15) and Peter Elliott (1:46.67). Another fast rising middle distance star, John Gladwin, took the AAA 1500m in a championship record of 3:35.93.

The Commonwealth Games in Edinburgh were seriously devalued by an African and Caribbean boycott because of the British Government's refusal to impose economic sanctions against the then apartheid state of South Africa. Not surprisingly, England's medal tally was the highest ever but there were many very worthy performances despite the unhelpful weather. Seb Coe had to withdraw from the 800m final on medical grounds but the race still proved memorable as Cram pulverised the opposition in a super-fast 1:43.22, while in a ludicrously slow 1500m (3:50.87) he simply toyed with his rivals, taking 24.9 for his final 200m. Black turned the tables on Clark to take the 400m in 45.57; Steve Ovett displayed his wondrous range by winning the 5000m in 13:24.11, outkicking Jack Buckner and Tim Hutchings (the AAA champion in 13:25.03) for an England clean-sweep; Jon Solly added the 10,000m crown (27:57.42) to his AAA victory in 27:51.76; and there were field event wins by AAA champions Billy Cole in the shot (19.01m at Crystal Palace, 18.16m at Meadowbank), Dave Smith in the hammer (68.72m, 74.06m) and Dave Ottley with the new specification javelin (80.24m, 80.62m), plus Andy Ashurst in the pole vault (5.30m), John Herbert in the triple jump (windy 17.27m), Daley Thompson in the decathlon (8663) and the 4x400m team (3:07.19). Phil Beattie from N Ireland took the 400m hurdles in 49.60. Competition was much tougher in most events at the European Championships in Stuttgart, but there was plenty of British success there too: Linford Christie at 100m (10.15), Black at 400m (UK record of 44.59), Coe at 800m (1:44.50, followed in by Scotland's Tom McKean and Cram), Cram at 1500m (3:41.09 with Coe second), Buckner at 5000m (13:10.15 with Hutchings third), the 4x400m team (2:59.84) and, inevitably, Thompson in the decathlon (8811).

1987 (Crystal Palace)

TWO OF BRITAIN'S brightest young prospects, John Regis and Jon Ridgeon, were the stars of the show. Until a couple of weeks earlier, the racing form of Regis was giving cause for concern as he was struggling to break 21 sec while the previous year he was Europe's fastest at 20.41. His shrewd coach, John Isaacs, was unperturbed as training was geared towards hitting top form at these Championships, and so it proved. On the first day he ran his fastest 100m time of 10.37 for second place to Dwayne Evans (USA), 10.33, and in Sunday's 200m he retained his title in the fabulous time of 20.25, 0.01 ahead of Evans, to break a string of records: UK all-comers, championship and English. Only one Briton, Scotsman Allan Wells with 20.21 for the 1980 Olympic silver medal, had ever run faster. Another English record fell in the 110m hurdles where Ridgeon ran 13.36 for a four-metre victory over Welsh rugby star Nigel Walker with world record holder

Renaldo Nehemiah (who was reinstated by the IAAF after having turned pro footballer with the San Francisco 49ers in 1982) third, a long way from the form he exhibited at this meeting six years earlier when he clocked 13.17. Ridgeon had set a UK record of 13.29 earlier in the season in Zagreb but English records had to be established in England or Wales. Colin Jackson had to withdraw because of injury, and a number of other big names experienced a meeting they would rather forget.

Roger Black could finish only fourth in the 400m, Steve Cram fifth in the 800m and Dave Moorcroft seventh in the 1500m after a fast heat, with Steve Ovett having to scratch from the final of that event with a foot injury. Mark Rowland, destined to gain an Olympic bronze medal the following year, fell at the last barrier in the steeplechase. The long jump produced a win by Mike Powell (USA) with 7.94m. His best at the time was 8.27m ... and four years later he would set the world record which still stands of 8.95m. Mick Hill, the British javelin record holder with 85.24m, threw 81.68m for a championship record using the "new" implement, and Ian McCombie set new figures of 41:16.14 for the 10,000m walk. The most inspirational winner was Eric McCalla in the triple jump with the very reasonable distance of 16.86m. The wonder was that he could jump at all, for in 1985 he had suffered 95% kidney failure and in April 1986 he underwent a kidney transplant.

Britain's only winner at the World Championships in Rome was Fatima Whitbread in the women's javelin, but a number of medals were scooped up by the men. There were silvers for Peter Elliott in the 800m (personal best of 1:43.41), Ridgeon (equalling his UK record of 13.29) and the 4x400m team of Derek Redmond (45.11), Kriss Akabusi (44.48), Regis (43.93!) and Black (43.96) with a European record of 2:58.86. Bronze awards went to Linford Christie (10.14) in the 100m after Ben Johnson's retrospective disqualification, Regis in the 200m (20.18, just 0.02 behind the winner), Jack Buckner at 5000m (13:27.74) and Jackson in the sprint hurdles (13.38). Redmond won his 400m semi in a UK record 44.50, which would have sufficed for second in the final, but there he ran 45.06 to place fifth.

1988 (Birmingham)

HISTORY WAS MADE as, after years of fraught discussions, the outdoor Kodak AAA and TSB Women's AAA Championships were staged as a combined meeting, with the men leaving their previous London home for Birmingham's Alexander Stadium. It was the first time the AAA Championships had been held in Birmingham since 1890! The three-day meeting assumed extra significance as it incorporated the Olympic Trials with the first two in each event automatically selected for Seoul subject to having acquired the requisite qualifying standard.

The big winner was Linford Christie; the big loser Seb Coe. Christie at last (and for the only time) achieved the sprint double he coveted, becoming the first Briton to do so since McDonald Bailey in 1953. Followed home in both races by John Regis, Christie took the 100m in a championship record of 10.15 and 200m in a personal best of 20.46. Hopes of the first Coe v Steve Ovett clash on a British track in the 1500m came to nought after an out-of-sorts Coe could finish only fourth in his heat in 3:45.01 and was eliminated. In the final, won in 3:44.48 by Peter Elliott thanks to a 51.5 last lap, Ovett was among those blown away, placing fourth and out of the Olympic team. With Steve Cram – winner of the 800m in an impressive championship record of 1:44.16 – already pre-selected for the 1500m the other two places went to Elliott and his AAA runner-up Steve Crabb. Coe's last chance of an Olympic berth was at 800m. No problem there for Cram and second placed Tom McKean but the third spot was at the discretion of the selectors. They voted 4-2 in favour of Coe but that decision was controversially over-ruled by the BAAB Council, the final arbiters, who voted 11-10 for Elliott. Elliott went on to place fourth in the Olympic 800m in 1:44.12, with neither Cram nor McKean advancing beyond the quarter-finals, prior to taking the silver medal at 1500m in 3:36.15 with Cram fourth in 3:36.24 and Crabb failing to survive his semi-final. A deeply frustrated Coe, meanwhile, ran 1:43.93 and 3:35.72 in late summer races.

Christie proved to be the most successful member of the Olympic team with silver medals in the 100m behind Carl Lewis in a European record of 9.97 after the infamous disqualification of Ben Johnson and in the 4x100m relay where he took over from Elliot Bunney, Regis and Mike McFarlane to set a UK record of 38.28. He also placed fourth in the 200m in a British record of 20.09. Another silver medallist was sprint hurdler Colin Jackson who followed up his AAA win in 13.29 (13.27 heat) with 13.28 in Seoul. Remarkably, three Britons made the final with Jon Ridgeon fifth and Tony Jarrett sixth. The other medallist was Mark Rowland, content to clock a very ordinary 8:32.60 for his AAA steeplechase win ("I am just a novice really at the event ... I still cannot hurdle") but running eyeballs out for third place in the Olympics with the still standing and totally unthreatened UK record of 8:07.96. Hampered by a thigh injury, Daley Thompson failed in his bid to secure an unprecedented third Olympic decathlon title but won new admirers for a gutsy display which saw him finish fourth with 8306 points. It proved to be the last decathlon he would complete. Back at the AAA Championships one of the most notable performances was the championship record of 44.93 for 400m by Kriss Akabusi, selected for the Olympic 400m hurdles (he placed sixth) but here elevating himself to equal third with David Jenkins on the UK all-time list behind Derek Redmond and Roger Black.

1989 (Birmingham)

AT LAST IT happened – Seb Coe v Steve Ovett on a British track – but it was no contest. One month short of his 33rd birthday Coe finally won his first and only AAA 1500m title, and in suitably dramatic fashion. Approaching the bell he almost fell, having to hurdle over the sprawled body of Steve Crabb and losing some 20m to the leaders before he was able to recover sufficiently to set off in pursuit in eighth place. It looked an impossible task, even for Coe at his best, but he was equal to the challenge. Running with supreme pace judgement, Coe caught the leader, Tony Morrell, early in the finishing straight to gain a remarkable victory in 3:41.38, clocking 25.4 for the last 200m despite having strained a hamstring while jumping over Crabb. As for Ovett, who was greatly upset to learn that he had been offered money by Promotions Officer Andy Norman to run whereas Coe hadn't, he finished ninth and later broke down and wept during an ITV interview. Coe ended his last full season of competition ranked no 1 in Britain at both 800m (1:43.38, his fastest for four years) and 1500m (3:34.05, his best for three years).

Two national records fell at these the 100th staging of the AAA Championships: Dalton Grant high jumped 2.33m for a UK and championship record (he had cleared 2.35m indoors earlier in the year) while Stewart Faulkner set an English long jump record of 8.13m. Steve Backley, aged 20 and already the UK record holder with the "new" javelin (85.86m), broke the championship record with 83.16m, while Colin Jackson – the European record holder at 13.11 – narrowly missed Renaldo Nehemiah's 110m hurdles championship record with 13.19. Linford Christie retained his 100m title by a huge margin in 10.16 and Jonathan Edwards collected his first AAA triple jump championship with a relatively modest 16.53m. A month later he broke into world class with a leap of 17.28m.

BRITISH RECORDS AT 1 JANUARY 1990
100m: 9.97 Linford Christie 1988; 200m: 20.09 Christie 1988; 400m: 44.50 Derek Redmond 1987; 800m: 1:41.73 Seb Coe 1981; 1000m: 2:12.18 Coe 1981; 1500m: 3:29.67 Steve Cram 1985; Mile: 3:46.32 Cram 1985; 2000m: 4:51.39 Cram 1985; 3000m: 7:32.79

Dave Moorcroft 1982; 2M: 8:13.51 Steve Ovett 1978; 5000m: 13:00.41 Moorcroft 1982; 10,000m: 27:23.06 Eamonn Martin 1988; Half Marathon: 60:59 Steve Jones 1986; Marathon: 2:07:13 S Jones 1985; 3000mSC: 8:07.96 Mark Rowland 1988; 110mH: 13.11 Colin Jackson 1988 & 1989; 400mH: 48.12 David Hemery 1968; HJ: 2.34 Dalton Grant 1989 (2.35 indoors 1989); PV: 5.65 Keith Stock 1981; LJ: 8.23 Lynn Davies 1968; TJ: 17.57 Keith Connor 1982; SP: 21.68 Geoff Capes 1980; DT: 64.32 Bill Tancred 1974 (unratified: 65.16 Richard Slaney 1985); HT: 77.54 Martin Girvan 1984; JT: 85.90 Steve Backley 1989; Decathlon: (re-scored on 1985 tables) 8847 Daley Thompson 1984; 3000m Walk: 11:24.4 Mark Easton 1989; 10,000m Walk: 40:06.65 Ian McCombie 1989; 20km Walk: 1:22:03 McCombie 1988; 50km Walk: 3:57:48 Les Morton 1989.

THE NINETIES

THE SUPREME STARS of the 1980s – Seb Coe, Steve Ovett, Steve Cram and Daley Thompson, all global champions and world record breakers – were a hard act to follow, but the 1990s featured a trio whose achievements were similarly awe-inspiring ... Linford Christie, Colin Jackson and Jonathan Edwards. Christie was the only British male to strike Olympic gold during the decade (he was joined in Barcelona in 1992 by Sally Gunnell) while Jackson and Edwards won world titles and set long-standing world records. Jackson's 12.91 110m hurdles in 1993 was not beaten for 13 years and his 7.30 for the indoor 60m hurdles in 1994 remains unbroken, as does Edwards' 18.29m triple jump in 1995. At the European level British athletes continued to perform with distinction in a wide range of events, continental titles being won in the 100m, 200m, 400m, 800m, 110m and 400m hurdles, triple jump, javelin and both relays. However, pickings were slim in what were the traditionally strong middle and long distance events (1500m-marathon including steeplechase) with just three silver medals.

Huge changes occurred in respect of the administration of British athletics, with the AAA wielding considerable influence. In June 1990 AAA General Committee approved a constitution for a new Federation as well as a drastically altered AAA. As AAA spokesman Tony Ward said: "There will be fundamental changes to the way athletics is run in Britain. Power will be devolved upwards by the various national and regional bodies rather than downwards by the central authority from now on. It's an important step in our history."

A key date was 17 March 1991 when Extraordinary General Meetings of the British Amateur Athletic Board (BAAB), AAA and Women's AAA at Birmingham University transformed the future course of the sport's administration. The BAAB, founded in 1932 and affiliated to the IAAF as the governing association for the UK, decided by 220 votes to none to replace itself by the British Athletic Federation (BAF). The AAA voted 835-39 and the WAAA 80-0 in favour of BAF's creation. At the same time, the AAA and WAAA, after co-existing for nearly 70 years, finally merged to form what would be known as the AAA of England, with Her Majesty The Queen as Patron. Tony Ward commented: "The coming together of the men's and women's associations is perhaps the most notable of the changes. Many counties who have long since made this move have recognised the benefits. Amalgamation will also mean the equal development of men's and women's athletics with the expertise at present only available to half the sport becoming available to all." Another consequence was that the Athletic Association of Wales, which had been part of the AAA since 1928, now seceded to become an autonomous body.

It was on 1 October 1991 that the AAA of England officially came into being, adopting a new Memorandum and Articles of Association. On the same day the WAAA ceased its activities and transferred its funds to the new body and four days later, at the AAA of England's first Council meeting, Marea Hartman (the long-serving Hon. Secretary of the WAAA and Chairman of the BAAB) was elected President, with David Cropper as Chairman, Derek Johnson as Hon. Secretary and Geoff Clarke as Hon. Treasurer. The new Association would be responsible for the co-ordination and development of athletics in England in conjunction with the Regional Associations. Its total reserves as at 30 September 1991 were £2,267,679 of which £1,040,323 was being transferred to BAF and £100,000 to the Athletic Association of Wales.

BAF, whose Patron was the Duke of Edinburgh (previously President of the BAAB), also officially began life on 1 October 1991, bringing together for the first time all the clubs of the UK under a single umbrella organisation with every affiliated club and athletic body in the UK entitled to attend and vote on major constitutional matters and the election of officers. The inaugural Chief Executive (chosen from over 150 applicants) was Malcolm Jones, previously the AAA's Financial Controller, and the first honorary officers were Arthur McAllister as President, Dr Bill Evans as Chairman, IAC Chairman Dave Bedford as Secretary and John Lister as Treasurer. The fact that Dave Bedford and Derek Johnson were serving as officers of the new governing bodies was indicative of the level of co-operation which now existed between the athletes and the administration, and the IAC was eventually disbanded as BAF took over such services as medical insurance, screening and an athletes' helpline.

BAF's responsibilities included the co-ordination and disciplinary procedures of all doping matters, and this proved to be a monumental burden, contributing to its financial ruin. A number of high profile doping positives rocked British athletics during the 1990s, the most costly being that attributed to Diane Modahl in a test carried out in Portugal in June 1994.

In December 1994 the BAF Disciplinary Committee came to the unanimous decision that a doping offence had been committed and banned Mrs Modahl for four years. Following a protracted fight to clear her name, the IAAF Council reinstated her in March 1996, conceding that the test was unreliable. British scientists had proved that urine samples that were not properly stored, as in Mrs Modahl's case, could become bacterially degraded.

The athlete sued BAF for £480,000 for loss of earnings, medical and legal fees incurred while suspended – later rising to £1 million to include punitive damages. The action was contested by BAF whose own legal expenses led in part to the body's acute financial problems which resulted in BAF going into administration in October 1997. The High Court in London rejected Mrs Modahl's claim in December 2000.

During its six years of existence BAF, despite launching many useful initiatives, appeared to be constantly in a state of crisis, a situation not helped by various power struggles within the Federation. Malcolm Jones resigned as Chief Executive in 1993, to be replaced by Professor Peter Radford, the former world record holder at 200m and 220 yards, as Executive Chairman. At the 1994 AGM Dave Bedford was ousted as Hon. Secretary by Matt Frazer with Ken Rickhuss becoming Chairman. Also that year Frank Dick resigned as Director of Coaching following a reduction in the development budget and Andy Norman was dismissed as Director of Promotions in the wake of the suicide of noted journalist Cliff Temple. Mary Peters succeeded Arthur McAllister as President at the 1996 AGM, where John Lister stood down as Hon. Treasurer.

With the AAA of England declining to bail out the financially ailing BAF its future looked bleak, the accounts showing a deficit of £324,000 in 1996, and there was a further shock when Prof. Radford announced his resignation in January 1997. In July 1997 former world 5000m record holder Dave Moorcroft (who in 1993 had set a world veterans mile record of 4:02.53) defeated 127 other applicants to be appointed the new Chief Executive ... but within days of his beginning work in October he had to announce the devastating news that BAF had been placed in the hands of the administrators after declaring a substantial cash shortfall which included payments of £860,000 yet to be made to athletes who had competed in BAF meetings. The pain was widespread as, in order to maximise the return to BAF's creditors, the administrators quickly made redundant several employees including nine national coaches or development officers.

An interim body, UK Athletics 98, was set up with £300,000 of funding from the UK Sports Council to act as agents for the administrators managing the affairs of BAF, while a steering group, chaired by Sir Chris Chataway (the former world 5000m record holder), identified the needs of a new governing body. In May 1998 UK Athletics 98 was able to announce that agreement had been reached with the administrators of BAF over the ownership of the sport's commercial rights and with the AAA of England ("a great step forward," said Athletics 98 Chief Executive Dave Moorcroft) to ensure that the AAA Championships would be held as a combined UK Trials event for at least the next four years.

It was also revealed that Fast Track, a new company formed by former European and Commonwealth 400m hurdles champion Alan Pascoe, had been appointed to stage televised events and seek sponsors for British athletics. In July 1998 the AAA of England announced its backing for the new proposals. A General Committee statement read: "The AAAoE is strongly supportive of a clear role for a new UK body, setting and monitoring policy for performance, competition and development throughout the UK. We are firmly committed to supporting such a UK body and ensuring its success."

A brochure entitled "A new future for athletics in the UK" was distributed to more than 1600 affiliated athletic clubs and associations, setting out the structure and aims of the new organisation, and later in the year UK Athletics 98 received an overwhelming vote of confidence following the most extensive review conducted by any sport within Britain with 97% of the clubs which took part voting in favour of the proposals. Clubs were invited also to vote for President of the new governing body, UK Athletics, with 1968 Olympic 400m hurdles champion David Hemery the winner. "It's a great honour to be elected by the clubs to this position," he said. "The President will be an ambassador and also a conscience for the sport, working to select the best people to run athletics in the UK. I look forward to taking up the challenge." Sir Arthur Gold, who was elected President of the AAA of England in 1995 following Dame Marea Hartman's death the previous year, commented: "I warmly welcome the election of David Hemery as President of the proposed new governing body. He has standards of true sportsmanship." As the year ended, Dave Moorcroft was appointed Chief Executive Officer of UK Athletics. "The last 15 months have seen great turbulence within the sport," he said. "But, in the course of our year-long consultation process and an outstanding year of athletic performances, we have hopefully reached a point where we have solid foundations on which to build a fantastic future for the sport. There are still many challenges ahead but I think we have the will, the people and the vision to face them with confidence."

UK Athletics came into existence in January 1999 and the future looked bright with a lucrative BBC television contract worth £17.5 million over four years and increasing lottery funding for top athletes. That summer CGU Insurance (which merged with Norwich Union in 2000) and UKA announced a new four year £10 million sponsorship package, which not only provided title sponsorship for all the major British meetings (including the AAA Championships) but included investment in a broad range of grassroots and development initiatives.

Meanwhile the AAA of England retained its healthy financial situation, the accounts presented to the AGM in February 1999 indicating a surplus of £1,150,945. Roy Mitchell, who had succeeded Derek Johnson in 1994, remained Hon. Secretary, while David Cropper and Geoff Clarke continued as Chairman of General Committee and Hon. Treasurer respectively as they had throughout the existence of the AAAoE. Cropper would later say that his greatest achievement as Chairman was setting up a Management Board, making the members directors of AAA of England Ltd.

For many years the Association had plans for development and from 1985-86 there were Development Officers in the Territorial Associations. After considerable discussion a Major Development Strategy was established. This was to be funded by a substantial English Sports Council grant but would require significant financial support from the AAA and the three Territorial Associations. In 1999 Lorretta Sollars was appointed Head of Development with a team of Regional Development Co-ordinators based in the English Sports Council regions, and at its peak ten RDCs were in post. The plan required rigorous targets to be met in many areas of development as well as working in an increasing number of national multi-sports programmes. The availability of full-time professional support for clubs and athletes was seen as a real benefit, but the constraint of meeting Sport England objectives caused difficulties to some clubs who had different aspirations. In 2003 1992 and 1996 Olympian Alison Wyeth replaced Ms Sollars on her appointment as a Regional Director of Sport England.

The decade saw the sport at the elite level become openly professional at last. The trust fund arrangement was disbanded and athletes via their agents could be paid whatever they could earn in prize money, bonuses, sponsorship, advertising and promotional deals. There was big money available. In 1999, for example, Jamie Baulch and Colin Jackson won $50,000 apiece for their victories at the World Indoor Championships; Kenya's Joyce Chepchumba collected a total of $230,000 for winning the London Marathon in a world best for a women-only race (plus a substantial appearance fee); and Wilson Kipketer of Denmark and Gabriela Szabo of Romania shared a million dollar jackpot in the IAAF's Golden League. On a more modest level, British athletes of a certain standard could, from May 1997, receive grants via Performance Athlete Services (PAS) from the government's Lottery Sports Fund.

As rewards for top performances increased so too did the number of athletes prepared to resort to doping and it was a sad sign of the times that the entry form for the AAA

High flyers all. Top (left) DALTON GRANT, 1994 European Indoor and 1998 Com-monwealth Games champion with best marks of 2.36m outdoors and 2.37m indoors; (right) STEVE SMITH, UK record holder with 2.37m outdoors and 2.38m indoors, bronze medallist at the 1993 World Championships and 1996 Olympics; (below): Britain's triumphant 4x400m relay team at the 1991 World Championships: (from left) DEREK REDMOND, KRISS AKABUSI, JOHN REGIS and ROGER BLACK

STEVE BACKLEY

Britain's greatest ever male thrower. He set three world javelin records (91.46m in 1992 still the unapproached British record), won four European and three Commonwealth Games titles, and gained three Olympic medals – two silver and a bronze. He also won six AAA titles between 1989 and 2004

LINFORD CHRISTIE
The peak of a brilliant if controversial career as he celebrates his Olympic 100m victory in Barcelona in 1992. Clocking 9.96 he became at 32 the oldest man to win this title, displacing the 1980 champion Allan Wells. The following year Christie added the World title in his best time of 9.87, just 1/100th of a second outside Carl Lewis' world record. He won a record number of eight AAA 100m titles between 1986 and 1996

COLIN JACKSON

Leaping for joy after not only winning the 1993 World title for 110m hurdles in Stuttgart but setting a world record of 12.91 in the process. Although an Olympic title eluded him, the Welshman won every other honour in the sport and after 17 years still holds the world record for the indoor 60m hurdles at 7.30. He was AAA champion no fewer than 11 times between 1986 and 2002

Clockwise from top left: JON BROWN,
AAA 5000m champion in 1993 who later
became a successful marathoner, as did
EAMONN MARTIN, three times AAA
5000m champion; ROGER BLACK, 1996
Olympic 400m runner-up; JON RIDGEON, 1996 AAA 400m hurdles champion –
nine years after taking the 110m hurdles crown

JONATHAN EDWARDS
Pictured during his day of days at the 1995 World Championships in Gothenburg when in the first round he shattered his own world triple jump record of 17.98m with 18.16m and then with his second jump cut the sand at an astonishing 18.29m (60 feet) – a distance which has yet to be threatened. He won the Olympic title five years later

Top: (left) ROBERT WEIR, nine times AAA discus champion between 1983 and 2002 (and 1982 hammer champion); IWAN THOMAS (30), UK 400m record holder; (middle): DARREN CAMPBELL (13) wins 1998 AAA 100m in 10.22 into a 1.7m wind; (bottom): JASON GARDENER (158) runs a windy 10.02 for victory in 1999 with DWAIN CHAMBERS (78) second

Clockwise from top left: The injury plagued decathlete DEAN MACEY, who nonetheless struck silver (1999) and bronze (2001) at the World Championships and was Commonwealth Games champion in 2006; JOHN MAYOCK, winner of more AAA 1500m titles (six between 1995 and 2001) than anyone else; CHRIS RAWLINSON, AAA 400m hurdles champion six times on the trot (1999-2004); TONY JARRETT, perpetually overshadowed by Colin Jackson but a brilliant sprint hurdler who was second in the 1993 and 1995 World Championships and was Commonwealth Games champion in 1998. His solitary AAA title came in 2001, 13 years after the first of his numerous second places

Clockwise from top left: MARLON DEVONISH, the 2003 World Indoor 200m champion, has won seven AAA titles outdoors – two at 100m and five at 200m; two more of the mainstays of British sprinting in DWAIN CHAMBERS (left) and MARK LEWIS-FRANCIS; CARL MYERSCOUGH, the biggest man in British athletics who broke Geoff Capes' long standing British shot put record in 2003 with 21.92m; and MICK JONES, the 2002 Commonwealth Games hammer champion who has won six AAA titles and finished in the first three 15 times between 1986 and 2005

Top left: British long jump record holder (at 8.30m) GREG RUTHERFORD, who was 18 when he won his first AAA senior title in 2005; NATHAN DOUGLAS, who triple jumped a massive 17.64m when winning the 2005 AAA title; (below) Tasting the fruits of victory – Britain's 4x100m relay team at the 2004 Olympics in Athens: from left: MARK LEWIS-FRANCIS, MARLON DEVONISH, DARREN CAMPBELL and JASON GARDENER

PHILLIPS IDOWU
Gold medals so far at 2006 Commonwealth Games, 2007 European Indoors, 2008
World Indoors, 2009 World Championships and 2010 European Championships.
Second in 2008 Olympics … ? in London 2012

MO FARAH
The most successful British male distance runner for many years, he completed a 5000m/10,000m double at the 2010 European Championships and achieved one of his great ambitions that summer when breaking Dave Moorcroft's British (and former world) 5000m record with 12:57.94

Clockwise from top left: SIMEON WILLIAMSON (left) clocked a remarkable 10.05 100m into a 1.8m wind well ahead of DWAIN CHAMBERS at the 2009 UK Championships; MICHAEL RIMMER, winner of the national 800m title five years running since 2006; DAI GREENE, 2010 European and Commonwealth 400m hurdles champion; ANDY TURNER, won the same title double at 110m hurdles

Coaching genius GEOFF DYSON with his wife, the former MAUREEN GARDNER

SIR ARTHUR GOLD, AAA of England President 1995–2000

DAME MAREA HARTMAN, the first President of the AAA of England, 1991–1994

AAA officers – clockwise from top left: GEORGE BUNNER, Chairman 2004–2007; BARRY WILLIS, Hon. Secretary 1965–1982; CHRIS CARTER, Chairman since 2009; WALTER NICHOLLS, Hon. Secretary since 2004. (Photograph of Chris Carter by Sheri Whiting Photography)

AAA TROPHIES
Top left: The C.W.F. Pearce Trophy, presented to the winner of the javelin at the AAA Championships
Top right: The C.B. Lawes Trophy, presented to the winner of the mile, and later 1500m
Above: The Earl of Jersey Trophy, presented by the first Chairman of the AAA. It was awarded to winners of the 4 miles championship, subsequently (from 1932) the 3 miles and (from 1969) the 5000m
Right: The Harvey Memorial Cup, awarded to the best AAA champion of the year

Championships now included the following declaration which had to be signed by the athlete: "I have not made use of any doping substances and I will not do so in order to improve my athletic performance. I am aware that drug testing may take place."

The combined AAA/WAAA Indoor Championships in 1991 were the last to be staged at RAF Cosford, the much appreciated but somewhat geographically remote venue since 1965. From 1992 until 2001 they were held each year at the magnificently equipped National Indoor Arena in the centre of Birmingham. Among the decade's highlights were championship records of 20.46 for 200m by Julian Golding and 45.71 for 400m by Solomon Wariso in 1998, 7.43 for 60m hurdles by Colin Jackson in 1990 and a 5.61m pole vault by Nick Buckfield in 1996.

The saddest feature of writing a history of athletics is recording the deaths of those who contributed so much to the sport and there was a heavy toll throughout the 1990s. In 1991 we lost that great coach, TV commentator and conscience of the sport, Ron Pickering, former AAA Treasurers Ray Stroud and John Martell, and the world record breaking Gordon Pirie; in 1992 that most popular of British team managers Les Jones died, as did one of his predecessors, Pat Sage, while the never to be forgotten Arthur Wint, Jamaica's 1948 Olympic 400m champion but so much part of the post-war British athletics scene, also passed away. As mentioned earlier, Dame Marea Hartman – President of the AAA of England – died in 1994. The following year saw the demise of 1936 Olympic hero Godfrey Brown and former BAAB and BAF Chairman Dr Bill Evans. Jimmy Green, founder and long-time editor of *Athletics Weekly*, died in 1998, as did former British team manager and AAA Chairman Les Golding, while 1999 took from us the barrier-breaking marathoner Jim Peters and Steve Ovett's coach Harry Wilson.

Highlights from each of the AAA Championships meetings 1990-1999

1990 (Birmingham)

THE 1500m MAY still have been Britain's parade event but there was little evidence of that in these Panasonic AAA/ WAAA Championships, staged in sweltering conditions. Seb Coe had recently retired, Peter Elliott (who earlier in the year had won the Commonwealth Games title in 3:33.39 followed by a world indoor record of 3:34.21) was absent and Steve Cram, bothered by an Achilles tendon injury, qualified for but pulled out of the final. That left just Steve Ovett, who wished to support the meeting but was aware he was not in good shape. In what proved to be his AAA swan-song he surprised himself by making the final but there he was never a factor, placing a distant eighth as Welshman Neil Horsfield won in 3:44.70. Tom McKean, the Scot who was one of two Britons to have struck gold at the European Indoor Championships in Glasgow (Linford Christie being the other), ran a fine 800m to clock 1:44.44 – which would have won all but one previous AAA title – but had to settle for second to William Tanui (1:44.14). It was a remarkable and controversial event, for Tanui had broken Cram's championship record of 1:44.16 in his heat with 1:43.94 and fellow-Kenyan Robert Kibet won his heat in 1:44.29, both using the meeting as an opportunity for fast time trials.

Christie, winner of the Commonwealth title in a windy 9.93, had a roller-coaster experience in the 100m. Suffering from cramp in both calves, he only qualified for the final as a fastest loser but he ran well in the final only to lose a photo finish decision against former world record holder Calvin Smith (USA) in 10.21 as he celebrated a little too early. Of Britain's other newly minted Commonwealth champions in Auckland, Marcus Adam placed only fifth in the 200m won by John Regis in 20.28, 10,000m gold medallist Eamonn Martin took the 5000m in 13:32.07, Welshman Colin Jackson (who had set a European and Commonwealth record of 13.08 in Auckland) clocked 13.23 in the high hurdles and Simon Williams finished second in the shot to Paul Edwards. Choosing not to compete (like Elliott) in the AAA Championships as their selection for the European Championships in Split was assured were Kriss Akabusi, who had won the 400m hurdles in 48.89, and Steve Backley, who had set a Commonwealth javelin record in Auckland of 86.02m, which he later extended to 89.58m in Stockholm, to become the first British man to become a field event world record breaker, and 90.98m at Crystal Palace.

The European Championships a month after the AAA Championships proved a memorable occasion for the British men's team which accumulated a record eight gold medals and even topped the Soviet Union on the basis of first-eight placings. It was a triumphant moment in the career of the BAAB's Director of Coaching, Frank Dick, and everyone else who had worked so hard to improve the standard of men's athletics in this country. Christie (10.00w) and Backley (87.30m) led the onslaught on August 28, followed next day by Akabusi – who was thrilled to break David Hemery's historic British and former world record of 48.12 with a 47.92 timing in the 400m hurdles – and McKean who front-ran to 800m victory in 1:44.76. August 30 saw two more victories thanks to Regis (20.11 200m) and Roger Black (45.08 400m); and on the final two days Colin Jackson (13.18) and the 4x400m team of Paul Sanders (45.85), Akabusi (44.48), Regis (43.93 for his fourth medal of the week) and Black (43.96) for the fastest ever non-American time of 2:58.22 increased the tally.

1991 (Birmingham)

THE LAST OF the pre-BAF Championships, incorporating selection trials for the World Championships in Tokyo, featured a championship best in the 100m by Linford

Christie. He clocked a wind assisted 10.02 semi-final before taking the final in 10.14 a metre clear of John Regis. The 400m was a much closer race, the judges taking nearly ten minutes to determine that Derek Redmond (46.07) had prevailed over Mark Richardson (46.08) and Ade Mafe (46.09). Redmond would, in Tokyo, play his part in one of British athletics' most memorable moments when Roger Black (44.7), himself (44.0), Regis (44.22) and Kriss Akabusi (44.59) famously beat the crack US squad for the world 4x400m relay title in the European and Commonwealth record time of 2:57.53. In addition to Christie's exploit there were two other championship records. Mick Hill threw the javelin 84.54m and Tony Jarrett set an English record of 13.13 in his 110m hurdles heat but withdrew from the final because of a calf muscle twinge. Barrington Williams won his first AAA long jump title at the age of 35, leaping 7.94m (he became champion again three years later), while in the triple jump the American showman Willie Banks trumped Jonathan Edwards' 16.50m with 16.60m on the final jump of the competition. Little did anyone suspect then that Edwards would, four years later, succeed Banks as world record holder.

The 4x400m relay provided the British men's team with its only victory in Tokyo (Liz McColgan won the women's 10,000m) but Roger Black took silver in the 400m (44.62) and there were bronze medals for Jarrett (13.25), Akabusi with a British 400m hurdles record of 47.86 and the 4x100m team of Jarrett, Regis, Darren Braithwaite and Christie (38.09). Such was the standard of performance that Christie set a European and Commonwealth 100m record of 9.92 and Dalton Grant a British high jump record of 2.36m ... in fourth place.

1992 (Birmingham)

AS THE MEETING incorporated the Olympic Trials it was appropriate that Britain's only male gold medallist in Barcelona should prove the star of the show. Clocking what was then his fastest legal 100m time on a British track of 10.09, Linford Christie streaked to victory by over two metres from Jason Livingston, who during the winter had become European indoor 60m champion in 6.53. Dubbed "Baby Ben" as a smaller version of Ben Johnson, Livingston unfortunately resembled the Canadian in other ways as he failed a random drugs test, was sent home from Barcelona 48 hours before his 100m heat and was banned for four years. Christie only narrowly failed to complete the sprint double, finishing 2/100ths behind John Regis (20.27) in the 200m. Colin Jackson underlined his status as Olympic favourite by taking the 110m hurdles in 13.15 but at the Games he injured himself after an outstanding 13.10 heat and could place only seventh in the final in 13.46, his Canadian training partner Mark McKoy striking gold in 13.12. Tony Jarrett, AAA runner-up in 13.23, finished fourth in 13.26.

The British heroes in Barcelona were Christie with his 9.96 100m victory and Sally Gunnell, the 400m hurdles champion in 53.23. British men claimed three bronze medals. Kriss Akabusi, an unstraining AAA winner in 49.16, was pulled to a UK 400m hurdles record of 47.82 in a race won by Kevin Young (USA) in the still unapproached world record time of 46.78; Steve Backley, who had thrown the javelin a world record 91.46m in New Zealand in January and produced a AAA championship record of 88.14m, managed only 83.38m but that sufficed for third place at the Olympics; and the 4x400m team of Roger Black, David Grindley, Akabusi and Regis ran 2:59.73 behind the USA and Cuba.

It was a bleak Games for Derek Redmond, who had placed second in the AAA 400m (45.14), won by Trinidad's Alvin Daniel in a championship record of 44.84 with Grindley third in 45.41. Feeling in the form of his life after winning his heats in 45.03 and 45.02, Redmond pulled a hamstring in his semi and, helped by his dad, Jim, heartrendingly hobbled to the finish. That put paid to his relay hopes too, and just to compound the agony Grindley broke Redmond's

British record with 44.47 in the other semi before going on to place sixth in the final in 44.75.

There was a British record also in the 200m where Regis equalled Christie's figures of 20.09 in his semi, a time which would have earned the silver medal in the final, but by then Regis was too tired and he slumped to sixth in 20.55. Steve Smith, AAA high jump winner with a UK junior record of 2.31m, cleared 2.29m in the Olympic qualifying round before placing 12th in the final with 2.24m, but ended the year brilliantly in Seoul at the World Junior Championships. Raising his personal best three times he finished up with 2.37m, equalling the world junior record and setting a new Commonwealth and British senior record. Another to redeem himself late in the season was Jonathan Edwards, who had managed only a paltry 15.76m in the Olympic triple jump qualifying contest. Competing in the World Cup in Havana he offered a glimpse of what was to come by winning with 17.34m.

1993 (Birmingham)

LINFORD CHRISTIE WAS once again foiled in his bid for a sprint double … this time not by any of his opponents, but by himself! Having comfortably won his sixth 100m title in 10.13 and with arch-rival John Regis deciding not to contest the 200m, Christie looked all set. But in the heats, with only winners automatically qualifying for the final, he was simply careless. Many metres ahead entering the straight, he eased up too drastically and was caught on the line by Solomon Wariso, 21.41-21.42, and that was the end of Christie's involvement in the 200m. Another of Britain's greatest athletes, Steve Cram, came unstuck in the 1500m. Although he had placed third in Oslo's Dream Mile the previous weekend in 3:52.17 he could manage only fourth in 3:40.60 as Matthew Yates sprinted to victory in 3:38.75. The classiest mark of the weekend came from Colin Jackson with his 13.15 sprint hurdles and almost inevitably Tony Jarrett (13.37) was runner-up. He was fated to finish second to Jackson at the AAA Championships eight times between 1988 and 2002, winning the title just once (2001) in the Welshman's absence.

Australia's Olympic high jump bronze medallist Tim Forsyth, second to Smith in last year's meeting on count-back at 2.31m, this time turned the tables in the high jump, 2.32m to Smith's 2.30m. Jon Brown, destined to finish fourth in the Olympic marathons of seven and 11 years hence, claimed the 5000m title in 13:35.67. Two other more youthful athletes who would go on to achieve high honours made their AAA debuts. Jason Gardener (17) was seventh in his 100m heat in 10.87 and Iwan Thomas (19) was fifth in his 400m heat in 48.36.

The World Championships in Stuttgart the following month produced three gold medals for British athletes, each with a stunning performance. Both Jackson (12.91 110m hurdles) and Sally Gunnell (52.74 400m hurdles) set world records and Christie's European and Commonwealth 100m record of 9.87 with a wind of only 0.3m/sec was adjudged superior to Carl Lewis's world record of 9.86 with a 1.2m tailwind. At 33 Christie became the oldest man to win a global title at the distance. Jackson became the first Briton to set a new world record in the sprint hurdles since his namesake Clement Jackson with 16.0 in 1865! Jarrett was runner-up to Jackson yet again, but this time he showed just what a brilliant athlete he was in his own right by lowering his English record to 13.00 for fourth place on the world all-time list. It was the first time British athletes had ever finished first and second in any World Championships event. Regis came so close to becoming world 200m champion. Ahead of Carl Lewis at 100m in 10.28 and 150m in 14.93 he was edged out near the finish by Namibia's Frank Fredericks (19.85). Regis's time of 19.94 was a British record and the fastest by a European at or near sea level. The all-medallist 4x100m relay team of Jackson, Jarrett, Regis and Christie picked up silverware behind the USA in the European record time of 37.77, and there were bronze medals for Smith, who equalled his Commonwealth high jump record of 2.37m, Jonathan Edwards (17.44m triple jump) and Mick Hill (82.96m javelin).

1994 (Sheffield)

YET AGAIN IT was Linford Christie who provided the headlines at these KP AAA Championships, held for the first time at Sheffield's Don Valley Stadium. In capturing his seventh 100m title, matching the record of McDonald Bailey, he clocked the fastest time yet seen in Britain of 9.91, albeit assisted by a hefty 3.7m/sec gust of wind. There were other notable times in his slipstream with Toby Box and Mike Rosswess running 10.07 and Jason John 10.08. There was impressive depth also in the 400m with four men inside 45.50, led by Roger Black (44.94), returning after a year out while suffering from the debilitating Epstein Barr virus, and in the triple jump where Jonathan Edwards set an English native (i.e. best mark in England) and championship record of 17.39m and two others registered 16.95m or better. The javelin featured a close duel with Mick Hill's 84.60m opener prevailing against Steve Backley's final throw of 84.24m. Rob Denmark, in his track debut at the distance, won the 10,000m by nearly half a lap in 28:03.34. A couple of interesting names to finish third were Gary Lough in the 1500m – he would set a Northern Irish record of 3:34.76 the following year and marry Paula Radcliffe in 2000 – and Lloyd Cowan in the 110m hurdles. He ran his lifetime best of 13.75 that season but became better known as the coach of Olympic and world 400m champion Christine Ohuruogu. Barrington Williams regained the long jump title with 7.77m, aged 38, while former British pole vault record holder and Superstars legend Brian Hooper (41), in his farewell AAA appearance 21 years after winning his first title, levered himself over 4.75m for tenth place. He cleared 5.01m later in the season.

It was another good year internationally for British athletes. Colin Jackson was the star of the indoor season, setting a still standing world record of 7.30 for 60m hurdles and winning both that event (7.41) and the flat 60m (6.49) at the European Indoor Championships in Paris, just missing Christie's new European record of 6.48. Steve Smith high jumped a Commonwealth record of 2.38m, while Dalton Grant was only 1cm below that when capturing the European indoor title. At the outdoor European Championships, in Helsinki, British men won five gold medals through Christie (10.14), Du'aine Ladejo (45.09 400m), Jackson (13.08), Backley (85.20m) and the 4x400m team (2:59.13). Christie (9.91), Jackson (13.08) and Backley (82.74) emerged as winners also in the Commonwealth Games in Victoria, British Columbia, along with Denmark (13:23.00 5000m), Welshman Neil Winter (5.40m pole vault), Julian Golley (17.03m triple jump), Matt Simson (19.49m shot) and the England 4x400m squad (3:02.14).

1995 (Birmingham)

CONTROVERSIAL ACTIONS INVOLVING Linford Christie and Colin Jackson attracted most of the media attention at the KP National Championships, incorporating the AAA Championships and World Championships Trials. When Christie finished fourth in his heat in 10.93, easing off drastically after feeling tightness in a tendon behind his right knee, it was assumed that was the end of his involvement in the meeting. However, Christie felt he could benefit from another race that day and asked if he could run as a guest in the final as there was a spare lane. "As a gesture to him and the crowd" he was granted permission, although some fans booed when he appeared for the final. Although he finished first in 10.18 the title went to Darren Braithwaite in 10.33, having set a personal best of 10.12 in his semi-final. Dwain Chambers, then 17, made his senior AAA debut, finishing seventh in his semi in 10.57. Jackson, who tweaked a hamstring in his 100m heat, withdrew from the semis and a statement was made that he would not be competing for several days while he underwent treatment.

However, the very next day Jackson won a 110m hurdles race in Italy in 13.32! That led to a very public dispute between the athlete and BAF Executive Chairman Peter Radford, one of the consequences being that Jackson was unable to defend his world title in Gothenburg. Meanwhile, Tony Jarrett failed to capitalise on his great rival's absence from the AAA 110m hurdles as he had opted to go instead for the 200m where he placed fourth in 20.67 in a race won by John Regis in 20.37, having won his semi in a personal best of 20.50. Other top performances included a 44.94 400m by Mark Richardson, a 2.35m high jump by Steve Smith and a 17.13m triple jump by Francis Agyepong. Apart from a few successful Irish visitors these were the last Championships to feature overseas title winners with the Australians Rohan Robinson and Sean Carlin capturing the 400m hurdles and hammer respectively.

It was another triple jumper, Jonathan Edwards, who emerged that year as British athletics' brightest star. Having suffered the previous year from the Epstein Barr virus he approached the 1995 season with caution. He started promisingly, breaking Keith Connor's British record with 17.58m, and two weeks later in the European Cup in Lille he created a worldwide sensation with wind assisted clearances of 18.43m and 18.39m. Suddenly the world record of 17.97m by Willie Banks was within his sights, and in Salamanca he added a centimetre to that mark. But that was small beer to what he achieved at the World Championships. He opened with a resounding 18.16m and one round later improved to 18.29m, becoming in effect the Bob Beamon of his event. No one since has threatened that phenomenal world record, the nearest approach being 18.09m by Kenny Harrison (USA) in 1996.

There were two British silver medallists in Gothenburg: Jarrett (for the second time) with 13.04 in the hurdles and Steve Backley with 86.30m in the javelin. Earlier in the year Christie had become the first British sprinter since Peter Radford in 1960 (20.5 200m/220 yards) to set a world record when registering 20.25 for the indoor 200m, also clocking 6.47 for a European 60m record at the same meeting in Liévin.

1996 (Birmingham)

RESPONDING TO THE request of the British Olympic team selectors and the wishes of the athletes themselves, this edition of the Championships, sponsored by Securicor, was confined to athletes eligible to compete for Britain. Chris Carter, at the time Secretary of BAF's Track & Field Commission, remarked: "The response from spectators, coaches and athletes is that we must continue with this format. I think it was brilliant." BAF Council Chairman Ken Rickhuss said: "Everybody I've spoken to says it was the best AAA Championships they remember. It takes me back to the days at the White City." It was indeed a meeting to savour, with a capacity crowd of 15,000 present for the final day. Exciting competition was assured as the first two in each event were automatically chosen for the team for Atlanta subject to having achieved the required qualifying standard and only two of Britain's top Olympic hopes – Jonathan Edwards and Steve Backley – were unable to compete because of injury problems. They were selected subject to fitness ... and both went on to win medals in Atlanta.

In what was his farewell AAA Championships appearance, Linford Christie not only notched up a record eighth title in the 100m but his 10.04 was a championship record based on legal times (he had run a windy 9.91 in 1994). However, he failed by a whisker to complete the sprint double, leading into the straight in the 200m but being pipped on the line by John Regis, 20.54 for both. That was Regis's sixth victory in the event, one short of McDonald Bailey's record. Roger Black won a great 400m in a championship and British record of 44.39 – an improvement of 0.20 sec over his previous personal best, set fully ten years earlier. The place times were spectacular also as European indoor champion Du'aine Ladejo ran 44.66, Iwan Thomas 44.69

and Jamie Baulch finding 44.72 sufficing only for a relay spot. Despite pain in his knee, Colin Jackson equalled Tony Jarrett's championship record of 13.13 in the 110m hurdles for his seventh AAA title, and there was a new champion-ship and British record in the pole vault when Nick Buck-field cleared 5.71m at his final attempt. One of the most satisfying victories was that of Jon Ridgeon in the 400m hurdles in 49.16. His only previous senior AAA title was at 110m hurdles in 1987 when he was Jackson's arch-rival and in the meantime his career had been constantly inter-rupted by the necessity for four Achilles tendon operations.

Although no gold medals came Britain's way in Atlanta, the team performed commendably. Black fulfilled all his realistic ambitions by finishing second (44.41) to the all-conquering American, Michael Johnson, in the 400m to become the first British medallist in that event since Godfrey Brown 60 years earlier. Edwards triple jumped the excellent distance of 17.88m but had to settle for silver behind an inspired Kenny Harrison (USA) whose 18.09m remains to this day the closest anyone has got to Edwards' world record of 18.29m. Backley's opening javelin throw of 87.44m wasn't quite long enough to hold off Jan Zelezny, the Czech throwing 88.16m in the second round, and a fourth silver medal materialised in the 4x400m relay where the Anglo-Welsh combination of Thomas (44.92), Baulch (44.19), Mark Richardson (43.62; the fastest split of the race) and Black (43.87) ran their socks off to clock a European and Commonwealth record of 2:56.60 behind the Americans' 2:55.99.

Steve Smith high jumped 2.35m for a bronze, the first medal in this event by a British Isles representative since Irishman Con Leahy in 1908. However, there were disappointments in the 100m and 110m hurdles. Usually such a steady starter, Christie was thrown out of the 100m final for two breaks, as was Jarrett in his hurdles quarter-final. Jackson, who never approached his very best form that year due to injury and motivational problems, placed fourth in the final in 13.19, 2/100ths away from a bronze medal but well behind the 12.95 which won the race for Allen Johnson (USA).

1997 (Birmingham)

ALTHOUGH SEPARATE UK Championships were discontinued after 1993, there was again a parting of the ways as the BAF went ahead with their British Champ-ionships (incorporating the World Championship Trials) in Birmingham in July while the AAA of England staged their own Championships, sponsored by View From, in the same stadium six weeks later. Although there were over 800 entries few of Britain's leading athletes supported the meeting which came soon after the World Championships. In only one event – Francis Agyepong's 16.71m triple jump – was the winning mark superior to that at the BAF meeting. The British Championships had thrown up such noteworthy performances as a British 400m record of 44.36 by Iwan Thomas, a rare 110m hurdles victory by Tony Jarrett over Colin Jackson (13.33-13.39) and throws of 63.74m by Robert Weir and 86.20m by Steve Backley. Pick of the AAA winners were two sprinters who would achieve great distinction and long careers at the top in Jason Gardener (10.31 100m) and Marlon Devonish (20.65 200m), and Weir who collected his sixth discus title (61.60m). The towering figure of Carl Myerscough, a 17-year-old schoolboy who would succeed Geoff Capes as British shot put record holder with 21.92m six years later, opened his senior AAA account with second place at 16.99m.

On the international plane, the British men's team won the European Cup and four silver medals – or so we thought then – were gained at the World Championships in Athens through Jackson (13.05), Jonathan Edwards (17.69m), Backley (86.80m) and the 4x400m team (2:56.65), while the 4x100m team finished third. However, in 2008 a member of the winning USA 4x400m squad, Antonio Pettigrew (who died in 2010), admitted he was taking performance enhancing drugs at the time and the IAAF retrospectively disqualified the American team. Thus, belatedly, Iwan Thomas (44.8), Roger Black (44.2), Jamie Baulch (44.08) and Mark Richardson (43.57) were awarded the gold medals.

1998 (Birmingham)

WITH THE MEETING serving also as selection trials for the European Championships in Budapest and Commonwealth Games in Kuala Lumpur, the Bupa AAA Championships regained its status as a must for all of Britain's leading athletes and this was reflected in the standard of performance. The standout event once again was the 400m where Roger Black found his cracking time of 44.71 merited only fourth place! With just the first two home assured of selection for Budapest, the other place being awarded at the discretion of the selectors, a dramatic final was anticipated and the fans were not disappointed as Iwan Thomas, the British record holder with 44.36, prevailed in 44.50 ahead of Mark Richardson (44.62), while in the final desperate strides Black, despite running his finest race for two years, was passed by the astonishing if somewhat unpredictable Solomon Wariso (the 1994 200m champion), who improved his personal best from 45.70 in the previous day's semis to 44.68. Black, in his final season, had set his heart upon bidding for an unprecedented third European 400m title, but to his chagrin the selectors offered that third spot instead to Wariso. It was a shame that headwinds (1.7m in the 100m and 1.5m in the 200m) robbed the sprinters of some really spectacular times but as it was Darren Campbell (coached by Linford Christie) clocked 10.22 just 0.01 ahead of Dwain Chambers (who had the previous year set a world junior record of 10.06) and Scotsman Doug Walker took the longer race in 20.35. Of the more established stars, Colin Jackson took the hurdles in 13.37, inevitably pursued by Tony Jarrett (13.42), Dalton Grant the high jump with 2.20m, Jonathan Edwards the triple jump with 17.12m (with 19-year-old Phillips Idowu sixth with 15.90m) and Steve Backley the javelin with 84.78m. It was Jackson's eighth AAA title since 1986, matching Don Finlay's record haul between 1932 and 1949 ... and he was certainly not finished yet.

Having already retained the European Cup, the British men's team flew to Budapest in good heart and performed brilliantly. The UK athletics governing body may have been in a state of flux (BAF had gone into administration in October 1997) but the athletes were delivering. With eight gold medals and numerous top eight placings the GB team topped all the rankings in Budapest. Crowned European champion were Campbell (10.04), Walker (20.53, leading a clean sweep of the medals), Thomas (44.52), Jackson (13.02), Edwards (17.99m), Backley (89.72m) and both relay teams (38.52 and 2:58.68). Successful at the Commonwealth Games were England's Julian Golding (20.18 200m), Jarrett (13.47), Grant (2.31m), Larry Achike (17.10m triple jump), Robert Weir (64.42m discus) and the 4x100m team (38.20), while Thomas won the 400m (44.52) for Wales.

1999 (Birmingham)

AS FAR AS most people were concerned, 1999 was the last year of the 20th century and these CGU AAA Championships brought the millennium to a satisfactory close. Colin Jackson made history by winning a ninth 110m hurdles title, the most in any track event, and in the absence of Tony Jarrett he romped home by the massive margin of seven metres in a just-windy 13.24. Another prolific champion, Robert Weir, chalked up his seventh discus victory (61.35m) since 1983, although those with long memories might have recalled that his very first AAA title came in the hammer in 1982. Helped by assisting winds of just over the limit the sprinters posted quick times. Jason Gardener, who had recently become the second fastest ever European (after Linford Christie) with 9.98, ran 10.02

ahead of a slow-starting Dwain Chambers (10.07), and Julian Golding with a championship record of 20.20 beat Marlon Devonish (20.36). Jamie Baulch took the 400m in 45.36.

Steve Backley clicked into top form after a moderate start to the season with a throw of 87.59m, having earlier fouled an effort which landed in the region of 90m. John Mayock, the 1998 European indoor 3000m champion, won the fourth of his record number of six 1500m titles in 3:39.12, and there was a welcome return after injury for Steve Smith, high jump winner at 2.28m. At 19 the 2.09m (6ft 10in) tall Carl Myerscough apparently became one of the youngest ever throwing event champions, putting the shot 18.97m, but it transpired that he had failed a drugs test some weeks earlier and the title was later awarded instead to Mark Proctor. Chambers would also later serve a drugs-related suspension, as would Christie, who had emerged from retirement early in 1999 to run 6.57 for the indoor 60m and tested positive. The British governing body, UKA, cleared him but the IAAF imposed a two-year ban.

Jackson won everything going that year, for in Maebashi (Japan) he not only captured the World Indoor 60m hurdles title (at the fifth attempt) in 7.38 but went on to regain his world 110m hurdles crown in Seville in 13.04. Baulch also shone at the World Indoors, taking the 400m in 45.73 to become the first Briton to win a global 400m title since Eric Liddell at the 1924 Olympics, and he also contributed a dazzling 44.78 anchor leg to ensure the British 4x400m team took third place. There was bronze also for Gardener, whose 60m time of 6.46 was a European record. British revelation of the year was decathlete Dean Macey, who had been World Junior silver medallist in 1996 with a score of 7480 points. Due to injuries which would bedevil him throughout his career that had remained his best until he scored a sensational 8347 in May and then 8556 for the silver medal in Seville in August, performances which marked him out as easily Britain's second finest all-rounder behind Daley Thompson. The 4x100m team of Gardener, Darren Campbell, Devonish and Chambers clocked a European record of 37.73 for a close second to the Americans, while Chambers (9.97) and Jonathan Edwards (17.48m) collected bronze medals.

BRITISH RECORDS AT 1 JANUARY 2000
100m: 9.87 Linford Christie 1993; 200m: 19.94 John Regis 1993 (unratified 19.87 in 1994); 400m: 44.36 Iwan Thomas 1997; 800m: 1:41.73 Seb Coe 1981; 1000m: 2:12.18 Coe 1981; 1500m: 3:29.67 Steve Cram 1985; Mile: 3:46.32 Cram 1985; 2000m: 4:51.39 Cram 1985; 3000m: 7:32.79 Dave Moorcroft 1982; 2M: 8:13.51 Steve Ovett 1978; 5000m: 13:00.41 Moorcroft 1982; 10,000m: 27:18.14 Jon Brown 1998; Half Marathon: 60:59 Steve Jones 1986; Marathon: 2:07:13 S Jones 1985; 3000mSC: 8:07.96 Mark Rowland 1988; 110mH: 12.91 Colin Jackson 1993; 400mH: 47.82 Kriss Akabusi 1992; HJ: 2.37 Steve Smith 1992 & 1993 (2.38 indoors 1994); PV: 5.80 Nick Buckfield 1998; LJ: 8.23 Lynn Davies 1968; TJ: 18.29 Jonathan Edwards 1995; SP: 21.68 Geoff Capes 1980; DT: 66.64 Perriss Wilkins 1998; HT: 77.54 Martin Girvan 1984; JT: 91.46 Steve Backley 1992; Decathlon: 8847 Daley Thompson 1984; 3000m Walk: 11:24.4 Mark Easton 1989; 10,000m Walk: 40:06.65 Ian McCombie 1989; 20km Walk: 1:22:03 McCombie 1988; 50km Walk: 3:51:37 Chris Maddocks 1990.

THE TWENTY-FIRST CENTURY

THE FIRST DECADE or so of the new millennium proved to be a tumultuous period for the sport in this country, a roller coaster of a ride for all concerned. Happily, there were several truly memorable achievements by English athletes – notably Paula Radcliffe's phenomenal world marathon records, Kelly Holmes' Olympic double and other Olympic golds for Jonathan Edwards, the men's 4x100m relay team, Denise Lewis and Christine Ohuruogu – but there were unprecedented lows too. There was just one victory for the men at the 2006 European Championships, while only one bronze medal apiece (in the 4x100m relay) was obtained by the men's team at the 2005 and 2007 World Championships. However, there was a notable change of fortunes at the 2010 European Championships in Barcelona where British men accumulated no fewer than 15 medals, five of them gold – four by English athletes and one by a Welshman. British records in the men's events were scarce, the only new outdoor bests coming in the 5000m, long jump and shot. Back on the positive side the men's team won the European Cup in 2000 and 2008 but were almost relegated in 2005, while what was originally celebrated as a glorious victory in 2002 turned into a humiliating fourth place as points were deducted retrospectively when Dwain Chambers admitted he had taken performance enhancing drugs that year. The inaugural European Team Championships in 2010 saw the British team finish a commendable second to Russia.

There were several other doping cases for the authorities to investigate and act upon and one of them, involving Diane Modahl (who was eventually cleared and unsuccessfully sued the British Athletic Federation for a million pounds in lost earnings, legal and medical fees and punitive damages), proved so costly that it was a major factor in BAF's financial collapse. It was succeeded as the internationally recognised governing body for British athletics by United Kingdom Athletics (UKA), which in turn experienced its problems in a fast changing sport. The AAA of England survived, reverting to simply the AAA in 2007, but its status and functions were reduced as the entire UK athletics administration was restructured.

Another example of the ups and downs of the decade concerned the staging of the two greatest events in athletics: the Olympic Games and World Championships. UKA's Chief Executive Dave Moorcroft announced in January 2000 that, despite the disappointing news that athletics would not be accommodated within the new national stadium to be built at Wembley, a bid to hold the 2005 World Championships in London was being submitted to the IAAF. Great was the joy among the British athletics community when the IAAF Council unanimously agreed in April 2000 to award the prestigious meeting to London. A high powered presentation team, including Chris Smith representing the British Government, had convinced the IAAF that a 50,000 capacity stadium designed specifically for athletics would be built at Picketts Lock in the Lee Valley Regional Park.

Lamine Diack, the IAAF President, enthused: "This will be the first time in the history of the World Championships that an event is held in a venue designed only for our sport." It all seemed too good to be true ... and so it proved.

In October 2001 the whole ambitious scheme collapsed ignominiously when Tony Blair's Government reneged on its promise to finance the building of the stadium at a cost to the taxpayer of some £110 million. Richard Caborn, the Minister for Sport, explained: "We could not justify spending that money on a stadium. The decision we took was for the good of sports in this country."

Embarrassed by its *volte-face*, the Government promised to compensate the sport by providing £41 million over five years to UK Athletics, although there were long delays before most of it was advanced and the strings attached were to force major changes to the way athletics was run. At the time of the announcement, in May 2002, a delighted Dave Moorcroft declared: "The £41 million funding package represents the most significant financial investment the sport has ever received. Athletics now has a huge opportunity to realise its aspirations and to move forward to achieve its full potential in the coming years." Of the sum involved, £5 million was earmarked for track refurbishment throughout the UK, £5 million for high performance centres in London, £11 million for an indoor facility at Picketts Lock, and £20 million for grassroots projects outlined in UKA's On Track document. This plan, signed by AAA of England Chairman David Cropper as well as by Moorcroft and representatives of the Scottish, Welsh and Northern Irish governing bodies, would focus on helping clubs, competition structure, coaching, schools development, school and club links, event-specific groups and better medical support, and efforts were made to discover from the clubs and other parties how best the money could be spent..

In view of the Picketts Lock fiasco, which was very damaging to the international standing of British athletics, it would have been reasonable to assume that it would be a long time before another major sporting occasion would be entrusted to this country, but in July 2005 – this time with the full backing of Tony Blair and his Government – London unexpectedly pipped Paris for the honour of staging the 2012 Olympic Games. Much of the credit for the International Olympic Committee's decision went to Lord (Sebastian) Coe. Twice winner of the 1500m gold medal, he achieved another Olympic triumph of legendary proportions by successfully leading London's bid. Thanks to his personal prestige, tireless lobbying and an inspirational final presentation, London beat Paris 54-50 in the final round of voting. Lamine Diack, who took part in the ballot, stated: "The IAAF is pleased that London will host these Games in 2012 because Great Britain has always been a great country for sport and particularly our sport of athletics. I was impressed by the plans to develop sporting facilities over the next years, and I would like to underline the fact that Britain will now have a permanent, state of the art stadium for athletics, and this is something we are very pleased about." The bid promised that the 80,000-seat Olympic stadium in East London would be converted after the Games to a 25,000-seat multi-purpose venue to be used mainly for athletics. In fact, negotiations continued as to the precise capacity and functions of the stadium following the Games but the retention of the running track is guaranteed and a bid has been made to stage the 2017 edition of the IAAF World Championships there. The legacy for the sport of such a stadium will be incalculable and at last British athletics would have its own home.

Here, year by year, is a summary of the most significant developments affecting UK and English athletics during the decade.

2000

SIR ARTHUR GOLD stepped down as AAA of England President due to ill health, to be succeeded by Seb Coe – the third Olympic champion (after Lord Burghley and Harold Abrahams) to hold that office. He had been created a peer earlier in the year. Ten AAA Regional Development Co-ordinators were appointed, the areas covered being the South West, South, South East, London, East, East

Midlands, West Midlands, North West, Yorkshire and North East. Funded through a partnership including the AAA, the three Area Athletic Associations and Sport England, the appointees' role was to co-ordinate the activities of professional staff and voluntary officers to implement the AAA's Development Plan, working closely with clubs, county and area associations and local authorities.

The death occurred of former British Olympic and English team manager Cecil Dale.

2001

DIANE MODAHL, THE 1990 Commonwealth Games 800m champion, lost her High Court action against BAF. The World Class Potential Plan, designed to help up to 140 particularly promising English athletes and funded to the tune of £2 million per year for four years by the Sport England Lottery Fund, was announced. It was formulated by the UKA Performance department under its Director Max Jones at the request of the AAA of England and Sport England. Lottery funding of athletes, which began in 1997 under a plan drawn up by the then BAF Director of Coaching Malcolm Arnold, continued to be of benefit to all of Britain's top athletes and for 2001-2002 a total of 86 athletes received support. In September the sport's biggest ever sponsorship deal was revealed: £20 million to UKA over five years from Norwich Union (formerly CGU). Apart from title sponsorship of several major meetings, including the AAA Championships, around 20% of the money would be ploughed into grassroots schemes like Sports Hall Athletics.

Deaths during the year included 1936 Olympic 4x400m relay gold medallist Bill Roberts, former AAA National Coach Bill Marlow, and Ron Goodman, AAA President from 1984 to 1986.

2002

AS REFERRED TO earlier, the big news of the year was the £41 million compensation over five years to be channelled through UKA, and another boost was the announcement that the Government would contribute £14.1 million to help elite competitors across all the Olympic sports prepare for the Games in Athens in 2004. It was a good year in the stadium with the Commonwealth Games in Manchester (with considerable input by AAA of England officials) voted a huge success. With David Hemery having completed his two four-year terms, he was succeeded as President of UKA by another iconic figure in fellow Olympic champion Lynn Davies.

Death claimed one of the most influential men in British and European athletics, former AAA President Sir Arthur Gold; former National Coach Lionel Pugh; ex-BAF Chairman Ken Rickhuss; and 1960 Olympic 4x100m relay bronze medallist and later British Olympic team manager Nick Whitehead.

2003

A TOTAL OF £5 million was released to pay for local track refurbishment but the rest of the £41 million of Government funding, to be distributed by Sport England, was held back due to a fundamental disagreement between the AAA of England and UKA over the latter's modernisation plan. Sport England insisted in September that differences within the sport had to be resolved by April 2004 before the money could be handed over. The body's Chief Executive, Roger Draper, warned: "Athletics has got to start singing with one voice – and the clock's ticking. The money's there but we're getting frustrated. We want one plan and one cheque we can give to UKA that we know will be spent wisely." However, the AAA Management Board rejected the basic premise of the plan: that England scraps the traditional three area associations (South, Midlands and North), to be replaced by nine regional hubs. David Cropper remained hopeful. "We've got to keep talking. There is a solution that can meet most people's needs and the sport's needs. This is an opportunity we won't get again."

As the AAA of England and UKA were unable to come to an agreement on the best way forward, at year's end Sport England and UK Sport announced an independent review, led by Sir Andrew Foster, former controller of the Audit Commission, to scrutinise the athletics set-up and determine by April 2004 whether the sport was structured to provide good value for the lottery funding involved. As Sport England Chairman Patrick Carter commented: "Sport England has recently announced a rationalisation of the way it funds sports' governing bodies and we expect them all to be accountable for delivering results in return for the public funds they receive. We expect to see results in athletics, both in driving up participation levels and in success at the highest level." Sir Andrew said: "We will be asking probing questions because we must come up with real solutions and we will not duck the tough issues."

The sport mourned the death of one of the major figures in British athletics history: Chris Brasher, the 1956 Olympic steeplechase champion, prize winning journalist and broadcaster, and founder of the London Marathon.

2004

DAVID CROPPER, THE AAA 800m champion of 1969, decided to step down as AAA of England Chairman, a post he had filled since 1991, and was succeeded by George Bunner, AAA Junior half mile champion of 1950. Cropper explained: "It is not good for an individual at an association to stay too long. It's time to move on and give someone else a chance." Another major development was that Seb Coe did not stand for re-election as AAAoE President, that position being filled by Sir Rodney Walker, a former Chairman of UK Sport, while Walter Nicholls, a former Chairman of the North of England AA, was elected Hon. Secretary.

When the composition of the Foster Working Group was announced, George Bunner was included as the only representative of the AAAoE and the three Territories. That was clearly unacceptable and Sir Andrew agreed that each of the Territories be represented: by Geoff Durbin (Midlands), Chris Carter (South) and Walter Nicholls (North).

The Foster Report, published in May, called for a complete re-organisation of the structure of athletics, including the formation of English (later changed to England) Athletics. Government "legacy" money totalling £21 million would be dependent on acceptance of the 33 key recommendations. The Report urged: "English regions to be managed by a new body – English Athletics – with operational responsibility for delivering all aspects of athletics in England except the management of elite athletes and anti-doping work. The balance between its streamlined central office and the nine regions [hubs] should be its defining feature, with everything possible devolved to regional level." The Report added: "AAA of England and three English Territories to take full part in design of new organisation, which would assume full responsibility for delivering athletics in England's nine regions. Current talent and skills within AAA of England and Territories – both paid and voluntary – must not be lost." Dave Moorcroft, for UKA, said: "We will accept it. We are really glad that he said it was not a sport in crisis, but a sport at a crossroads. We now have a way forward." George Bunner, in the invidious position of chairing an organisation about to lose much of its power and influence, said: "We all want to work together. There will be difficulties, but healthy debate can bring things forward."

At its first meeting following circulation of the Report, the AAAoE's Management Board agreed with 28 of the 33 recommendations and sought clarification with regard to the other five. Later in May the AAAoE agreed with 31 of the points and following a meeting between themselves and UKA it was agreed to send a letter to all of England's club secretaries pointing out that there was broad agreement with the Foster recommendations. The letter read: "The (AAAoE) Management have agreed unanimously to welcome and to accept the broad proposals outlined in the Report. We are pleased to see that there will be a strong and defining role for England and we all look forward to being part of the team that re-structures the sport in England. We will at all stages consult and advise our member clubs of any major changes that are likely to be made. We hope that you will all join and support England as we re-shape our future." Jack Buckner, the 1986 European 5000m champion, was appointed in August by Sir Andrew Foster (Chairman of UK Sport's Athletics Project Board) as Project Director charged with managing the Board's work over the next 18 months to help achieve the objectives outlined in the Foster Report by working closely with all the key parties involved.

In November it was announced that Buckner had appointed Peter Radcliffe, Paula's father, to act as Chairman of an interim body, England Athletics 2005, set up to oversee the establishment of England Athletics and its key appointments. Sir Andrew said: "Real progress is now being made in our reform of athletics, with the key recommendation of a new England Athletics well underway." Bunner's reaction was: "There is no question of this being imposed on us. We've got to modernise and will be working hard to co-operate in the interests of athletics in England."

A statement issued in December and signed by Sir Andrew Foster, Dave Moorcroft, George Bunner, Peter Radcliffe and Jack Buckner had this to say about the future of the AAAoE: "It has been agreed that many of the current functions of AAAoE will pass to England Athletics after the Commonwealth Games in April 2006. However, the future of the organisation remains in the hands of its members: the clubs in England. They may choose to wind up the company after the handover, but this will be their decision. In the 18 months leading up to the handover, AAAoE's role will continue as now. This is particularly important with a Commonwealth Games approaching, and the aim will be to minimise disruption for athletes and their support team at this important time. The heritage of the AAAoE is an important aspect of the sport's history. It is premature to assume the AAA Championships will not have a role in the sport's competition structure. Equally importantly, the experience and knowledge of individuals in AAAoE and the Territories must be retained as far as possible in the new England Athletics."

The situation was that under the Foster recommendations the AAAoE was about to lose all former authority and funding and was left with little choice but to take a seat at the discussions in order to exert some influence on the proposals for the implementation of the Report. The alternative was for the AAAoE to stand aside and end up in the wilderness with no longer any meaningful role in the sport.

Those who passed away that year included legendary marathoner Jack Holden (days before his 97th birthday), long-time AAA Championships Secretary Roy Tilling (the AAA Junior indoor 1500m champion in 1970), former Welsh National Coach and 1938 Empire Games mile champion Jim Alford, and Derek Johnson, the 1956 Olympic 800m silver medallist who became a prominent campaigner in the International Athletes' Club and South of England AAA before serving for two years as Hon. Secretary of the AAAoE.

2005

JACK BUCKNER ORGANISED a series of public con-sultation meetings all over England to enable athletes, coaches and club officials to question himself and others involved in implementing the Foster Report. As a result of these discussions and concerns by the AAAoE some of the original recommendations were modified. One of the main recommendations was that the territories be retained. A further step towards taking on board the views of the clubs was the organising in September of a poll of all 1492 clubs in the UK, asking four questions alongside explanatory text. (1) Local Delivery: Does your club support these proposals for the decentralisation of athletics delivery? (2) Governance & Accountability: Does your club support the proposed accountability plans for athletics in the UK? (3) Finance: Does your club support the proposed financial direction for athletics in the UK? (4) Membership & Data: Does you club support implementing the membership scheme as presented here? Of the 465 clubs who participated, 58.6% to 34.6% (6.8% no view) were in favour of the Local Delivery plan, 55.6% to 35.8% (8.5% no view) voted for Governance & Accountability, and the Finance plan was approved by 50.3% to 40.5% (9.2% no view). However, there was a vote against Membership & Data by 53.6% to 41.4% (5.0% no view).

Meanwhile, at an Extraordinary General Meeting of the AAAoE in late October it was decided to return at some time in the future to the historically important name of AAA (that happened when a new constitution was adopted in 2007) and preserve the Association's assets and rights to the AAA Championships. Sir Rodney Walker, the President, proclaimed: "I would like to tell the world that the AAA has voted to retain its identity and to engage constructively with the new management of athletics in England. If you are seen not to engage in the new structure you will render yourselves irrelevant." In November former sprinter Dr Alan Harrison was named as England Athletics' first Chief Executive, but that there was still significant resistance among the clubs for change could be gauged from the vote at an Emergency General Meeting in December when the proposal "The AAA of England agrees that all governance of Athletics in England will be transferred to a new body, England Athletics Ltd" received 378 votes in favour and 301 against. That was a percentage vote of 55.2% in favour but 75% was needed for the motion to succeed.

The deaths occurred of former Principal National Coach and AAA long and triple jump champion Denis

Watts; England's 1938 Empire Games team captain Sandy Duncan, who was Secretary General of the British Olympic Association from 1948 to 1974; and Roy Mitchell, Hon. Secretary of the AAAoE between 1993 and 2000.

2006

ENGLAND ATHLETICS CAME into being on April 1, replacing the AAAoE as the country's governing body to which all 1230 clubs became automatically affiliated. It had earlier been announced by Sport England that in addition to the £21 million of Government funding that had already been granted for capital projects, mainly indoor facilities and track refurbishment, £13.3 million would be forwarded to UKA over three years to support its business plan and an additional £1,345,000 would go to England Athletics. Sport England released the money after it was satisfied that the sport had moved towards the modernisation recommended in the Foster Report. Dr Alan Harrison, England Athletics' Chief Executive, welcomed the cash injection. "This funding gives an essential boost to our ability to increase athlete participation and success for 2012. It is key to increasing the profile of athletics in England and will enable investment in the training of coaches and officials from the volunteer community, opening up capacity for greater participation of athletes at grassroots level through the clubs."

At the AGM of the AAAoE it was resolved by an overwhelming majority that the Association should "modernise its Memorandum and Articles of Association and put in place a management structure which would take recognition of the organisational changes to the sport of athletics in England which would become effective from 1 April 2006." Strong evidence of the support of the Association's policies in the face of considerable criticism was reflected in George Bunner gaining 71% of the vote as he was re-elected AAAoE Chairman for the next year by beating off a challenge from former international steeplechaser John Bicourt._He said he was gratified that the new England body would be totally in charge of its own affairs, and added: "The AAA will still have a task, certainly for the next few years. Its new role will not be governing but using its finance, expertise and influence to strongly support the lifeblood of the sport, its competitions and its representative teams in all disciplines."

In addition to the Sport England legacy payment, UK Athletics received another massive financial boost with the announcement that Norwich Union (now Aviva) had agreed to sponsorship over six years from 1 January 2007 worth £50 million, making UKA the wealthiest national governing body in the world. In addition to support packages for elite athletes and the title sponsorship of several major televised meetings, the company would be investing in grassroots and schools athletics. The good news didn't end there, for UK Sport allocated £6.6 million for athletics in the 2006-07 financial year, £6.8 million in 2007-08 and £6.9 million in 2008-09. The level of support from then until the 2012 London Olympics would be dependent on results at the Beijing Olympics in 2008. British athletes considered to be of Olympic medal potential could receive lottery funding of £23,930 per year, possibly the highest figure anywhere in the world.

The AAA Championships, inaugurated in 1880 and acknowledged as one of the world's most prestigious meetings, came to an end in Manchester with July's 117th edition. At first UKA declined to include AAA in the title of the meeting, designated the Norwich Union European Trials, but eventually, after a concerted campaign by the AAAoE, agreement was reached with UKA, England Athletics and Fast Track and the event was labelled the Norwich Union European Trials Incorporating the UK Championships and AAA of England Championships. However, the vast majority of athletes referred to it, as they always had, as the AAA Championships. That was the name they had grown up with and had affection for. Walter Nicholls, Hon. Secretary of the AAAoE, said: "We believe the history and tradition of this Association should not be forgotten and can best be preserved by the continuance of championships in its name." UKA and Fast Track deemed otherwise and subsequently the "Trials" from 2007 onwards have included only UK Championships or National Championships in their title. Under a previous agreement the AAAoE was entitled to a considerable income from the Championships, including the "gate money", whereas re-titling the Championships has enabled UKA, supported by Fast Track, to retain all revenue.

In August came the unexpected news that Dave Moorcroft had resigned as Chief Executive of UKA. He explained: "Athletics now has the system, funding, facilities and most importantly the people in place to take the sport into the next phase of its development. I have been Chief Executive for nine challenging and rewarding years and I have decided it is the right time to let someone new take the helm and lead the sport through to 2012." He left office early in 2007.

During the year Sport England ceased to fund the Development Plan and its professional staff, who were then later employed by England Athletics.

Deaths this year included Arthur McAllister, who was variously Chairman and President of the AAA , Chairman of the BAAB and President of BAF; former National Coach and twice AAA pole vault champion Ian Ward; 1960 Olympic 50km walk champion Don Thompson; 3 miles world record breaker Freddie Green; 1948 Olympic 4x100m relay silver medallist and Welsh rugby legend Ken Jones; and Sydney Wooderson (at age 92), a world record breaker at 800m, 880 yards and the mile who was one of the most beloved as well as most distinguished of all British athletes.

2007

TWO MEN WITH little experience of athletics administration but well versed in financial affairs were appointed to the two key posts at UKA. Ed Warner, a recreational runner

(3:19 marathon) with the Fittleworth Flyers in Sussex, a businessman and financial journalist, became the inaugural part-time Chairman.

"My job," he explained when his appointment was announced in January, "is to ensure the sport is properly governed, that the strategy agreed by key stake-holders is implemented and that I can act as a lightning rod in good times and bad." One of his first tasks was to help find a Chief Executive to replace the departed Dave Moorcroft, and that proved to be Niels de Vos, a 1:57.2 800m runner who was Commercial Director of the Manchester Commonwealth Games in 2002 and currently Chief Executive of the Sale Sharks rugby union club. "Athletics was my sport as a youngster," he said, "and has been my lifelong passion."

With England Athletics having taken over most of its traditional functions, many people assumed the AAA of England would disappear but that body felt it still had much to offer the sport and at the start of the year the AAAoE announced a series of initiatives. As George Bunner stressed: "The AAA want to be supportive of the sport going forward and want to be of benefit to the athletes." This they would do in several ways, not least in the establishment of the "AAA Tom Pink Memorial Relays & AAA Field Events Challenge For Young People". The late Alice and Lewis Pink, parents of Tom Pink, a Mitcham AC middle distance runner who died at 18 in a road accident in 1971, left a substantial bequest to the Association in acknowledgement and appreciation of the positive influence which athletics had on the life of their son. The AAAoE made use of that funding to organise a series of "fun" relays for kids aged under 11 and under 13. The Tom Pink Relays moved around the country and in 2010, for example, were staged in Birmingham's National Indoor Arena with hundreds of boys and girls from the Midlands, plus a team from Madrid, enjoying themselves immensely as well as developing a love of competition as they participated in such events as "Chasing Kelly" (a continuous relay for a team of five girls attempting to cover

1500m in a time faster than Kelly Holmes' UK record of 3:57.90) and "Chasing Steve" (a similar event for boys with Steve Cram's UK record of 3:29.67 the target).

Field events included standing long jump and triple jump, weight for height and distance, and throwing a soft javelin. The programme has proved another huge success for its mastermind, George Bunner, the man who created Sportshall Athletics in 1976. Sportshall Athletics, which has developed over the years to cater for youngsters aged 4 to 16, has introduced countless thousands of children to the joys of athletics and now forms a key part of the Aviva UKA Academy, launched in 2009 with the objective of giving every child in the country the opportunity to get involved in athletics by 2012.

Although he would continue to play an important role in the Association's affairs, 75-year-old Bunner stepped down as Chairman at the AGM in March, to be succeeded by Graham Jessop who paid this tribute: "George has provided statesmanlike leadership for the Association during a period of major change. The commitment, enthusiasm, vision and energy which George brought to the sport has been second to none and the Association can now move forward with confidence in its new role." In accordance with the resolution passed at the 2006 AGM, a new amended constitution was presented to the meeting. With the support of 86% of the clubs who voted this was passed, together with a change of name back to the plain old and familiar AAA. It was also agreed that the AAA's functions should include the holding of athletics competitions; supporting and co-operating with other athletics bodies; maintaining a dialogue with the Territorial Associations, regional bodies and clubs; promoting the traditions of the AAA; ensuring proper use of AAA trophies; retaining the long established AAA standards scheme; and looking after the interests of the sport's voluntary sector. In other words, there was still much good and useful work to be done even if the AAA's powers of old had gone. Over at England Athletics, Chief Executive Dr Alan Harrison announced that he wished to leave. The post was advertised, seeking a candidate who "will inspire, motivate and develop enthusiastic teams of staff and volunteers to deliver results locally and nationally for all age groups and athletics disciplines".

Sir Arthur Marshall, the oldest of all AAA champions (a member of the winning Achilles Club team in the 1925 mile medley relay) and who was a reserve for the 1924 Olympic 4x400m, died at 103. The ever controversial Andy Norman, once the most powerful figure in British athletics, made it only to 64.

2008

EARLY IN THE year the post of England Athletics Chief Executive was filled by Mike Summers, Project Manager for UKA's Road Running Leadership Group and an international marketing director. John Graves, Chairman of England Athletics, told *Athletics Weekly*: "He has learned the sport very quickly, he's got business skills, marketing skills which we desperately need, and he is also very committed and passionate." Explaining the different spheres of influence between UKA and England Athletics, Summers stated: "UKA is responsible for the development of UK-wide policy, promotion and financing alongside elite athlete funding and GB teams. England Athletics (as with Wales, Scotland and Northern Ireland) is charged with implementing the strategy at a local and regional level, leading the sport in our cities, schools, clubs and communities across the country." Among the priorities were establishing a registration system for England's 110,000 members of the 1270 affiliated clubs and building a nationwide network of highly motivated coaches at all levels.

Aware of the sport's rich heritage, England Athletics inaugurated the England Athletics Hall of Fame. An independent panel of experts, chaired by Olympic relay gold medallist Darren Campbell, drew up a short list of 11 all-time greats with the public invited to vote for five, and the first inductees (six as there was a tie for fifth place) were, in alphabetical order, Roger Bannister, Seb Coe, Sally Gunnell, David Hemery, Steve Ovett and Daley Thompson. The panel also inducted three personalities for their very special contribution to the sport: Geoff Dyson (Chief National Coach 1947-61), Chris Brasher (Olympic gold medallist and founder of the London Marathon) and David Coleman (BBC television's voice of athletics for so many years). David Holding was included for his achievements as a wheelchair racer.

There was splendid news for England Athletics, in the throes of restructuring its organisation, at the end of the year. Its application for Sport England funding was successful and £20.4 million was awarded for the period 2009-2013 subject to performance monitoring criteria.

In September UKA announced that Charles van Commenee had been appointed to the newly created role of Head Coach, taking up his duties full-time in January 2009. The Dutchman, with 27 years of experience including coaching Denise Lewis to the Olympic heptathlon gold medal in 2000, would oversee the UK Sport funded World Class Performance Programme. "There is genuine talent here in the UK, and my challenge is to ensure that potential translates to medal success."

Meanwhile, the AAA continued with its work, one of its initiatives being the setting up of a charity, Athletics for the Young, to award grants to athletes under 23 who are in full time education or equivalent and not receiving other funding. Close to 200 athletes benefited in 2009.

Two distinguished coaches died during the year, both aged 88: Allan Malcolm, who in 1948 was appointed one of the first AAA National Coaches, and Peter Coe, who guided his son Seb to the highest of honours.

2009

CHRIS CARTER, THE former British record holder for 800m and 880 yards who took over from Graham Jessop as

AAA Chairman at its AGM in March, issued this statement in July to explain the functions and challenges of the AAA these days.

"Since the formation of the AAA in 1880 athletics worldwide has gone through numerous changes in all aspects of communication, organisation, specification, coaching and attitudes. The AAA underwent a fundamental change only three years ago when it ceased to be the governing body for the sport in England after more than 125 years. There were many outside reasons for this change but not least was that all outside sources of funding were withdrawn which meant the Association was unable to continue in the same way. However painful the loss of governing body status was, the Association has remained positive and is committed to ensure the Association's influence and finances are used as effectively as possible to support the clubs and athletes in England.

"Although the demise of the Association has been greatly exaggerated in some quarters of the sport, the Association is determined to play its part within athletics in the years up to and beyond the 2012 London Olympics, arguably the greatest sporting festival in the country since 1948. Our contribution to developing initiatives for younger athletes, illustrated by the successful Tom Pink Relay programme, is specifically designed to meet the important objective of stimulating and encouraging interest in athletics. It also serves to keep our younger athletes in the sport longer, thus ensuring many will stay to ensure a thriving and successful sport at the highest level.

"Our commitment to the upper levels of the sport is demonstrated by the support given to Northern Athletics in their senior development initiative being held in conjunction with an outdoor Tom Pink Relays meeting. This style of initiative will continue with support for other competition providers giving the opportunity to introduce innovative competition. In our discussions with England Athletics we hope to re-establish an England Track & Field Championship under the title of the internationally well respected AAA Championship, the oldest national championship in the world.

"The transitional period is now over and the Amateur Athletic Association is committed to going forward in partnerships with other like-minded athletic bodies for the common good of athletics in England."

The second wave of England Athletics Hall of Fame inductees comprised Steve Backley, Steve Cram, Jonathan Edwards, Ann Packer, Mary Rand, Dorothy Tyler, Alf Shrubb and Sydney Wooderson, with Harold Abrahams and Lord Burghley (both Olympic gold medallists and holder of numerous leading posts as administrators) together with coach Malcolm Arnold and coach/TV commentator Ron Pickering nominated for special services to the sport. Visually impaired Paralympian Noel Thatcher was also inducted.

Godfrey Rampling, one of the heroes of the victorious 1936 Olympic 4x400m relay team, died soon after celebrating his 100th birthday. The death occurred also of Fred Holder (95), who served as Hon. Secretary and/or Treasurer of the IAAF between 1970 and 1984.

2010

ALTHOUGH THE AAA was not included in the meeting's title, this season saw the creation of the England Athletics Senior Championships – the first such meeting since English Championships, open only to athletes born in England and Wales, were staged from 1923 to 1925. There was a link with the AAA, though, as some of the title winners were presented with historic AAA trophies. As Andy Day, England Athletics' head of competition, said: "As well as the history of our sport we also want to build for the future and we hope that some of the athletes winning titles in Gateshead will go on to emulate the feats of some of the icons of our sport who have won these trophies in the past. When you look at some of the names on these trophies it shows how many truly great national champions we have had over a wide range of events."

Third-year inductees into the England Athletics Hall of Fame were Kelly Holmes, Brendan Foster, Linford Christie, Walter George and Albert Hill, with former Chief National Coaches John Le Masurier and Denis Watts and *Athletics Weekly* founder/editor Jimmy Green nominated for special services to the sport.

Deaths during the year included former National Coach Wilf Paish, who trained Tessa Sanderson among others; Albert Webster, a member of a world record 4 x 880 yards relay team in 1951; Doug Wilson, the 1946 AAA mile champion; Tony Ward, co-founder of the National Athletics League; and Chris Goudge, AAA 440y hurdles champion in 1959. Former UK high hurdles record holder Peter Hildreth died in February 2011.

Highlights from each of the AAA or UK Championships meetings 2000-2010

2000 (Birmingham)

DARREN CAMPBELL CAME tantalisingly close to joining McDonald Bailey and Linford Christie as the only Britons since Frederick Reid back in 1932 to complete a AAA sprint double. Competing in what was styled the Norwich Union Olympic Trials & AAA Championships, Campbell closed at the end to finish just 1/100th of a second behind Dwain Chambers over 100m, 10.11-10.12, before upsetting the 200m specialists the following day with a 20.49 victory. Both races were run into the wind. Mark Lewis-Francis, at the time the world's fastest ever 17-year-old with a sensational 10.10 clocking the previous week, finished third in 10.24 but told the selectors that he did not wish to be considered for the Olympic team as his goal was the World Junior title, which he duly won by a big margin in 10.12. John Mayock equalled Sydney Wooderson's record of five 1500m/mile titles (1935-39) with a modest time of 3:45.29 but he rated as merely a beginner compared to Colin Jackson with AAA 110m hurdles title no 10 in 13.54 against a strong wind (with Tony Jarrett second for a seventh time) and Robert Weir with his eighth discus title (62.13m) 17 years after his first.

Responding immediately to Nick Nieland's lifetime javelin best of 85.09m, Steve Backley provided one of the meeting's highlights with a throw of 86.70m. Phillips Idowu, his hair dyed purple on this occasion, took advantage of Jonathan Edwards' absence to notch up his first AAA triple jump title (16.87m), while Chris Rawlinson took the 400m hurdles in 48.95. Who would have realised it, but buried deep in the results was a future star in Andy Baddeley; aged 18, he placed 13th of 14 runners in his 1500m heat in 3:54.15. Six years later he would win the title and in 2008 he would become the sixth Briton to crack 3:50 for the mile.

It was altogether an eventful year on the track. Jason Gardener (6.49 60m) and Welshman Christian Malcolm (20.54 200m) struck gold at the European Indoor Championships, while despite the absence of eight first choice representatives the British men's team beat Germany by half a point to carry off the European Cup at Gateshead with individual victories by Campbell (10.09w), Malcolm (20.45), Jamie Baulch (46.64 400m), Rawlinson (48.84), Larry Achike (windy 17.31m triple jump) and the 4x100m relay team (38.41). Britain's two gold medals at the Sydney Olympics came from Edwards in the triple jump (17.71m), with Achike and Idowu also in the top six, and the women's heptathlon courtesy of Denise Lewis, while Campbell (20.14) and Backley (89.85m) came up with brilliant performances to earn silver medals behind the controversial Konstadinos Kedéris (20.09) and the incomparable Jan Zelezny (90.17m). But for a debatable judging decision in the discus favouring the eventual winner, Erki Nool, Dean Macey (8567) would have finished third instead of fourth in the decathlon; and that – the most frustrating of places – was the fate also of Chambers in the 100m, and Jon Brown, the 1993 AAA 5000m champion, in the marathon.

2001 (Birmingham)

DWAIN CHAMBERS EMPHASISED his high level consistency when clocking 10.01 in cool conditions to retain his 100m title. following marks of 10.01 in Seville and 10.00 in Lausanne. He was chased home by Mark Lewis-Francis in 10.12. Although the now suspended but retired anyway Linford Christie is credited with the championship record of 9.91 in 1994 that was a wind-assisted time and his fastest ever legal time on a British track was 10.04 in the 1996 Championships. Next day Chambers set a personal best of 20.65 behind Marlon Devonish (20.52) and Christian Malcolm (20.63) in the 200m which was not contested by Olympic silver medallist Darren Campbell who, hampered by a leg injury, had wound up sixth in the 100m. Despite having been down with flu days earlier, Jonathan Edwards put his younger challengers in their place in decisive fashion. After running through on his first attempt he produced a championship record of 17.59m in round two and called it a day. His winning margin over Larry Achike was fully 60cm with defending champion Phillips Idowu third on 16.88m.

John Mayock (3:44.05) won his sixth 1500m title, a record; Tony Jarrett (13.66) finally became 110m hurdles champion, 13 years after the first of his numerous second places; and Chris Rawlinson only narrowly missed Ed Moses' 1979 championship record in the 400m hurdles with 48.68. There was quite an age range on view: Lloyd Finch (17) won the inaugural 5000m walk title in 20:47.23, whereas Chris Black – champion in 1976, 1977 and 1983 and now competing with an artificial hip – finished eighth in the hammer at 51.

Daniel Caines' 400m victory in 45.75 at the AAA Indoor Championships in Birmingham made him favourite for the World Indoor title in Lisbon, which he duly won in 46.40. Malcolm (20.76) and Edwards (17.26m) picked up silver medals and Lewis-Francis, who would win the European Junior 100m in 10.09w later in the year, was third in the 60m (6.51). The outdoor World Championships in Edmonton, Canada, proved a disappointment for the British team. Edwards performed brilliantly by winning with 17.92m, but the only other medallist was Dean Macey whose 8603 decathlon score earned him the bronze.

2002 (Birmingham)

MOST OF THE excitement in the men's events at the Norwich Union European Trials & AAA Championships was generated in the sprints where several leading contenders for European Championships selection (first two in each event automatically won their places for Munich subject to having achieved UKA's standards) took advantage of the warm weather and favourable winds to clock quick times. Dwain Chambers elected to miss the 100m, assuming he would be given the discretionary third selection spot, in order to bid for a 200m place, but his plans went awry when he was left completely at the start of the final and took no meaningful part in a race won by Marlon Devonish in a just windy championship record of 20.18 ahead of Darren Campbell (20.26) and Christian Malcolm (20.29). The previous day Campbell, the reigning European champion, had won selection for the 100m when his 10.11 gained him second place just ahead of Jason Gardener (10.13) with Mark Lewis-Francis – despite encountering a left hamstring problem two strides from the finish – an outstanding winner in 10.06.

Another defending European champion, Colin Jackson, collected his final AAA outdoor title (a record 11th) in 13.40 with – you guessed it – Tony Jarrett (13.52) the runner-up. European Junior champion Tim Benjamin won the 400m in 45.73 and Chris Rawlinson was pushed to a good time (48.68) in the 400m hurdles by Anthony Borsumato's personal best of 48.90. Pick of the field event winners was Phillips Idowu with 17.02m in the triple jump while Robert Weir, now aged 41, collected a record ninth discus title (58.22m). Nick Buckfield, who had raised the British indoor pole vault record to 5.81m in February, had been hampered since by Achilles tendon problems and found 5.35m sufficed for victory, while Chris Tomlinson – who had succeeded Lynn Davies as British long jump record holder with 8.27m in April – was beaten by Darren Ritchie, 7.93m (a Scottish record) to 7.82m.

The year had got off to a promising start when ever reliable Gardener (6.49) and Jackson (7.40) won European Indoor titles over 60m, flat and hurdles, and there was jubilation when the British men regained the European Cup with wins by Chambers (10.04), Devonish (20.27), Daniel Caines (45.14 400m), Jackson (13.15), Tomlinson (8.17m), Jonathan Edwards (17.19m) and both relay teams (38.65 and 3:00.57). The hugely successful Commonwealth Games in Manchester, the first time they had been staged in England since 1934, yielded gold medals for Michael East (3:37.35 1500m), Rawlinson (49.14), Nathan Morgan (8.02m long jump), Edwards (17.86m with Idowu excelling himself with 17.68m for silver), Mick Jones (72.55m hammer), Steve Backley (86.81m) and both relays (38.62 and 3:00.40). The European Championships in Munich, shortly afterwards, produced victories by Chambers (9.96), Jackson (13.11), Backley (88.54m) and both relays (38.19 and 3:01.25). Ultimately, that haul of European medals proved less impressive as Chambers failed a doping test the following year and after admitting taking drugs also in 2002 all his results from 1 January 2002 were annulled. Out went his European 100m title, the 4x100m team lost their gold medals as Chambers was anchorman, and after deducting his points for winning the 100m the European Cup squad dropped from first to fourth. He also forfeited a 9.87 100m time in Paris which had equalled Linford Christie's European record.

2003 (Birmingham)

UNDERSTANDABLY THE FANS were let down by the number of prominent names who gave these Norwich

Union World Trials & AAA Championships a miss, and the standard in some events was quite appalling for the national championships of a major athletics power. For example, the 5000m winning time was the slowest ever and for the first time in over 40 years only one man threw the javelin beyond 70m. As Chris Rawlinson, winner of the 400m hurdles for the fifth year running (49.24), commented: "For trials, I support three past the post, like the Americans have. It would eliminate the drop-outs. If you are too injured to compete three weeks before the Worlds, chances are you are not going to be winning a medal anyway. The national championships are our chance to compete at home and say thank you to our supporters, to give something back."

On the men's side there were only two performances of the highest world class ... and one of them was by Dwain Chambers, who would later test positive for drugs and have his result annulled. He clocked 10.08 for 100m into a 1.6m/sec headwind in damp conditions, easing up before the line. Darren Campbell, second in 10.19, was subsequently awarded the title. The other literally towering performance of the meeting was Carl Myerscough's championship record of 21.55m in the shot, the old mark being American Al Feuerbach's 21.37m from 1974. There was another record of sorts as the margin of victory, close to four metres, was the widest in AAA Championships history. Myerscough had, the previous month, broken Geoff Capes' Commonwealth record of 21.68m set in 1980 with a massive put of 21.92m.

Like Chambers, Myerscough is banned for life from Olympic competition as he served a two-year drugs ban in 2000/2001. Perhaps the most keenly awaited race was the 200m, with five top class performers chasing three team places for Paris. The dramatic outcome was that Julian Golding, the 1998 Commonwealth champion who had been close to retiring after injuries and illness, prevailed over Christian Malcolm (20.39) in 20.37, his fastest for four years. Darren Campbell (20.49) edged out world indoor champion Marlon Devonish (20.50) for third while Chris

Lambert, who headed the UK year list at 20.34, finished fifth. Mick Hill, with a modest throw of 76.35m, won the javelin for the seventh time since 1987, equalling the record by Dave Travis (1965-1974). Without question the outstanding performance of the year, perhaps any year, was Paula Radcliffe's incredible world record of 2:15:25 in the London Marathon. She scaled the heights at the same time that British men's marathoning plumbed the depths, so we had the unique situation that she won her AAA title (held in conjunction with London) with a faster time than Chris Cariss (2:17:57) posted for his title. Indeed, Paula topped the UK marathon list for 2003, followed by Mark Steinle (2:09:17 the previous year) at 2:15:41. Never before in British athletics history, in a standard event, had a woman surpassed all the men!

The British team performance at the World Championships proved deeply disappointing with only Campbell excelling himself. He finished third, just one tantalising hundredth of a second behind the 100m winner, Kim Collins, in 10.08 – and again a mere 0.01 sec separated him from a bronze medal in the 200m as he placed fourth in 20.39. He later played his part in a fine British showing in the 4x100m relay, the team finishing a close second in 38.08 to the USA's 38.06, but because Chambers (fourth in the 100m in 10.08) anchored that squad the silver medals were subsequently taken away. Shockingly, the only other top eight placing in an individual event was Rawlinson's sixth in the 400m hurdles (48.90) as Myerscough failed to reach the shot final and (bearing out Rawlinson's opinion) even such distinguished AAA Championship absentees as Jonathan Edwards (12th) and Steve Backley (9th) failed to make their mark.

2004 (Manchester)

NINETY-SEVEN YEARS had passed since the AAA Championships were last staged in Manchester ... and probably even more since the meeting was held in such cold weather. Incorporating the Norwich Union Olympic Trials, this was the first major event at the Manchester Regional Arena, a 6000-seat stadium which was constructed around what had been the warm-up track for the 2002 Commonwealth Games, but despite the chilly, wet and windy conditions there were a number of splendid performances. Who, at the start of the season, could have predicted that Nathan Douglas would win the AAA triple jump title and make the Olympic team for Athens? Never in his wildest dreams could Douglas have foreseen what would happen in the Trials. With Jonathan Edwards retired and Phillips Idowu a non-starter through injury the thought that he might actually win must have entered his mind but, with a personal best of 16.49m to his name, he could hardly countenance the Olympic A standard of 16.95m. He was pleased enough to reach a new best of 16.56m in the fourth round, so imagine his feelings when – with the final jump of the contest – he landed at precisely 16.95m!

The classiest event was the 100m in which 2/100ths separated the first three with Jason Gardener (winner of the World Indoor 60m in 6.49 in March) clocking 10.22 against a 1.2m/sec wind, Darren Campbell 10.23 and Mark Lewis-Francis 10.24. An injury sustained when he fell at the finish of that 100m kept Campbell out of the 200m final where Chris Lambert, following an impressive 20.59 heat, won in a disappointing 20.94, the slowest winning time since 1977. One of the best performances was Carl Myerscough's 20.84m shot but he was ineligible for Olympic selection. Chris Rawlinson chalked up his sixth consecutive 400m hurdles title (50.04), one short of Harry Whittle's record sequence between 1947 and 1953. Fifteen years after his first AAA victory, Steve Backley won the javelin for a sixth and final time with a throw of 81.25m.

Even more of a "golden oldie" was 40-year-old Mick Jones who threw the hammer 72.04m, also his sixth title which equalled the record in his event set by Tom Nicolson between 1903 and 1912. There was an unusual occurrence in the 5000m walk where twins Dominic (20:11.35) and Daniel (20:47.19) King filled first two places.

The Athens Olympics will, of course, always be remembered fondly for Kelly Holmes' fabulous 800m/ 1500m double but those two gold medals along with that of the 4x100m team of Gardener, Campbell, Marlon Devonish and Lewis-Francis who held on by 1/100th from the Americans in 38.07, tended to distract from the fact that in the individual men's events not a single medal was gained. Closest to the podium were the fourth places of Jon Brown (again) in the marathon in 2:12:26, Backley (84.13m) and decathlete Dean Macey (8414). Shockingly, only one British man made a track final: Michael East, sixth at 1500m in 3:36.33.

2005 (Manchester)

TOP MARK OF the Norwich Union World Trials & AAA Championships, held in gloriously hot and sunny weather, was undoubtedly the triple jump of 17.64m by Nathan Douglas to add 5cm to the championship record set by Jonathan Edwards in 2001. He first jumped beyond 17m in June with 17.11m, improved to 17.27m and here he jumped 17.36m in the first round before sailing out to 17.64m in the second. It moved him to third on the UK all-time list behind Edwards (18.29m in 1995) and Phillips Idowu (17.68m in 2002), who at this meeting placed a distant third with 16.29m. While there were several encouraging marks by up-and-coming athletes, there was otherwise little of really top world quality although there was a fine 200m duel between Christian Malcolm (20.65) and Marlon Devonish (20.66) run into a 1.4m headwind. Devonish had looked superb in his 100m semi (10.19 into a 1.5m wind) but fell foul of the false start rule, leaving Jason Gardener (who had won the European Indoor 60m in 6.55) to take his fourth 100m title from Mark Lewis-Francis, the times of 10.26 and 10.30 slowed by a 1.0m headwind. Those who had despaired of late of the passive tactics of British middle distance men were encouraged by the front-running of Nick McCormick in the 1500m. His brave strategy enabled him to run a personal best (3:37.05) and just hold on to beat Andy Baddeley (3:37.08), Michael East (3:37.23) and Chris Mulvaney (3:37.74). Never before in the event's history had four men broken 3:38. Carl Myerscough won both the shot (20.27m) and discus (58.48m), the first such double since Brian Oldfield (USA) in 1980 and the first ever by a British thrower.

The World Championships in Helsinki saw Paula Radcliffe crowned marathon champion but, as in Paris 2003 and Athens 2004, the men's team under-performed. The only medal was a bronze by the 4x100m team (38.27). In individual events, the only placing in the top eight was fifth in the 400m by Welshman Tim Benjamin in 44.93.

2006 (Manchester)

THE FULL UNWIELDY title of the meeting was the Norwich Union European Trials Incorporating the UK Championships and AAA of England Championships and, sadly, this was the last occasion on which the AAA would feature in the name of the senior national track and field championships. From an international standpoint the top performances came from Greg Rutherford in the long jump, Phillips Idowu in the triple jump and Andy Turner in the 110m hurdles, but the meeting – held during a heatwave – was notable also for Marlon Devonish's sprint double (10.19/20.69), the first since Linford Christie in 1988. Rutherford (19) bounced back after a nightmarish display in the European Cup when he registered a personal worst of 5.98m with a personal best of 8.26m which missed Chris Tomlinson's UK record by a single centimetre. Hoping for around 17.20m, Idowu opened with 17.50m, his best for four years. He fouled his next two efforts and then quit a competition in which defending champion Nathan Douglas was left 51cm behind. Turner's wind assisted time of 13.24 had only been bettered in any conditions by two

Britons: Colin Jackson and Tony Jarrett. For the second year running, Carl Myerscough gained a shot (20.00m) and discus (61.04m) double, while Nick Nieland – coached by Steve Backley – retained his javelin title with a throw of 80.56m. He had first been a AAA winner back in 1996.

It was another busy year internationally but again the gold medal count was modest. Winners at the Commonwealth Games in Melbourne in March were Idowu (17.45m), Nieland (80.10m) and Dean Macey (8143 decathlon), while the only victory at the European Championships in Gothenburg in August came in the 4x100m relay (38.91). The 4x400m team finished second in 3:01.63, as did Mo Farah in the 5000m (13:44.79), Rutherford (8.13m) and Douglas (17.21m).

2007 (Manchester)

DESIGNATED THE NORWICH Union World Trials and UK Championships, this was the last nationally important meeting to be staged at the Manchester Regional Arena – to the relief of many spectators. The venue, at the mercy of the elements, was particularly unappreciated on this occasion by the competitors as well as the fans as blustery conditions all weekend conspired to downgrade performances. Marlon Devonish, at 31, became the first man since McDonald Bailey in 1953 to retain both sprint titles, but it was close each time. On a track he described as slow, Devonish ran 10.31 in the 100m, into a 2m/sec wind, to win by 1/100th from Craig Pickering, while in the 200m the newly crowned European Junior champion Alex Nelson was overtaken only in the last ten metres as Devonish prevailed in 20.79. But for the ever troublesome wind Andrew Steele (45.70) and Martyn Rooney (45.93) might have run the 400m in the low 45s and the laudable front running 800m victory by Michael Rimmer (1:47.06) would have been appreciably quicker. European cross country champion Mo Farah won his first national track title, clocking 13:40.19 for 5000m. The most exciting field event action came in the long jump where Nathan Morgan led throughout until Chris Tomlinson, who had recently extended the UK record to 8.29m, came up with a winning 7.99m at his final attempt. Steve Lewis moved to equal third on the UK all-time list by pole vaulting 5.61m.

The European Indoor Championships, in Birmingham, threw up three British victories for the men's team. Jason Gardener (6.51) and Pickering (6.59) went one-two in the 60m, as did Phillips Idowu (17.56m) and Nathan Douglas (17.47m) in the triple jump, and the 4x400m team triumphed in 3:07.04. The World Championships in Osaka were a much more demanding test with just one bronze medal (4x100m team in 37.90) being brought home from Japan on the men's side although Christine Ohuruogu and Nicola Sanders excelled themselves by finishing first and second in the women's 400m, together with bronze medals for the 4x400m team and heptathlete Kelly Sotherton. Individually, the highest placed men were Devonish (10.14), Farah (13:47.54) and Idowu (17.09m) ... all sixth in their events.

2008 (Birmingham)

WITH BRITISH ATHLETICS' biggest ever sponsor Norwich Union having changed its name it was back to Birmingham for the Aviva National Championships (incorporating the Team GB Selection Trials). Already the world triple jump leader in Olympic year with 17.75m when winning the World Indoor title (breaking Jonathan Edwards' UK indoor record) and 17.55m outdoors, Phillips Idowu was the star of the show as he jumped 17.58m from behind the board, costing him upwards of 20cm. Behind him, Larry Achike and Nathan Douglas both reached 17.18m, the first time three men exceeded 17m in a British championship. The other big talking point was a superb 100m final which saw Dwain Chambers – in his second post-drugs ban comeback – clock 10.00, the fastest legitimate time by a Briton since his own 9.99 in 2001 and also the quickest by a home athlete on a British track. His times of 9.87 in Paris and 9.98 at Crystal Palace in 2002 were among those annulled as a result of his confession that he was taking performance enhancing drugs at the time. Chambers was ruled ineligible to represent Britain in the Beijing Olympics and so British hopes rested on runner-up Simeon Williamson, the European Under-23 champion, who improved his personal best to 10.03 to rank fourth on the UK all-time list. Suffering from a virus, Marlon Devonish placed only seventh in the 100m and scratched from the 200m which went to a rejuvenated Christian Malcolm in 20.52.

Also a victim of a virus, and competing against medical advice, Chris Tomlinson (silver medallist in the World Indoor Championships) finished fifth in the long jump won in fine style by Greg Rutherford with 8.20m. Other highlights included a 45.31 400m by Martyn Rooney, a personal best 2.30m high jump by Tom Parsons ahead of former Jamaican Germaine Mason (2.27m) and a 5.60m vault by Steve Lewis, who unsuccessfully attempted a UK record of 5.82m.

A month earlier the British men scored a convincing victory in the European Cup in Annecy with wins in the 100m (Tyrone Edgar 10.20), 200m (Devonish 20.52), 400m (Rooney 45.33), 3000m (Andy Baddeley 8:01.28), triple jump (Idowu 17.46m) and the 4x100m team (38.48). Christine Ohuruogu's 400m triumph and Tasha Danvers' unexpected bronze medal in the 400m hurdles captured most of the attention at the Beijing Olympics but the men's team had its moments too as Idowu (17.62m) and Mason (personal best equalling 2.34m with two other Britons making the high jump final) struck silver. Again the trackmen overall were disappointing, best placed being Malcolm (5th in 20.40 after a 20.25 semi) and Rooney (6th in 45.12 after a personal best 44.60 semi). None of the 100m runners made even the semis and the final straw came when the 4x100m team was disqualified in the heats. All credit, though, to the 4x400m team which clocked a splendid 2:58.81, the best British time for ten years with Rooney clocked at 43.73 on the anchor leg, but still good only for fourth.

2009 (Birmingham)

THE 100m CLAIMED centre stage at these Aviva World Trials & UK Championships. Simeon Williamson was the winner, his margin of victory over Dwain Chambers being surprisingly wide at 0.17 sec – but then Williamson was running the race of his life. The time of 10.05, close to his personal best of 10.03, was impressive enough but what made this such a stunning achievement was that the temperature was only 15°C and there was a headwind of 1.8m/sec. Using an American formula which attempts to evaluate sprint performances according to wind readings, that 10.05 equated to 9.95 with zero wind and 9.85 with the maximum allowable wind of 2m/sec!

Two notable winning streaks: Michael Rimmer (1:46.47) collected his fourth consecutive 800m title to break the record of three held by among others Olympic champions Alfred Tysoe (1898–1900), Tom Hampson (1930–32) and Steve Ovett (1974–76); and Carl Myerscough (19.87m) won the shot for the seventh time in a row, equalling the run of Irishman Denis Horgan between 1893 and 1899. History was made also in the hammer, won by Alex Smith with a personal best of 69.79m. It was a rare instance of a father and son winning national titles as David Smith was AAA hammer champion five years running (1984–88). Alex's younger brother Peter, competing alongside the seniors, threw the 6kg implement 76.67m for a British junior record. Phillips Idowu took only one triple jump attempt, reaching 17.05m, and that held up – just – against Nathan Douglas (17.01m) ... but greater deeds were in the offing.

Chambers' best form of the year occurred in March when, at the European Indoor Championships, he set a European 60m record of 6.42 in his semi and won the final in 6.46. Britain's other gold medallist in Turin was Mo Farah with a championship record of 7:40.17 in the 3000m. Chambers registered a season's 100m best of 10.00 at the World Championships in Berlin but in that sensational race, won by Usain Bolt in a stunning world record of 9.58, he had to settle for sixth place. That was one position higher than Farah in the 5000m (13:19.69). Heroes of the British team were Idowu and Jessica Ennis, who were crowned world champions with 17.73m in the triple jump and a heptathlon score of 6731. The other medals from the men's team came in the relays with the 4x400m squad second in 3:00.53 and the 4x100m foursome third. Revelation of the team was William Sharman, a late selection for the 110m hurdles who went on to place fourth in a personal best of 13.30. Greg Rutherford, who had seized the UK long jump record from Chris Tomlinson with 8.30m in the qualifying competition (8.42m from take-off to landing), fell short in the final with 8.17m for fifth place.

2010 (Birmingham & Gateshead)

THE MEN'S 400m was the parade event at the Aviva European Trials & UK Championships in sunny Birmingham as Martyn Rooney won in a brisk 44.99 while four others – led by Michael Bingham – broke 46 sec. In all, 19 men bettered 47 sec. Dai Greene was the other top performer of the meeting as he lowered his European-leading 400m hurdles time to 48.77, leaving his training partner, fellow Welshman Rhys Williams, almost a full second behind. Much later in the summer Greene would only narrowly miss Kriss Akabusi's UK record with a time of 47.88 for a brilliant victory for the European team in the IAAF's inaugural Continental Cup. The closest men's race of the day came in the 110m hurdles where there was never more than inches between William Sharman (13.45) and Andy Turner (13.48). Dwain Chambers (32) reclaimed the 100m title in 10.14 into the wind with James Dasaolu a clear second in 10.23 after stumbling at the start. Mark Lewis-Francis, fifth in 10.42, appeared to have blown his chance of selection for the European Championships in Barcelona ... but he had a shock in store.

Another of the old guard, Christian Malcolm (31), swept to 200m victory in 20.77 ahead of 34-year-old Marlon

Devonish. Michael Rimmer was only 24 but he notched up a record fifth consecutive 800m title with a front running 1:47.22 notable for a second lap of 52.45. Phillips Idowu (who had been unwell all week) and Nathan Douglas, who train together under Aston Moore, scored an expected one-two in the triple jump. The wind was tricky, causing run-up problems, and between them they fouled seven times and each managed only one decent effort, Idowu's third round 17.12m overtaking Douglas's 17.03m opener. Chris Tomlinson long jumped a wind-aided 8.17m and encouraging too was the return to good form of Martyn Bernard who, despite wearing an exceptionally baggy pair of shorts, cleared 2.28m to win the high jump on countback against Tom Parsons. Carl Myerscough extended his record of consecutive shot titles to eight with 19.77m but was deprived of a double when Brett Morse threw 61.45m to become the first Welsh winner of the discus.

Earlier in the year, the top performance at the Aviva World Indoor Trials & UK Championships in Sheffield was Chambers' 60m in a swift 6.50 with former World Youth and World Junior 100m champion Harry Aikines-Aryeetey second in a personal best of 6.55. Chambers went even faster in Doha to be crowned World Indoor champion in the year's quickest time of 6.46. It was the first global title of his chequered career.

A significant development in 2010 was that separate England Athletics Senior Championships were staged in Gateshead in July. Held a month before the England selectors chose the Commonwealth Games team the meeting offered an opportunity for athletes to stake their claim for Delhi. The blustery conditions held down performances and the classiest mark came from 19-year-old Tremayne Gilling, son of 1978 Commonwealth Games 100m hurdles champion Lorna Boothe, who won the 100m in a personal best of 10.25.

The European Championships in Barcelona proved a huge success for the British team, which easily surpassed UK Sport's target of 10-15 medals with a record haul of

19, 15 of them by the men. Mo Farah claimed a 10,000m (28:24.99) and 5000m (13:31.18) double, the hurdling gold medals went to Andy Turner (13.28 110m) and David Greene (48.12 400m for a Welsh record), and Phillips Idowu added the European to his World triple jump title with a lifetime best of 17.81m. Later in the season Farah broke Dave Moorcroft's long-standing UK (and former world) 5000m record with 12:57.94 in Zürich, while at the inaugural IAAF Continental Cup, in Split, Greene won his event in 47.88, narrowly missing Kriss Akabusi's UK record of 47.82. England's men won 14 medals and Wales' three at the Commonwealth Games in Delhi, including victories by Leon Baptiste (20.45 200m), Turner (13.38 110m hurdles) and the 4x100m team (38.74) for England and Greene (48.52) for Wales.

BRITISH RECORDS AT 1 JANUARY 2011

100m: 9.87 Linford Christie 1993; 200m: 19.94 John Regis 1993 (unratified 19.87 in 1994); 400m: 44.36 Iwan Thomas 1997; 800m: 1:41.73 Seb Coe 1981; 1000m: 2:12.18 Coe 1981; 1500m: 3:29.67 Steve Cram 1985; Mile: 3:46.32 Cram 1985; 2000m: 4:51.39 Cram 1985; 3000m: 7:32.79 Dave Moorcroft 1982; 2M: 8:13.51 Steve Ovett 1978; 5000m: 12:57.94 Mo Farah 2010; 10,000m: 27:18.14 Jon Brown 1998; Half Marathon: 60:59 Steve Jones 1986; Marathon: 2:07:13 S Jones 1985; 3000mSC: 8:07.96 Mark Rowland 1988; 110mH: 12.91 Colin Jackson 1993; 400mH: 47.82 Kriss Akabusi 1992; HJ: 2.37 Steve Smith 1992 & 1993 (2.38 indoors 1994); PV: 5.80 Nick Buckfield 1998 (5.81 indoors 2002); LJ: 8.30 Greg Rutherford 2009; TJ: 18.29 Jonathan Edwards 1995; SP: 21.92 Carl Myerscough 2003; DT: 66.64 Perriss Wilkins 1998; HT: 77.54 Martin Girvan 1984; JT: 91.46 Steve Backley 1992; Decathlon: 8847 Daley Thompson 1984; 3000m Walk: 11:24.4 Mark Easton 1989; 10,000m Walk: 40:06.65 Ian McCombie 1989; 20km Walk: 1:22:03 McCombie 1988; 50km Walk: 3:51:37 Chris Maddocks 1990.

FROM AAA TO OLYMPIC CHAMPION

OF THE 28 British men who have won individual gold medals at the quadrennial Olympic Games between 1900 and 2000, 26 have AAA titles to their name. The only exceptions are Arnold Strode-Jackson (1912 Olympic 1500m champion), who never competed in the AAA Championships, and Chris Brasher (1956 Olympic steeplechase champion), whose highest AAA placing was second in 1952 and 1955. Here is the list in alphabetical order, showing Olympic victory year and event in brackets followed by AAA title wins.

Harold Abrahams (1924 100m) 1923 long jump, 1924 100y & long jump
Charles Bennett (1900 1500m) 1897-1899 4M, 1899 10M, 1900 1M
Lord Burghley (1928 400mH) 1926-1928, 1930 & 1932 440yH, 1929-1931 120yH
Linford Christie (1992 100m) 1986, 1988, 1989, 1991-1994 & 1996 100m, 1988 200m
Seb Coe (1980 & 1984 1500m) 1981 800m, 1989 1500m
Lynn Davies (1964 long jump) 1964, 1966-1969 long jump
Jonathan Edwards (2000 triple jump) 1989, 1994, 1998 & 2001 triple jump

Tommy Green (1932 50km walk) 1930 50km walk
Wyndham Halswelle (1908 400m) 1905, 1906 & 1908 440y
Tom Hampson (1932 800m) 1930-1932 880y
David Hemery (1968 400mH) 1966 120yH, 1968 440yH, 1970 110mH, 1972 400mH
Albert Hill (1920 800m & 1500m) 1910 4M, 1919 880y & 4M, 1921 1M
Percy Hodge (1920 3000m steeplechase) 1919-1921 & 1923 2M steeplechase
George Larner (1908 3500m & 10M walk) 1904, 1905 & 1908 2M walk, 1904, 1905 & 1911 7M walk
Eric Liddell (1924 400m) 1923 100y & 220y, 1924 440y
Douglas Lowe (1924 & 1928 800m) 1927 & 1928 440y & 880y
Ken Matthews (1964 20km walk) 1959, 1961-1964 2M walk, 1959-1961, 1963, 1964 7M walk, 1959-1964 10M walk, 1962 20M walk
Steve Ovett (1980 800m) 1974-1976 800m, 1979 1500m, 1980 1M
John Rimmer (1900 4000m steeplechase) 1900 4M
Arthur Russell (1908 3200m steeplechase) 1904-1906 steeplechase
Daley Thompson (1980 & 1984 decathlon) 1976 decathlon, 1977 long jump
Don Thompson (1960 50km walk) 1956-1962, 1966 50km walk, 1961 20M walk
Alfred Tysoe (1900 800m) 1897 1M & 10M, 1899 & 1900 880y
Emil Voigt (1908 5M) 1908 & 1909 4M, 1910 1M
Allan Wells (1980 100m) 1980 100m
Harold Whitlock (1936 50km walk) 1933, 1935-1939 50km walk, 1939 20M walk

Five of those Olympic champions gained their first important titles at AAA Youth and/or Junior Championships:
Seb Coe: 1973 Youth 1500m, 1975 Junior 1500m
Lynn Davies: 1961 Junior triple jump
David Hemery: 1963 Junior 120yH
Steve Ovett: 1971 & 1972 Youth 400m
Daley Thompson: 1975 Junior 100m & decathlon

BRITISH MEN'S HONOURS LIST

THIS LIST FEATURES more than 350 British male athletes who achieved particular international distinction between 1900 and the present day. Criteria for inclusion: placing in first three in the Olympics, World Championships (including cross country since it became an IAAF event in 1973) and World Indoor Championships; winner in individual events only in European Championships, European Indoor Games/Championships, Empire/Commonwealth Games, International (pre-IAAF) & European Cross Country Championships, and World Race Walking Cup, plus world record setters in the more commonly contested or significant events. Abbreviations used: Oly = Olympic Games; World = World Championships; World/Eur Ind = World/European Indoor Championships; Int/World/Eur CC = International/World/European Cross Country; Eur = European Championships; CG = Commonwealth Games. European records quoted only when not a world record and for metric distances, except for mile

ABRAHAMS Harold: 1 1924 Oly 100 (2 4x100); world record – 4x100 (42.0 - 1924)
ACHIKE Larry: 1 1998 CG TJ
ADAM Marcus: 1 1990 CG 200

ADCOCKS Bill: Eur record – Mar (2:12:17 & 2:10:48 - 1968)

AIKINES-ARYEETEY Harry: 3 2009 World 4x100

AINSWORTH-DAVIS John: 1 1920 Oly 4x100

AKABUSI Kriss: 2 1984 Oly 4x400, 2 1987 World 4x400, 1 1990 CG & Eur 400H, 3 1991 World 400H (1 4x400), 3 1992 Oly 400H (3 4x400)

ALDER Jim: 1 1966 CG Mar; world records - 30,000m (1:34:01.8 - 1964, 1:31:30.4 – 1970)

ALDRIDGE Robert: 1 1905 Int CC

ALFORD Jim: 1 1938 CG 1M

ANDERSON Gerard: World record – 440yH (56.8 – 1910); Eur record – 110m/120yH (15.2 - 1912)

ANDERSON Tim: 1 1950 CG PV

APPLEBY Fred: World records – 20,000m (1:06:42.2 – 1902), 15M (1:20:04.6 – 1902)

APPLEGARTH Willie: 3 1912 Oly 200 (1 4x100); world records – 200m/220y (21.2 – 1914), 4x100 (43.0 – 1912)

ARCHER Jack: 1 1946 Eur 100, 2 1948 Oly 4x100

ASHURST Andy: 1 1986 CG PV

BACKLEY Steve: (JT) 1 1990 CG, 1 1990 Eur, 3 1992 Oly, 1 1994 CG & Eur, 2 1995 World, 2 1996 Oly, 2 1997 World, 1 1998 Eur, 2 2000 Oly, 1 2002 CG & Eur; world records – (89.58 & 90.98 – 1990, 91.46 – 1992)

BAILEY George: 1 1930 CG steeplechase

BAILEY McDonald: 3 1952 Oly 100; world record – 100 (10.2 – 1951); Eur records – 200 (21.0 – 1950, 20.9 – 1950, 1951 & 1952)

BAKER Howard: Eur rec – HJ (1.95 - 1921)

BAKER Philip: 2 1920 Oly 1500

BANNISTER Roger: 1 1954 CG 1M, 1 1954 Eur 1500; world records - 1500 (3:43.0 – 1954), 1M (3:59.4 – 1954), 4x1M (16:41.0 – 1953); Eur records – 1500 (3:42.2 – 1954), 1M (3:58.8 – 1954)

BAPTISTE Leon: 1 2010 CG 200

BARRETT Henry: World best – Mar (2:42:31 - 1909)

BARRY Steve: 1 1982 CG 30km Walk

BATTY Mel: World record - 10M (47:26.8 - 1964)

BAULCH Jamie: 2 1996 Oly 4x400, 2 1997 World Ind 400, 1 1997 World 4x400, 1 1999 World Ind 400 (3 4x400), 3= 2003 World Ind 400 (3 4x400)

BEATTIE Phil: 1 1986 CG 400H

BEAVERS Walter: 1 1934 CG 3M

BEDFORD Dave: 1 1971 Int CC; world record - 10,000 (27:30.80 – 1973); Eur records – 5000 – 13:22.2 (1971) & 13:17.21 (1972), 10,000 – 27:47.0 (1971)

BENJAMIN Tim: 3 2003 World Ind 4x400

BENNETT Ainsley: 3 1983 World 4x400
BENNETT Todd: 3 1983 World 4x400, 2 1984 Oly 4x400, 1 1985 Eur Ind 400, 2 1985 World Ind 400, 1 1987 Eur Ind 400; world indoor record - 400 (45.56 - 1985)
BILLY Ikem: 3 1985 World Ind 800
BINGHAM Michael: 2 2009 World 4x400
BLACK Roger: 1 1986 CG & Eur 400, 2 1987 World 4x400, 2 1991 World 400 (1 4x400), 3 1992 Oly 4x400, 2 1996 Oly 400 (2 4x400), 1 1997 World 4x400
BLAGROVE Mike: World record - 4x1M (16:30.6 – 1958)
BLEWITT Charles: 2 1920 Oly 3000 team race, 1 1923 Int CC
BOULTER John: World record - 4x880y (7:14.6 - 1966)
BRADSTOCK Roald: World record - JT (81.74 - 1986)
BRAITHWAITE Darren: 3 1991 World 4x100, 2 1995 World Ind 60, 3 1997 World 4x100; world indoor record - 4x200 (1:22.11 - 1991)
BRASHER Chris: 1 1956 Oly 3000SC
BRIDGE Robert: World records – 15M Walk (1:56:41.4 – 1914), 2 hours (24,781m - 1914)
BRIGHTWELL Robbie: 1 1962 Eur 400, 2 1964 Oly 4x400
BROWN Godfrey: 2 1936 Oly 400 (1 4x400), 1 1938 Eur 400; Eur records – 400 (47.31 & 46.68 - 1936)
BROWN Jon: 1 1996 Eur CC
BROWN Phil: (4x400) 3 1983 World, 2 1984 Oly, 2 1987 World
BUCK Richard: 3 2010 World Ind 4x400
BUCKNER Jack: (5000) 1 1986 Eur, 3 1987 World
BULL Mike: 1 1970 CG PV, 1 1974 CG Dec
BUNNEY Elliot: 2 1988 Oly 4x100
BURGHLEY Lord: 1 1928 Oly 400H, 1 1930 CG 120yH & 440yH, 2 1932 Oly 4x400; world record – 440yH (54.2 – 1927); Eur records – 400H (54.8 – 1925, 54.0 & 53.4 - 1928)
BUTLER Guy: 2 1920 Oly 400 (1 4x400), 3 1924 Oly 400 (3 4x400)

CAINES Daniel: 1 2001 World Ind 400, 2 2003 World Ind 400 (3 4x400)
CAMPBELL Darren: 3 1997 World 4x100, 1 1998 Eur 100, 2 2000 Oly 200, 3 2003 World 100, 1 2004 Oly 4x100
CAPES Geoff: (SP) 1 1974 Eur Ind, 1 1974 CG, 1 1976 Eur Ind, 1 1978 CG
CARTER Chris: World record - 4x880y (7:14.6 - 1966)
CHAMBERS Dwain: 3 1999 World 100 (2 4x100), 2= 2008 World Ind 60, 1 2009 Eur Ind 60, 1 2010 World Ind 60
CHATAWAY Chris: 1 1954 CG 3M; world records - 3M (13:32.2 - 1954, 13:23.2 - 1955), 5000 (13:51.6 - 1954), 4x1M (16:41.0 - 1953)
CHIPCHASE Ian: 1 1974 CG HT

CHRISTIE Linford: 1 1986 Eur Ind 200, 1 1986 Eur 100, 3 1987 World 100, 1 1988 Eur Ind 60, 2 1988 Oly 100 (2 4x100), 1 1990 Eur Ind 60, 1 1990 CG & Eur 100, 2 1991 World Ind 60 & 200, 2 1991 World 4x100, 1 1992 Oly 100, 1 1993 World 100 (2 4x100), 1 1994 CG & Eur 100; world indoor records – 200 (20.25 – 1995), 4x200 (1:22.11 – 1991); Eur records – 100 (9.97 – 1988, 9.92 – 1991, 9.87 - 1993)
CHURCHER Harry: World records – 5M Walk (35:43.4 – 1948, 35:33.0 - 1949)
CLARK Duncan: 1 1950 CG HT
CLARK Peter: World record - 4x1M (16:30.6 – 1958)
CLARKE Chris: 3 2010 World Ind 4x400
CLOVER Charles: 1 1974 CG JT
COALES Bill: 1 1908 Oly 3M team race (3rd indiv)
COE Seb: 1 1977 Eur Ind 800, 1 1980 Oly 1500 (2 800), 1 1984 Oly 1500 (2 800), 1 1986 Eur 800; world records – 800 (1:42.33 – 1979, 1:41.73 – 1981), 1000 (2:13.40 – 1980, 2:12.18 – 1981), 1500 (3:32.1/3:32.03 – 1979), 1M (3:48.95 – 1979, 3:48.53 & 3:47.33 – 1981), 4x800 (7:03.89 – 1982); world indoor records – 800 (1:46.0 – 1981, 1:44.91 – 1983), 1000 (2:18.58 – 1983); Eur rec – 1500 (3:32.8 - 1979)
COLE Billy: 1 1986 CG SP
CONDON Allyn: 3 1999 World Ind 4x400
CONNOR Keith: (TJ) 1 1978 CG, 1 1982 CG & Eur, 3 1984 Oly; world indoor record – (17.31 - 1981)
COOK Garry: (4x400) 3 1983 World, 2 1984 Oly; world record - 4x800 (7:03.89 – 1982)
COOPER Bert: World records – 3000 Walk (12:38.2 – 1935), 5000 Walk (21:52.4 - 1935)
COOPER John: 2 1964 Oly 400H (2 4x400)
CORNES Jerry: 2 1932 Oly 1500; world record – 4x1500 (15:55.6 – 1931)
COTTERELL Joe: 1 1924 & 1929 Int CC
COTTRILL William: 3 1912 Oly CC team race
CRAM Steve: 1 1982 CG & Eur 1500, 1 1983 World 1500, 2 1984 Oly 1500, 1 1986 CG 800 & 1500, 1 1986 Eur 1500; world records - 1500 (3:29.67 - 1985), 1M (3:46.32 - 1985), 2000 (4:51.39 – 1985), 4x800 (7:03.89 - 1982)

D'ARCY Vic: 1 1912 Oly 4x100; world record – 4x100 (43.0 - 1912)
DAVIES John: World indoor record - 1000 (2:20.9 - 1970)
DAVIES Lynn: (LJ) 1 1964 Oly, 1 1966 CG & Eur, 1 1967 Eur Ind, 1 1970 CG
DEAKIN Joe: 1 1908 Oly 3M team race (individual winner)
DENMARK Rob: 3 1991 World Ind 3000, 1 1994 CG 5000
DEVONISH Marlon: 2 1999 World 4x100, 1 2003 World Ind 200, 1 2004

Oly 4x100, 3 2005 World 4x100, 3 2007 World 4x100, 3 2009 World 4x100
DISLEY John: 3 1952 Oly 3000SC
DRIVER Peter: 1 1954 CG 6M
DUNKLEY Ralph: World record - 4x1500 (15:27.2 - 1953)

EAST Michael: 1 2002 CG 1500
EATON William: 1 1936 Int CC
ECKERSLEY Harry: 1 1928 Int CC
EDGAR Tyrone: 3 2009 World 4x100
EDWARD Harry: 3 1920 Oly 100 & 200
EDWARDS Jonathan: (TJ) 3 1993 World, 1 1995 World, 2 1996 Oly, 2 1997 World, 1 1998 Eur Ind, 1 1998 Eur, 3 1999 World, 1 2000 Oly, 2 2001 World Ind, 1 2001 World, 1 2002 CG; world records – (17.98, 18.16 & 18.29 - 1995)
ELDON Stan: 1 1958 Int CC
ELLIOTT Geoff: 1 1954 & 1958 CG PV
ELLIOTT Peter: 2 1987 World 800, 2 1988 Oly 1500, 1 1990 CG 1500; world record - 4x800 (7:03.89 - 1982); world indoor record – 1500 (3:34.20 – 1990)
ELLIS Mike: 1 1958 CG HT
EMERY Jack: 1 1938 Int CC
ENGELHART Stan: 1 1930 CG 220y
EVANS Frank: World record - 4x880y (7:30.6 – 1951)
EVENSON Tom: 1 1930 & 1932 Int CC, 2 1932 Oly 3000SC
EYRE Len: 1 1950 CG 3M

FARAH Mo: 1 2006 Eur CC, 1 2009 Eur Ind 3000, 1 2010 Eur 5000 & 10,000, 1 2011 Eur Ind 3000
FERRIS Sam: 2 1932 Oly Mar
FINLAY Don: 3 1932 Oly 110H, 1 1934 CG 120yH, 2 1936 Oly 110H, 1 1938 Eur 110H; Eur records – 110H (14.4 – 1936, 14.3 - 1938)
FITZSIMONS John: 1 1966 CG JT
FLOCKHART Jim: 1 1937 Int CC
FLYNN Olly: 1 1978 CG 30km Walk
FORD Bernie: 3 1976 World CC
FOSTER Brendan: 1 1974 Eur 5000, 3 1976 Oly 10,000, 1 1978 CG 10,000; world records - 3000 (7:35.1 – 1974), 2M (8:13.68 – 1973); Eur record – 10,000 (27:30.3 - 1978)
FOWLER Roy: 1 1963 Int CC
FREEMAN Walter: 1 1921 Int CC
FRITH Bob: World indoor record – 50 (5.5 - 1963)

GARDENER Jason: 3 1999 World Ind 60, 2 1999 World 4x100, 1 2000 & 2002 Eur Ind 60, 3 2003 World Ind 60, 1 2004 World Ind 60, 1 2005 Eur Ind 60, 3 2005 World 4x100, 1 2007 Eur Ind 60

GILL Cyril: 3 1928 Oly 4x100

GLOVER Ernest: 3 1912 Oly CC team race

GOLDING Julian: 3 1997 World 4x100, 1 1998 CG 200

GOLLEY Julian: 1 1994 CG TJ

GOODWIN Reginald: 2 1924 Oly 10,000 Walk

GRAHAM Tim: 2 1964 Oly 4x400

GRANT Dalton: (HJ) 1 1994 Eur Ind, 1 1998 CG

GRANT Graeme: World record - 4x880y (7:14.6 - 1966)

GREEN Freddie: World record – 3M (13:32.2 – 1954)

GREEN Harry: World records – 2 hours (33,057m – 1913), 25M (2:29:04.0 – 1913); world best – Mar (2:38:16.2 track – 1913)

GREEN Tommy: 1 1932 Oly 50km Walk

GREENE David: 1 2010 Eur 400H, 1 2010 CG 400H

GREGORY Jack: 2 1948 Oly 4x100

GRIFFITHS Cecil: 1 1920 Oly 4x400

GRINDLEY David: 3 1992 Oly 4x400

GUNN Charles: 3 1920 Oly 10,000 Walk

HALLOWS Norman: 3 1908 Oly 1500

HALSWELLE Wyndham: 2 1906 Oly 400 (3 800), 1 1908 Oly 400

HAMPSON Tom: 1 1930 CG 880y, 1 1932 Oly 800 (2 4x400); world record – 800 (1:49.70 - 1932)

HARDY Roland: World records - 5M Walk (35:24.0 - 1951, 35:15.0 – 1952)

HARPER Ernie: 1 1926 Int CC, 2 1936 Oly Mar; world records – 25,000m (1:23:45.8 – 1929), 2 hours (33,653m – 1933)

HARRIS Aubrey: World record – 4x1500 (15:55.6 - 1931)

HARRISON Rob: 1 1985 Eur Ind 800

HAWTREY Henry: 1 1906 Oly 5M

HEARD Steve: 1 1989 Eur Ind 800

HEATLEY Basil: 1 1961 Int CC, 2 1964 Oly Mar; world record -10M (47:47.0 – 1961), world best – Mar (2:13:55 – 1964)

HEDGES Harry: World record – 4x1500 (15:55.6 – 1931)

HEGARTY Frank: 2 1920 Oly CC team race

HEMERY David: 1 1966 CG 120yH, 1 1968 Oly 400H, 1 1970 CG 110H, 3 1972 Oly 400H (2 4x400); world record – 400H (48.12 – 1968)

HENLEY Ernest: 3 1912 Oly 4x400

HENRY Cori: 3 2003 World Ind 4x400

HERBERT John: 1 1986 CG TJ

HERRIOTT Maurice: 2 1964 Oly 3000SC

HEWSON Brian: 1 1958 Eur 1500; world record - 4x1M (16:30.6 - 1958)
HIBBINS Fred: 3 1912 Oly CC team race
HIGGINS Peter: 3 1956 Oly 4x400
HILL Albert: 1 1920 Oly 800 & 1500 (2 3000 team race)
HILL Mick: 3 1993 World JT
HILL Ron: (Mar) 1 1969 Eur, 1 1970 CG; world records – 10M (47:02.2 & 46:44.0 – 1968), 15M (1:12:48.2 – 1965), 25,000m (1:15:22.6 – 1965); Eur records – Mar (2:10:30 & 2:09:28 - 1970)
HODGE Percy: 1 1920 Oly 3000SC
HOGAN Jim: 1 1966 Eur Mar; world record - 30,000m (1:32:25.4 - 1966)
HOLDEN Jack: 1 1933, 1934, 1935 & 1939 Int CC, 1 1950 CG & Eur Mar
HOLMES Cyril: 1 1938 CG 100y & 220y
HUMPHREYS Tom: 3 1912 Oly CC team race
HUNTER Alan: 1 1934 CG 440yH
HUTCHINGS Tim: 2 1984 & 1989 World CC
HUTSON George: 3 1912 Oly 5000 & 3000 team race

IBBOTSON Derek: 3 1956 Oly 5000; world records - 1M (3:57.2 - 1957), 4x1M (16:30.6 – 1958); Eur record – 1M (3:58.4 - 1957)
IDOWU Phillips: (TJ) 1 2006 CG, 1 2007 Eur Ind, 1 2008 World Ind, 2 2008 Oly, 1 2009 World, 1 2010 Eur

JACKSON Arnold: 1 1912 Oly 1500; Eur record – 1500 (3:56.8 - 1912)
JACKSON Colin: (110H) 3 1987 World, 2 1988 Oly, 1 1989 Eur Ind 60H, 1 1989 World Ind 60H, 1 1990 CG & Eur, 2 1993 World Ind 60H, 1 1993 World (2 4x100), 1 1994 Eur Ind 60 & 60H, 1 1994 CG & Eur, 2 1997 World Ind 60H, 2 1997 World, 1 1998 Eur, 1 1999 World Ind 60H, 1 1999 World, 1 2002 Eur Ind 60H, 1 2002 Eur; world record – 110H (12.91 – 1993), world best – 200H (22.63 – 1991), world indoor records – 60H (7.36 & 7.30 – 1994); Eur records – 110H (13.11 – 1988, 1989 & 1990, 13.08 – 1990, 13.06 & 13.04 – 1992, 12.97 - 1993)
JACOBS David: 1 1912 Oly 4x100; world record – 4x100 (43.0 - 1912)
JARRETT Tony: (110H) 3 1991 World (3 4x100), 2 1993 World (2 4x100), 3 1995 World Ind 60H, 2 1995 World, 1 1998 CG
JENKINS David: 1 1971 Eur 400, 2 1972 Oly 4x400
JOHNSON Derek: 1 1954 CG 880y, 2 1956 Oly 800 (3 4x400)
JOHNSTON Johnny: 2 1924 Oly 3000 team race
JOHNSTON Tim: World record - 30,000m (1:32:34.6 - 1965)
JONES Berwyn: World record - 4x110y (40.0 - 1963)
JONES David: 3 1960 Oly 4x100; world record - 4x110y (40.0 – 1963)
JONES Ken: 2 1948 Oly 4x100
JONES Mick: 1 2002 CG HT

JONES Ron: World record - 4x110y (40.0 - 1963)
JONES Steve: 3 1984 World CC; world best - Mar (2:08:05 – 1984)

KELLY Barrie: 1 1966 Eur Ind 60
KILBY Brian: 1 1962 Eur & CG Mar

LADEJO Du'aine: (400) 1 1994 Eur Ind, 1 1994 Eur, 1 1996 Eur Ind
LARNER George: 1 1908 Oly 3500m & 10M Walks; world records included
– 2M (13:11.4 – 1904), 5M (36:00.2 – 1905), 7M (50:50.8 – 1905), 10M
(1:15:57.4 – 1908) and 1 hour (13,275m - 1905)
LAW David: World record - 4x1500 (15:27.2 - 1953)
LERWILL Alan: 1 1974 CG LJ
LEVINE Nigel: 3 2010 World Ind 4x400
LEWIS-FRANCIS Mark: 3 2001 World Ind 60, 1 2004 Oly 4x100, 3 2005
World 4x100, 3 2007 World 4x100
LIDDELL Eric: 1 1924 Oly 400 (3 200); Eur record – 400 (47.6 - 1924)
LINDSAY Robert: 1 1920 Oly 4x400
LIVINGSTON Jason: 1 1992 Eur Ind 60
LLOYD JOHNSON Tebbs: 3 1948 Oly 50km Walk
LONDON Jack: 2 1928 Oly 100 (3 4x100)
LOWE Douglas: 1 1924 & 1928 Oly 800; Eur record – 800 (1:52.4 - 1924)
LUCKING Martyn: 1 1962 CG SP

MACDONALD Bernard: 2 1924 Oly 3000 team race (3rd indiv)
MACEY Dean: (Dec) 2 1999 World, 3 2001 World, 1 2006 CG
MACINTOSH Henry: 1 1912 Oly 4x100; world record – 4x100 (43.0 - 1912)
MAFE Ade: (200) 2 1985 World Ind, 1 1989 Eur Ind & World Ind, 3 1991
World Ind; world indoor record – 4x200 (1:22.11 - 1991)
MALCOLM Christian: 1 2000 Eur Ind 200, 2 2001 World Ind 200, 3 2005
World 4x100, 3 2007 World 4x100
MARTIN Eamonn: 1 1990 CG 10,000
MASON Germaine: 2 2008 Oly HJ
MATTHEWS Ken: (20km Walk) 1 1961 World Walk Cup, 1 1962 Eur, 1
1963 World Walk Cup, 1 1964 Oly
MAYOCK John: 1 1998 Eur Ind 3000
McCORQUODALE Alistair: 2 1948 Oly 4x100
McFARLANE Mike: 1= 1982 CG 200, 1 1985 Eur Ind 60, 2 1988 Oly 4x100
McGHEE Joe: 1 1954 CG Mar
McKEAN Tom: (800) 1 1990 Eur Ind, 1 1990 Eur, 1 1993 World Ind
McLEOD Mike: 2 1984 Oly 10,000
METCALFE Adrian: 2 1964 Oly 4x400
MILLIGAN Bill: World record – 4x880y (7:50.4 - 1920)

British Men's Honours List

MITCHELL Roy: 1 1978 CG LJ
MOORCROFT Dave: 1 1978 CG 1500, 1 1982 CG 5000; world record –
5000 (13:00.41 – 1982); Eur record – 3000 (7:32.79 - 1982)
MORGAN Nathan: 1 2002 CG LJ

NANKEVILLE Bill: World records – 4x880y (7:30.6 – 1951), 4x1500 (15:27.2
– 1953), 4x1M (16:41.0 – 1953)
NICHOL William: 2 1924 Oly 4x100; world record – 4x100 (42.0 – 1924)
NICHOLS Alfred: 1 1914 Int CC, 3 1920 Oly CC team race
NICOL George: 3 1912 Oly 4x400
NIELAND Nick: 1 2006 CG JT
NIHILL Paul: 2 1964 Oly 50km Walk, 1 1969 Eur 20km Walk, World best
– 20km Walk (1:24:50 – 1972
NOKES Malcolm: (HT) 3 1924 Oly, 1 1930 & 1934 CG; Eur record – 52.76
(1923)
NORRIS Fred: 1 1959 Int CC

OAKES Gary: 3 1980 Oly 400H
OTTLEY Dave: (JT) 2 1984 Oly, 1 1986 CG
OVETT Steve: 1 1978 Eur 1500, 1 1980 Oly 800 (3 1500), 1 1986 CG
5000; world records – 1500 (3:32.1/3:32.09 & 3:31.36 – 1980, 3:30.77 –
1983), 1M (3:48.8 – 1980, 3:48.40 – 1981), 2M (8:13.51 – 1978)
OWEN Edward: 2 1908 Oly 5M

PARLETT John: 1 1950 CG 880y, 1 1950 Eur 800; world record - 4x880y
(7:30.6 - 1951)
PASCOE Alan: 1 1969 Eur Ind 50H, 2 1972 Oly 4x400, 1 1974 CG & Eur
400H
PATERSON Alan: 1 1950 Eur HJ
PATRICK Adrian: 3 1999 World Ind 4x400
PAYNE Howard: 1 1962, 1966 & 1970 CG HT
PENNY Arthur: 1 1934 CG 6M
PETERS Jim: World bests – Mar (2:20:43 – 1952, 2:18:41 & 2:18:35 – 1953,
2:17:40 – 1954)
PICKERING Craig: 3 2007 World 4x100
PIRIE Gordon: 2 1956 Oly 5000; world records - 3000 (7:55.5 & 7:52.7 -
1956), 5000 (13:36.8 - 1956), 6M (28:19.4 - 1953), 4x1500 (15:27.2 – 1953)
PLUMB Arthur: World record – 20M Walk (2:43:38.0 – 1932)
POPE Alf: World records – 5M Walk (35:47.2 – 1932), 10,000 (44:42.4 –
1932), 7M (50:28.8 – 1932), 1 hour (13,308m – 1932)
PORTER Cyril: 3 1912 Oly CC team race
PRICE Berwyn: 1 1978 CG 110H

PRITCHARD Norman: 2 1900 Oly 200
PUGH Derek: 1 1950 Eur 400

RADFORD Peter: 3 1960 Oly 100 (3 4x100); world records - 200m/220y
(20.5 - 1960), 4x110y (40.0 - 1963), world indoor record - 50m (5.5 –
1958); Eur record – 100 (10.29 - 1958)
RAMPLING Godfrey: 2 1932 Oly 4x400, 1 1934 CG 440y, 1 1936 Oly
4x400
RANGELEY Walter: 2 1924 Oly 4x100, 2 1928 Oly 200 (3 4x100); world
record – 4x100 (42.0 - 1924)
RAWLINSON Chris: 1 2002 CG 400H
RAWSON Mike: 1 1958 Eur 800
REDMAN Frank: World record – 10M Walk (1:14:30.6 - 1934)
REDMOND Derek: (4x400) 2 1987 World, 1 1991 World
REGIS John: 3 1987 World 200, 2 1988 Oly 4x100, 1 1989 World Ind 200,
1 1990 Eur 200, 1 1991 World 4x400 (3 4x100), 3 1992 Oly 4x400, 2 1993
World 200 (2 4x100); world indoor record - 4x200 (1:22.11 - 1991)
REITZ Colin: 3 1983 World 3000SC
RENWICK George: 3 1924 Oly 4x400
REYNOLDS Martin: 2 1972 Oly 4x400
RICHARDS Tom: 2 1948 Oly Mar
RICHARDSON Mark: (4x400) 2 1996 Oly, 1 1997 World
RIDGEON Jon: 3 1985 World Ind 60H, 2 1987 World 110H
RIMMER John: 1 1900 Oly 5000 team race (2nd indiv) & 4000mSC
RIPLEY Richard: 3 1924 Oly 4x400
ROBERTS Bill: 1 1936 Oly 4x400, 1 1938 CG 440y
ROBERTSON Archie: 1 1908 Int CC, 1 1908 Oly 3M team race (2nd indiv)
(2 3200mSC); world record – 5000 (15:01.2 – 1908)
ROBINSON Sidney: 1 1900 Oly 5000 team race (2 2500mSC, 3 4000mSC)
ROONEY Martyn: 2 2009 World 4x400
ROSE Nick: 3 1980 World CC
ROSS Harold: World records – 15M Walk (1:59:12.6 – 1911), 2 hours
(24,256m - 1911)
ROWE Arthur: 1 1958 CG & Eur SP; Eur records – 18.59 (1959), 18.92 &
19.11 (1960), 19.19, 19.44 & 19.56 (1961)
ROWLAND Mark: 3 1988 Oly 3000SC
ROYLE Lancelot: 2 1924 Oly 4x100; world record – 4x100 (42.0 – 1924)
RUSSELL Arthur: 1 1908 Oly 3200mSC

SALISBURY John: 3 1956 Oly 4x400
SANDO Frank: 1 1955 & 1957 Int CC
SAUNDERS Geoff: 1 1951 Int CC

SAVIDGE John: 1 1954 CG SP

SCARSBROOK Stan: 1 1934 CG 2MSC

SCHOFIELD Sidney: World record – 25M Walk (3:37:06.8 – 1911)

SEAGROVE William: 2 1920 Oly 3000 team race

SEAMAN Don: World record - 4x1M (16:41.0 – 1953)

SEEDHOUSE Cyril: 3 1912 Oly 4x400

SEGAL Dave: 3 1960 Oly 4x100

SHARPE David: 1 1988 Eur Ind 800

SHENTON Brian: 1 1950 Eur 200

SHERWOOD John: (400H) 3 1968 Oly, 1 1970 CG

SHRUBB Alf: 1 1903 & 1904 Int CC; world records – 2M (9:11.0 – 1903, 9:09.6 – 1904), 3M (14:17.6 – 1903, 14:17.2 – 1904), 6M (29:59.4 – 1904), 10,000 (31:02.4 – 1904), 10M (50:40.6 – 1904), 1 hour (18,742m - 1904)

SIMMONS Tony: 2 1976 World CC

SIMPSON Alan: World indoor record - 5000 (13:58.4 - 1965)

SIMSON Matt: 1 1994 CG SP

SMITH Colin: 1 1958 CG JT

SMITH David: 1 1986 CG HT

SMITH Steve: (HJ) 3 1993 World Ind, 3 1993 World, 3 1996 Oly

SMOUHA Edward: 3 1928 Oly 4x100

SOLLY Jon: 1 1986 CG 10,000

SOUTTER James: 3 1912 Oly 4x400

SPEDDING Charlie: 3 1984 Oly Mar

SPENCER Edward: 3 1908 Oly 10M Walk

STALLARD Henry: 3 1924 Oly 1500; world record - 4x880y (7:50.4 - 1920)

STEWART Ian: 1 1969 Eur Ind 3000, 1 1969 Eur 5000, 1 1970 CG 5000, 3 1972 Oly 5000, 1 1975 Eur Ind 3000, 1 1975 World CC; Eur record – 5000 (13:22.8 - 1970)

STEWART Lachie: 1 1970 CG 10,000

STEWART Peter: 1 1971 Eur Ind 3000

STONELEY Crew: 2 1932 Oly 4x400

STRANG David: (1500) 2 1993 World Ind, 1 1994 Eur Ind

STRAW Charlie: 1 1906 Int CC

STRODE-JACKSON Arnold: see under JACKSON

SWEENEY Arthur: 1 1934 CG 100y & 220y

TAGG Mike: 1 1970 Int CC

TAITT Laurie: World indoor records – 60H (7.9 & 7.8 – 1963)

TATHAM Wilfrid: World record – 4x880y (7:50.4 - 1920)

THACKERY Carl: 3 1993 World Half Mar

THOMAS Iwan: 2 1996 Oly 4x400, 1 1997 World 4x400, 1 1998 Eur & CG 400

THOMAS Reggie: 1 1930 CG 1M; world record – 4x1500 (15:55.6 - 1931)

THOMPSON Daley: (Dec) 1 1978 CG, 1 1980 Oly, 1 1982 CG & Eur, 1 1983 World, 1 1984 Oly, 1 1986 CG & Eur; world records - (8648 - 1980, 8730 & 8774 - 1982, 8847 - 1984)
THOMPSON Don: 1 1960 Oly 50km Walk
THOMPSON Ian: 1 1974 CG & Eur Mar; Eur rec – 2:09:12 (1974)
TOBIN Rob: 2 2009 World 4x400
TOMLIN Stan: 1 1930 CG 3M
TOMLINSON Chris: 2 2008 World Ind LJ
TOMS Edward: 3 1924 Oly 4x400
TRAVIS David: 1 1970 CG JT
TREMEER Jimmy: 3 1908 Oly 400H; world record – 100 (10.8 - 1906)
TULLOH Bruce: 1 1962 Eur 5000
TURNER Andy: 1 2010 Eur 110H, 1 2010 CG 110H
TYSOE Alfred: 1 1900 Oly 800 & 5000 team race

UNDERWOOD Adam: 1 1907 Int CC

VARAH Mike: World record - 4x880y (7:14.6 - 1966)
VICKERS Stan: (20km Walk) 1 1958 Eur, 3 1960 Oly
VOIGT Emil: 1 1908 Oly 5M

WALKER Doug: 3 1997 World 4x100, 1 1998 Eur 200
WALKER Nigel: 3 1987 World Ind 60H
WALLWORK Ron: 1 1966 CG 20M Walk
WARHURST John: 1 1974 CG 20M Walk
WARISO Solomon: 3 1999 World Ind 4x400
WEBB Ernest: 2 1908 Oly 3500m & 10M Walks, 2 1912 Oly 10,000 Walk
WEBBER George: 2 1924 Oly 3000 team race
WEBSTER Albert: World record - 4x880y (7:30.6 – 1951)
WEBSTER Jack: 1 1925 Int CC
WEIR Robert: 1 1982 CG HT, 1 1998 CG DT
WELLS Allan: 1 1978 CG 100 (1= 200), 1 1980 Oly 100 (2 200), 1 1982 CG 100
WHEELER Mike: 3 1956 Oly 4x400
WHETTON John: (1500) 1 1966, 1967 & 1968 Eur Ind, 1 1969 Eur
WHITEHEAD Nick: 3 1960 Oly 4x100
WHITLOCK Harold: (50km Walk) 1 1936 Oly, 1 1938 Eur; world record – 30M Walk (4:29:31.8 - 1935)
WILDE Ricky: 1 1970 Eur Ind 3000; world indoor record - 3000 (7:46.85 – 1970)
WILLIAMS Conrad: (4x400) 2 2009 World, 3 2010 World Ind
WILLIAMS Simon: 1 1990 CG SP

WILLIAMSON Simeon: 3 2009 World 4x100
WILMSHURST Ken: 1 1954 CG LJ & TJ
WILSON Harold: 2 1908 Oly 1500 & CC team race; world record – 1500 (3:59.8 – 1908)
WILSON Jim: 1 1920 Int CC, 3 1920 Oly 10,000
WINTER Neil: 1 1994 CG PV
WOLFF Freddie: 1 1936 Oly 4x400
WOOD Alastair: Eur record – Mar (2:13:45 - 1966)
WOOD Ted: 1 1909 & 1910 Int CC
WOODERSON Sydney: 1 1938 Eur 1500, 1 1946 Eur 5000; world records – 800m/880y (1:48.4/1:49.2 – 1938), 1M (4:06.4 – 1937)
WORKMAN Herbert: Eur record – 800 (1:54.6 - 1901)
WRIGHT Dunkie: 1 1930 CG Mar
WRIGHTON John: 1 1958 Eur 400

YATES Matthew: 1 1992 Eur Ind 1500

AAA TROPHIES

AN IMPORTANT PART of the AAA's heritage and legacy is the array of trophies which, over the years, have been presented to many of the most celebrated of athletes from all over the world as well as from Britain. Here, with thanks to Jack Miller and Philip Andrew (who provided the images), are descriptions of a few of them.

THE HARVEY MEMORIAL CUP

THIS SILVER GILT cup was awarded annually to the competitor in the AAA Championships who was adjudged by the Championships Committee to be the best champion of the year. Charles Harvey had been a respected starter who became President of the Northern Counties' AA. He died in 1907 and the trophy was donated in his memory by his brother Gordon Harvey, MP. The trophy was first awarded in 1907 jointly to Alex Duncan, winner of the 4 miles and second at 10 miles, and Jack Morton, the 100 yards champion and runner-up in the 220 yards. Among subsequent winners were Olympic champions Robert Kerr (Canada), Albert Hill, Bevil Rudd (South Africa), Eric Liddell, Harold Abrahams, Harold Osborn (USA), Douglas Lowe, Lord Burghley, Lauri Lehtinen (Finland), Janusz Kusocinski (Poland), Arthur Wint (Jamaica), Ken Matthews,

Don Quarrie (Jamaica), Ed Moses (USA), Linford Christie and Jonathan Edwards plus such world record setters as Willie Applegarth, Otto Peltzer (Germany), Sydney Wooderson, McDonald Bailey, Roland Hardy, Jim Peters, Gordon Pirie, Freddie Green, Derek Ibbotson, Basil Heatley, John Pennel (USA), Ron Clarke (Australia), Ron Hill, Dave Bedford, Al Feuerbach (USA), Brendan Foster, Renaldo Nehemiah (USA) and Steve Cram. It just underlines how many of the all-time greats competed, and excelled, in the AAA Championships.

THE C B LAWES TROPHY

THIS TROPHY WAS presented first to the mile and later 1500 metres champion and is therefore one of the most prestigious of AAA trophies. Charles Bennet Lawes (1843-1911) was a fine oarsman, having won the Diamond Sculls at Henley in 1863 and stroking the Cambridge Boat Race crew in 1865. In 1866 he became the first winner of the Amateur Athletic Club (the AAA's forerunner) mile championship. He became a well known sculptor and at the age of 55 took up speed cycling and set English amateur records at one and 25 miles. In 1900 he succeeded to the family title and became Sir Charles B Lawes-Wittewronge, Bart. The trophy has been won by many of the greatest names in miling, among them Walter George (1880, 1882 & 1884), Albert Hill (1919 & 1921), Jack Lovelock of New Zealand (1934), Sydney Wooderson (1935-1939), Roger Bannister (1951, 1953 & 1954), Eamonn Coghlan of Ireland (1977), Steve Ovett (1979 & 1980), Steve Cram (1981-1983) and Seb Coe (1989).

THE EARL OF JERSEY TROPHY

THIS MAGNIFICENT TROPHY was donated by Victor Albert George Child-Villiers, 7th Earl of Jersey, and the first President of the AAA (1845-1915). He was runner-up in the 1865 Oxford v Cambridge mile and was on the

253

organising committee of the first Amateur Athletic Club Championships the following year. He resigned as AAA President in 1890 when he was appointed Governor-General of New South Wales. The trophy was originally presented to the winner of the four miles, but was re-engraved in 1932 when the championship distance was changed to three miles. In 1969 the metric distance of 5000m was adopted. The trophy has some particularly distinguished names engraved as holders including Walter George (1880, 1882 & 1884), Alf Shrubb (1901-1904), Albert Hill (1910), Hannes Kolehmainen (1911) and Paavo Nurmi (1922) of Finland, Sydney Wooderson (1946), Chris Chataway (1952 & 1955), Gordon Pirie (1953 & 1961), Derek Ibbotson (1956 & 1957), Ron Clarke of Australia (1965-1967), Ian Stewart (1969), Dave Bedford (1972), Brendan Foster (1973, 1974 & 1976) and Henry Rono of Kenya (1978).

THE C W F PEARCE TROPHY

THIS IS THE most unusual and certainly the heaviest of the AAA trophies. It was presented to the winner of the javelin championship. It is unusual not just for its design but also that it was not donated but acquired by the AAA in memory of its Hon Treasurer (since 1938) Claude W F Pearce, who was taken fatally ill at a AAA Committee meeting in 1947. Pearce had also amazingly been President of Herne Hill Harriers both before and after both World Wars, his terms of office being 1909-1910, 1919-1920 and 1938-1946. The bronze trophy is also distinctive for the detachable javelin. Holders of the trophy have included world record breakers Jorma Kinnunen of Finland (1966), Miklós Németh of Hungary (1980) and Steve Backley (1989, 1992 & 1998-2000). The most prolific winners were David Travis and Mick Hill who were champions seven times between 1965 & 1974 and 1987 & 2003 respectively.

PRESIDENTS AND OFFICERS OF THE AAA

1880–1890 The Earl of Jersey (1845–1915)

VICTOR ALBERT GEORGE CHILD-VILLIERS, 7th Earl of Jersey, won the mile at Eton in 1862, was runner-up to his successor as AAA President, Richard Webster, in the 1865 Oxford v Cambridge mile and helped organise the first Amateur Athletic Club (AAC) Championships, forerunner of the AAA Championships, in 1866. He resigned as President on being appointed Governor-General of New South Wales.

1891–1915 Viscount Alverstone (1842–1915)

AS RICHARD WEBSTER, he set a world amateur best of 10:07 ¼ for 2 miles at the 1865 Cambridge University Sports and won the mile and 2 miles in the Inter-Varsity Sports that year. He went on to enjoy a distinguished legal career. He was called to the bar in 1868; in 1885 he became Attorney-General and in 1900 he was raised to the peerage. Between 1900 and 1913 he was England's Lord Chief Justice, his cases including the Dr Crippen Trial in 1910.

1916–1930 Sir Montague Shearman (1857–1930)

THE AAC 100 yards champion in 1876 at age 19, he represented England against Ireland that year in the world's first international match. The inaugural AAA 440 yards champion in 1880, he was one of the three young men who effectively founded the AAA and was its first Honorary Secretary. His book *Athletics and Football*, first published in 1887, is acknowledged as a classic. He was called to the bar in 1881 and was involved in several high profile trials. He was knighted in 1914 when he became a judge.

1930–1936 Lord Desborough (1855–1945)

WILLIAM GRENFELL, Lord Desborough of Taplow, was a remarkable all-round sportsman. He set a Harrow School mile record which lasted over 60 years, played cricket against Eton, placed second in the 1876 Inter-Varsity 3 miles and rowed for Oxford, climbed the Matterhorn and swam across Niagara! He was an MP between 1880 and 1900 and made a peer in 1905; as Chairman of the British Olympic Association and an IOC representative he was heavily involved in the staging of the London Games of 1908.

1936–1976 The Marquess of Exeter (1905–1981)

COMPETING AS Lord Burghley, he set British records in all three hurdling events (120, 220 and 440 yards), including briefly a share of the world record at the longest event in 1927, before winning the 1928 Olympic 400m hurdles in Amsterdam, setting a British record of 53.4 in the process. Four years later, at the Los Angeles Games, he lowered that record to 52.2 in fourth place and contributed a 46.7 leg for Britain's silver medal winning 4x400m relay team. He won both the 120 and 440 yards hurdles at the inaugural Empire Games in 1930 and that year he ran 14.5 for the "highs", only 0.1 sec outside the world record.

Elected a Conservative MP from 1931 until in 1943 he was appointed Governor of Bermuda, he became a member of the International Olympic Committee in 1933 and was elected AAA President in 1936 (the youngest ever at 31), serving for 40 years. He was also IAAF President from 1946 to 1976 and as Chairman of the Organising Committee for the 1948 Olympics played a vital role in the success of the London Games.

1976–1978 Harold Abrahams (1899–1978)

EXCEEDING EVERYONE'S EXPECTATIONS, except possibly those of his coach Sam Mussabini, he became the first European to win the Olympic 100m, three times equalling the Olympic record of 10.6 at the "Chariots of Fire" Games in Paris in 1924. He followed with a silver medal in the 4x100m relay but that was effectively the end of his active career. In May 1925 he seriously damaged his leg while long jumping (his 7.38m leap in 1924 stood as the English native record for 32 years!) and turned to other ways he could serve athletics. A barrister by profession, he was a member of AAA General Committee from age 26 and was Hon. Treasurer of the BAAB from 1948 to 1968, BAAB Chairman from 1968 to 1975, and in 1976 fulfilled a life ambition by being elected AAA President. He was also for many years an influential member of the IAAF, was a prolific writer on the sport – notably as athletics correspondent of The Sunday Times from 1925 to 1967 – and provided radio commentaries for the BBC over an even longer period. He was also a noted historian and statistician.

1978–1984 Squire Yarrow (1905–1984)

A MOTOR RACING driver at Brooklands in his younger days, he did not take up running seriously until he was in his thirties. He found immediate success when he moved up to the marathon in 1938, finishing second in his debut, the Polytechnic race, and then winning the silver medal at the European Championships in Paris. He clocked his fastest time of 2:37:50 in 1939 and after war service in the RAF he was involved in the closest ever AAA Marathon, in 1946 at age 40, finishing just one fifth of a second ahead of Donald McNab Robertson! His main contribution to the sport, though, was as a tireless and popular official from the 1930s onwards.

1984–1986 Ron Goodman (1912–2001)

WHEN ELECTED PRESIDENT at the 1984 AGM he referred to so many of his predecessors being aristocrats and medallists and described himself – the first President not to have gone to either Oxford or Cambridge – as "the first of the scrubbers, the plebeians." A former sprinter and cross country runner with Herne Hill Harriers (which he joined at 16) he became the club's Hon. General Secretary in 1935, aged 23. Serving with the Royal Artillery during the war he won the Military Medal for bravery. He was Surrey County AAA President in 1967–68, Southern Counties AAA President in 1977–78, served as a member of the BAAB Council and was Chairman of AAA General Committee. His younger brother Doug Goodman (1919–2008) was also a prominent official and was British team manager at the 1976 Olympics and England team manager at three Commonwealth Games (1970–1978).

1986–1991 Arthur McAllister (1920–2006)

KNOWN THROUGHOUT THE sport as Arthur Mac, he was one of the key figures in British athletics. His first important post was as Coaching Secretary for the North of England and he gradually worked his way up to the highest levels of administration, serving as Chairman of the BAAB from 1975 to 1980 and acting as the British athletics team's Head of Delegation at the Moscow Olympics. From 1982 to 1986 he was Chairman of AAA General Committee. After five years as AAA President he served a further five years (1991–1996) as President of the British Athletic Federation.

1991–1994 Dame Marea Hartman (1920–1994)

INVOLVED IN THE sport for all of her adult life, first as a runner for Spartan Ladies AC and Surrey and then, from soon after the war, as an official, she rose to become the most influential woman in British athletics. She became Hon. Treasurer of the Women's AAA in 1950, took over as Hon. Secretary in 1960 and for over two decades was also the British women's team manager. She was at the heart of BAAB affairs, serving as Hon. Treasurer from 1972 to 1984 and as Chairman from 1989 to 1991. She was Chairman of the IAAF Women's Commission from 1968 to 1981 and did much to broaden the programme of events available to women. She finally came to terms with amalgamation and after her beloved WAAA merged with the AAA she was elected the first President of the AAA of England. She received the ultimate accolade for her services to the sport by being made a Dame a few months before her death. She was one of five "Women of Achievement" selected for a set of postage stamps issued in 1996.

1995– 2000 Sir Arthur Gold (1917– 2002)

AN INTERNATIONAL HIGH jumper in 1937 with a best of 1.90m when the British record stood at 1.95m, he was among the pioneers of British coaching, qualifying in his early twenties, and went on to fill practically every post of significance in British athletics. He succeeded Jack Crump as Hon. Secretary of the BAAB in 1965 and during his 12 years in that role he was also athletics Team Leader at the 1968, 1972 and 1976 Olympics. In 1992, as Chairman of the British Olympic Association, he was Commandant of the entire team at the Albertville and Barcelona Olympics. He was President of the European AA from 1976 to 1987, his firm stance on the dangers of drugs and over commercialisation making him one of the most respected figures in international sport, and he was knighted in 1984 for services to athletics. Ill health cut short his term as President of the AAA of England.

2000– 2004 Lord (Sebastian) Coe (1956–)

SEB COE ENJOYED one of the most successful careers of any athlete in history. Not only did he become the first man ever to retain a quadrennial Olympic 1500m title (1980 & 1984) and the only Briton to claim four individual Olympic medals (with 800m silvers in 1980 & 1984) but he set a number of world records which in their day were considered phenomenal. His 1:41.73 for 800m went unbeaten for 16 years and his 2:12.18 1000m for 18 years, both still the British records; other less durable but still mightily impressive world records included 1500m in 3:32.03 (1979) and the mile in 3:47.33 (1981). A Conservative MP from 1992 to 1997, he was created a life peer in 2000, is currently a Vice-President of the IAAF, and won immense public acclaim by leading London's successful 2012 Olympic bid.

2004– 2011 Sir Rodney Walker (1943–)

THIS FORMER SHOT putter's wide sporting background as an administrator includes being Chairman of Wakefield Trinity Rugby League FC between 1986 and 1993, the Rugby Football League between 1993 and 2002, the GB Sports Council between 1994 and 1996, and UK Sport between 1997 and 2003. He was also Chairman of Wembley National Stadium Ltd, the World Professional Billiards & Snooker Association for several years until 2009 and of the Manchester 2002 Commonwealth Games. He was knighted in 1996 for services to sport and designated Yorkshire's Man of the Year in 2008. He stood down as AAA President prior to the 2011 AGM.

PATRON

Her Majesty The Queen

HONORARY SECRETARIES

1880–1883 Sir Montague Shearman
1883–1906 Charles Herbert
1906–1915 Percy Fisher
1915–1931 Sir Harry Barclay
1931–1938 Douglas Lowe
1938–1947 Ernest Holt
1947–1965 Ernest Clynes
1965–1982 Barry Willis
1982–1991 Mike Farrell*
1991–1993 Derek Johnson
1993–2000 Roy Mitchell
2004– Walter Nicholls
* General (Professional) Secretary

HONORARY TREASURERS

1880–1910 Clement Jackson
1910–1932 William Barnard
1932–1938 Ernest Holt
1938–1947 Claude Pearce
1947–1957 Walter Jewell
1957–1960 Arthur Thwaites
1960–1966 Phil Gale
1966–1967 George Cooper
1967–1970 Frank Read
1970–1974 John Martell
1974–1980 Ray Stroud
1980–1985 John Martell
1985–1986 David Cropper
1986–1991 John Lister
1991–2001 Geoff Clarke
2001–2005 Keith Atkins

2006 Graham Jessop
2007–2008 Richard Float
2008–2009 Graham Jessop
2010– Martin Etchells

CHAIRMEN OF GENERAL COMMITTEE

(From 1946)
1946–1950 Arthur Turk
1950–1965 J Willie Turner
1966–1967 Sidney Best
1967–1969 Eric Kennell
1970–1975 Ron Goodman
1976–1980 Les Golding
1981–1986 Arthur McAllister
1987–1988 Bill Ferguson
1989–1991 Dr Bill Evans
1991–2004 David Cropper
2004– 2007 George Bunner
2007–2008 Graham Jessop*
2009– Chris Carter*
* General Committee was abolished under the new Constitution when the Association reverted to AAA in 2007 and the post was designated as Chairman

FOUNDER LIFE VICE-PRESIDENTS

R.J. Barrow; Miss N. Blaine MBE; Mrs F.M. Clarke MBE; Wg. Cdr. D.C. Davies OBE; Miss E.M. Holland MBE; Mrs J. Lindsay; Mrs M.M. Oakley; B.E. Willis OBE; G.A. Wright.

LIFE VICE-PRESIDENTS

D. Adams; G. Clarke; D. Cropper OBE; Mrs S. Deaves; Mrs J. Febery; Mrs P.M. Green; E. Nash; K.A. Oakley

MANAGEMENT BOARD (2011)

C. Carter – Chairman; W. Nicholls – Honorary Secretary; M. Etchells – Treasurer; A.G. Bunner MBE – Events Director; R.H. Float – Director; I. Byett – Director (Cross Country); E.C. Butcher – Director (Road Running); M. Neighbour – Regional Director; G. Durbin – Regional Director; B. Heywood – Regional Director; Ms F.P. Ratchford – Director.

AWARDS OF HONOUR

AAA AWARD OF HONOUR plaques were presented to any person approved by General Committee in recognition of outstanding service to Amateur Athletics and the AAA.

1948: E.H. Clynes, E.J. Holt, W.J. Pepper, A.W.H. Stringer, E.Tomlinson, J.W.Turner, A.S. Turk
1956: W.C. Jewell
1959: Cdr F.W. Collins, W. Butler, A.D. Thwaites
1960: S.G. Moss
1963: R. St. G.T. Harper, A.B. Wignall, J.D.B. Williams
1964: E. Neville, E.R.L. Powell, J.C.G. Crump
1966: E. Strickland
1967: L.J. Cohen
1968: H.M. Abrahams
1970: A.J.C. Kendall
1972: C.S.P. Dale, Lt Cdr C.A. Sinfield, A.E. Williams
1975: F. Davies, J. Forrester, L.H. Golding, J.C. Rice
1977: R.W. Goodman, B.E. Willis
1979: G.M. Adam, C.J. Harrison, A.A. Tomkins, S.A. Wright
1981: R.L. Stroud
1982: Sqd Ldr C.N. Cobb, Sir Arthur Gold, F.J. Martell, A.J. Norman, W. Rae
1983: Wing Cdr D.C. Davies, A.W. Eves, D.J.D. Goodman, F.A. Keen
1984: R.B Evans, J.E. Davies
1985: K. Finding
1986: J.W. Aspland
1987: A.G. McAllister
1988: W.J. Ferguson, A.H. Willmot
1989: D. Cropper, M.A. Farrell, K.W.B. Harris, R. Mitchell, R.V. Roberts
1990: R.A.Sales
2004: Marianne Lingen, E.Sutters
2007: G.Clarke, K.A.Oakley

AAA CHAMPIONS

Senior Men

AAA TITLE WINNERS from 1980 to 2006 inclusive; UK champions from 2007 to 2010. England Senior Championships were instituted in 2010 and winners are listed below the UK champions for that year. AAA champions from 1880 to 1979 were listed in *The Official Centenary History of the AAA* by Peter Lovesey

(Where the AAA title was won by an overseas athlete, the highest placed UK athlete is shown in brackets)

Venues: (AAA Championships) 1980–1987 London/Crystal Palace; 1988–1993 & 1995–2003 Birmingham; 1994 Sheffield; 2004–2006 Manchester; (UK Championships) 2007 Manchester; 2008–2010 Birmingham; (England Senior Championships) 2010 Gateshead

100 METRES

(Event instituted in 1880 at 100 yards; 100m since 1969)

1980	Allan Wells	10.36
1981	Mel Lattany USA	10.24
	(3, Drew McMaster 10.45)	
1982	Cameron Sharp	10.31
1983	Calvin Smith USA	10.30
	(2, Allan Wells 10.34)	
1984	Donovan Reid	10.42
1985	Ernest Obeng GHA	10.44
	(4, Lincoln Asquith 10.49)	
1986	Linford Christie	10.22

1987	Dwayne Evans USA	10.33
	(2, John Regis 10.37)	
1988	Linford Christie	10.15
1989	Linford Christie	10.16
1990	Calvin Smith USA	10.21w
	(2, Linford Christie 10.21)	
1991	Linford Christie	10.14
1992	Linford Christie	10.09
1993	Linford Christie	10.13
1994	Linford Christie	9.91w
1995	Darren Braithwaite	10.33
	(Linford Christie, guesting, won in 10.18)	
1996	Linford Christie	10.04
1997	Jason Gardener	10.31
1998	Darren Campbell	10.22
1999	Jason Gardener	10.02w
2000	Dwain Chambers	10.11
2001	Dwain Chambers	10.01
2002	Mark Lewis-Francis	10.06
2003	Darren Campbell	10.19
	(Dwain Chambers won in 10.08 but result later annulled due to drugs disqualification)	
2004	Jason Gardener	10.22
2005	Jason Gardener	10.26
2006	Marlon Devonish	10.19
2007	Marlon Devonish	10.31
2008	Dwain Chambers	10.00
2009	Simeon Williamson	10.05
2010	Dwain Chambers	10.14
	Tremayne Gilling	10.25

Most titles won: 8 Linford Christie 1986, 1988, 1989, 1991–1994, 1996. Most medals: 10 Christie

200 METRES

(Event instituted in 1902 at 220 yards; 200m since 1969)

1980	Mel Lattany USA	20.74
	(3, Trevor Hoyte 21.11)	
1981	Stanley Floyd USA	20.51
	(3, Mike McFarlane 20.92)	
1982	Don Quarrie JAM	20.79
	(2, Buster Watson 20.90)	
1983	Mel Lattany USA	20.61
	(2, Donovan Reid 21.00)	
1984	Todd Bennett	20.79w
1985	Ade Mafe	20.99
1986	John Regis	20.41
1987	John Regis	20.25
1988	Linford Christie	20.46
1989	Marcus Adam	20.78
1990	John Regis	20.28

AAA Champions

1991	Jon Drummond USA	20.61
	(2, Michael Rosswess 20.64)	
1992	John Regis	20.27
1993	Jeff Williams USA	20.47w
	(2, Toby Box 20.85)	
1994	Solomon Wariso	20.67w
1995	John Regis	20.37
1996	John Regis	20.54
1997	Marlon Devonish	20.65
1998	Doug Walker	20.35
1999	Julian Golding	20.20w
2000	Darren Campbell	20.49
2001	Marlon Devonish	20.52
2002	Marlon Devonish	20.18w
2003	Julian Golding	20.37
2004	Chris Lambert	20.94
2005	Christian Malcolm	20.65
2006	Marlon Devonish	20.69
2007	Marlon Devonish	20.79
2008	Christian Malcolm	20.52
2009	Toby Sandeman	20.69
2010	Christian Malcolm	20.77
	Chris Clarke	21.06

Most titles won: 7 McDonald Bailey 1946, 1947, 1949–1953. Most medals: 10 Marlon Devonish

400 METRES

(Event instituted in 1880 at 440 yards; 400m since 1969)

1980	Rod Milne	46.53
1981	Tony Darden USA	45.11
	(3, Garry Cook 46.25)	
1982	Mike Paul TRI	45.74
	(2, David Jenkins 45.93)	
1983	Darren Clark AUS	45.05
	(7, Ainsley Bennett 46.43)	
1984	Darren Clark AUS	45.66
	(4, Alan Slack 46.51)	
1985	Darren Clark AUS	45.45
	(2, Derek Redmond 45.52)	
1986	Darren Clark AUS	44.94
	(2, Roger Black 45.16)	
1987	Gabriel Tiacoh CIV	45.10
	(2, Derek Redmond 45.17)	
1988	Kriss Akabusi	44.93
1989	Phil Brown	46.26
1990	Howard Burnett JAM	45.52
	(6, Lewis Samuel 46.73)	
1991	Derek Redmond	46.07
1992	Alvin Daniel TRI	44.84
	(2, Derek Redmond 45.14)	

1993	Kennedy Ochieng KEN	45.32
	(2, Ade Mafe 45.64)	
1994	Roger Black	44.94
1995	Mark Richardson	44.94
1996	Roger Black	44.39
1997	Kent Ulyatt	46.86
1998	Iwan Thomas	44.50
1999	Jamie Baulch	45.36
2000	Mark Richardson	45.55
2001	Mark Richardson	45.79
2002	Tim Benjamin	45.73
2003	Daniel Caines	45.56
2004	Tim Benjamin	45.58
2005	Tim Benjamin	45.52
2006	Tim Benjamin	46.00
2007	Andrew Steele	45.70
2008	Martyn Rooney	45.31
2009	Rob Tobin	45.84
2010	Martyn Rooney	44.99
	Nick Leavey	46.52

Most titles won: 6 David Jenkins 1971–1976. Most medals: 9 Jenkins

800 METRES

(Event instituted in 1880 at 880 yards; 800m since 1969)

1980	Omer Khalifa SUD	1:47.43
	(3, Paul Forbes 1:48.31)	
1981	Sebastian Coe	1:45.41
1982	Peter Elliott	1:45.61
1983	William Wuycke VEN	1:45.44
	(2, Peter Elliott 1:45.64)	
1984	Steve Cram	1:46.84
1985	José-Luis Barbosa BRA	1:45.48
	(5, John Gladwin 1:47.08)	
1986	Steve Cram	1:46.15
1987	Peter Elliott	1:48.71
1988	Steve Cram	1:44.16
1989	Ikem Billy	1:48.01
1990	William Tanui KEN	1:44.14
	(2, Tom McKean 1:44.44)	
1991	Tom McKean	1:45.67
1992	Curtis Robb	1:45.16
1993	Martin Steele	1:47.83
1994	Craig Winrow	1:48.45
1995	Curtis Robb	1:46.78
1996	Curtis Robb	1:47.61
1997	James Nolan IRL	1:51.47
	(2, Noel Edwards 1:51.73)	
1998	Jason Lobo	1:49.68
1999	Mark Sesay	1:48.03
2000	James McIlroy	1:50.08

AAA Champions

2001	Neil Speaight	1:49.63
2002	James McIlroy	1:50.09
2003	Ricky Soos	1:47.51
2004	Sam Ellis	1:49.19
2005	Tim Bayley	1:48.54
2006	Michael Rimmer	1:47.20
2007	Michael Rimmer	1:47.06
2008	Michael Rimmer	1:49.13
2009	Michael Rimmer	1:46.47
2010	Michael Rimmer	1:47.22
	Darren St Clair	1:49.58

Most titles won: 5 Michael Rimmer 2006–2010. Most medals: 6 Noel Carroll IRL

1500 METRES

(Event instituted in 1880 at 1 mile; 1500m since 1969 except for 1980)

1980	Steve Ovett	4:04.40 (mile)
1981	Steve Cram	3:36.82
1982	Steve Cram	3:36.14
1983	Steve Cram	3:41.69
1984	Peter Elliott	3:39.66
1985	Marcus O'Sullivan IRL	3:40.27
	(3, Alistair Currie 3:41.09)	
1986	John Gladwin	3:35.93
1987	Steve Crabb	3:41.23
1988	Peter Elliott	3:44.48
1989	Sebastian Coe	3:41.38
1990	Neil Horsfield	3:44.70
1991	Matthew Yates	3:40.88
1992	Kevin McKay	3:37.51
1993	Matthew Yates	3:38.75
1994	Kevin McKay	3:40.59
1995	John Mayock	3:40.55
1996	John Mayock	3:37.03
1997	Richard Ashe	3:54.37
1998	John Mayock	3:39.38
1999	John Mayock	3:39.12
2000	John Mayock	3:45.29
2001	John Mayock	3:44.05
2002	Anthony Whiteman	3:38.24
2003	Michael East	3:42.29
2004	Chris Mulvaney	3:50.14
2005	Nick McCormick	3:37.05
2006	Andy Baddeley	3:41.18
2007	Andy Baddeley	3:43.25
2008	Tom Lancashire	3:38.92
2009	Jermaine Mays	3:41.26
2010	Andy Baddeley	3:41.49
	Nick McCormick	3:42.67

Most titles won: 6 John Mayock 1995, 1996, 1998–2001. Most medals: 7 Bill Nankeville & Mayock

3000 METRES

(Event instituted in 1989; discontinued after 1999)

1989	Matt Giusto USA	8:00.38
	(2, Tony Leonard 8:04.92)	
1990	John Walker NZL	8:05.01
	(2, Matthew Clarkson 8:06.22)	
1991	Tom Hanlon	8:02.11
1992	Frank O'Mara IRL	7:59.97
	(2, Michael Quinn 8:03.85)	
1993	Joseph Keter KEN	7:56.39
	(5, Spencer Barden 8:07.44)	
1994	Bashir Hussain	8:19.28
1995	Nick Hopkins	8:11.86
1996	Matt O'Dowd	8:30.11
1997	Cormac Finnerty IRL	8:08.83
	(2, Allen Graffin 8:15.54)	
1998	Nick Comerford	8:11.98
1999	Andy Graffin	8:07.58

5000 METRES

(Event instituted in 1932 at 3 miles; 5000m since 1969)

1980	Harald Hudak FRG	13:51.71
	(2, Dick Callan 13:52.49)	
1981	Eamonn Coghlan IRL	13:20.36
	(4, Geoff Smith 13:26.33)	
1982	Wilson Waigwa KEN	13:29.32
	(2, Tim Hutchings 13:30.53)	
1983	Steve Harris	13:38.63
1984	Ray Flynn IRL	13:19.52
	(2, Nick Rose 13:22.00)	
1985	David Lewis	13:42.82
1986	Tim Hutchings	13:25.03
1987	Jack Buckner	13:25.02
1988	Eamonn Martin	13:50.03
1989	Mark Rowland	13:32.05
1990	Eamonn Martin	13:32.07
1991	Eamonn Martin	13:32.99
1992	Jack Buckner	13:22.50
1993	Jon Brown	13:35.67
1994	Dermot Donnelly	13:52.63
1995	Rob Denmark	13:37.57
1996	John Nuttall	13:48.35
1997	Kris Bowditch	13:53.12
1998	Karl Keska	13:41.61
1999	Rob Denmark	13:34.17
2000	Andres Jones	13:45.86
2001	Jon Wild	13:52.72
2002	Jon Wild	13:52.59

AAA Champions

2003	Andy Graffin	13:56.59
2004	Chris Thompson	13:42.10
2005	Mark Carroll IRL	13:48.90
	(2, Mark Miles 13:58.18)	
2006	Peter Riley	13:46.68
2007	Mo Farah	13:40.19
2008	Andy Vernon	13:54.26
2009	Scott Overall	13:57.75
2010	Chris Thompson	13:48.15
	Mark Draper	14:06.51

Most titles won: 3 Bruce Tulloh 1959, 1962, 1963; Ron Clarke AUS 1965–1967; Brendan Foster 1973, 1974, 1976; Eamonn Martin 1988, 1990, 1991. Most medals: 5 Tulloh
(4 Miles 1880–1931; most titles won: 4 Alf Shrubb 1901–1904; 5 medals)

10,000 METRES

(Event instituted in 1932 at 6 miles; 10,000m since 1969)
(Venues: staged at main championships except for 1989 Birmingham; 1990 Gateshead; 1991 Cardiff; 1992 Sheffield; 1993 London (Crystal Palace); 1995 Loughborough; 1997–1998 Bedford; 1999–2001 & 2003–2008 Watford; 2002 Manchester)

1980	Nick Rose	28:11.98
1981	Barry Smith	28:06.13
1982	Julian Goater	28:02.45
1983	Charlie Spedding	28:08.12
1984	Steve Jones	28:09.97
1985	Kevin Ryan USA	28:50.70
	(2, Karl Harrison 28:52.46)	
1986	Jon Solly	27:51.76
1987	Steve Harris	28:35.07
1988	Steve Binns	28:40.14
1989	Eamonn Martin	28:13.69
1990	Richard Nerurkar	28:05.16
1991	Carl Thackery	28:37.52
1992	Eamonn Martin	28:02.56
1993	Paul Evans	28:17.49
1994	Rob Denmark	28:03.34
1995	Gary Staines	28:49.29
1996	Rob Denmark	28:20.80
1997	Mark Steinle	29:27.98
1998	Dermot Donnelly	28:43.17
1999	Paul Evans	28:34.62
2000	Andres Jones	28:00.50
2001	Glynn Tromans	28:31.33
2002	Rob Denmark	28:43.42
2003	Karl Keska	27:56.37
2004	Matt O'Dowd	29:05.08
2005	Gavin Thompson	28:40.58
2006	Dominic Bannister	29:31.26

2007	Phil Nicholls	28:40.85
2008	Anthony Ford	28:30.39
2009	Andy Vernon	28:43.41
2010	James Walsh	29:04.62

Most titles won: 5 Dave Bedford 1970–1974. Most medals: 5 Frank Sando, Bedford & Rob Denmark
(10 Miles 1880–1972; most titles won: 5 Ron Hill 1965–1969)

3000 METRES STEEPLECHASE

(Steeplechase instituted in 1880; distance varied until 1912; 2 miles 1913–1953; 3000m from 1954)

1980	Roger Hackney	8:39.38
1981	Ken Martin USA	8:29.25
	(2, Graeme Fell 8:31.80)	
1982	Roger Hackney	8:28.98
1983	Colin Reitz	8:28.42
1984	Domingo Ramón ESP	8:23.12
	(2, Paul Davies-Hale 8:24.07)	
1985	Brian Diemer USA	8:31.51
	(2, Kevin Capper 8:38.11)	
1986	Eddie Wedderburn	8:33.03
1987	Eddie Wedderburn	8:24.78
1988	Mark Rowland	8:32.60
1989	Colin Walker	8:35.73
1990	Philip Barkutwo KEN	8:22.22
	(2, Tom Hanlon 8:22.60)	
1991	Colin Walker	8:38.02
1992	Colin Walker	8:25.15
1993	Colin Walker	8:33.45
1994	Justin Chaston	8:28.28
1995	Spencer Duval	8:24.64
1996	Justin Chaston	8:29.19
1997	Spencer Duval	8:45.91
1998	Christian Stephenson	8:32.76
1999	Christian Stephenson	8:44.42
2000	Christian Stephenson	8:28.21
2001	Ben Whitby	8:32.68
2002	Ben Whitby	8:40.12
2003	Stuart Stokes	8:40.10
2004	Justin Chaston	8:33.69
2005	Andrew Lemoncello	8:33.93
2006	Jermaine Mays	8:39.95
2007	Andrew Lemoncello	8:42.57
2008	Adam Bowden	8:36.17
2009	Luke Gunn	8:46.87
2010	Luke Gunn	8:37.35
	Stuart Stokes	8:35.79

Most titles won: 8 Maurice Herriott 1959, 1961–1967. Most medals: 9 Herriott

110 METRES HURDLES

(Event instituted in 1880 at 120 yards; 110m since 1969)

1980	Rod Milburn USA	13.69
	(2, Mark Holtom 13.71)	
1981	Renaldo Nehemiah USA	13.17
	(3, Mark Holtom 13.75)	
1982	Mark Holtom	13.88
1983	Tonie Campbell USA	13.41
	(5, Mark Holtom 13.96)	
1984	Nigel Walker	13.78
1985	Henry Andrade USA	13.83
	(2, Nigel Walker 13.98)	
1986	Colin Jackson	13.51
1987	Jon Ridgeon	13.36
1988	Colin Jackson	13.29
1989	Colin Jackson	13.19
1990	Colin Jackson	13.23
1991	David Nelson	13.55
1992	Colin Jackson	13.15
1993	Colin Jackson	13.15
1994	Andy Tulloch	13.70
1995	Neil Owen	13.63
1996	Colin Jackson	13.13
1997	Damien Greaves	14.02
1998	Colin Jackson	13.37
1999	Colin Jackson	13.24w
2000	Colin Jackson	13.54
2001	Tony Jarrett	13.66
2002	Colin Jackson	13.40
2003	Damien Greaves	13.66
2004	Robert Newton	13.72
2005	Allan Scott	13.62
2006	Andy Turner	13.24w
2007	Andy Turner	13.54
2008	Andy Turner	13.58
2009	Andy Turner	13.47
2010	William Sharman	13.45
	Lawrence Clarke	14.0

Most titles won: 11 Colin Jackson 1986, 1988–1990, 1992, 1993, 1996, 1998–2000, 2002. Most medals: 11 Don Finlay (between 1929 & 1949!) & Jackson

400 METRES HURDLES

(Event instituted in 1914 at 440 yards; 400m since 1969)

1980	James King USA	49.50
	(2, Bill Hartley 50.04)	
1981	Gary Oakes	49.69
1982	James King USA	50.25
	(4, Mike Whittingham 51.13)	

1983	David Lee USA	49.18
	(2, Steve Sole 49.95)	
1984	Martin Gillingham	50.24
1985	Ahmed Hamada BRN	49.82
	(2, Max Robertson 50.16)	
1986	Max Robertson	49.52
1987	Max Robertson	49.51
1988	Max Robertson	50.23
1989	Max Robertson	50.30
1990	Nat Page USA	50.06
	(2, Max Robertson 50.22)	
1991	Max Robertson	49.98
1992	Kriss Akabusi	49.16
1993	Gary Cadogan	50.60
1994	Peter Crampton	49.82
1995	Rohan Robinson AUS	49.21
	(2, Gary Cadogan 49.70)	
1996	Jon Ridgeon	49.16
1997	Charles Robertson-Adams	51.01
1998	Paul Gray	49.81
1999	Chris Rawlinson	49.62
2000	Chris Rawlinson	48.95
2001	Chris Rawlinson	48.68
2002	Chris Rawlinson	48.68
2003	Chris Rawlinson	49.24
2004	Chris Rawlinson	50.04
2005	Matt Elias	49.67
2006	Rhys Williams	49.28
2007	Dale Garland	49.79
2008	Rick Yates	49.50
2009	David Greene	49.07
2010	David Greene	48.77
	David Hughes	49.73

Most titles won: 7 Harry Whittle 1947–1953. Most medals: 8 Max Robertson

HIGH JUMP

(Event instituted in 1880)

1980	Carlo Thränhardt FRG	2.23
	(2, Mark Naylor 2.20)	
1981	James Frazier USA	2.23
	(2, Mark Naylor 2.20)	
1982	Takao Sakamoto JPN	2.24
	(3, Geoff Parsons 2.18)	
1983	Leo Williams USA	2.29
	(5, Geoff Parsons 2.20)	
1984	Francisco Centelles CUB	2.30
	(4, Geoff Parsons 2.22)	
1985	Milt Ottey CAN	2.28
	(4=, Dalton Grant 2.20)	
1986	Geoff Parsons	2.23

AAA Champions

1987	Geoff Parsons	2.24
1988	Geoff Parsons	2.28
1989	Dalton Grant	2.33
1990	Dalton Grant	2.28
1991	Hollis Conway USA	2.31
	(2, Geoff Parsons 2.28)	
1992	Steve Smith	2.31
1993	Tim Forsyth AUS	2.32
	(2, Steve Smith 2.30)	
1994	Brendan Reilly	2.24
1995	Steve Smith	2.35
1996	Steve Smith	2.31
1997	Mark Mandy IRL	2.20
	(2, Brendan Reilly 2.15)	
1998	Dalton Grant	2.20
1999	Steve Smith	2.28
2000	Ben Challenger	2.22
2001	Ben Challenger	2.17
2002	Dalton Grant	2.20
2003	Ben Challenger	2.24
2004	Ben Challenger	2.23
2005	Ben Challenger	2.27
2006	Martyn Bernard	2.25
2007	Martyn Bernard	2.24
2008	Tom Parsons	2.30
2009	Germaine Mason	2.24
2010	Martyn Bernard	2.28
	Robbie Grabarz	2.23

Most titles won: 6 Howard Baker 1910, 1912, 1913, 1919–1921. Most medals: 13 Dalton Grant (1987–2004)

POLE VAULT

(Event instituted in 1880)

1980	Brian Hooper	5.59
1981	Earl Bell USA	5.50
	(3, Keith Stock 5.20)	
1982	Tomomi Takahashi JPN	5.51
	(3, Jeff Gutteridge 5.20)	
1983	Jeff Gutteridge	5.35
1984	Jeff Gutteridge	5.40
1985	Kory Tarpenning USA	5.40
	(5, Keith Stock 5.20)	
1986	Brian Hooper	5.30
1987	Jeff Gutteridge	5.35
1988	Simon Arkell AUS	5.10
	(2, Mike Edwards 5.00)	
1989	Mike Edwards	5.20
1990	Paul Benavides USA	5.30
	(2, Mike Edwards 5.25)	

1991	Tim Bright USA	5.50
	(3, Mike Edwards 5.30)	
1992	Ian Tullett	5.30
1993	Simon Arkell AUS	5.60
	(6, Ian Tullett 5.10)	
1994	Andy Ashurst	5.30
1995	Nick Buckfield	5.50
1996	Nick Buckfield	5.71
1997	Tim Thomas	5.30
1998	Kevin Hughes	5.40
1999	Kevin Hughes	5.50
2000	Kevin Hughes	5.50
2001	Paul Williamson	5.30
2002	Nick Buckfield	5.35
2003	Nick Buckfield	5.50
2004	Tim Thomas	5.45
2005	Nick Buckfield	5.50
2006	Steve Lewis	5.40
2007	Steve Lewis	5.61
2008	Steve Lewis	5.60
2009	Luke Cutts	5.55
2010	Joe Ive	5.35
	Luke Cutts	5.40

Most titles won: 7 Tom Ray 1881, 1882, 1884–1888. Most medals: 10 Ray, Brian Hooper (1971–1987) & Mike Edwards

LONG JUMP

(Event instituted in 1880)

1980	Arnie Robinson USA	7.92
	(2, Gus Udo 7.64)	
1981	Larry Myricks USA	8.38
	(2, Roy Mitchell 7.60)	
1982	Junichi Usui JPN	7.94w
	(2, John Herbert 7.94w)	
1983	Mike Conley USA	7.82
	(2, Fred Salle 7.56w)	
1984	Fred Salle	7.59
1985	Dannie Jackson USA	7.89
	(2, Derrick Brown 7.80)	
1986	Derrick Brown	8.07w
1987	Mike Powell USA	7.94
	(3, Keith Fleming 7.50)	
1988	Stewart Faulkner	7.98
1989	Stewart Faulkner	8.13
1990	Stewart Faulkner	8.05
1991	Barrington Williams	7.94
1992	David Culbert AUS	7.85
	(3, Mark Forsythe 7.66)	
1993	Fred Salle	7.72

1994	Barrington Williams	7.77
1995	Fred Salle	7.66
1996	Darren Ritchie	7.86
1997	Steve Phillips	7.57
1998	Nathan Morgan	8.11
1999	Steve Phillips	7.79
2000	George Audu	7.89
2001	Nathan Morgan	7.80
2002	Darren Ritchie	7.93
2003	Darren Ritchie	7.74
2004	Chris Tomlinson	7.84
2005	Greg Rutherford	7.79
2006	Greg Rutherford	8.26
2007	Chris Tomlinson	7.99
2008	Greg Rutherford	8.20
2009	Chris Tomlinson	8.03
2010	Chris Tomlinson	8.17w
	J J Jegede	7.72

Most titles won: 6 Peter O'Connor IRL 1901–1906. Most medals: 8 Roy Cruttenden & Lynn Davies

TRIPLE JUMP

(Event instituted in 1914)

1980	Paul Jordan USA	16.49
	(2, Aston Moore 16.49)	
1981	Aston Moore	16.66
1982	Ken Lorraway AUS	17.19w
	(2, John Herbert 16.91)	
1983	Mike Conley USA	16.49
	(2, Eric McCalla 16.10)	
1984	Lázaro Betancourt CUB	16.93
	(5, John Herbert 16.39)	
1985	Willie Banks USA	17.22
	(3, John Herbert 16.85)	
1986	Joseph Taiwo NGR	16.99w
	(3, Mike Makin 16.67w)	
1987	Eric McCalla	16.86
1988	John Herbert	17.12
1989	Jonathan Edwards	16.53
1990	John Herbert	16.61
1991	Willie Banks USA	16.60
	(2, Jonathan Edwards 16.50)	
1992	Julian Golley	16.81
1993	Francis Agyepong	16.05
1994	Jonathan Edwards	17.39
1995	Francis Agyepong	17.13
1996	Francis Agyepong	17.12
1997	Francis Agyepong	16.71
1998	Jonathan Edwards	17.12

1999	Larry Achike	16.73w
2000	Phillips Idowu	16.87
2001	Jonathan Edwards	17.59
2002	Phillips Idowu	17.02
2003	Larry Achike	16.55
2004	Nathan Douglas	16.95
2005	Nathan Douglas	17.64
2006	Phillips Idowu	17.50
2007	Tosin Oke	16.59
2008	Phillips Idowu	17.58
2009	Phillips Idowu	17.05
2010	Phillips Idowu	17.12
	Julian Golley	15.34w

Most titles won: 6 Wim Peters NED 1927–1930, 1935, 1937 & Phillips Idowu 2000, 2002, 2006, 2008–2010. Most medals: 9 Fred Alsop & Francis Agyepong

SHOT

(Event instituted in 1880)

1980	Brian Oldfield USA	21.25
	(2, Geoff Capes 20.10)	
1981	Mike Winch	18.36
1982	Mike Winch	18.90
1983	Mike Carter USA	20.80
	(2, Mike Winch 18.02)	
1984	Mike Winch	18.39
1985	Billy Cole	17.88
1986	Billy Cole	19.01
1987	Paul Edwards	17.26
1988	Simon Williams	17.78
1989	Simon Williams	18.73
1990	Paul Edwards	19.00
1991	Paul Edwards	18.92
1992	Paul Edwards	19.08
1993	Matt Simson	18.79
1994	Paul Edwards	18.32
1995	Mark Proctor	18.81
1996	Matt Simson	18.82
1997	Steph Hayward	17.26
1998	Mark Proctor	19.50
1999	Mark Proctor	17.83
	(Carl Myerscough won with 18.97	
	but result later annulled due to drugs disqualification)	
2000	Steph Hayward	18.24
2001	Mark Proctor	18.38
2002	Mark Proctor	18.54
2003	Carl Myerscough	21.55
2004	Carl Myerscough	20.84
2005	Carl Myerscough	20.27
2006	Carl Myerscough	20.00
2007	Carl Myerscough	19.39

2008	Carl Myerscough	20.15
2009	Carl Myerscough	19.87
2010	Carl Myerscough	19.77
	Scott Rider	18.43

Most titles won: 13 Denis Horgan IRL 1893–1899, 1904, 1905, 1908–1910, 1912.
Most medals: 14 Horgan

DISCUS

(Event instituted in 1914)

1980	Brian Oldfield USA	61.46
	(2, Peter Tancred 59.46)	
1981	John Powell USA	62.46
	(5, Robert Weir 57.42)	
1982	Brad Cooper BAH	63.70
	(2, Robert Weir 58.14)	
1983	Robert Weir	59.76
1984	Robert Weir	62.50
1985	Juan Martínez CUB	65.72
	(3, Paul Mardle 58.28)	
1986	Richard Slaney	59.62
1987	Paul Mardle	57.34
1988	Paul Mardle	58.06
1989	Paul Mardle	57.90
1990	Abi Ekoku	57.58
1991	Werner Reiterer AUS	59.56
	(2, Simon Williams 58.08)	
1992	Werner Reiterer AUS	61.78
	(2, Abi Ekoku 58.02)	
1993	Robert Weir	57.44
1994	Kevin Brown	58.60
1995	Nick Sweeney IRL	60.34
	(2, Robert Weir 60.18)	
1996	Robert Weir	60.02
1997	Robert Weir	61.60
1998	Robert Weir	62.82
1999	Robert Weir	61.35
2000	Robert Weir	62.13
2001	Glen Smith	59.99
2002	Robert Weir	58.22
2003	Emeka Udechuku	57.26
2004	Emeka Udechuku	61.60
2005	Carl Myerscough	58.48
2006	Carl Myerscough	61.04
2007	Emeka Udechuku	60.83
2008	Emeka Udechuku	59.35
2009	Emeka Udechuku	56.93
2010	Brett Morse	61.45
	Emeka Udechuku	57.50

Most titles won: 9 Robert Weir 1983, 1984, 1993, 1996–2000, 2002. Most medals: 13 Weir (1982–2002)

HAMMER

(Event instituted in 1880)

1980	Martin Girvan	68.72
1981	Martin Girvan	68.98
1982	Robert Weir	71.92
1983	Chris Black	75.40
1984	Dave Smith	72.40
1985	Dave Smith	77.30
1986	Dave Smith	68.72
1987	Dave Smith	70.60
1988	Dave Smith	72.08
1989	Jud Logan USA	72.34
	(2, Paul Head 70.32)	
1990	Paul Head	72.68
1991	Sean Carlin AUS	72.58
	(2, Mick Jones 66.72)	
1992	Sean Carlin AUS	74.60
	(2, Paul Head 70.94)	
1993	Paul Head	72.32
1994	Peter Vivian	70.80
1995	Sean Carlin AUS	73.40
	(2, Mick Jones 69.44)	
1996	Dave Smith II	72.58
1997	Paul Head	70.66
1998	Mick Jones	72.13
1999	Mick Jones	74.25
2000	Mick Jones	71.51
2001	Mick Jones	74.40
2002	Mick Jones	72.26
2003	Bill Beauchamp	69.33
2004	Mick Jones	72.04
2005	Andy Frost	72.09
2006	Andy Frost	69.15
2007	Andy Frost	71.02
2008	Mike Floyd	69.68
2009	Alex Smith	69.79
2010	Alex Smith	70.68
	Mike Floyd	69.93

Most titles won: 6 Tom Nicolson 1903–1905, 1907, 1909, 1912; Mick Jones 1998–2002, 2004. Most medals: 15 Howard Payne & Jones (1986–2005)

JAVELIN

(Event instituted in 1914)

1980	Miklós Németh HUN	83.34
	(3, Dave Ottley 80.38)	
1981	Mike O'Rourke NZL	83.72
	(3, Dave Ottley 79.36)	
1982	Dave Ottley	80.54

1983	Mike O'Rourke NZL	84.88
	(2, Dave Ottley 78.80)	
1984	Dave Ottley	81.34
1985	Dave Ottley	88.32
1986	Dave Ottley	80.24
1987	Mick Hill	81.68
1988	Dave Ottley	80.34
1989	Steve Backley	83.16
1990	Mick Hill	81.22
1991	Mick Hill	84.54
1992	Steve Backley	88.14
1993	Colin Mackenzie	81.44
1994	Mick Hill	84.60
1995	Mick Hill	80.54
1996	Nick Nieland	83.06
1997	Mark Roberson	77.22
1998	Steve Backley	84.78
1999	Steve Backley	87.59
2000	Steve Backley	86.70
2001	Mark Roberson	80.80
2002	Mick Hill	77.86
2003	Mick Hill	76.35
2004	Steve Backley	81.25
2005	Nick Nieland	78.30
2006	Nick Nieland	80.56
2007	Nick Nieland	73.95
2008	Michael Allen	75.07
2009	Mervyn Luckwell	77.70
2010	James Campbell	74.00
	Brett Byrd	67.80

Most titles won: 7 David Travis 1965, 1968, 1970–1974; Mick Hill 1987, 1990, 1991, 1994, 1995, 2002, 2003. Most medals: 15 Hill (1985–2004)

DECATHLON

(Scores per tables in use at the time)
(Event instituted in 1928)
(Venues: 1980 Cwmbran; 1981–1983, 1985 & 2008 Birmingham; 1984 London (Copthall); 1986 & 2002 Wrexham; 1987–1991, 1995, 2000, 2003–2004, 2006–2007 & 2009 Stoke; 1992 & 1997 Sheffield; 1993–1994 Horsham; 1996, 2001 & 2010 Bedford; 1998 Derby; 1999 & 2005 Hexham)

1980	Brad McStravick	7663
1981	Colin Boreham	7639
1982	Fidelis Obikwu	7535
1983	Kevin Atkinson IRL	7353
	(2, Ken Hayford 7317)	
1984	Kevin Atkinson IRL	7451
	(2, Ken Hayford 7431)	
1985	Greg Richards	7456
1986	Greg Richards	7336

1987	Ken Hayford	7388
1988	Eugene Gilkes	7529
1989	Alex Kruger	7646
1990	Brian Taylor	7567
1991	Eric Hollingsworth	7631
1992	Alex Kruger	7582
1993	Barry Walsh IRL	7275
	(2, Barry Thomas 7121)	
1994	Barry Thomas	7458
1995	Steve Rogers	7295
1996	Barry Thomas	7701
1997	Alexis Sharp	7500
1998	Rafer Joseph	7126
1999	Paul Jones	6922
2000	Alex Kruger	6975
2001	John Heanley	7129
2002	Adrian Hemery	6620
2003	Paul Tohill	6962
2004	Louis Evling-Jones	7405w
2005	Ben Hazell	7193
2006	Dean Showler-Davis	7146
2007	Ben Hazell	7528
2008	Daniel Awde	7704
2009	Guy Stroud	7258
2010	David Guest	7727

Most titles won: 4 Leslie Pinder 1951–1954. Most medals: 5 Pinder, Pan Zeniou, Mike Corden, Brad McStravick & Alex Kruger

3000 METRES TRACK WALK

(Event instituted in 1901 at 2 miles; 3000m since 1969; discontinued after 1986)
(1986 race, organised by RWA, held in London (Copthall))

1980	Steve Barry	12:00.44
1981	Roger Mills	11:44.68
1982	Roger Mills	11:58.18
1983	Dave Smith AUS	11:36.04
	(2, Phil Vesty 11:48.03)	
1984	Phil Vesty	11:42.94
1985	Ian McCombie	11:41.73
1986	Murray Day NZL	12:04.0
	(2, Chris Smith 12:23.0)	

Most titles won: 10 Roger Mills 1969, 1972–1974, 1976–1979, 1981, 1982

5000 METRES TRACK WALK

(Event instituted in 2001 to replace 10,000m)

2001	Lloyd Finch	20:47.23
2002	Steve Hollier	20:41.29
2003	Steve Hollier	20:59.46
2004	Dominic King	20:11.35

2005	Colin Griffin IRL	20:44.45
	(2, Dominic King 21:07.50)	
2006	Colin Griffin IRL	19:43.40
	(3, Dominic King 21:21.16)	
2007	Dominic King	20:57.90
2008	Dan King	21:06.37
2009	Scott Davis	22:40.63
2010	Alex Wright	20:11.09

10,000 METRES TRACK WALK

(Event instituted in 1880 at 7 miles; 10,000m since 1969; discontinued after 2000)

(Venues: 1980–1981 London (Parliament Hill); 1982 London (West London); 1983 Kirkby; 1984 Birmingham; 1985 London (Copthall); 1994 Horsham)

1980	Roger Mills	43:21.2
1981	Steve Barry	43:22.4
1982	Steve Barry	41:14.7
1983	Steve Barry	40:54.7
	(slightly under-distance; 14cm per lap)	
1984	Ian McCombie	41:33.0
1985	Murray Day NZL	43:35.3
	(2, Roger Mills 43:48.9)	
1986	Ian McCombie	41:42.28
1987	Ian McCombie	41:16.14
1988	Ian McCombie	41:36.51
1989	Mark Easton	41:39.93
1990	Mark Easton	41:32.80
1991	Ian McCombie	41:24.69
1992	Martin Rush	41:46.42
1993	Martin Bell	42:29.63
1994	Darrell Stone	43:09.28
1995	Darrell Stone	41:10.11
1996	Steve Partington	42:29.73
1997	Philip King	42:32.32
1998	Martin Bell	41:48.81
1999	Andi Drake	42:14.69
2000	Matt Hales	43:12.85

Most titles won: 5 Roland Hardy 1950–1953, 1955; Ken Matthews 1959–1961, 1963, 1964; Brian Adams 1975–1979; Ian McCombie 1984, 1986–1988, 1991

ROAD RUNNING

(First British finisher)

5 KILOMETRES

(Held only in 2005 & 2006)

2005	Mark Miles	13:58
2006	Chris Davies	13:56

10 KILOMETRES

(Event instituted in 1984)

1984	Steve Jones	27:59
1985	Jack Buckner	28:13
1986	Steve Harris	27:58
1987	Jack Buckner	28:18
1988	Eamonn Martin	28:35
1989	Peter Tootell	29:39
1990	Ian Manners	30:10
1991	Nigel Adams	28:50
1992	Rob Denmark	28:36
1993	Justin Hobbs	28:45
1994	Justin Hobbs	29:07
1995	Paul Taylor	29:20
1996	Dale Laughlin	30:28
1997	Rob Birchall	29:22
1998	Nick Wetheridge	29:45
1999	Mark Morgan	29:13
2000	Mike Openshaw	29:13
2001	Rob Denmark	28:53
2002	Allen Graffin	29:45
2003	Rob Whalley	29:44
2004	Glyn Tromans	29:50
2005	Peter Riley	28:54
2006	Peter Riley	29:02
2007	Willard Chinhanhu	29:18
2008	Ian Boneham	29:44
2009	Chris Thompson	29:32
2010	Andy Vernon	29:12

10 MILES

(Event instituted in 1983; discontinued after 1999)

1983	Bob Westwood	48:20
1984	Steve Anders	48:48
1985	Bernie Ford	48:21
1986	Karl Harrison	47:40
1987	David Lewis	47:20
1988	Mike Cadman	47:47
1989	Sam Carey	48:21
1990	Chris Buckley	48:15
1991	Nigel Adams	47:14
1992	Kevin McCluskey	47:44
1993	Martin Hula	48:15
1994	Carl Udall	47:56
1995	Steve Knight	51:08
1996	Mark Flint	48:14
1997	Andrew Pearson	47:32
1998	Glynn Tromans	47:25
1999	Matt O'Dowd	48:58

HALF MARATHON

(Event instituted in 1984)

1984	Allister Hutton	65:17
1985	Steve Jones	61:14
1986	Steve Jones	60:59
1987	Allister Hutton	62:28
1988	Steve Jones	61:58
1989	Mike McLeod	62:39
1990	Mark Flint	62:10
1991	Steve Brace	63:50
1992	Colin Walker	63:59
1993	Steve Brace	65:00
1994	Mark Hudspith	63:37
1995	Andy Green	64:39
1996	Justin Hobbs	63:41
1997	Spencer Duval	64:50
1998	Ian Hudspith	64:22
1999	Malcolm Price	66:12
2000	Nick Wetheridge	64:09
2001	Kassa Tadesse	64:04
2002	Mark Hudspith	64:17
2003	Ian Hudspith	63:32
2004	David Anderson	65:32
2005	Huw Lobb	66:52
2006	Dave Mitchinson	67:08
2007	Phil Wicks	64:43
2008	Tomas Abyu	64:14
2009	Mark Miles	64:11
2010	Andi Jones	64:45
2011	Nick Swinburn	65:44

MARATHON

(Event instituted in 1925)
(Since 1983, where different, first Briton to finish in London Marathon as well as AAA champion is listed)

1980	Ian Thompson	2:14:00
1981	Hugh Jones	2:14:07
1982	Steve Kenyon	2:11:40
1983	Mike Gratton	2:09:43
1984	Charlie Spedding	2:09:57
1985	Steve Jones	2:08:16
1986	Hugh Jones	2:11:42
1987	Hugh Jones	2:10:11
1988	Kevin Forster	2:10:52
1989	Tony Milovsorov	2:09:54
1990	Allister Hutton	2:10:10
1991	Dave Long	2:10:30
1992	Paul Evans	2:10:36
1993	Eamonn Martin	2:10:50

1994	Eamonn Martin	2:11:05
1995	Paul Evans	2:10:31
1996	Paul Evans	2:10:40
1997	Richard Nerurkar	2:08:36
	(AAA champion: Paul Evans 2:09:18)	
1998	Jon Brown	2:11:11
	(AAA champion: Mark Hudspith	2:14:19)
1999	Jon Brown	2:09:44
	(AAA champion: Mark Hudspith	2:15:11)
2000	Mark Steinle	2:11:18
	(AAA champion: Mark Hudspith	2:15:16)
2001	Mark Steinle	2:10:46
2002	Mark Steinle	2:09:17
2003	Chris Cariss	2:17:57
2004	Jon Brown	2:13:39
2005	Jon Brown	2:09:31
2006	Peter Riley	2:14:31
2007	Dan Robinson	2:14:14
2008	Dan Robinson	2:13:10
2009	Andi Jones	2:15:20
2010	Andrew Lemoncello	2:13:40
2011	Lee Merrien	2:14:27

Most titles won: 6 Donald McNab Robertson 1932–1934, 1936, 1937, 1939

100 KILOMETRES

(Event first staged as AAA championship in 1989)

1989	Trevor Hawes	6:43:55
1990	Don Ritchie	6:49:29
1991	Erik Seedhouse	6:42:03
1992	Don Ritchie	6:51:54
1993	Greg Dell	6:58:32
1994	Paul Taylor	7:35:03
1995	Steve Moore	7:17:47
1996	Steve Moore	7:17:16
1997	Steve Moore	7:04:22
1998	Steve Moore	6:57:33
1999	William Sichel	7:32:19
2000	Steve Moore	7:14:57
2001	Chris Finill	7:24:20
2002	Dennis Walmsley	7:07:39
2003	Dennis Walmsley	7:05:12
2004	Brian Hennessey	7:07:23
2005	Dominic Croft	7:23:48
2006	Matthew Lynas	7:17:40
2007	Jez Bragg	7:04:46
2008	Dominic Croft	7:21:45
2010	Brian Cole	7:07:21
2011	Craig Stewart	7:01:36

6-STAGE ROAD RELAY

(Event instituted in 1969; distances varied until 2001)

Year	Team	Time
1980	Tipton	1:44:11
1981	Aldershot Farnham & D	1:57:36
1982	Tipton	1:54:35
1983	Shaftesbury	1:43:11
1984	Stretford	1:38:32
1985	Gateshead	1:34:28
1986	Gateshead	1:24:27
1987	Gateshead	1:45:40
1988	Swansea	2:26:05
1989	Stretford	1:41:38
1990	Bingley	1:47:19
1991	Swansea	1:47:32
1992	Tipton	1:41:15
1993	Blackheath	1:46:25
1994	Bingley	1:57:15
1995	Bingley	1:45:20
1996	Bingley	1:40:39
1997	Birchfield	1:40:36
1998	Birchfield	1:44:16
1999	Cardiff	1:42:46
2000	Morpeth	1:44:14
2001	Belgrave	1:45:28
2002	Belgrave	1:44:24
2003	Belgrave	1:45:22
2004	Belgrave	1:44:35
2005	Belgrave	1:46:30
2006	Newham & Essex B	1:44:46
2007	Belgrave	1:44:30
2008	Belgrave	1:45:18
2009	Newham & Essex B	1:43:14
2010	Bedford & County	1:45:42

12-STAGE ROAD RELAY

(Event instituted in 1967)

Year	Team	Time
1980	Bristol	4:00:37
1981	Tipton	4:05:33
1982	Aldershot Farnham & D	4:03:01
1983	Birchfield	4:05:16
1984	Tipton	4:04:43
1985	Tipton	4:04:52
1986	Tipton	4:02:58
1987	Gateshead	4:02:56
1988	Gateshead	4:02:01
1989	Tipton	4:03:49
1990	Tipton	4:03:43
1991	Tipton	4:04:13

1992	Tipton	4:04:51
1993	Shaftesbury Barnet	4:06:24
1994	Swansea	4:06:26
1995	Blackheath	4:03:04
1996	Bingley	4:02:06
1997	Salford	4:06:37
1998	Birchfield	4:07:06
1999	Tipton	4:06:22
2000	Salford	4:08:04
2001	Tipton	4:10:27
2002	Belgrave	4:04:51
2003	Belgrave	4:08:55
2004	Aldershot Farnham & D	4:10:15
2005	Belgrave	4:08:36
2006	Newham & Essex B	4:10:08
2007	Leeds City	4:11:31
2008	Leeds City	4:09:40
2009	Belgrave	4:04:43
2010	Newham & Essex B	4:09:12
2011	Tipton	4:10:36

ROAD WALKING
(under aegis of Race Walking Association)

10 KILOMETRES
(Event instituted in 2005)

2005	Dominic King	45:01
2006	Daniel King	43:49
2007	Daniel King	44:30
2008	Daniel King	43:52
2009	Brendan Boyce	44:40
2010	Alex Wright	42:38

10 MILES
(Event instituted in 1947)

1980	Roger Mills	68:45
	(course 60 yards short)	
1981	Mike Parker NZL	73:37
	(2, Graham Morris 74:52)	
1982	Steve Barry	68:01
1983	Steve Barry	66:41
1984	Ian McCombie	67:32
1985	Ian McCombie	66:32
1986	Ian McCombie	66:35
1987	Ian McCombie	67:36
1988	Ian McCombie	67:22
1989	Ian McCombie	65:39
	(course 63m short)	

AAA Champions

1990	Ian McCombie	68:36
1991	Ian McCombie	68:17
1992	Ian McCombie	69:42
1993	Les Morton	73:16
1994	Chris Cheeseman	73:17
1995	Chris Maddocks	69:11
1996	Andy Penn	71:14
1997	Steve Partington	75:34
1998	Andi Drake	71:14
	(1999–2007 not held)	
2008	Darrell Stone	73:41
2009	Ben Wears	70:22
2010	Darrell Stone	73:49
2011	Alex Wright	70:46

Most titles won: 9 Ian McCombie 1984–1992

20 KILOMETRES

(Event instituted in 1965)

1980	Mike Parker NZL	1:29:20
	(2, Amos Seddon 1:29:41)	
1981	Mike Parker NZL	1:31:08
	(2, Dennis Jackson 1:32:28)	
1982	Steve Barry	1:28:51
1983	Steve Barry	1:23:15
1984	Ian McCombie	1:25:34
1985	Ian McCombie	1:22:37
1986	Ian McCombie	1:27:14
1987	Les Morton	1:31:17
1988	Ian McCombie	1:23:31
1989	Andi Drake	1:26:55
1990	Sean Martindale	1:27:37
1991	Mark Easton	1:25:36
1992	Chris Maddocks	1:23:38
1993	Andy Penn	1:25:57
1994	Chris Cheeseman	1:29:11
1995	Darrell Stone	1:27:44
1996	Darrell Stone	1:26:44
1997	Andy Penn	1:28:41
1998	Martin Bell	1:27:22
1999	Chris Maddocks	1:26:22
2000	Darrell Stone	1:27:08
2001	Andy Penn	1:31:09
2002	Andi Drake	1:24:43
2003	Andy Penn	1:28:52
2004	Daniel King	1:31:01
2005	Daniel King	1:32:55
2006	Dominic King	1:31:26
2007	Andy Penn	1:35:24
2008	Scott Davis	1:38:22

| 2009 | Luke Finch | 1:28:31 |
| 2010 | Tom Bosworth | 1:31:06 |

Most titles won: 6 Paul Nihill 1965, 1966, 1968, 1969, 1971, 1972

35 KILOMETRES

(Event instituted in 1908 at 20 miles)

1980	Amos Seddon	2:40:04
1981	Bob Dobson	2:48:30
1982	David Jarman	2:48:41
1983	Carl Lawton	2:58:44
1984	Paul Blagg	3:03:54
1985	Dennis Jackson	2:41:03
1986	Chris Maddocks	2:47:54
1987	Chris Berwick	2:56:38
1988	Chris Maddocks	2:45:09
1989	Darrell Stone	2:50:44
1990	Les Morton	2:50:50
1991	Stuart Phillips	2:55:21
1992	Les Morton	2:59:38

20 MILES

| 1993 | Sean Martindale | 2:33:58 |

30 KILOMETRES

| 1994 | Chris Maddocks | 2:22:45 |

20 MILES

1995	Gareth Brown	2:41:36
1996	Chris Cheeseman	2:35:15
1997	Chris Cheeseman	2:34:04
1998	Les Morton	2:43:01

35 KILOMETRES

1999	Darrell Stone	2:49:45
2000	Chris Cheeseman	2:51:20
2001	Mark Easton	2:55:00
2002	Martin Young	3:04:39
2003	Andi Drake	2:54:36
2004	Nathan Adams	3:06:25

(Event discontinued after 2004)

Most titles won: 6 Harold Ross 1908, 1910, 1912–1914, 1920; Paul Nihill 1963–1965, 1968, 1969, 1971

50 KILOMETRES

(Event instituted in 1930)

1980	Dennis Jackson	4:16:25
1981	Barry Graham	4:10:46
1982	Adrian James	4:14:11
1983	Barry Graham	4:24:18
1984	Paul Blagg	4:20:31
1985	Les Morton	4:19:09
1986	Chris Berwick	4:23:22
1987	Les Morton	4:23:40
1988	Les Morton	4:17:05
1989	Les Morton	4:21:19
1990	Chris Berwick	4:33:23
1991	Les Morton	4:15:48
1992	Chris Maddocks	4:13:25
1993	Les Morton	4:03:55
1994	Les Morton	4:32:25
1995	Les Morton	4:01:36
1996	Chris Cheeseman	4:22:42
1997	Mark Easton	4:07:45
1998	Tim Watt	4:32:00
1999	Chris Cheeseman	4:31:08
2000	Darrell Stone	4:21:23
2001	Mike Smith	4:33:17
2002	Mike Smith	4:42:58
2003	Mike Smith	5:00:41
2004	Steve Partington	4:30:08
2005	Scott Davis	4:47:34
2006	Scott Davis	4:52:51
2007	Scott Davis	4:35:39
2008	Scott Davis	4:29:25
2009	Scott Davis	4:30:28
2010	Scott Davis	4:28:29

Most titles won: 8 Don Thompson 1956–1962, 1966; Les Morton 1985, 1987–1989, 1991, 1993–1995

LONG DISTANCE

(Event instituted in 1979; 100 kilometres 1979–1985; 100 miles 1987–1999, 2001, 2003–2009; 24 hours 2000, 2002; * track race)

1979	Peter Hodkinson	9:46:36
1980	Ian Richards	9:45:46
1981	Graham Young	9:36:23
1982	Chris Berwick	10:02:03
1983	Brian Adams	10:13:16
1984	not held	
1985	Ted Shillabeer	9:41:54*
1986	not held	
1987	John Cannell	17:55:10

1988	Richard Brown	17:00:35
1989	Ted Shillabeer	18:11:08
1990	Richard Brown	17:54:28
1991	Richard Brown	17:52:47
1992	Richard Brown	18:50:29
1993	Chris Berwick	17:57:07
1994	Richard Brown	18:39:42
1995	Richard Brown	19:27:16
1996	not held	
1997	Chris Flint	20:21:41*
1998	not held	
1999	Richard Brown	19:08:16
2000	Ian Statter	193.114km
2001	Bob Dobson	19:46:11
2002	Kevin Perry	182.591km*
2003	Peter Ryan	19:57:35
2004	Ian Statter	20:10:31
2005	Sean Hands	19:02:57
2006	Sean Hands	19:16:03
2007	Chris Flint	21:14:40
2008	Ian Richards	19:37:11*
2009	Richard Brown	20:12:44

Most titles won: 8 Richard Brown 1988, 1990–1992, 1994, 1995, 1999, 2009

CROSS COUNTRY

(under aegis of English Cross Country Union/Association)
(Event instituted in 1877)
(Distance varied; Individual and team winners)

1980	Nick Rose	45:15	Tipton
1981	Julian Goater	44:39	Tipton
1982	Dave Clarke	42:19	Tipton
1983	Tim Hutchings	37:28	Aldershot, Farnham & District
1984	Eamonn Martin	41:50	Aldershot, Farnham & District
1985	David Lewis	44:30	Aldershot, Farnham & District
1986	Tim Hutchings	47:25	Tipton
1987	Dave Clarke	47:04	Gateshead
1988	Dave Clarke	44:14	Birchfield
1989	David Lewis	44:26	Tipton
1990	Richard Nerurkar	44:56	Valli
1991	Richard Nerurkar	43:11	Bingley
1992	Eamonn Martin	40:29	Tipton
1993	Richard Nerurkar	42:52	Bingley
1994	David Lewis	42:35	Blackheath
1995	Spencer Duval	42:35	Blackheath
1996	John Nuttall	40:35	Bingley
1997	Steffan White	45:53	Tipton
1998	Dominic Bannister	44:45	Bingley

1999	Justin Pugsley	38:32	Tipton
2000	Glynn Tromans	40:19	Tipton
2001	Mike Openshaw	36:52	Bingley
2002	Sam Haughian	39:26	Bingley
2003	Matt Smith	41:54	Leeds City
2004	Glynn Tromans	41:24	Belgrave
2005	Glynn Tromans	37:53	Salford
2006	Peter Riley	38:53	Leeds City
2007	Frank Tickner	37:31	Leeds City
2008	Tom Humphries	32:03	Leeds City
2009	Frank Tickner	38:02	Newham & Essex Beagles
2010	Andy Vernon	38:01	Aldershot Farnham & District
2011	Steve Vernon	35:11	Leeds City

Most titles won: 4 Percy Stenning 1877–1880; Alf Shrubb 1901–1904

AAA INDOOR CHAMPIONS

AAA title winners from 1980 to 2006 inclusive; UK champions from 2007 to 2011 (Where the title was won by an overseas athlete, the highest placed UK athlete is shown in brackets)
Venues: 1935–1939 & 1962–1964 London (Wembley); 1965–1991 Cosford; 1992–2001 & 2003 Birmingham; 2002 Cardiff; 2004–2011 Sheffield

60 METRES

(Event instituted in 1935 at 70 yards; 60 yards 1962–1967; 60m from 1968)

1980	Cameron Sharp	6.74
1981	Selwyn Clarke	6.8
1982	Harry King	6.75
1983	Selwyn Clarke	6.75
1984	Ernest Obeng GHA	6.79
	(2, Buster Watson 6.82)	
1985	Ronald Desruelles BEL	6.65
	(2, Mike McFarlane 6.66)	
1986	Ernest Obeng GHA	6.72
	(3, Cameron Sharp 6.75)	
1987	Elliot Bunney	6.62
1988	Lincoln Asquith	6.62
1989	Linford Christie	6.55
1990	Linford Christie	6.61
1991	Linford Christie	6.63
1992	Jon Drummond USA	6.60
	(2, Jason John 6.63)	
1993	Mark McKoy CAN	6.56
	(2, Colin Jackson 6.60)	
1994	Michael Rosswess	6.56
1995	Michael Rosswess	6.63
1996	Michael Rosswess	6.68

1997	Jason Livingston	6.58
1998	Darren Braithwaite	6.57
1999	Jason Gardener	6.57
2000	Jason Gardener	6.53
2001	Christian Malcolm	6.72

(John Skeete won in 6.59 but result
later annulled due to drugs disqualification)

2002	Jason Gardener	6.52
2003	Mark Lewis-Francis	6.58
2004	Jason Gardener	6.49
2005	Jason Gardener	6.60
2006	Tim Abeyie	6.64
2007	Craig Pickering	6.58
2008	Dwain Chambers	6.56
2009	Dwain Chambers	6.51
2010	Dwain Chambers	6.50
2011	Dwain Chambers	6.57

Most titles won: 5 Jason Gardener 1999, 2000, 2002, 2004, 2005

200 METRES

(Event instituted in 1965 at 220 yards; 200m from 1968)

1980	Phil Brown	22.1
1981	Linford Christie	21.9
1982	Linford Christie	21.75
1983	Earl Tulloch	21.66
1984	Ade Mafe	21.38
1985	Mel Lattany USA	21.36

(2, Linford Christie 21.49)

1986	Ade Mafe	21.25
1987	Linford Christie	21.23
1988	Linford Christie	21.36
1989	Linford Christie	20.95
1990	Marcus Adam	21.25
1991	Linford Christie	21.28
1992	Jon Drummond USA	21.40

(2, Stewart Weathers 21.62)

1993	Jason John	21.17
1994	Phil Goedluck	21.16
1995	Solomon Wariso	20.87
1996	Doug Turner	21.06
1997	Jamie Baulch	20.84
1998	Julian Golding	20.46
1999	Marcus Adam	20.77
2000	Christian Malcolm	20.74
2001	Allyn Condon	20.60
2002	Doug Turner	21.24
2003	Allyn Condon	20.69
2004	Paul Brizzel IRL	20.98

(2, Tim Abeyie 21.02)

AAA Champions

2005	Paul Hession IRL	21.01
	(2, Chris Lambert 21.03)	
2006	Tim Abeyie	20.96
2007	Rikki Fifton	21.06
2008	Chris Clarke	20.98
2009	Leon Baptiste	21.04
2010	Leon Baptiste	20.90
2011	Danny Talbot	20.89

Most titles won: 6 Linford Christie 1981, 1982, 1987–1989, 1991

400 METRES

(Event instituted in 1965 at 440 yards; 400m from 1968)

1980	Terry Whitehead	48.4
1981	Ainsley Bennett	47.6
1982	Paul Dunn	48.11
1983	Ainsley Bennett	47.06
1984	Walter McCoy USA	48.23
	(2, Terry Whitehead 48.65)	
1985	Todd Bennett	46.83
1986	Roger Black	47.22
1987	Todd Bennett	47.12
1988	Mark Thomas	47.34
1989	Phil Brown	47.64
1990	Danny Harris USA	46.73
	(2, Gary Cadogan 47.50)	
1991	Ade Mafe	47.18
1992	Ade Mafe	46.47
1993	Sunday Bada NGR	46.34
	(3, Mark Morris 47.89)	
1994	Du'aine Ladejo	46.54
1995	Mark Hylton	46.56
1996	Mark Hylton	46.45
1997	Mark Hylton	46.24
1998	Solomon Wariso	45.71
1999	Allyn Condon	47.14
2000	Daniel Caines	46.89
2001	Daniel Caines	45.75
2002	Robert Daly IRL	47.58
	(2, Tim Benjamin 47.60)	
2003	Daniel Batman AUS	45.93
	(3=, Cori Henry & Mark Hylton 47.20)	
2004	Robert Daly IRL	46.68
	(3, Jamie Baulch 47.70)	
2005	David Gillick IRL	46.45
	(2, Dale Garland 47.05)	
2006	Rob Tobin	45.90
2007	Gareth Warburton	48.02
2008	Richard Buck	46.53
2009	Richard Buck	46.41

| 2010 | Richard Buck | 47.54 |
| 2011 | Nigel Levine | 46.76 |

Most titles won: 4 Jim Aukett 1971–1974

800 METRES

(Event instituted in 1937 at 880 yards; 800m from 1968)

1980	Simon Larder	1:51.0
1981	Paul Forbes	1:50.3
1982	Chris McGeorge	1:50.4
1983	Milovan Savic YUG	1:50.92
	(3, Paul Forbes 1:51.32)	
1984	Phil Norgate	1:50.27
1985	Ikem Billy	1:49.85
1986	David Sharpe	1:49.48
1987	Tony Morrell	1:48.66
1988	Tony Morrell	1:49.70
1989	David Sharpe	1:51.32
1990	Tom McKean	1:46.49
1991	Martin Steele	1:49.43
1992	Martin Steele	1:47.78
1993	Tom McKean	1:47.27
1994	Tom McKean	1:48.46
1995	Martin Steele	1:49.17
1996	Martin Steele	1:51.21
1997	James Nolan IRL	1:49.42
	(2, Eddie King 1:49.60)	
1998	Wilson Kirwa KEN	1:47.85
	(4, Bradley Donkin 1:48.94)	
1999	Andy Hart	1:49.41
2000	Luke Kipkoech KEN	1:51.72
	(2, Dominic Hall 1:52.14)	
2001	Eddie King	1:49.98
2002	James McIlroy	1:51.10
2003	Neal Speaight	1:51.99
2004	Ahmed Ismail SUD	1:49.39
	(2, James McIlroy 1:50.32)	
2005	James McIlroy	1:47.94
2006	Jimmy Watkins	1:49.00
2007	James Brewer	1:49.03
2008	Richard Hill	1:48.26
2009	Ed Aston	1:48.82
2010	Andrew Osagie	1:50.21
2011	Joe Thomas	1:47.87

Most titles won: 4 Martin Steele 1991, 1992, 1995, 1996

1500 METRES

(Event instituted in 1962 at 1 mile; 1500m from 1968)

| 1980 | Malcolm Edwards | 3:46.9 |

1981	Roger Hackney	3:44.4
1982	Graham Williamson	3:40.72
1983	Stuart Paton	3:46.65
1984	Steve Crabb	3:44.47
1985	Rob Harrison	3:42.95
1986	Rob Harrison	3:47.49
1987	Malcolm Edwards	3:47.52
1988	Gareth Brown	3:56.10
1989	Andrew Geddes	3:47.39
1990	Kip Cheruiyot KEN	3:44.12
	(2, Alistair Currie 3:45.26)	
1991	Mark Scruton	3:51.98
1992	Joseph Chesire KEN	3:43.34
	(3, Jason Dullforce 3:43.96)	
1993	Jason Dullforce	3:45.05
1994	Atoi Boru KEN	3:42.25
	(2, Ian Campbell 3:43.05)	
1995	Grant Graham	3:55.68
1996	Terry West	3:49.90
1997	Niall Bruton IRL	3:49.23
	(2, Ian Campbell 3:49.92)	
1998	Joe Mills	3:50.30
1999	Eddie King	3:40.24
2000	Gareth Turnbull IRL	3:44.06
	(2, Eddie King 3:44.39)	
2001	Angus Maclean	3:48.02
2002	Anthony Whiteman	3:52.44
2003	James Thie	3:41.84
2004	Michael East	3:44.93
2005	Neil Speaight	3:45.87
2006	Colin McCourt	3:41.71
2007	Chris Warburton	3:56.47
2008	James McIlroy	3:44.90
2009	Mo Farah	3:40.57
2010	Colin McCourt	4:04.83
2011	Nick McCormick	3:45.30

Most titles won: 6 John Whetton 1963–1968

3000 METRES

(Event instituted in 1937 at 2 miles; 3000m from 1968)

1980	Dick Callan	8:00.0
1981	Sebastian Coe	7:55.2
1982	Ken Newton	7:52.95
1983	Colin Reitz	7:53.19
1984	Gary Staines	8:04.72
1985	David Lewis	7:58.41
1986	David Lewis	7:49.61
1987	Adrian Passey	7:52.87
1988	Mike McLeod	8:06.07

1989	Paul Larkins	7:58.84
1990	Rob Denmark	7:54.41
1991	Rob Denmark	7:54.83
1992	John Mayock	8:01.54
1993	Paul Larkins	8:05.10
1994	Matt Barnes	7:56.08
1995	Steve Green	8:08.71
1996	Matt Skelton	8:00.48
1997	Darius Burrows	8:04.71
1998	Rod Finch & Dave Taylor	8:00.37
1999	Phillip Tulba	8:07.46
2000	Rob Whalley	8:02.40
2001	Mark Miles	8:19.89
2002	Michael East	8:18.41
2003	Mo Farah	8:05.58
2004	Andy Graffin	8:06.59
2005	Mo Farah	7:56.86
2006	James Thie	8:06.55
2007	Mo Farah	7:50.86
2008	Nick McCormick	8:16.73
2009	Nick McCormick	7:54.73
2010	Andy Vernon	8:00.70
2011	Andy Baddeley	7:54.60

Most titles won: 3 Ian McCafferty 1967–1969; Ian Stewart 1972, 1973, 1975; Ray Smedley 1974, 1976, 1977; Mo Farah 2003, 2005, 2007

2000 METRES STEEPLECHASE

(Event instituted in 1967; discontinued after 1985)

1980	Paul Bettridge	5:45.3
1981	Ron Harris	5:32.9
1982	Peter Barratt	5:33.2
1983	Colin Walker	5:38.45
1984	Colin Walker	5:35.38
1985	Colin Walker	5:35.92

Most titles won: 4 Ron McAndrew 1967, 1970, 1972, 1973

60 METRES HURDLES

(Event instituted in 1935 at 70 yards; 60 yards 1962–1967; 60m from 1968)

1980	David Wilson	7.99
1981	Peter Kelly	8.21
1982	Mark Holtom	7.8
1983	Mark Holtom	7.93
1984	Mark Holtom	7.98
1985	Jon Ridgeon	7.71
1986	Alan Tapp	7.96
1987	Jon Ridgeon	7.66
1988	Jon Ridgeon	7.68

AAA Champions

1989	Colin Jackson	7.52
1990	Colin Jackson	7.43
1991	Thomas Kearns IRL	7.73
	(3, Hugh Teape 7.79)	
1992	Colin Jackson	7.55
1993	Colin Jackson	7.55
1994	Hugh Teape	7.73
1995	Paul Gray	7.83
1996	Neil Owen	7.81
1997	Colin Jackson	7.54
1998	Tony Jarrett	7.59
1999	Colin Jackson	7.59
2000	Tony Jarrett	7.65
2001	Dominic Bradley	7.84
2002	Colin Jackson	7.60
2003	Dominic Girdler	7.78
2004	Mohammed Sillah-Freckleton	7.68
2005	Allan Scott	7.58
2006	Andy Turner	7.70
2007	Andy Turner	7.55
2008	Allan Scott	7.61
2009	Chris Baillie	7.74
2010	Callum Priestley	7.69
2011	Andy Turner	7.61

Most titles won: 7 Colin Jackson 1989, 1990, 1992, 1993, 1997, 1999, 2002

HIGH JUMP

(Event instituted in 1935)

1980	Andrew McIver	2.15
1981	Mark Naylor	2.18
1982	Alex Kruger	2.12
1983	Geoff Parsons	2.20
1984	Dariusz Biczysko POL	2.25
	(2, Geoff Parsons 2.20)	
1985	Alain Metellus CAN	2.23
	(5=, John Hill & Leroy Lucas 2.09)	
1986	Geoff Parsons	2.30
1987	Henderson Pierre	2.15
1988	Geoff Parsons	2.27
1989	Nick Saunders BER	2.30
	(2, Dalton Grant 2.24)	
1990	Nick Saunders BER	2.25
	(2, Dalton Grant 2.25)	
1991	Geoff Parsons	2.24
1992	Steinar Hoen NOR	2.25
	(2, Geoff Parsons 2.20)	
1993	Dalton Grant	2.25
1994	Brendan Reilly	2.28
1995	Geoff Parsons	2.24

1996	Mike Robbins	2.19
1997	Mark Mandy IRL	2.22
	(2, Ben Challenger 2.21)	
1998	Ben Challenger	2.27
1999	Ben Challenger	2.25
2000	Stuart Ohrland	2.19
2001	Samson Oni	2.20
2002	Ben Challenger	2.17
2003	Dalton Grant	2.25
2004	Ben Challenger	2.20
2005	Robert Mitchell	2.20
2006	Martyn Bernard	2.24
2007	Martyn Bernard	2.23
2008	Samson Oni	2.30
2009	Darwin Edwards LCA	2.22
	(2, Robbie Grabarz 2.19)	
2010	Samson Oni	2.25
2011	Tom Parsons	2.31

Most titles won: 5 Geoff Parsons 1983, 1986, 1988, 1991, 1995

POLE VAULT

(Event instituted in 1935)

1980	Keith Stock	4.80
1981	Brian Hooper	5.40
1982	Jeff Gutteridge	5.00
1983	Steve Smith USA	5.25
	(3, Keith Stock 5.10)	
1984	Mariusz Klimczyk POL	5.30
	(2, Keith Stock 5.25)	
1985	Vasiliy Bubka URS	5.60
	(4, Keith Stock 5.10)	
1986	Andy Ashurst	5.20
1987	Jeff Gutteridge	5.30
1988	Andy Ashurst	5.10
1989	Andy Ashurst	5.20
1990	Andy Ashurst	5.20
1991	Peter Widén SWE	5.51
	(2, Andy Ashurst 5.30)	
1992	Galin Nikov BUL	5.45
	(2, Andy Ashurst 5.45)	
1993	Martin Voss DEN	5.30
	(3, Kevin Hughes 5.00)	
1994	Peter Widén SWE	5.45
	(5=, Andy Ashurst 5.20)	
1995	Paul Williamson	5.20
1996	Nick Buckfield	5.61
1997	Kevin Hughes	5.20
1998	Nick Buckfield	5.30
1999	Nick Buckfield	5.30
2000	Ben Flint	5.35

2001	Tim Thomas	5.35
2002	Nick Buckfield	5.50
2003	Viktor Chistiakov AUS	5.60
	(2, Tim Thomas 5.30)	
2004	Ashley Swain	5.50
2005	Ashley Swain	5.25
2006	Steve Lewis	5.40
2007	Steve Lewis	5.50
2008	Steve Lewis	5.61
2009	Steve Lewis	5.65
2010	Steve Lewis	5.56
2011	Max Eaves	5.61

Most titles won: 8 Mike Bull 1967–1972, 1974, 1977

LONG JUMP

(Event instituted in 1935)

1980	Tony Henry	7.56
1981	Aston Moore	7.49
1982	Tony Henry	7.59
1983	Dimitrios Delifotis GRE	7.47
	(2, Eddie Starrs 7.34)	
1984	Derrick Brown	7.52
1985	Liu Yuhuang CHN	7.67
	(2, Derrick Brown 7.64)	
1986	John King	7.49
1987	Barrington Williams	7.64
1988	John King	7.65
1989	Barrington Williams	7.88
1990	Stewart Faulkner	8.03
1991	Vernon George USA	7.84
	(2, Barrington Williams 7.81)	
1992	Mark Forsythe	7.85
1993	Matias Ghansah SWE	7.63
	(2, Paul Johnson 7.60)	
1994	Mattias Sunneborn SWE	7.50
	(3, Fred Salle 7.39)	
1995	Barrington Williams	7.55
1996	Chris Davidson	7.60
1997	Steve Phillips	7.54
1998	Chris Davidson	7.43
1999	Chris Davidson	7.62
2000	Chris Tomlinson	7.57
2001	Chris Tomlinson	7.41
2002	Gable Garenamotse BOT	8.01
	(2, André Fernandez 7.22)	
2003	Chris Tomlinson	7.90
2004	Chris Tomlinson	7.80
2005	Nathan Morgan	7.96
2006	Leigh Smith	7.56

2007	Bernard Yeboah	7.50
2008	Chris Tomlinson	7.80
2009	Chris Tomlinson	7.72
2010	Greg Rutherford	7.94
2011	Ezekiel Ewulo	7.60

Most titles won: 6 Chris Tomlinson 2000, 2001, 2003, 2004, 2008, 2009

TRIPLE JUMP

(Event instituted in 1965)

1980	David Johnson	15.64
1981	Aston Moore	15.90
1982	Aston Moore	16.46
1983	David Johnson	15.68
1984	Al Joyner USA	16.54
	(2, John Herbert 16.33)	
1985	Zou Zhenxian CHN	16.50
	(4, Francis Agyepong 15.66)	
1986	Craig Duncan	15.62
1987	Arne Holm SWE	16.38
	(2, Eric McCalla 16.03)	
1988	Eric McCalla	16.06
1989	Francis Agyepong	16.17
1990	Francis Agyepong	16.05
1991	Joe Sweeney	15.93
1992	Vernon Samuels	16.24
1993	Tosi Fasinro	15.89
1994	Francis Agyepong	16.55
1995	John Herbert	16.48
1996	Francis Agyepong	16.55
1997	Femi Akinsanya	16.37
1998	Julian Golley	16.49
1999	Julian Golley	16.22
2000	Julian Golley	16.56
2001	Julian Golley	16.22
2002	Tosin Oke	15.95
2003	Tosin Oke	16.61
2004	Julien Kapek FRA	16.32
	(2, Femi Akinsanya 15.79)	
2005	Phillips Idowu	17.30
2006	Nathan Douglas	16.55
2007	Nathan Douglas	17.19
2008	Phillips Idowu	17.24
2009	Julian Golley	16.07
2010	Tosin Oke NGR	16.76
	(2, Nick Thomas 16.22)	
2011	Ben Williams	15.88

Most titles won: 5 Julian Golley 1998–2001, 2009

SHOT

(Event instituted in 1935)

1980	Mike Winch	18.74
1981	Mike Winch	18.38
1982	Mike Winch	18.82
1983	Mike Winch	18.84
1984	Mike Winch	18.52
1985	Billy Cole	17.32
1986	Billy Cole	18.48
1987	Graham Savory	17.52
1988	Paul Edwards	17.78
1989	Matt Simson	18.21
1990	Paul Edwards	17.79
1991	Paul Edwards	18.58
1992	Paul Edwards	19.15
1993	Paul Edwards	18.47
1994	Paul Edwards	18.95
1995	Lee Newman	17.30
1996	Shaun Pickering	17.88
1997	Lee Newman	18.10
1998	Shaun Pickering	18.95
1999	Gary Sollitt	17.26
2000	Steph Hayward	17.67
2001	Emeka Udechuku	18.19
2002	Erik van Vreumingen NED	17.38
	(2, Gary Sollitt 16.66)	
2003	Scott Rider	17.60
2004	Rutger Smith NED	19.85
	(2, Emeka Udechuku 18.12)	
2005	Emeka Udechuku	17.64
2006	Emeka Udechuku	17.89
2007	Garrett Johnson USA	18.98
	(2, Chris Gaviglio 18.05)	
2008	Garrett Johnson USA	20.66
	(2, Emeka Udechuku 18.06)	
2009	Mark Edwards	18.90
2010	Mark Edwards	17.40
2011	Scott Rider	17.96

Most titles won: 7 Mike Winch 1973, 1979–1984

HEPTATHLON

(Event instituted in 1987 (Octathlon); Heptathlon since 1991)

1987	Mark Luscombe	6191
1988	Mark Bishop	5918
1989	Mark Bishop	6306
1990	Bill Jewers	5998
1991	Bill Jewers	5230
1992	Alex Kruger	5700

1993	Alex Kruger	5888
1994	Barry Thomas	5366
1995	Anthony Brannen	5877
1996	Steve Rogers	5252
1997	Brett Heath	4989
1998	Joe Naughton IRL	5384
	(2, Paul Jones 4954)	
1999	Du'aine Ladejo	5607
2000	Paul Jones	5277
2001	John Heanley	5148
2002	Barry Thomas	5403
2003	John Heanley	5499
2004	John Heanley	5464
2005	Edward Dunford	5438
2006	Louis Evling-Jones	5563
2007	Kevin Sempers	5367
2008	Edward Dunford	5722
2009	Kevin Sempers	5580
2010	Richard Reeks	5629
2011	Francis Baker	5407

Most titles won: 3 John Heanley 2001, 2003, 2004

3000 METRES WALK

(Event instituted in 1997; discontinued after 2002)

1997	Andy Penn	12:14.42
1998	Martin Bell	12:08.61
1999	Andi Drake	11:56.72
2000	Robert Heffernan IRL	11:38.20
	(2, Martin Bell 12:03.12)	
2001	Robert Heffernan IRL	11:19.27
	(2, Andi Drake 12:02.24)	
2002	Robert Heffernan IRL	11:10.02
	(3, Andi Drake 11:58.49)	

UNDER-23

(Instituted in 1999)

100 METRES

1999	Christian Malcolm	10.20w
2000	Jon Barbour	10.32
2001	Jon Barbour	10.13w
2002	Tyrone Edgar	10.31w
2003	Tyrone Edgar	10.28
2004	Tim Abeyie	10.79
2005	Gibril Bangura SLE	10.41
	(2, James Ellington 10.42)	

AAA Champions

2006	Craig Pickering	10.35w
2007	Simeon Williamson	10.22
2008	James Dasaolu	10.40
2009	Rion Pierre	10.34
2010	Leevan Yearwood	10.31w

200 METRES

1999	Christian Malcolm	21.01
2000	Jon Barbour	21.04
2001	Jon Barbour	20.8w
2002	Dominic Papura	21.15
2003	Chris Lambert	20.58
2004	Tim Abeyie	21.25
2005	Rikki Fifton	21.21
2006	Leon Baptiste	21.03
2007	Rikki Fifton	21.10
2008	Jeffrey Lawal-Balogun	21.33w
2009	Toby Sandeman	20.72
2010	Ryan Oswald	21.23

400 METRES

1999	David Naismith	46.95
2000	Daniel Caines	46.82
2001	David Naismith	47.13
2002	Ian Lowthian	49.01
2003	Allan Stuart	46.72
2004	Rob Tobin	46.27
2005	Rabah Yusuf SUD (2, Gareth Warburton 47.05)	46.69
2006	Richard Buck	46.77
2007	Rabah Yusuf SUD (2, Richard Buck 46.63)	46.04
2008	Ben Higgins	47.68
2009	Nigel Levine	46.30
2010	Luke Lennon-Ford	47.16

800 METRES

1999	Alasdair Donaldson	1:49.02
2000	Chris Moss	1:50.11
2001	Chris Moss	1:53.0
2002	Sam Ellis	1:53.17
2003	Tim Bayley	1:48.68
2004	Damien Moss	1:50.01
2005	Gareth Balch	1:53.33
2006	Chris Gowell	1:53.16
2007	Richard Hill	1:47.59

2008	Joe Thomas	1:52.33
2009	Andrew Osagie	1:47.70
2010	Joseph Durrant	1:52.54

1500 METRES

1999	Matthew Dixon	3:47.38
2000	Angus Maclean	3:47.21
2001	Angus Maclean	3:47.6
2002	Chris Bolt	3:53.19
2003	Chris Thompson	3:47.73
2004	Chris Warburton	3:57.27
2005	Chris Warburton	3:52.15
2006	Alan Wales	3:49.93
2007	Ross Toole	3:52.51
2008	Andy Vernon	3:54.0
2009	James Brewer	3:44.45
2010	Daniel Clorley	3:50.98

5000 METRES

1999	Sam Haughian	14:09.21
2000	Stephen Hepples	14:40.85
2001	Adam Sutton	14:25.84
2002	James Fewtrell	14:26.58
2003	Mo Farah	13:58.58
2004	Phil Nicholls	14:23.26
2005	Scott Overall	14:17.88
2006	Moumin Geele SOM	14:41.45
	(2, Phil Wicks 14:45.64)	
2007	Andy Vernon	14:25.21
2008	Jonathan Mellor	14:11.88
2009	Jonathan Taylor	14:27.28
2010	Craig Gundersen	14:50.33

3000 METRES STEEPLECHASE

1999	Ben Whitby	8:59.29
2000	Iain Murdoch	9:01.32
2001	Andrew Franklin	8:51.4
2002	Adam Bowden	9:12.76
2003	Adam Bowden	8:42.92
2004	Stephen Murphy	9:09.80
2005	Mark Buckingham	8:58.11
2006	Samater Farah	9:11.31
2007	Chris Hart	9:06.25
2008	Glen Watts	9:13.89
2009	Stephen Lisgo	9:08.47
2010	Tom Wade	9:07.19

AAA Champions

110 METRES HURDLES

1999	Duncan Malins	14.29
2000	Duncan Malins	14.10
2001	Robert Newton	14.0w
2002	Dominic Girdler	14.0
2003	Robert Newton	13.89
2004	Allan Scott	13.84
2005	David Hughes	13.90
2006	William Sharman	13.49
2007	Nicholas Gayle	14.14
2008	Gianni Frankis	13.76w
2009	Gianni Frankis	13.95
2010	Lawrence Clarke	13.60w

400 METRES HURDLES

1999	James Hillier	51.30
2000	Matt Elias	51.51
2001	Matt Elias	50.1
2002	Steve Surety	51.8
2003	Steven Green	51.13
2004	Elliott Wood AUS	51.14
	(2, Richard Blake-Smith 51.34)	
2005	Rhys Williams	50.43
2006	Ben Carne	52.57
2007	Iain McDonald	51.86
2008	Rick Yates	52.20
2009	Lloyd Gumbs	50.36
2010	Andrew Howell	51.44

HIGH JUMP

1999	Daniel Graham	2.11
2000	Robert Mitchell	2.19
2001	Samson Oni	2.18
2002	Robert Mitchell	2.13
2003	Samson Oni	2.18
2004	Tom Parsons	2.15
2005	Martyn Bernard	2.24
2006	Adam Scarr	2.22
2007	Adam Scarr	2.23
2008	Nick Stanisavljevic	2.14
2009	Robbie Grabarz	2.14
2010	Alan McKie	2.10

POLE VAULT

1999	Mark Davis	5.10
2000	Ben Flint	5.25

2001	Scott Simpson	5.20
2002	Ashley Swain	5.15
2003	Mark Beharrell	5.35
2004	Mark Christie	4.95
2005	Keith Higham	5.00
2006	Paul Walker	4.95
2007	Joe Ive	5.40
2008	Luke Cutts	5.10
2009	Luke Cutts	5.41
2010	Luke Cutts	5.25

LONG JUMP

1999	Darren Thompson	7.52
2000	Stuart Wells	7.28
2001	Chris Tomlinson	7.61
2002	Mark Awanah	7.60w
2003	Alex Hall	7.73w
2004	Jonathan Moore	7.75w
2005	Jonathan Moore	7.47
2006	Chris Kirk	7.41
2007	Oliver McNeillis	7.23
2008	Lee Blaymire	7.28
2009	Jamie Blundell	7.39
2010	Daniel Gardiner	7.56w

TRIPLE JUMP

1999	Phillips Idowu	16.09w
2000	Nick Thomas	15.93
2001	Nick Thomas	15.54
2002	Tosin Oke	16.27w
2003	Nathan Douglas	16.30
2004	Nathan Douglas	16.42
2005	Jonathan Moore	15.75
2006	Gary White	15.47
2007	Gary White	15.74
2008	John Carr	15.09
2009	John Carr	15.52
2010	Trevor Okoroafor	16.00w

SHOT

1999	Emeka Udechuku	16.88
	(Carl Myerscough won with 17.99 but	
	result later annulled due to drugs disqualification)	
2000	Emeka Udechuku	17.66
2001	Emeka Udechuku	17.90
2002	David Readle	16.91

2003	Marcus Gouldbourne	16.32
2004	Nick Vince	14.59
2005	Sam Westlake-Cann	16.03
2006	Chris Gearing	17.12
2007	Kieren Kelly	17.84
2008	Kieren Kelly	17.84
2009	James Stevenson	17.85
2010	Daniel Carlin	14.70

DISCUS

1999	Emeka Udechuku	55.90
	(Carl Myerscough won with 58.99 but	
	result later annulled due to drugs disqualification)	
2000	Emeka Udechuku	53.87
2001	Emeka Udechuku	59.84
2002	Luke Rosenberg	50.48
2003	Scot Thompson	55.27
2004	Josh Lamb	49.43
2005	Simon Cooke	49.64
2006	Leslie Richards	51.38
2007	Leslie Richards	53.94
2008	Chris Scott	51.93
2009	Brett Morse	54.78
2010	Chris Scott	59.90

HAMMER

1999	Matthew Bell	60.42
2000	Matthew Bell	61.51
2001	Andy Frost	61.30
2002	Andy Frost	63.05
2003	Carl Saggers	59.81
2004	Carl Saggers	63.17
2005	Carl Saggers	65.49
2006	Matthew Richards	51.83
2007	Amir Williamson	61.41
2008	Amir Williamson	64.91
2009	Mark Dry	69.40
2010	Peter Smith	69.92

JAVELIN

1999	Robert Charlesworth	60.92
2000	Daniel Carter	71.90
2001	David Parker	75.53
2002	Phil Sharpe	71.09
2003	Jon Lundman	64.24
2004	Anthony Lovett	67.30

2005	Alex van der Merwe	71.49
2006	Alex van der Merwe	64.64
2007	James Hopley	66.12
2008	James Campbell	71.88
2009	James Campbell	70.07
2010	James Campbell	73.41

DECATHLON

| 2008 | Daniel Awde | 7704 |
| 2009 | Guy Stroud | 7258 |

10,000 METRES WALK

1999	Robert Heffernan IRL	43:49.80
	(3, Matt Hales 45:38.01)	
2000	not held	
2001	not held	
2002	Nathan Adams	46:22.2
2003	Dominic King	43:27.93
2004	Daniel King	43:52.86
2005	Daniel King	44:40.35
2006	Luke Finch	47:59.51

(Discontinued after 2006)

JUNIOR (UNDER-20)

100 METRES

(Event instituted in 1931 at 100 yards; 100m since 1969)

1980	Darren Bills	10.74
1981	Lincoln Asquith	10.7
1982	Lincoln Asquith	10.45w
1983	Lincoln Asquith	10.29w
1984	Elliot Bunney	10.40
1985	Elliot Bunney	10.38w
1986	David Kirton	10.62
1987	Marcus Adam	10.69
1988	Darren Braithwaite	10.34w
1989	Steve Gookey	10.63
1990	Jason Livingston	10.39
1991	Darren Campbell	10.46
1992	Darren Campbell	10.48
1993	Danny Joyce	10.46w
1994	Julian Golding	10.52
1995	Jamie Henthorn	10.64
1996	Dwain Chambers	10.42
1997	Dwain Chambers	10.41
1998	Christian Malcolm	10.17w

AAA Champions

1999	Mark Lewis-Francis	10.38
2000	Mark Lewis-Francis	10.46
2001	Tyrone Edgar	10.17w
2002	Karl Forde	10.6w
2003	Leon Baptiste	10.43
2004	Leon Baptiste	10.51
2005	Simeon Williamson	10.24
2006	Harry Aikines-Aryeetey	10.49
2007	Leevan Yearwood	10.30
2008	James Alaka	10.52
2009	Max Galliers	10.54
2010	David Bolarinwa	10.47

200 METRES

(Event instituted in 1931 at 220 yards; 200m since 1969)

1980	Phil Brown	21.53
1981	Donovan Reid	21.10
1982	Paul Dunn	21.40
1983	Lincoln Asquith	21.06
1984	Derek O'Connor IRL	21.19
	(2, Elliot Bunney 21.30)	
1985	Richard Ashby	21.83
1986	Marcus Adam	21.09
1987	Marcus Adam	21.30
1988	Lloyd Stapleton	21.17
1989	Wayne McDonald	21.05w
1990	Mark Smith	20.85w
1991	Darren Campbell	21.31w
1992	Darren Campbell	21.01
1993	Danny Joyce	21.60w
1994	Julian Golding	21.02
1995	Mark Hylton	21.4
1996	Christian Malcolm	21.32
1997	Christian Malcolm	20.48w
1998	Christian Malcolm	20.32w
1999	Chris Lambert	21.47
2000	Tim Benjamin	20.95w
2001	Dwayne Grant	20.4w
2002	Leon Baptiste	21.41w
2003	Leon Baptiste	21.64
2004	Leon Baptiste	21.07w
2005	Somto Eruchie	21.02
2006	Alex Nelson	21.05
2007	Alex Nelson	20.99
2008	Richard Kilty	21.40
2009	Sebastian Tully-Middleton	21.55
2010	Kieran Showler-Davis	20.75

400 METRES

(Event instituted in 1931 at 440 yards; 400m since 1969)

1980	Roy Dickens	46.77
1981	Todd Bennett	46.6
1982	Paul Dunn	47.34
1983	Mark McMahon	47.79
1984	Derek Redmond	46.35
1985	Roger Black	47.33
1986	Gary Patterson	47.54
1987	Gary Patterson	47.80
1988	Wayne McDonald	47.15
1989	Wayne McDonald	46.93
1990	Mark Richardson	47.79
1991	Mark Richardson	45.72
1992	Carl Southam	46.74
1993	Guy Bullock	46.96
1994	Mark Hylton	46.94
1995	Geoff Dearman	47.55
1996	Geoff Dearman	47.55
1997	Michael Parper	47.10
1998	Alloy Wilson	48.04
1999	Adam Buckley	47.71
2000	Ian Tinsley	48.19
2001	Rob Tobin	47.3
2002	Adam Charlton	48.95
2003	Adam Charlton	46.88
2004	Rabah Yusuf SUD	47.51
	(2, Richard Buck 47.84)	
2005	Martyn Rooney	46.44
2006	Grant Baker	46.98
2007	Nigel Levine	46.69
2008	Chris Clarke	47.08
2009	Chris Clarke	46.55
2010	Nathan Wake	47.37

800 METRES

(Event instituted in 1931 at 880 yards; 800m since 1969)

1980	John Blackledge	1:52.53
1981	Chris McGeorge	1:48.4
1982	Philip Verschueren	1:50.38
1983	Darryl Taylor	1:50.12
1984	Paul Williams	1:51.46
1985	Paul Williams	1:52.68
1986	Kevin McKay	1:51.77
1987	Kevin McKay	1:50.69
1988	Kevin McKay	1:51.70
1989	Craig Winrow	1:57.19
1990	Mark Sesay	1:55.6

1991	Noel Edwards	1:51.70
1992	Paul Walker	1:50.54
1993	Hezekiel Sepeng RSA	1:47.69
	(4, Simon Saxby 1:51.66)	
1994	Paul Byrne AUS	1:48.25
	(2, Eddie King 1:48.93)	
1995	Andy Blackmore	1:50.8
1996	James Nolan IRL	1:49.95
	(2, Tom Lerwill 1:50.21)	
1997	Neil Kirk	1:50.89
1998	Chris Moss	1:50.09
1999	Nic Andrews	1:53.13
2000	Chris Mulvaney	1:51.40
2001	Ricky Soos	1:56.97
2002	Ricky Soos	1:50.21
2003	Chris Reynolds	1:49.30
2004	Chris Gowell	1:53.00
2005	Michael Rimmer	1:49.82
2006	James Mills	1:52.68
2007	James Brewer	1:48.23
2008	James Shane	1:52.33
2009	Robbie Schofield	1:49.82
2010	Niall Brooks	1:47.29

1500 METRES

(Event instituted in 1931 at 1 Mile; 1500m since 1969)

1980	Jack Buckner	3:50.94
1981	Phil Dixon	3:44.60
1982	Stuart Paton	3:43.06
1983	Enda Fitzpatrick IRL	3:47.17
	(2, Paul Wynn 3:47.19)	
1984	Neil Horsfield	3:45.85
1985	Neil Horsfield	3:47.38
1986	Steve Halliday	3:52.05
1987	Steve Halliday	3:54.62
1988	Simon Brown	3:46.08
1989	Martin Forder	4:04.07
1990	Curtis Robb	3:55.98
1991	Curtis Robb	3:49.69
1992	Matt Hibberd	3:48.38
1993	Neil Caddy	3:51.21
1994	Paul Cleary AUS	3:49.45
	(3, Neil Caddy 3:49.94)	
1995	Des Roache	3:45.6
1996	Andrew Walker IRL	3:47.21
	(2, Grant Cuddy 3:49.36)	
1997	Matthew Dixon	3:49.00
1998	Chris Livesey	3:53.79
1999	Chris Bolt	3:47.09

2000	Chris Thompson	3:48.93
2001	Derek Watson	3:50.1
2002	Derek Watson	3:58.73
2003	Tom Lancashire	3:49.33
2004	Tom Lancashire	3:48.30
2005	Anthony Moran	3:54.94
2006	Kris Gauson	3:50.31
2007	Ricky Stevenson	3:51.34
2008	David Forrester	4:12.99
2009	Simon Horsfield	3:46.92
2010	Ronnie Sparke	3:50.38

3000 METRES

(Event instituted in 1964 at 2 Miles; 3000m since 1969; discontinued after 2007)

1980	John Doherty	7:59.86
1981	Paul Davies-Hale	7:59.55
1982	David Topham	8:12.58
1983	Cyrille Laventure FRA	7:59.83
	(2, Jon Richards 8:03.33)	
1984	Enda Fitzpatrick IRL & David Miles	8:15.09
1985	James Piper	8:16.27
1986	Darren Mead	8:09.93
1987	Rob Denmark	8:16.00
1988	John Mayock	8:20.67
1989	Mike Proudlove	8:24.12
1990	Robert Kettle	8:26.36
1991	Steffan White	8:24.50
1992	Luke Veness	8:18.14
1993	Chris Elliott	8:21.61
1994	Chris Elliott	8:31.20
1995	Matt O'Dowd	8:25.0
1996	James Thie	8:34.17
1997	Michael East	8:23.28
1998	David Hibbert	8:27.93
1999	Neil Bangs	8:41.71
2000	Richard Ward	8:24.73
2001	not held	
2002	Matthew Bowser	8:20.38
2003	not held	
2004	Mark Buckingham	8:24.69
2005	Adam Hickey	8:22.50
2006	Tom Bilham	8:16.26
2007	David Forrester	8:31.66

5000 METRES

(Event instituted in 1973)

1980	Brian O'Keeffe IRL	14:34.90
	(2, Andrew Bristow 14:35.8)	

1981	Tony Leonard	14:08.38
1982	Paul O'Callaghan IRL	14:12.45
	(2, Peter Tootell 14:16.68)	
1983	Richard Carter	14:12.61
1984	Paul Taylor	14:07.85
1985	Paul Taylor	14:16.89
1986	Darrell Smith	14:28.97
1987	Clark Murphy	14:39.19
1988	Jon Dennis	14:14.27
1989	Jon Dennis	14:19.93
1990	Malcolm Campbell	14:44.5
1991	Steffan White	14:43.66
1992	Spencer Barden	14:26.27
1993	Enoch Skosana RSA	14:24.69
	(2, Darius Burrows 14:28.03)	
1994	Blair Martin NZL	14:35.77
	(2, Darius Burrows 14:45.90)	
1995	Alan Dunleavy IRL	14:26.54
	(2, Allen Graffin 14:30.42)	
1996	Andres Jones	14:39.57
1997	Alan Vaughan	15:29.76
1998	Sam Haughian	14:39.00
1999	Stephen Hepples	15:09.89
2000	Nicholas Goodliffe	14:47.15
2001	Ed Prickett	15:01.03
2002	Tom Sharland	14:32.2
2003	Tom Humphries	14:36.81
2004	Ryan McLeod	14:40.80
2005	Andy Vernon	14:44.39
2006	Adam Hickey	14:47.4
2007	Lee Carey	14:54.93
2008	Abdirisak Ahmed	14:46.92
2009	Simon Lawson	14:39.03
2010	Josh Gorecki	14:48.24

STEEPLECHASE

(Event instituted in 1931 at ¾ Mile; 1 Mile from 1956; 1500m from 1958; 2000m from 1965; 3000m from 1987)

1980	Tom Conlon IRL	5:51.79
	(2, Ken Baker 5:58.6)	
1981	Ken Baker	5:42.94
1982	Ken Baker	5:38.01
1983	Andrew Rodgers	5:43.18
1984	John Hartigan	5:49.48
1985	Tom Hanlon	5:45.87
1986	Tom Hanlon	5:41.18
1987	Mark Wortley	9:03.26
1988	Spencer Duval	9:10.86
1989	Mike Proudlove	9:16.24

1990	Kevin Toher	9:25.1
1991	Rob Hough	9:10.60
1992	Stuart Kefford	9:09.21
1993	Daniel Furmidge	9:20.81
1994	Chris Elliott	9:09.47
1995	Kevin Nash	9:07.22
1996	Ben Whitby	8:59.09
1997	Andrew Robinson	9:07.70
1998	Chris Thompson	9:06.20
1999	Iain Murdoch	9:07.8
2000	Adam Bowden	9:14.12
2001	Jermaine Mays	9:10.8
2002	Mohammed Al-Banai KSA	9:16.98
	(2, Frank Tickner 9:18.88)	
2003	Peter Kellie	9:13.63
2004	Mark Buckingham	9:03.54
2005	Chris Hart	9:16.08
2006	Jon Pepper	9:13.67
2007	Phil Norman	9:10.16
2008	James Wilkinson	9:12.21
2009	Ben Nagy	9:10.76
2010	Matthew Graham	9:06.91

110 METRES HURDLES

(Event instituted in 1931 at 120 yards (3'3"); 110m (3'3") since 1969; 110m (3'6")
from 1973; (3'3") from 2006)

1980	Nigel Walker	15.07
1981	Nigel Walker	14.47
1982	Kieran Moore	14.59
1983	Kieran Moore	14.82
1984	Jon Ridgeon	13.92
1985	Colin Jackson	14.17
1986	David Nelson	14.21
1987	Paul Gray	14.08
1988	Paul Gray	14.39
1989	Brian Taylor	14.30w
1990	Richard Harbour	14.27w
1991	Richard Harbour	14.67
1992	Neil Owen	14.36
1993	Kevin Lumsdon	14.32w
1994	John Whelan IRL	14.38
	(3, James Archampong 14.50)	
1995	Damien Greaves	14.4w
1996	Damien Greaves	14.20
1997	Richard Sear	14.45
1998	Ben Warmington	14.24w
1999	Robert Newton	14.27
2000	Chris Baillie	13.84
2001	Dominic Girdler	14.2

2002	David Hughes	14.68w
2003	David Hughes	14.49
2004	Jordan Fleary	14.49w
2005	Daniel Davis	14.60
2006	Gianni Frankis	13.68
2007	Gianni Frankis	13.66
2008	Edirin Okoro	13.68w
2009	Lawrence Clarke	13.78
2010	Ben Kelk	13.87w

400 METRES HURDLES

(Event instituted in 1967 at 440 yards; 400m since 1969)

1980	Paul Goacher	51.66
1981	Phil Beattie	53.3
1982	Phil Beattie	51.15
1983	Martin Briggs	51.45
1984	Andrew Abrahams	52.24
1985	Phil Harries	54.63
1986	Peter Campbell	52.80
1987	Bob Brown	52.49
1988	Peter Campbell	51.99
1989	Matthew Birchall	53.73
1990	Tim Gwynne	54.56
1991	Gary Jennings	52.26
1992	Noel Levy	52.42
1993	Eugene v.d Westhuizen RSA	53.11
	(2, Jason Toal 54.08)	
1994	Matt Beckenham AUS	52.58
	(3, Alex Hunte 53.09)	
1995	Matt Douglas	52.21
1996	Mark Rowlands	52.38
1997	Mark Rowlands	51.88
1998	Richard McDonald	52.63
1999	Richard McDonald	52.15
2000	Jeff Christie	52.83
2001	Jeff Christie	51.8
2002	Steven Green	51.6
2003	Rupert Gardner	51.4
2004	Richard Davenport	51.11
2005	Adel Jaber Assiri KSA	52.18
	(2, David Greene 52.19)	
2006	Toby Ulm	52.58
2007	Toby Ulm	51.60
2008	Nathan Woodward	53.06
2009	Niall Flannery	51.07
2010	Jack Green	51.54

HIGH JUMP

(Event instituted in 1931)

1980	Claude Moseley	2.08
1981	David Watson	2.10
1982	Mark Lakey	2.10
1983	John Hill	2.10
1984	Dalton Grant	2.12
1985	John Hill	2.13
1986	Andy Hutchinson	2.08
1987	John Holman	2.04
1988	Marlon Huggins	2.05
1989	Brendan Reilly	2.13
1990	Brendan Reilly	2.20
1991	Brendan Reilly	2.25
1992	Adrian Anderson	2.11
1993	Jagan Hames AUS	2.18
	(3=, Damon Rutland 2.05)	
1994	Jagan Hames AUS	2.21
	(3, Stuart Ohrland 2.14)	
1995	James Brierley	2.16
1996	James Brierley	2.21
1997	Ben Challenger	2.15
1998	Martin Lloyd	2.09
1999	Robert Mitchell	2.14
2000	Luke Crawley	2.15
2001	Chuka Enih-Snell	2.14
2002	Mark Crowley	2.15
2003	Martyn Bernard	2.10
2004	Nick Stanisavljevic	2.15
2005	Nick Stanisavljevic	2.15
2006	Robbie Grabarz	2.12
2007	Alan McKie	2.12
2008	Matthew Owens	2.09
2009	Sam Bailey	2.09
2010	Sam Bailey	2.09

POLE VAULT

(Event instituted in 1931)

1980	Tim Anstiss	4.80
1981	Richard Hooper	4.40
1982	Billy Davey	5.00
1983	Billy Davey	5.10
1984	Andy Ashurst	4.90
1985	Paul Wray	4.60
1986	Paul Phelps	4.80
1987	Mike Edwards	4.95
1988	Ian Tullett	4.85
1989	Duncan Pearce	4.70
1990	Neil Winter	5.00

AAA Champions

1991	Warren Siley	5.10
1992	Neil Winter	5.35
1993	Neil Winter	5.40
1994	Neil Young	4.75
1995	Matt Filsbell AUS	4.80
	(2, Christian Linskey 4.70)	
1996	Christian Linskey	5.10
1997	Christian Linskey	5.10
1998	Christian Linskey	5.00
1999	Ashley Swain	4.60
2000	Mark Beharrell	4.90
2001	Richard Hurren	4.60
2002	Richard Hurren	4.60
2003	Mark Christie	5.00
2004	Steve Lewis	4.80
2005	Steve Lewis	5.00
2006	Luke Cutts	5.15
2007	Scott Huggins	4.80
2008	Scott Huggins	4.95
2009	Andrew Sutcliffe	5.10
2010	Matt Devereux	5.10

LONG JUMP

(Event instituted in 1931)

1980	Trevor Sinclair	7.24
1981	Hugh Whyte	7.44
1982	Gary Pullen	7.41w
1983	Femi Abejide	7.34
1984	Ian Ward	7.51w
1985	Barry Nevison	7.23w
1986	Darren Gomersall	7.31
1987	Stewart Faulkner	7.86
1988	Stewart Faulkner	7.90
1989	Wayne Griffith	7.35w
1990	Peter Banks AUS	7.29w
	(2, Eric Scott 7.10w)	
1991	Steve Phillips	7.31
1992	Carl Howard	7.48w
1993	Carl Howard	7.52
1994	Shane Hair AUS	7.58
	(2, Chris Davidson 7.46w)	
1995	Dean Stevens AUS	7.35
	(2, Nathan Morgan 7.23)	
1996	Nathan Morgan	7.65
1997	Nathan Morgan	7.55
1998	Stuart Wells	7.38w
1999	Steven Shalders	7.23
2000	Chris Tomlinson	7.59
2001	Jonathan Moore	7.98w

2002	Jonathan Moore	7.57w
2003	Chris Kirk	7.64
2004	Greg Rutherford	7.24
2005	Oliver McNeillis	7.43w
2006	Luke Thomas	7.34
2007	Andrew Jones	7.65w
2008	Jamie Blundell	7.28
2009	Daniel Gardiner	7.29
2010	Kadeem Greenidge-Smith	7.59w

TRIPLE JUMP

(Event instituted in 1950)

1980	Conroy Brown	15.57w
1981	Steven Anderson	15.45
1982	Vernon Samuels	15.80
1983	Vernon Samuels	15.69
1984	Michael McDonald	15.37w
1985	David Emanuel	15.25w
1986	Lawrence Lynch	15.07
1987	Chike Chukwolozie	15.11
1988	Peter Akwaboah	15.42
1989	Julian Golley	15.14
1990	Tosi Fasinro	15.83w
1991	Tosi Fasinro	16.19w
1992	Larry Achike	15.31
1993	Larry Achike	16.28w
1994	Tayo Erogbogbo	15.92
1995	Marvin Bramble	15.23
1996	James Peacock	15.04
1997	Phillips Idowu	15.86
1998	Jonathan Wallace	15.76w
1999	Tosin Oke	15.70w
2000	Steven Shalders	15.12
2001	Nathan Douglas	15.06
2002	Kevin Thompson	15.07
2003	Gary White	14.99
2004	Moussa Qarqaran KSA	15.52w
	(2, Gary White 15.15w)	
2005	Jude Beimers	14.92
2006	Matthew Burton	14.99
2007	Jeremy Odametey	15.01
2008	Ben Williams	15.76w
2009	Ben Williams	15.70
2010	Batabunde Amosu	15.39

SHOT

(Event instituted in 1931 with 5.44kg; 6.25kg in 1971/1972; 7.26kg/16lb from 1973)

1980	Tony Zaidman	15.85
1981	Tony Zaidman	16.36
1982	Billy Cole	16.30
1983	Billy Cole	16.79
1984	Billy Cole	16.92
1985	Chris Ellis	16.44
1986	Matt Simson	14.63
1987	Matt Simson	14.84
1988	Matt Simson	17.39
1989	Matt Simson	17.89
1990	Mark Davies	15.35
1991	Scott Hayes	15.00
1992	Scott Hayes	15.34
1993	Mark Edwards	15.17
1994	Justin Anlezark AUS	15.85
	(3, Bill Fuller 15.08)	
1995	Felix Hyde GHA	17.38
	(3, Bill Fuller 15.64)	
1996	Carl Myerscough	15.82
1997	Carl Myerscough	17.41
1998	Carl Myerscough	19.24
1999	David Readle	16.15
2000	Greg Beard	15.59
2001	Greg Beard	16.23
2002	Sam Westlake-Cann	16.42
2003	Chris Gearing	16.93
2004	Chris Gearing	17.97
2005	Jamie Williamson	18.14
2006	Jamie Williamson	17.39
2007	Jay Thomas	17.53
2008	Jamie Stevenson	18.47
2009	Curtis Griffith-Parker	18.65
2010	Anthony Oshodi	17.39

DISCUS

(Event instituted in 1931 with 1.5kg; 1.75kg in 1971/1972; 2kg from 1973; 1.75kg from 2002)

1980	Robert Weir	51.80
1981	Paul Mardle	49.68
1982	Peter Weir	51.08
1983	Kevin Brown	48.52
1984	Neil Boyton	46.92
1985	Simon Williams	49.20
1986	Stephen Ayre	48.12
1987	Nick Sweeney IRL	48.16
	(2, Matt Symonds 45.98)	

1988	Neal Brunning	47.88
1989	Neal Brunning	51.66
1990	Glen Smith	48.28
1991	Glen Smith	49.72
1992	Lee Newman	51.22
1993	Frits Potgieter RSA	59.12
	(2, Robert Russell 52.14)	
1994	Justin Anlezark AUS	49.54
	(2, James South 47.86)	
1995	Bruce Robb	46.34
1996	Carl Myerscough	50.60
1997	Carl Myerscough	53.86
1998	Emeka Udechuku	60.97
1999	Luke Rosenberg	51.05
2000	Scot Thompson	50.07
2001	Greg Beard	47.20
2002	Roger Bate	49.99
2003	Simon Cooke	49.43
2004	Simon Cooke	57.93
2005	Sam Herrington	50.86
2006	Chris Scott	52.39
2007	Brett Morse	56.15
2008	Brett Morse	55.30
2009	Curtis Griffith-Parker	59.66
2010	Lawrence Okoye	63.92

HAMMER

(Event instituted in 1951 with 5.44kg; 6.25kg in 1971/1972; 7.26kg from 1973; 6kg from 2002)

1980	Robert Weir	63.48
1981	David Smith	60.86
1982	Mick Jones	61.28
1983	Paul Head	62.92
1984	Paul Head	64.42
1985	Garrett Halpin IRL	61.22
	(2, Andrew Tolputt 59.94)	
1986	Andrew Tolputt	59.46
1987	Gareth Cook	56.16
1988	Gareth Cook	61.06
1989	Jason Byrne	64.72
1990	Paddy McGrath IRL	58.18
	(2, Matthew Spicer 56.90)	
1991	Stuart Spratley	56.44
1992	Malcolm Croad	56.22
1993	Matthew Dwight AUS	62.18
	(2, Karl Andrews 60.16)	
1994	Karl Andrews	65.30
1995	Jeff Ayres AUS	56.06
	(3, Matthew Bell 54.00)	

1996	John Thompson IRL	57.54
	(2, John Urquhart 56.32)	
1997	Matthew Bell	58.96
1998	Andrew Grierson	54.12
1999	Ross Thompson	55.32
2000	John Osazuwa NGR	62.87
	(2, Andy Frost 58.75)	
2001	Thomas Dempsey	56.33
2002	Carl Saggers	64.81
2003	Karim Chester	62.13
2004	Alex Smith	65.79
2005	Amir Williamson	62.73
2006	Alex Smith	72.85
2007	Alex Smith	68.72
2008	Peter Smith	71.05
2009	Peter Smith	74.45
2010	Nick Miller	66.79

JAVELIN

(Event instituted in 1931 with 700gm; 800gm from 1961; specification changed in 1986)

1980	Colin Mackenzie	71.46
1981	Roald Bradstock	76.20
1982	Colin Mackenzie	70.28
1983	Mick Hill	71.62
1984	Gary Jenson	67.54
1985	Gary Jenson	74.80
1986	Mark Roberson	73.68
1987	Steve Backley	69.88
1988	Roddy James	61.66
1989	Myles Cottrell	71.74
1990	Nick Nieland	64.46
1991	James Hurrion	64.98
1992	Duncan McDonald	60.60
1993	Duncan McDonald	65.16
1994	Shane Wyle AUS	69.64
	(4, Stuart Faben 66.30)	
1995	Paul Cooper	61.68
1996	David Parker	66.94
1997	David Parker	71.06
1998	David Parker	72.95
1999	David Parker	73.56
2000	Phill Sharpe	71.79
2001	Alex van der Merwe	64.04
2002	Alex van der Merwe	68.85
2003	Alex van der Merwe	67.21
2004	Lee Doran	66.14
2005	Stuart Harvey	66.00
2006	James Campbell	69.02

2007	James Campbell	71.09
2008	Bonne Buwembo	65.73
2009	Matthew Hunt	69.69
2010	Dan Pembroke	72.43

DECATHLON

(Event instituted in 1971 with junior implements; senior implements from 1973;
IAAF junior implements from 2002)

1980	Eugene Gilkes	7117
1981	Cliff Dickenson	6375
1982	Ken Hayford	6830
1983	Mark Luscombe	6312
1984	John Garner	6846
1985	Malachy Sheridan IRL	6517
	(2, Robert Laing 6191)	
1986	Rafer Joseph	6612
1987	Trevor Sloman	6030
1988	David Bigham	6690
1989	Jim Stevenson	6663
1990	David Bigham	7367
1991	Barry Thomas	7035
1992	Andrew Weston	5938
1993	Gavin Sunshine	6006
1994	Brett Heath	6579
1995	Roger Hunter	6925
1996	David Ralson	6199
1997	Erik Toemen	6052
1998	Darren Hatton	6477
1999	Jason McDade	6413
2000	James Wright	6007
2001	Steve Hughes	6151
2002	Edward Dunford	6583
2003	William Sharman	6976
2004	Kevin Sempers	7014
2005	Oliver McNeillis	6528
2006	Daniel Awde	7009
2007	Joe Lancaster	6639
2008	Daniel Gardiner	7207
2009	Daniel Gardiner	7567
2010	Ashley Bryant	7342

TRACK WALK

(Event instituted in 1947 at Mile; 3000m from1969; 10,000m from 1973 except
for 5000m in 2008)

1980	Gordon Vale	45:06.24
1981	Gordon Vale	42:06.35
1982	Phil Vesty	47:54.38

1983	Tim Berrett	43:21.28
1984	David Hucks	46:11.38
1985	Ian Ashforth	45:04.37
1986	Darrell Stone	45:15.68
1987	Darrell Stone	44:09.29
1988	Jon Vincent	45:19.11
1989	Carl Walmsley	51:26.82
1990	Guy Jackson	46:50.69
1991	Philip King	45:40.64
1992	David Cullinane IRL	44:13.91
	(2, Scott Davis 45:30.02)	
1993	Philip King	46:07.60
1994	Dion Russell AUS	43:26.22
1995	Jamie Costin IRL	44:12.51
1996	Jamie Costin IRL	44:55.20
	(3, Matt Hales 50:17.25)	
1997	Thomas Taylor	48:44.42
1998	Thomas Taylor	45:56.16
1999	Lloyd Finch	45:52.39
2000	Colin Griffin IRL	46:45.31
	(2, Daniel King 48:25.61)	
2001	Lloyd Finch	44:29.4
2002	Dominic King	42:49.8
2003	Nick Ball	49:38.49
2004	Luke Finch	46:48.40
2005	Nick Ball	45:36.24
2006	Nick Ball	43:50.94
2007	not held	
2008	Mark O'Kane	24:10.10
2009	Alex Wright	48:18.98
2010	Mark O'Kane	47:04.42

RWA 10 KILOMETRES ROAD WALK

(Event instituted in 1951 at 5 miles; 10km from 1976)

1980	Richard Dorman	43:18
1981	Phil Vesty	43:19
1982	Phil Vesty	43:59
1983	Martin Rush	45:15
1984	Tim Berrett	44:31
1985	Darrell Stone	44:25
1986	Darrell Stone	43:56
1987	Gareth Brown	45:33
1988	Gareth Holloway	46:25
1989	Kieron Butler	48:01
1990	Guy Jackson	47:55
1991	Kieron Butler	46:11
1992	Philip King	46:09
1993	Philip King	43:23
1994	Scott Davis	46:55

1995	Steve Hollier	46:52
1996	Stuart Monk	46:26
1997	Scott Taylor	48:01
1998	Michael Kemp	43:53
1999	Nathan Adams	51:34
2000	Dominic King	45:52
2001	Lloyd Finch	45:30
2002	Dominic King	42:21
2003	Luke Finch	46:09
2004	Luke Finch	46:02
2005	Nick Ball	44:05
2006	Nick Ball	44:47
2007	Ben Wears	50:39
2008	Ben Wears	45:23
2009	Mark O'Kane	47:46
2010	Mark O'Kane	48:11

UNDER-17

100 METRES

(Event instituted in 1968 at 100 yards; 100m from 1969)

1980	Lincoln Asquith	10.91
1981	Roger Hunter	10.7
1982	Gary Thomas	10.68w
1983	Elliot Bunney	10.66w
1984	Phil Goedluck	10.77w
1985	Ivan Collinge	10.78w
1986	Ray Burke	11.2
1987	Adrian Smith	11.15
1988	Duncan Game	10.74w
1989	David Jackson	10.69w
1990	Darren Campbell	10.81
1991	Danny Joyce	10.73
1992	Kevin Mark	10.76
1993	Trevor Cameron	10.72
1994	Dwain Chambers	10.76
1995	Christian Malcolm	10.85
1996	Steven Daly	11.01
1997	Matthew Russell	10.83
1998	Mark Lewis-Francis	10.49
1999	Karl Forde	10.66w
2000	Monu Miah	10.79
2001	Rikki Fifton	10.60w
2002	James Ellington	10.69
2003	Craig Pickering	10.7
2004	Harry Aikines-Aryeetey	10.66
2005	Gerald Phiri	10.75
2006	Olufunmi Sobodu	10.49
2007	Jordan Huggins	10.51

2008	Deji Tobais	10.86
2009	Jordan Arthur	10.72
2010	Chijindu Ujah	10.83

200 METRES

(Event instituted in 1967 at 220 yards; 200m from 1969)

1980	Lincoln Asquith	21.88
1981	Roger Hunter	21.44
1982	Gary Thomas	21.81
1983	Richard Ashby	21.63
1984	Marcus Adam	21.66
1985	Lloyd Stapleton	22.60
1986	Joe Lees	22.23
1987	Chris Blower	22.10
1988	Mark Richardson	21.47
1989	David Jackson	
	& Darren Campbell	21.72w
1990	Mark Walcott	21.90w
1991	John McAdorey	22.00
1992	Guy Bullock	22.03
1993	Trevor Cameron	21.56
1994	Matthew Clements	21.8
1995	Philip Perigo	21.77
1996	Ben Lewis	21.85
1997	Ben Lewis	21.63
1998	Tim Benjamin	21.15w
1999	Adam Rogers	21.64
2000	Monu Miah	21.45
2001	Rikki Fifton	21.48w
2002	Julian Thomas	22.10
2003	Jamahl Alert-Khan	21.20
2004	Harry Aikines-Aryeetey	21.76
2005	Chris Clarke	21.61
2006	Olufunmi Sobodu	21.46
2007	Andrew Robertson	21.51w
2008	Deji Tobais	21.63w
2009	Liam Clowes	21.62
2010	Tom Holligan	21.89

400 METRES

(Event instituted in 1968 at 440 yards; 400m from 1969)

1980	Paul Harmsworth	49.66
1981	Chris Thompson	48.4
1982	Kurt Moreby	49.64
1983	Adrian Hardman	49.09
1984	Mark Tyler	48.41
1985	Gareth Bakewell	49.66

1986	David McKenzie	49.05
1987	Paul Wood	49.32
1988	Adrian Patrick	49.95
1989	David Simpson	49.16
1990	Mark Spoors	51.65
1991	Guy Bullock	48.63
1992	Nick Budden	49.51
1993	Mark Hylton	48.87
1994	Ian Horsburgh	49.2
1995	Richard McNabb	48.93
1996	David Naismith	48.60
1997	Richard Attlee	49.61
1998	Aaron Evans	49.13
1999	Russell Nicholls	48.73
2000	Craig Erskine	50.01
2001	Richard Davenport	49.74
2002	Simon Toye	48.42
2003	Richard Buck	47.71
2004	Kris Robertson	47.08
2005	Chris Clarke	49.10
2006	Jordan McGrath	49.17
2007	Nathan Wake	48.44
2008	Ben Sturgess	48.36
2009	Greg Louden	48.46
2010	Jay Younger	48.49

800 METRES

(Event instituted in 1967 at 880 yards; 800m from 1969)

1980	Paul Wynn	1:57.45
1981	Darryl Taylor	1:57.3
1982	Paul Williams	1:53.37
1983	Albert James	1:54.12
1984	Paul Causey	1:54.12
1985	Davey Wilson	1:56.35
1986	Paul Burgess	1:54.70
1987	Craig Winrow	1:54.81
1988	Mark Sesay	1:57.51
1989	Steve Johnson	1:56.14
1990	Jon Murray	1:54.25
1991	Jayme Adams	1:54.23
1992	Scott West	1:54.72
1993	Alasdair Donaldson	1:54.39
1994	Michael Combe	1:54.57
1995	Neil Kirk	1:55.65
1996	Ross Fittall	1:56.74
1997	Nic Andrews	1:56.67
1998	Matthew Thomson	1:56.79
1999	Stephen Tompson	1:55.49
2000	Adam Davies	1:56.50
2001	Michael Rimmer	1:55.67

AAA Champions

2002	Michael Rimmer	1:53.81
2003	Grant Baker	1:53.19
2004	Mark Mitchell	1:50.90
2005	Dean Goodman	1:55.11
2006	James Shane	1:53.77
2007	Adam Moore	1:55.46
2008	Thomas Atkinson	1:55.65
2009	Tom Guy	1:53.58
2010	Patrick Monaghan	1:57.32

1500 METRES

(Event instituted in 1968 at 1 Mile; 1500m from 1969)

1980	David Brockwell	4:02.2
1981	Clifton Bradeley	3:52.78
1982	David Miles	3:58.82
1983	Neil Horsfield	3:55.09
1984	Terry West	3:55.84
1985	William Mullaney IRL	3:53.27
	(2, Darren Mead 3:54.98)	
1986	Jason Lobo	3:59.84
1987	Glen Stewart	3:58.77
1988	Mark Sesay	3:56.07
1989	Dave Robertson	3:54.62
1990	Simon Young	4:08.1
1991	Jayme Adams	4:01.58
1992	Ed Bowen	4:01.29
1993	Alasdair Donaldson	4:02.60
1994	Andy Graffin	3:59.11
1995	Gareth Turnbull	3:58.15
1996	Sam Boden	3:59.84
1997	Russell Pittam	4:04.0
1998	Richard Ward	4:00.89
1999	Malcolm Hassan	3:56.83
2000	Ian Munro	3:58.62
2001	Mark Shankey	3:57.10
2002	Lee Bowron	3:58.19
2003	Richard Newton	3:55.49
2004	Kris Gauson	3:56.34
2005	Jordon West	4:02.94
2006	David Forrester	3:57.74
2007	Josh Moody	3:59.40
2008	Alex Cornwell	3:59.13
2009	Tom Curr	3:55.73
2010	Luke Carroll	4:05.09

3000 METRES

(Event instituted in 1964 at 2 Miles; 3000m from 1969)

| 1980 | Jon Richards | 8:26.92 |
| 1981 | Clifton Bradeley | 8:31.41 |

1982	David Miles	8:34.80
1983	Richard Findlow	8:32.30
1984	Steve Fury	8:29.09
1985	Darren Mead	8:27.36
1986	Jason Lobo	8:40.30
1987	Jon Brown	8:32.93
1988	Keith Cullen	8:38.72
1989	Stuart Poore	8:44.50
1990	Chris Yates	8:46.98
1991	Neil Caddy	8:45.08
1992	Kevin Farrow	8:36.24
1993	Alasdair Donaldson	8:56.18
1994	Allen Graffin	8:51.62
1995	Steven Lawrence	8:52.59
1996	Graham Ferguson	8:48.68
1997	Daniel Samuels	9:00.76
1998	Stephen Bates	8:53.65
1999	Mo Farah	8:29.88
2000	Glenn Raggett	8:59.46
2001	Luke Northall	8:43.20
2002	Craig Ivemy	8:38.43
2003	James Philipson	8:44.54
2004	Robert Pickering	8:30.17
2005	James Shane	8:49.15
2006	Abdirisak Ahmed	8:35.79
2007	Jeremy Gilmour	8:43.56
2008	Paul Thompson	8:39.49
2009	Gordon Benson	8:42.18
2010	Gordon Benson	8:39.98

1500 METRES STEEPLECHASE

(Event instituted in 1967 at 1000m; 1500m from 1973)

1980	Lee Price	4:20.69
1981	John Hartigan	4:18.78
1982	Kevin Howard	4:20.37
1983	Robert Deakin	4:20.5
1984	David Caton	4:23.64
1985	Stephen Arnold	4:16.31
1986	Spencer Duval	4:18.33
1987	David Tune	4:23.00
1988	John Denham	4:25.48
1989	Stuart Kefford	4:21.75
1990	Mark McDowell	4:25.33
1991	Matthew Kelso	4:21.59
1992	Innes Harding	4:23.17
1993	Stuart Stokes	4:22.7
1994	Robert Brown	4:18.20
1995	David Mitchinson	4:23.17
1996	David Mitchinson	4:22.81

AAA Champions

1997	John Rice	4:23.50
1998	Mark Griffith	4:22.89
1999	Liam Reale IRL	4:18.20
	(2, James Bailey 4:22.68)	
2000	Daniel Lewis	4:26.26
2001	William Docherty	4:27.51
2002	Chris Hart	4:20.72
2003	Daniel Russell	4:22.67
2004	Ben Wilson	4:26.00
2005	Stephen Scullion	4:20.32
2006	James Wilkinson	4:25.01
2007	Noel Collins	4:18.74
2008	Ben Coldray	4:25.83
2009	Jack Partridge	4:20.69
2010	Alex Brecker	4:32.83

100 METRES HURDLES (3'0")

(Event instituted in 1968 at 110 yards; 100m from 1969)

1980	Hugh Teape	13.12
1981	Paul Brice	13.27
1982	Derek Wilson	13.26
1983	Jon Ridgeon	13.12
1984	Brett St Louis	13.06
1985	Brett St Louis	13.05
1986	James Wright	13.29
1987	Mark Purser	13.43
1988	Damon Bainbridge	13.48
1989	Berian Davies	13.01w
1990	Neil Owen	12.99w
1991	Steve Markham	12.90
1992	Ciaran Cash IRL	13.13
	(2, Grant Adams 13.16)	
1993	Matthew Clements	12.68
1994	Damien Greaves	13.0
1995	Chris Hargrave	13.34
1996	David O'Leary	13.30
1997	Andy Turner	12.97
1998	Nathan Palmer	12.96w
1999	Tristan Anthony	12.61
2000	Brenden Harmse RSA	12.83
	(2, Edward Dunford 13.18)	
2001	Edward Dunford	13.16
2002	Tom Stimson	13.48
2003	Craig France	13.16
2004	Daniel Maynard	13.11
2005	Julian Adeniran	13.17
2006	James McLean	12.78w
2007	James McLean	12.95
2008	Jack Meredith	12.80

| 2009 | Themba Luhana | 12.93 |
| 2010 | Jake Porter | 13.18 |

400 METRES HURDLES

(Event instituted in 1978)

1980	Martin Briggs	53.14
1981	David Wild	55.3
1982	David Wild	54.49
1983	Philip Parkinson	55.58
1984	Thomas Haynes	54.77
1985	Andrew Nelson	55.63
1986	Bob Brown	53.69
1987	Craig Street	57.39
1988	Matthew Birchall	55.29
1989	Nat Scott	54.92
1990	Kevin Darcy IRL	55.9
	(2, John Bell 56.3)	
1991	Noel Levy	54.58
1992	Tim Burrow	55.48
1993	Matt Douglas	54.73
1994	Mark Rowlands	53.30
1995	Ruben Tabares	54.52
1996	Richard McDonald	52.81
1997	Robert Newton	54.9
1998	Nange Ursell	55.32
1999	Jeffrey Christie	54.66
2000	Rhys Williams	54.91
2001	Rupert Gardner	54.98
2002	Richard Davenport	53.08
2003	Craig Glanville	53.25
2004	Andrew Howell	54.64
2005	David Martin	53.11
2006	Nathan Woodward	52.25
2007	Niall Flannery	53.60
2008	Jack Green	53.46
2009	Ben Jones	54.34
2010	Sean Adams & Jacob Paul	53.68

HIGH JUMP

(Event instituted in 1968)

1980	Mike Powell	2.00
1981	Mark Lakey	2.10
1982	Mark Lakey	2.10
1983	Leroy Lucas	2.11
1984	Nick Hay	2.04
1985	John Hopper	2.00
1986	Hopeton Lindo	2.01
1987	Glen Carpenter	1.94

AAA Champions

1988	Brendan Reilly	2.07
1989	Brendan Reilly	2.09
1990	Stephen Hughes	1.90
1991	Stanley Osuide	2.12
1992	Stuart Ohrland	2.02
1993	Martin Pate	2.00
1994	Darren Joseph	1.96
1995	Danny Graham	2.03
1996	Martin Lloyd	2.00
1997	Ken McKeown	2.06
1998	Ken McKeown	2.00
1999	Brian Hall	2.05
2000	Chuka Enih-Snell	2.06
2001	Martyn Bernard	1.99
2002	Oliver Sweeney	1.91
2003	Nick Stanisavljevic	2.00
2004	Darren Hammond	1.99
2005	Tom Mather	2.01
2006	Garry Coulter	1.94
2007	Jason Harvey	2.04
2008	Joe Kent	1.99
2009	Jonathan Heath	1.99
2010	Jonathan Heath	1.95

POLE VAULT

(Event instituted in 1968)

1980	Billy Davey	4.50
1981	Jimmy Lewis	4.20
1982	Steve Fuller	3.80
1983	Richard Quixley	4.00
1984	Gary Jackson	4.20
1985	Ian Lewis	4.20
1986	Robert Bond	4.20
1987	Mark Grant	4.10
1988	Mark Hodgkinson	4.30
1989	Neil Winter	4.40
1990	Neil Winter	5.00
1991	Simon Gaines	4.20
1992	Neil Turner	4.00
1993	Neil Young	4.30
1994	Stephen McLennan	4.20
1995	Christian Linskey	4.81
1996	Richard Smith	4.45
1997	Richard Smith	4.50
1998	Chris Type	4.35
1999	Cameron Johnston	4.50
2000	Mark Christie	4.30
2001	Chris Tremayne	4.50
2002	Keith Higham	4.50
2003	Carl Titman	4.10

2004	Alex Williams	4.50
2005	Andy Marsh	4.30
2006	Andy Marsh	4.80
2007	Ben Gregory	4.50
2008	Gregor MacLean	4.30
2009	Richard Humby	4.30
2010	Daniel Gardner	4.40

LONG JUMP

(Event instituted in 1968)

1980	Hugh Davidson	7.01w
1981	Ian Ward	6.74
1982	Barry Nevison	7.07
1983	Peter Shearman	6.81
1984	David Roughley	7.09
1985	Stewart Faulkner	6.96w
1986	Marcus Browning	6.62
1987	Kevin Liddington	6.96
1988	Zac Kerin	6.91w
1989	Jonathon Kron IRL	7.08w
	(2, Ennyina Chukukere 6.88w)	
1990	Oni Onuorah	6.95w
1991	Mike Jarvis	6.71
1992	James Clawley	6.82
1993	Nicholas Gordon	6.81
1994	Nathan Morgan	6.80
1995	Geoffrey Ojok	6.83w
1996	Alistair Gudgeon	6.57
1997	David Mountford	6.79w
1998	Darrell Aldridge	7.14w
1999	Darrell Aldridge	7.14w
2000	Jonathan Moore	7.46
2001	Onen Eyong	7.28w
2002	Bernard Yeboah	7.32w
2003	Ike Obuka-Mba	6.79
2004	Oliver McNeillis	7.50w
2005	Andrew Bullimore	7.21w
2006	Matthew Parnell	6.98
2007	Adam Timms	6.86w
2008	Dwyte Smith	7.16
2009	James Lelliott	6.92
2010	Feron Sayers	6.96

TRIPLE JUMP

(Event instituted in 1968)

1980	Steven Anderson	14.98
1981	Vernon Samuels	15.12w
1982	Steve Folkard	14.28

1983	Colin Slinn	13.90
1984	Lawrence Lynch	14.84
1985	Darren Gomersall	14.87w
1986	Junior Campbell	15.19
1987	Mark Gregory	14.06
1988	Zac Kerin	14.63w
1989	Dave Reeve	14.28w
1990	Carl Howard	14.20w
1991	Ezra Clarke	14.28
1992	Jason Bennett	14.27
1993	Marvin Bramble	15.14
1994	Dean Macey	14.26
1995	Jonathan Wallace	14.48w
1996	Peter Francis	13.78
1997	Steven Shalders	14.04
1998	Steven Shalders	15.38w
1999	Jonathan Moore	15.46w
2000	Jonathan Moore	15.67
2001	Enyloma Anomelechi	14.15w
2002	Graham Jackson	14.29w
2003	Shaun Batt	13.95
2004	Lanre Ali-Balogun	14.81
2005	Sean Wynter	14.06w
2006	Trevor Okoroafor	13.88
2007	Nathan Fox	15.10
2008	Tunde Amosu	15.08w
2009	Julien Allwood	14.58
2010	Jimi Tele	14.68

SHOT

(Event instituted in 1968; 10lb; 5kg from 1971)

1980	Martin Nutty IRL	16.33
	(2, Billy Cole 15.50)	
1981	Chris Ellis	18.58
1982	Chris Ellis	18.51
1983	Mitchell Smith	15.56
1984	Simon Williams	16.32
1985	Colm Moran IRL	16.91
	(2, Martin Fletcher 15.40)	
1986	Matt Simson	18.15
1987	Chris Symonds	15.82
1988	Jason Mulcahy	15.99
1989	Jason Mulcahy	16.42
1990	Bryan Kelly	15.99
1991	Mark Edwards	16.21
1992	Piers Selby	16.44
1993	Bill Fuller	16.54
1994	Emeka Udechuku	16.46
1995	Emeka Udechuku	17.41

1996	David Readle	16.89
1997	Adrian Cluskey	16.97
1998	Greg Beard	16.49
1999	Greg Beard	18.41
2000	Carl Saggers	17.34
2001	Eoin Leen IRL	18.33
	(2, Peter Cranfield 16.04)	
2002	Chris Gearing	17.05
2003	Chris Gearing	18.34
2004	Mathew Evans	16.17
2005	Jay Thomas	17.75
2006	Curtis Griffith-Parker	18.17
2007	Curtis Griffith-Parker	19.32
2008	Reece Thomas	17.19
2009	Matthew Halton	16.26
2010	Joshua Newman	15.91

DISCUS

(Event instituted in 1968; 1kg; 1.5kg from 1971)

1980	Neil Boyton	49.58
1981	Neil Boyton	48.70
1982	Keith Homer	49.04
1983	Matt Symonds	47.84
1984	Matt Symonds	51.52
1985	Guy Litherland	50.96
1986	Jason Byrne	48.36
1987	Chris Symonds	51.74
1988	Glen Smith	54.60
1989	Julian Willett	52.14
1990	Stephen Tinker	45.22
1991	Ashley Knott	50.02
1992	Ian McLaughlin	47.92
1993	Matthew Bundock	51.14
1994	Emeka Udechuku	51.26
1995	Emeka Udechuku	58.00
1996	Luke Rosenberg	48.56
1997	Simon D. Williams	52.24
1998	James Rumbold	47.03
1999	Greg Beard	52.13
2000	Carl Saggers	50.07
2001	Garry Hagan	50.01
2002	Andrew Thomas	52.84
2003	Sam Herrington	54.42
2004	Chris Scott	51.33
2005	Curtis Griffith-Parker	51.55
2006	Curtis Griffith-Parker	49.73
2007	Curtis Griffith-Parker	57.70
2008	Zane Duquemin	51.70
2009	Liam Biddlecombe	53.06
2010	Chris Barnes	51.55

HAMMER

(Event instituted in 1968; 10lb; 5kg from 1971)
1980	Tony Kenneally	68.04
1981	Paul Head	72.00
1982	Gary Halpin IRL	67.98
	(2, Vaughan Cooper 60.52)	
1983	Andrew Tolputt	67.34
1984	Andrew Tolputt	76.28
1985	Gareth Cook	63.50
1986	Peter Vivian	66.66
1987	Peter Vivian	66.38
1988	Adrian Johnson	59.24
1989	Jon Bond	60.12
1990	Malcolm Croad	61.44
1991	Alan McNicholas	61.22
1992	Nick Steinmetz	61.74
1993	Nick Steinmetz	68.48
1994	Matthew Bell	60.54
1995	James Hawkins	56.44
1996	Andrew Grierson	59.66
1997	Matthew Sutton	62.74
1998	Matthew Sutton	71.45
1999	Carl Saggers	61.75
2000	Carl Saggers	63.69
2001	Paul Farley	56.94
2002	Simon Bissell	63.18
2003	Alex Smith	66.46
2004	Alex Smith	73.25
2005	James Bedford	65.82
2006	Peter Smith	75.02
2007	Michael Jennings	61.39
2008	Andrew Jordon	61.09
2009	Andrew Elkins	63.16
2010	Ashley Gilder	63.35

JAVELIN (700gm)

(Event instituted in 1968)
1980	Dave Messom	58.10
1981	Mick Hill	60.12
1982	Lee Peters	59.04
1983	Gary Jenson	67.92
1984	Jon Clarke	60.26
1985	Paul Bushnell	60.56
1986	Roddy James	60.16
1987	David Bigham	56.08
1988	Stuart Hinton	57.20
1989	Alistair Gidley	59.16
1990	James Hurrion	58.82

1991	Tim Eldridge	65.68
1992	Tim Eldridge	59.18
1993	Sean O'Hanlon	60.50
1994	Mark Francis	61.86
1995	David Parker	65.16
1996	Tim Kitney	62.22
1997	Phillip Sharpe	63.52
1998	Richard Lainson	54.70
1999	Andrew Hall AUS	65.14
	(2, Matthew Dingley 55.19)	
2000	Alex van der Merwe	59.08
2001	Lee Doran	58.32
2002	Sam Kelvey	60.66
2003	Stuart Harvey	60.93
2004	James Campbell	65.39
2005	Bonne Buwembo	56.89
2006	Daniel Pembroke	61.46
2007	Harry Hollis	58.90
2008	Pieter Snyman	64.35
2009	Steven Turnock	62.55
2010	Robin Danaher	63.23

DECATHLON

(Event instituted in 1991 at Octathlon; Decathlon from 2002)

1991	Richard Hodgson	4657
1992	Chris Hindley	4886
1993	Matt Douglas	5102
1994	Trevor McGlynn	4545
1995	Marc Newton	4974
1996	Ed Coats	5158
1997	Robert Hollinger	4891
1998	Dominic Girdler	5210
1999	Tim Howell	4643
2000	Edward Dunford	5420
2001	Edward Dunford	5636
2002	Louis Moore	6501
2003	Andrew Staniland	6283
2004	Oliver McNeillis	6556
2005	Will Lambourne	5879
2006	Daniel Gardiner	6154
2007	David Guest	6530
2008	Jamie Courtney	6084
2009	Michael Downie	6420
2010	Jacob Paul	5637

TRACK WALK

(Event instituted in 1968 at 1 Mile; 2000m from 1969; 3000m from 1976; 10,000m from 1986; 5000m from 1991)

| 1980 | Tim Berrett | 14:09.71 |

AAA Champions

1981	Tim Berrett	13:23.76
1982	David Hucks	13:33.33
1983	Nathan Kavanagh	13:12.84
1984	not held	
1985	Paul Whitehouse	13:55.75
1986	Russell Hutchings	47:53.45
1987	Jon Vincent	48:53.17
1988	David Lawrence	51:55.14
1989	Stuart Tilbury	51:02.15
1990	Philip King	46:34.50
1991	Philip King	21:31.18
1992	Pierce O'Callaghan IRL	23:38.65
	(2, Ben Allkins 24:36.06)	
1993	Jamie Costin IRL	23:48.29
	(2, Matt Dunne 26:04.24)	
1994	Scott Taylor	28:00.12
1995	Stuart Monk	24:39.7
1996	Matt Hales	23:49.89
1997	David Kidd IRL	22:57.2
	(2, Thomas Taylor 23:34.4)	
1998	Colin Griffin IRL	23:41.47
	(2, Nathan Adams 24:42.02)	
1999	Andy Parker	23:22.81
2000	Andy Parker	22:48.91
2001	Luke Finch	23:50.61
2002	Luke Finch	23:56.41
2003	Nick Ball	22:59.03
2004	Nick Ball	22:30.26
2005	Ben Wears	24:09.16
2006	Ben Wears	22:48.35
2007	Matthew Halliday	24:14.82
2008	Jonathan Hobbs	25:27.80
2009	Jonathan Hobbs	25:24.31
2010	Jamie Higgins	29:31.30

RWA 5 KILOMETRES ROAD WALK

(Event instituted in 1961 at 3 miles; 5km from 1976)

1980	Tim Berrett	23:46
1981	Tim Berrett	22:39
1982	David Hucks	22:29
1983	Nathan Kavanagh	22:39
1984	Kirk Taylor	22:42
1985	D White (short course)	21:58
1986	Jon Vincent	22:13
1987	Jon Vincent	-
1988	Martin Young	23:31
1989	Jonathan Deakin	24:13
1990	Philip King	23:28
1991	Philip King	22:21

1992	Ben Allkins	23:42
1993	Guy Bailey	24:53
1994	David Crane	26:17
1995	Stuart Monk	24:16
1996	Michael Kemp	23:23
1997	Thomas Taylor	22:41
1998	Dominic King	24:24
1999	Lloyd Finch	22:06
2000	James Davis	22:56
2001	Luke Finch	22:35
2002	Luke Finch	22:04
2003	Nick Ball	23:32
2004	Lewis Hayden	24:44
2005	not held	
2006	Ben Wears	22:10
2007	Mark O'Kane	25:03
2008	Jonathan Hobbs	25:47
2009	Jonathan Hobbs	25:49
2010	Nathan Duncan	26:27

RWA 10 KILOMETRES ROAD WALK

(Event instituted in 2005)

2005	Simon Hambridge	50:03
2006	not held	
2007	Ben Wears	48:19
2008	Jonathan Hobbs	54:04
2009	Jonathan Hobbs	52:37

UNDER-15

(Instituted 1991)

100 METRES

1991	Cephas Howard	11.64
1992	Courage Edo	11.10
1993	Chris Blake	11.22
1994	André Duffus	11.25
1995	Wayne Gray	11.29w
1996	Joe Brown	11.38
1997	Tristan Anthony	11.11
1998	Tom Hyde	11.27
1999	Steven Fowles	11.17w
2000	Jamie Gill	11.24
2001	Craig Pickering	11.00w
2002	Andrew Watkins	11.07
2003	Gerald Phiri	11.2
2004	Yusuf Aliu	11.34
2005	Antonio Infantino	11.12

AAA Champions

2006	Deji Tobais	11.0
2007	Lawrence Owen	11.17w
2008	David Bolarinwa	11.22
2009	Nathan Hanson	11.22
2010	Alex Kiwomya	10.98

200 METRES

1991	Cephas Howard	23.14
1992	Matthew Clements	22.54
1993	Chris Blake	22.69
1994	André Duffus	22.7
1995	Ben Lewis	23.08
1996	Tristan Anthony	23.03
1997	Mark Lewis-Francis	23.02
1998	Tom Hyde	22.40w
1999	Stuart Haley	22.99
2000	James Ellington	22.46w
2001	Jamahl Alert-Khan	22.58
2002	Andrew Watkins	22.41
2003	Ricardo Francis	22.92
2004	Chris Clarke	22.48
2005	Tony Corrigan	22.46
2006	Rhion Samuel	22.21
2007	James Armstrong	22.51
2008	Akeem Akintokun	23.20
2009	Nathan Hanson	22.96
2010	Michael Tapa Mekomou	22.53

400 METRES

1991	Nian Jarvis	51.69
1992	Eoin McKinney	51.78
1993	Ken Elliott	53.20
1994	Marc Newton	51.0
1995	Ian Lowthian	50.65
1996	Aaron Evans	50.88
1997	Michael Snow	51.17
1998	Craig Erskine	51.84
1999	Daniel Petros	51.7
2000	Richard Davenport	51.4
2001	Craig Glanville	51.93
2002	Kris Robertson	52.06
2003	Thomas Duffield	50.91
2004	James Peden	51.56
2005	Matthew Lumm	50.77
2006	Matthew Webster	50.07
2007	Thomas Bensted	51.24
2008	Farren Morgan	51.53
2009	Omari Carr-Miller	51.22
2010	Aaron Pitt	49.99

800 METRES

1991	James Nolan IRL	2:00.29
	(2, Tim Whiteside 2:02.00)	
1992	Russell Cartwright	2:05.04
1993	Michael Combe	2:00.30
1994	Lee Hughes	2:03.05
1995	Austin Ferns	2:01.26
1996	Colin Joyce	2:03.23
1997	Brian McIlroy	2:02.54
1998	Chris Stoves	2:03.47
1999	Richard Dowse	2:02.25
2000	Michael Rimmer	1:56.9
2001	Matthew Wood	2:00.97
2002	Grant Prendergast	1:58.79
2003	Alastair Smith	2:00.46
2004	James Shane	1:58.39
2005	Abdi Risak Ahmed SUD	1:58.22
	(2, Adam Moore 1:58.83)	
2006	Joshua Moody	1:59.75
2007	Rikkie Letch	2:00.66
2008	Luke Carroll	2:01.84
2009	James McMurray	2:01.34
2010	Sean Molloy	2:01.75

1500 METRES

1991	Stuart Bond	4:15.35
1992	Dale Canning	4:17.58
1993	Matthew Dixon	4:14.72
1994	Sam Boden	4:13.9
1995	Stephen Holmes	4:16.68
1996	Richard King	4:15.13
1997	Chris Iddon	4:09.55
1998	Amanuel Tshaye	4:17.85
1999	Chris Reynolds	4:14.38
2000	Lee Bowron	4:04.63
2001	Ross Toole	4:15.61
2002	Adam Hickey	4:08.03
2003	Jordan West	4:06.5
2004	Simon Lawson	4:07.75
2005	Ryan Parker	4:11.14
2006	Shane Quinn IRL	4:04.19
	(2, James Senior 4:09.77)	
2007	Peter Devaney	4:15.44
2008	Karnvir Hayer	4:08.61
2009	Jack Gleave	4:13.75
2010	Ahmed Hassan	4:09.00

3000 METRES

1991	Stuart Bond	9:14.95
1992	Chris Old	9:16.52
1993	Elliot Hankins	9:33.9
1994	Simon Bentley	9:25.08
1995	Gareth Melvin	9:19.47
1996	Richard Ward	9:13.60
1997	Mo Farah	8:47.48
1998	Phil Nicholls	9:12.72
1999	Shugri Omar	9:15.37
2000	Tom Snow	9:16.98
2001–2007 not held		
2008	Richard Charles	9:05.16
2009	Peter Chambers	9:20.95
2010	Adam Howard	9:11.71

80 METRES HURDLES (2'9")

1991	Tony Lashley	11.17w
1992	Matthew Clements	10.98
1993	Ian Cawley	11.27
1994	Thomas Benn	11.41
1995	Robert Hollinger	11.11
1996	Sebastian Bastow	11.38
1997	Chris Tye-Walker	11.4
1998	Edward Dunford	11.45
1999	Edward Dunford	10.99
2000	Richard Alexis-Smith	11.21
2001	Richard Alexis-Smith	10.68w
2002	Daniel Maynard	10.87
2003	Daniel Evans	11.50
2004	Andrew Smith	11.27
2005	James McLean	11.05
2006	Brad Garside	11.00
2007	Cameron Goodall	11.44w
2008	Godwin Gyeabohr	11.18
2009	James Taylor	11.22
2010	Luke Jenkins	11.26

HIGH JUMP

1991	Brad Knowles	1.86
1992	Lee Bloomfield	1.85
1993	Robert Holton	1.89
1994	Jamie Dalton	1.84
1995	Neil Dixon	1.87
1996	Ken McKeown	1.91
1997	Brian Hall	1.94
1998	Chuka Enih-Snell	1.95

1999	Mark Bidwell	1.93
2000	Daniel Segerson	1.79
2001	Alan Hassall	1.86
2002	David Shields	1.90
2003	Gregory Simey	1.87
2004	Philip Collins	1.90
2005	Richard Byers	1.93
2006	David Guest	1.86
2007	Alex Cox	1.88
2008	Ross Walker-Smart	1.91
2009	Feron Sayers	1.90
2010	Nicholas Hunt	1.89

POLE VAULT

1991	Neil Young	3.70
1992	Martin Parley	3.55
1993	Christian Linskey	3.75
1994	Christian Linskey	4.10
1995	Richard Smith	4.11
1996	Andrew Corey	3.90
1997	Andrew MacDonald	3.60
1998	Alan Jervis	3.50
1999	Tom McDowell	3.35
2000	Steve Lewis (20.5.86)	3.70
2001	Carl Titman	3.35
2002	James Hoad	3.60
2003	Steven Lewis (12.3.89)	3.30
2004	Andrew Marsh	3.60
2005	Tony Hillier	3.90
2006	Cameron Walker-Shepherd	3.60
2007	Lewis Newton	3.60
2008	Eric Martin	3.70
2009	Tadgh Healy	3.60
2010	Harry Coppell	3.50

LONG JUMP

1991	David Gilkes	6.30w
1992	Courage Edo	6.37
1993	Ronnie Ingram	6.13w
1994	Kevin Hibbins	6.03
1995	Richard Gawthorpe	5.86
1996	Richard Phelan IRL (2, Mark Awanah 6.13)	6.21
1997	Mark Awanah	6.71
1998	Jordon Lau	6.68w
1999	Onen Eyong	6.72w

AAA Champions

2000	Gary Wilson	6.67
2001	Ryan Thomas	6.34w
2002	Darryl Thomas	6.48
2003	Jamie Jones	5.93
2004	Juan de Leon Padmore	6.39
2005	Tony Corrigan	6.62w
2006	Ding Yang	6.30
2007	Ciaran Dolan	6.39
2008	Ashley Wren	6.51w
2009	Feron Sayers	6.59
2010	Ross Maxwell	6.47

TRIPLE JUMP

1991	Kori Stennett	13.11
1992	Richard Crayford	12.28
1993	Mike McKernan	13.00
1994	Daniel Hutchinson	13.29
1995	Michael Ferraro	12.39
1996	Leon Burnett	13.31
1997	John Davies	13.27
1998	Andrew Harris	12.78
1999	Edward Dunford	13.17w
2000	Graham Jackson	12.59
2001	William Harwood	12.86w
2002	Rhyan Thomas	12.04
2003	Sean Wynter	12.97
2004	Chris Bartlett	13.20
2005	Nathan Fox	14.11
2006	Dwyte Smith	13.67
2007	Julien Allwood	13.27w
2008	Jimi Tele	13.49w
2009	Joshua Olawore	12.92
2010	Montel Nevers	13.24

SHOT (4kg)

1991	Ian McLaughlin	15.41
1992	Sudip Burman-Roy	15.15
1993	David Irwin	15.04
1994	Jamie Hunt	14.85
1995	Adrian Cluskey	15.18
1996	Paul Archer	14.96
1997	Greg Beard	16.11
1998	Carl Saggers	15.64
1999	Eoin Leen IRL	16.19
	(2, Garry Hagan 15.14)	
2000	Andrae Davis	16.11
2001	Daniel Hepplewhite	15.61

2002	Shane Birch	14.99
2003	Jay Thomas	17.44
2004	Mark Tough	14.48
2005	Curtis Griffith-Parker	17.56
2006	Anthony Oshodi	18.03
2007	Joshua Newman	15.02
2008	Joshua Newman	16.47
2009	Christopher Clarke	14.57
2010	Lewis Barnes	15.09

DISCUS (1.25kg)

1991	Ian McLaughlin	43.50
1992	Ben Walker	48.76
1993	Emeka Udechuku	48.96
1994	Carl Myerscough	39.16
1995	Simon Williams	44.88
1996	Liam Walsh	45.88
1997	Anthony Smith	43.50
1998	Carl Saggers	43.36
1999	Jim Healy IRL	46.48
(2, Simon Bulley 46.06)		
2000	Simon Bissell	47.10
2001	Sam Herrington	49.10
2002	Shane Birch	45.85
2003	Elliot Price	45.62
2004	Jamie Stevenson	43.08
2005	Curtis Griffith-Parker	55.39
2006	Anthony Oshodi	46.21
2007	Liam Biddlecombe	46.61
2008	Jake Armstrong	45.96
2009	Nicholas Percy	43.77
2010	Matthew Blandford	45.62

HAMMER (4kg)

1991	Nick Steinmetz	59.90
1992	Robin Walker	50.82
1993	Adam Devonshire	55.58
1994	James Hawkins	57.28
1995	Ross Kidner	54.14
1996	Matthew Sutton	62.58
1997	Joseph Kompani	55.22
1998	Carl Saggers	60.15
1999	Peter Cranfield	52.32
2000	Simon Bissell	54.47
2001	Gavin Hill	51.03
2002	Matt Lambley	62.18
2003	Kaine Harrington	50.44
2004	Joe Stockton	58.40

2005	Mike Jennings	52.66
2006	Andrew Jordan	56.20
2007	Craig Murch	58.86
2008	Sam Foster	53.82
2009	Ashley Gilder	63.52
2010	Fellan McGuigan	60.05

JAVELIN (600 gm)

(Specification changed from 1999)

1991	Alistair Christmas	52.88
1992	Simon Forster	49.88
1993	Martin Stringer	53.88
1994	Clifton Green	55.62
1995	Philips Olwenu	55.54
1996	Richard Lainson	60.34
1997	Anthony Lovett	53.66
1998	James Deacon-Brown	53.46
1999	Mark Lindsay	47.70
2000	Thomas Rees	47.33
2001	Ben Lee	48.18
2002	Adam Akehurst	48.24
2003	Alexander Shepherd	55.90
2004	Bonne Buwembo	57.78
2005	Ashley Bryant	55.70
2006	Ryan Stewart	54.63
2007	Matti Mortimore	62.33
2008	Liam Downer	47.72
2009	Oliver Bradfield	52.53
2010	Oliver Bradfield	65.26

PENTATHLON

(Instituted 1992)

1992	Scott Walker	2644
1993	Ian Leaman	2703
1994	Marc Newton	3032
1995	Richard Gawthorpe	2816
1996	Chris Jenkins	2775
1997	Mark Awanah	3129
1998	Chuka Enih-Snell	3039
1999	Edward Dunford	3403
2000	Louis Moore	2838
2001	Pepi Nanci	2974
2002	Lewis Robson	3129
2003	Gregor Simey	3293
2004	Anthony Shurmer	2767
2005	Edward Mourbey	2945
2006	David Guest	3227
2007	Cameron Irwin	2880

2008	Jacob Gardiner	2701
2009	Feron Sayers	3024
2010	Aled Price	2698

3000 METRES WALK

1991	Matthew Cross	16:08.72
1992	Robert Warren	19:35.37
1993	Matt Hales	15:45.2
1994	Matt Hales	14:51.12
1995	John Murphy	14:48.4
1996	Lloyd Finch	15:02.70
1997	Lloyd Finch	13:52.79
1998	Lloyd Finch	13:29.59
1999	James Davis	14:04.41
2000	Luke Finch	14:09.93
2001	Luke Davis	15:47.32
2002	Nick Ball	14:43.39
2003	Lewis Hayden	14:14.56
2004	Antonio Cirillo	15:49.32
2005	Antonio Cirillo	14:54.81
2006	Chris Ball	15:48.72
2007	Hamish Hall	14:48.86
2008	Maks Orzel	17:13.24
2009	Evan Lynch IRL	15:10.45
	(2, Ben Parsons 17:20.68)	
2010	Guy Thomas	17:55.55

RWA 3 KILOMETRES ROAD WALK

(Event instituted at 2 miles in 1972; 3km from 1976)

1991	Robert Mecham	14:26
1992	Robert Mecham	15:05
1993	Matt Hales	14:21
1994	Matt Hales	14:28
1995	John Murphy	14:11
1996	Nathan Adams	15:01
1997	Lloyd Finch	14:08
1998	Lloyd Finch	12:58
1999	James Davis	14:19
2000	Luke Davis	14:53
2001	Luke Davis	15:07
2002	Nick Ball	14:42
2003	Lewis Hayden	14:23
2004	Callum Taylor	15:26
2005	Mark O'Kane	15:08
2006	Chris Ball	15:54
2007	Chris Ball	15:56
2008	Hamish Hall	15:02
2009	James Green	16:50
2010	Alex Eaton	16:27

INDOORS

UNDER-20
(not previously listed in AAA Centenary History)

60 METRES

(Instituted in 1965 at 60 yards; 60m from 1968)

1965	Alan Dudley	6.6
1966	Ralph Banthorpe	6.5
1967	Peter Wiltshire	6.5
1968	Paul Machin	7.0
1969	Paul Pinnington	7.0
1970	Adrian Thomas	6.8
1971	Colin Nimmo	6.9
1972	Garry Peters	6.9
1973	Paul Evans	7.0
1974	Gareth Edwards	6.8
1975	Daley Thompson	6.9
1976	David Baptiste	6.8
1977	Daley Thompson	6.9
1978	Mike McFarlane	6.75
1979	Mike McFarlane	6.8
1980	Mike Powell	6.85
1981	Mike Powell	6.8
1982	Steve Graham	6.92
1983	Steve Graham	6.83
1984	Elliot Bunney	6.89
1985	Elliot Bunney	6.75
1986	Martin Waldron	6.83
1987	Jamie Henderson	6.73
1988	Jamie Henderson	6.78
1989	Jason Urron	6.87
1990	Jason Livingston	6.73
1991	David Jackson	6.91
1992	Peter Maitland	6.82
1993	Carl Howard	6.86
1994	Jason Gardener	6.77
1995	Martin Giraud	6.76
1996	Dwain Chambers	6.7
1997	Dwain Chambers	6.66
1998	Christian Malcolm	6.82
1999	Jon Barbour	6.77
2000	Tim Benjamin	6.83
2001	Mark Lewis-Francis	6.67
2002	Andrew Matthews	6.88
2003	Monu Miah	6.87
2004	James Ellington	6.79

2005	Simeon Williamson	6.73
2006	Harry Aikines-Aryeetey	6.67
2007	Harry Aikines-Aryeetey	6.67
2008	Jordan Huggins	6.70
2009	Andrew Robertson	6.77
2010	Jordan Huggins	6.73
2011	Emmanuel Stephens	6.87

200 METRES

(Instituted in 1969)

1969	Paul Pinnington	22.9
1970	Stewart Atkins	23.2
1971	not held	
1972	not held	
1973	not held	
1974	not held	
1975	William May	22.7
1976	Daley Thompson	22.5
1977	Mike McFarlane	22.5
1978	Mike McFarlane	22.0
1979	Mike McFarlane	22.0
1980	Mike Powell	22.4
1981	Donovan Reid	22.3
1982	Steve Eden	22.0
1983	Steve Eden	22.20
1984	Neil Thompson	22.16
1985	John Regis	21.93
1986	Marcus Adam	22.02
1987	Marcus Adam	21.86
1988	Darren Braithwaite	22.16
1989	Jason Livingston	22.19
1990	Jason Livingston	21.91
1991	Steve Rees	22.08
1992	Darren Walker	22.20
1993	Allyn Condon	21.40
1994	Andrew Walcott	21.67
1995	Mark Hylton	21.52
1996	Dwain Chambers	21.47
1997	Christian Malcolm	21.26
1998	Christian Malcolm	21.43
1999	Chris Lambert	21.67
2000	Tim Benjamin	21.06
2001	Tim Benjamin	20.78
2002	Paul Hession IRL	21.61
	(2, Paul Whitehouse 21.78)	
2003	Darragh Graham IRL	21.75
	(2, James Ellington 21.84)	
2004	Alex Williams	21.55
2005	Wade Bennett-Jackson	21.26

2006	Rion Pierre	21.23
2007	Danny Doyley	21.22
2008	James Alaka	21.87
2009	Junior Ejehu	21.62
2010	Liam Clowes	21.49
2011	Liam Clowes	21.39

400 METRES

(Instituted in 1962 at 440 yards; 400m from 1969)

1962	Dennis Osborne	53.6
1963	Mike Hauck	54.5
1964	Peter Fuller	52.6
1965	not held	
1966	not held	
1967	not held	
1968	not held	
1969	Ricky Taylor	49.8
1970	Gary Armstrong	51.3
1971	Norman Gregor	51.9
1972	Steve Ware	50.0
1973	Glen Cohen	49.6
1974	Brian Jones	49.1
1975	Peter Hoffmann	49.5
1976	Martin Francis	49.7
1977	Andy Kerr	49.5
1978	Neil Jackson	49.7
1979	Neil Jackson	48.3
1980	Roy Dickens	49.1
1981	Eugene Gilkes	48.5
1982	John Weston	49.2
1983	Chris Thompson	49.0
1984	Neil Thompson	49.09
1985	Roger Black	48.19
1986	Gary Patterson	49.33
1987	Gary Patterson	48.80
1988	Jason Walbyoff	49.89
1989	Craig Winrow	49.50
1990	Kent Ulyatt	48.95
1991	Kent Ulyatt	49.02
1992	Carl Southam	47.84
1993	Guy Bullock	47.65
1994	Matt Douglas	48.39
1995	Hugh Kerr	48.39
1996	Neil Jennings	48.9
1997	Kris Stewart	48.12
1998	Alloy Wilson	47.84
1999	Alloy Wilson	48.15
2000	Sam Ellis	49.1
2001	Adam Rogers	48.11

2002	David McCarthy IRL	46.66
	(2, Rob Tobin 46.80)	
2003	Adam Charlton	48.09
2004	Philip Taylor	48.47
2005	Bruce Tasker	48.86
2006	Bruce Tasker	47.74
2007	Robert Davis	47.90
2008	Jordan McGrath	47.67
2009	Ross McDonald	48.53
2010	Jack Green	48.01
2011	Josh Street	48.11

800 METRES

(Instituted in 1965 at 880 yards; 800m from 1968)

1965	Dave Wilcox	1:58.4
1966	Bob Steele	1:57.2
1967	Bob Steele	1:56.2
1968	Phil Lewis	1:54.2
1969	John Cherry	1:52.6
1970	Glenn Page	1:56.8
1971	Barry Smith	1:52.8
1972	Alan Mottershead	2:01.4
1973	Tony Dyke	1:52.6
1974	Wayne Tarquini	1:52.6
1975	Malcolm Edwards	1:55.0
1976	Nigel Field	1:57.1
1977	Garry Cook	1:51.7
1978	Terry Young	1:52.6
1979	Chris McGeorge	1:52.8
1980	Mark Rowland	1:54.3
1981	Peter Elliott	1:52.3
1982	Andy Myatt	1:50.9
1983	Ikem Billy	1:54.52
1984	Dave Baptiste	1:53.57
1985	John Evans	1:52.34
1986	Paul Causey	1:53.80
1987	Paul Causey	1:54.81
1988	Martin Forder	1:54.57
1989	Paul Burgess	1:52.93
1990	Craig Winrow	1:54.90
1991	David Grindley	1:52.99
1992	Shane Daly IRL	1:51.90
	(2, Paul Walker 1:52.09)	
1993	David Matthews IRL	1:53.04
	(2, Eddie King 1:53.85)	
1994	Eddie King	1:50.55
1995	James Nolan IRL	1:52.88
	(2, Andrew Young 1:53.38)	
1996	James Nolan IRL	1:54.03
	(2, Andrew Young 1:55.25)	

AAA Champions

1997	Matthew Dixon	1:51.3
1998	Gareth Beard	1:53.13
1999	Ian Tinsley	1:54.60
2000	Paul Gilbert	1:54.07
2001	Andy Fulford	1:55.52
2002	Gareth Balch	1:55.27
2003	Stephen Davies	1:52.76
2004	David Proctor	1:55.79
2005	Kieran Flannery	1:51.06
2006	James Brewer	1:51.68
2007	Ed Aston	1:52.88
2008	Rick Ward	1:54.69
2009	Adam Cotton	1:51.69
2010	Guy Learmonth	1:50.25
2011	Guy Learmonth	1:49.11

1500 METRES

(Instituted in 1969)

1969	Joe Brolly	3:57.9
1970	Roy Tilling	4:00.0
1971	Dave Moorcroft	3:55.8
1972	Timothy Butt	3:55.8
1973	Barrie Moss	3:56.2
1974	Keith Newton	4:04.1
1975	Sebastian Coe	3:54.4
1976	Kevin Glastonbury	3:54.0
1977	Kevin Glastonbury	3:55.0
1978	Colin Clarkson	3:55.9
1979	Nigel Harper	3:56.8
1980	Chris McGeorge	3:49.4
1981	Chris McGeorge	3:49.0
1982	Ken Baker	3:49.7
1983	Alan Parr	3:55.71
1984	Enda Fitzpatrick IRL	3:49.92
	(2, Alistair Currie 3:51.59)	
1985	Brian Scally	3:56.55
1986	Sam Wallace	4:03.24
1987	Sam Wallace	3:54.96
1988	Gavin Burren	3:58.57
1989	Gavin Burren	3:54.59
1990	Brian Treacy	3:52.26
1991	Curtis Robb	3:52.91
1992	Matt Hibberd	3:51.26
1993	Mark Griffin	3:53.36
1994	Stuart Overthrow	4:02.49
1995	Des Roache	3:57.06
1996	Andrew Walker IRL	3:52.43
	(2, Alasdair Donaldson 3:53.01)	
1997	Matthew Dixon	3:54.94

1998	Andrew Ingle	3:59.77
1999	Jonathan Stewart	3:55.82
2000	Mark Pollard	3:58.56
2001	Richard Ward	4:01.07
2002	Ian Carter	4:04.20
2003	Colin Costello IRL	3:53.33
	(2, Tom Snow 3:56.80)	
2004	Colin Costello IRL	3:49.98
	(2, Tom Snow 3:53.48)	
2005	Colin Costello IRL	3:55.89
	(2, Ross Toole 3:57.14)	
2006	James Mills	3:57.58
2007	Brian Markham IRL	4:03.56
	(2, Nathan Riding 4:07.97)	
2008	Noel Collins IRL	4:04.63
	(2, James Griffiths 4:04.71)	
2009	Chris Carter	3:56.90
2010	Paul Robinson IRL	3:52.73
	(3, John McDonnell 3:53.81)	
2011	Adam Cotton	3:51.43

3000 METRES

(Instituted in 1962 at 2 Miles; 3000m from 1968)

1962	David Prior	9:29.6
1963	Allan Rushmer	9:24.6
1964	Roy Young	9:13.2
1965	Chris Stewart	9:14.2
1966	Ken Bartlett	9:21.0
1967	Trevor Jefferies	9:26.2
1968	John Harrison	8:32.4
1969	John Boggis	8:28.4
1970	Jim Kendrick	8:47.6
1971	Dennis Coates	8:31.2
1972	Stephen Lawrence	8:34.4
1973	Stephen Lawrence	8:25.0
1974	Glyn Harvey	8:30.4
1975	Mike Longthorn	8:28.2
1976	Sean Cahill	8:38.0
1977	James Espir	8:30.4
1978	Keith Irvine	8:16.6
1979	Colin Reitz	8:18.0
1980	Phil Dixon	8:39.2
1981	Gary Staines	8:21.8
1982	Roger Bradley	8:22.4
1983	Paul Richley	8:28.14
1984	Nick Flanagan	8:27.53
1985	Adrian Iszatt	8:28.51
1986	Joe Dunbar	8:41.28
1987	Paddy Mulhall	8:31.46

1988	Justin Hobbs	8:23.03
1989	Jon Brown	8:27.91
1990	Malcolm Campbell	8:37.19
1991	Richard Blakely	8:40.10
1992	not held	
1993	not held	
1994	Andy Renfree	8:42.81
1995	not held	
1996	Mark Miles	8:40.73
1997	Paul Reilly IRL	8:41.93
	(2, James Muir 8:44.21)	
1998	Iain Murdoch	8:48.29
1999	Simon Kellie	9:28.93
2000	Richard Ward	8:33.06
2001	Richard Ward	8:27.53
2002	Paul Moores	8:37.79
2003	Tommy Davies	8:48.12
2004	David Bishop	8:37.74
2005	Ross Toole	8:31.73
2006	David Bishop	8:44.94

(discontinued after 2006)

60 METRES HURDLES

(Instituted in 1971 at 3'3" hurdles; 3'6" from 1973; 3'3" from 2006)

1971	Peter Kelly	8.2
1972	Stephen James	8.2
1973	Richard Palmer	8.3
1974	Jonathan Roberts	8.3
1975	Mark Hatton	8.2
1976	Ian Ratcliffe	8.3
1977	Mark Holtom	8.2
1978	Philip Johnson	8.53
1979	Austin Drysdale	8.5
1980	Ross Willard	8.50
1981	Nigel Walker	8.2
1982	Nigel Walker	8.01
1983	Martin Briggs	8.26
1984	Jon Ridgeon	8.20
1985	Colin Jackson	7.99
1986	David Nelson	8.01
1987	Brett St Louis	7.86
1988	Brian Taylor	8.25
1989	Andy Gill	8.34
1990	Richard Hunter	8.26
1991	Jamie Quarry	8.35
1992	Noel Levy	8.36
1993	Kevin Lumsdon	8.16
1994	James Archampong	8.01
1995	James Archampong	8.08

1996	Ross Baillie	8.19
1997	Trevor McGlynn IRL	8.16
	(2, Christopher Hargrave 8.31)	
1998	Chris Baillie	8.10
1999	Chris Baillie	8.01
2000	Chris Baillie	7.95
2001	Dominic Girdler	7.99
2002	Edward Dunford	8.38
2003	Nicholas Gayle	8.35
2004	Nicholas Gayle	8.14
2005	Daniel Davis	8.40
2006	Robert James	7.92
2007	Gianni Frankis	7.76
2008	Alex Al-Ameen	7.98
2009	Jack Meredith	7.76
2010	Andrew Pozzi	7.67
2011	Andy Pozzi	7.79

HIGH JUMP

(Instituted in 1969)

1969	David Wilson	1.93
1970	David Wilson	1.95
1971	Paul Hambley	1.82
1972	Gus McKenzie	2.03
1973	Alan Dainton	1.90
1974	Martyn Shorten	2.00
1975	David Harris	1.93
1976	Milton Palmer	2.03
1977	Derrick Morais	2.05
1978	Vince Clemmens	2.05
1979	Ossie Cham	2.05
1980	Ossie Cham	2.11
1981	Ossie Cham	2.10
1982	Geoff Parsons	2.13
1983	John Hill	2.01
1984	Leroy Lucas	2.10
1985	Dalton Grant	2.15
1986	Andy Hutchinson	2.04
1987	John Munroe	2.05
1988	Chris Innes	2.07
1989	Hopeton Lindo	2.12
1990	Brendan Reilly	2.21
1991	Brendan Reilly	2.20
1992	Steve Smith	2.10
1993	Andrew Lynch	2.11
1994	James Brierley	2.15
1995	Michael Robbins	2.15
1996	Darren Joseph	2.15
1997	Ben Challenger	2.16

1998	Colin McMaster	2.10
1999	Jason McDade	2.10
2000	Jamie Russell	2.05
2001	Chuka Enih-Snell	2.14
2002	Martin Aram	2.10
2003	Martyn Bernard	2.13
2004	Adam Scarr	2.09
2005	Nick Stanisavljevic	2.02
2006	Robbie Grabarz	2.15
2007	Alan McKie	2.09
2008	Chris Baker	2.06
2009	Scott Johnson	2.09
2010	Sam Bailey	2.10
2011	Allan Smith	2.04

POLE VAULT

(Instituted 1970)

1970	Steve Chappell	4.20
1971	Brian Hooper	4.35
1972	Stephen Clark	4.11
1973	Girish Patel	4.00
1974	Keith Stock	4.30
1975	Willoughby Best	4.45
1976	Keith Stock	4.30
1977	Daley Thompson	4.40
1978	Tim Anstiss	4.30
1979	Tim Anstiss	4.40
1980	David Hooper	4.60
1981	Billy Davey	4.60
1982	Billy Davey	5.10
1983	Frank Evers IRL	4.60
	(2, Andy Ashurst 4.60)	
1984	Andy Ashurst	5.00
1985	Paul Wray	4.50
1986	Mike Edwards	4.71
1987	Mike Edwards	4.80
1988	Ian Tullett	4.70
1989	Dylan McDermott	4.70
1990	Warren Siley	4.80
1991	Nick Buckfield	4.70
1992	Neil Winter	5.00
1993	Paul Williamson	4.80
1994	Ian Wilding	4.70
1995	Neil Young	4.70
1996	Craig Guite	4.60
1997	Christian Linskey	5.00
1998	Christian Linskey	4.70
1999	Christian Linskey	5.21
2000	Mark Beharrell	4.80

2001	Daniel Broadhead	4.50
2002	Richard Hurren	4.90
2003	Keith Higham	4.90
2004	Keith Higham	5.05
2005	Alex Williams	4.60
2006	Luke Cutts	5.00
2007	Luke Cutts	5.40
2008	Andy Marsh	5.00
2009	Andrew Sutcliffe	4.70
2010	Andrew Sutcliffe	5.30
2011	George Sharp	4.70

LONG JUMP

(Instituted 1969)

1969	Ian Anderson	6.72
1970	Stewart Atkins	6.97
1971	Don Porter	6.76
1972	Ian Hardie	6.82
1973	Stephen Wright	6.95
1974	Trevor Paice	6.95
1975	Albert Earle	6.81
1976	Daley Thompson	7.21
1977	Daley Thompson	7.20
1978	Gus Udo	7.28
1979	Trevor Sinclair	7.24
1980	John King	7.03
1981	David van Dyke	7.14
1982	Jeremy Pilling	7.02
1983	Fred Salle	7.13
1984	Lynton Boardman	7.22
1985	Barry Nevison	7.20
1986	Nick Riley	7.27
1987	Garry Slade	7.32
1988	Stewart Faulkner	7.81
1989	Kevin Liddington	7.50
1990	Richard Perry	6.95
1991	Chris Cotter	7.24
1992	Steve Smith	7.06
1993	Essop Merrick	6.88
1994	Chris Davidson	7.21
1995	Ciaran McDonagh IRL (2, Nathan Morgan 7.18)	7.37
1996	David Clerihew	7.24
1997	Nick Dowsett	6.82
1998	Stuart Wells	7.13
1999	Chris Tomlinson	7.44
2000	Chris Tomlinson	7.48
2001	Thomas Roe	6.88
2002	Jason Comissiong	7.07

AAA Champions

2003	Ryan James	7.12
2004	Samuel Jegede	7.24
2005	Greg Rutherford	7.60
2006	John Carr	6.96
2007	Andrew Jones	7.18
2008	Jamie Blundell	7.25
2009	Dwyte Smith	7.24
2010	James Davies	7.13
2011	James Davies	7.19

TRIPLE JUMP

(Instituted 1970)

1970	Matthew Cannavan	13.56
1971	Matthew Cannavan	13.76
1972	Stefan Nowak	14.00
1973	Frank Attoh	14.18
1974	Aston Moore	14.77
1975	Aston Moore	15.68
1976	Keith Connor	15.20
1977	Eric McCalla	14.51
1978	Megarry Effiong	15.19
1979	Stephen Metcalfe	14.49
1980	John Herbert	15.15
1981	Mike Makin	15.60
1982	Vernon Samuels	15.20
1983	Steven Anderson	15.14
1984	Ronnie Corbin	15.37
1985	Richard Edwards	14.49
1986	Mark Seeley	15.05
1987	Paul Johnson	15.30
1988	Patrick Teape	14.79
1989	Junior Campbell	15.27
1990	Julian Golley	15.27
1991	Dave Reeve	15.05
1992	Ezra Clarke	14.83
1993	Larry Achike	15.94
1994	Larry Achike	15.48
1995	Kori Stennett	14.59
1996	Marvin Bramble	15.04
1997	Jon Wallace	15.44
1998	Nicholas Thomas	15.20
1999	Tosin Oke	15.66
2000	Chris Tomlinson	15.31
2001	Kevin Thompson	14.36
2002	Kevin Thompson	14.93
2003	Christian Campbell	14.28
2004	Christian Campbell	15.16
2005	James Townsend	14.41
2006	Jude Beimers	15.23

2007	Stefan Tseng Ke Chen SIN	14.82
	(2, Trevor Okoroafor 14.62)	
2008	Stefan Tseng Ke Chen SIN	15.71
	(2, Nonso Okolo 14.88)	
2009	Babatunde Amosu	15.19
2010	Ben Williams	15.95
2011	Joe Lawrence	15.10

SHOT

(Instituted 1966 at 5.44kg; 6.25kg from 1971; 7.26kg from 1974; 6kg from 2003)

1966	Geoff Capes	16.57
1967	not held	
1968	not held	
1969	Jon Wood	15.53
1970	John Corbett	16.83
1971	Peter Wilson	14.18
1972	Peter Sharman	14.59
1973	Peter Sharman	14.11
1974	Ian Lindley	14.23
1975	Paul Buxton	15.75
1976	Andy Vince	13.75
1977	Andy Vince	14.91
1978	Tony Zaidman	14.30
1979	Graham Savory	15.52
1980	Tony Zaidman	16.16
1981	Tony Zaidman	16.49
1982	Billy Cole	16.33
1983	Chris Ellis	16.21
1984	Billy Cole	17.00
1985	Chris Ellis	16.73
1986	Simon Williams	16.18
1987	Matt Simson	15.68
1988	Matt Simson	17.60
1989	Matt Simson	18.14
1990	Mark Davies	15.54
1991	David Condon	15.14
1992	Bryan Kelly	14.53
1993	John Tyler	14.36
1994	Simon Fricker	14.17
1995	Bruce Robb	14.38
1996	Carl Myerscough	15.13
1997	Carl Myerscough	16.85
1998	Emeka Udechuku	17.02
1999	David Readle	15.57
2000	Greg Beard	15.39
2001	Greg Beard	16.10
2002	Sam Westlake-Cann	14.57
2003	Dave Dawson	16.07
2004	Chris Gearing	17.72

2005	Chris Gearing	18.57
2006	Jamie Williamson	17.05
2007	Jay Thomas	17.01
2008	Jamie Stevenson	18.01
2009	Curtis Griffith-Parker	18.51
2010	Robert Mohan	17.56
2011	Andrew Doyle	16.15

HEPTATHLON

(Instituted in 1987 at Octathlon; Heptathlon since 1991 except for Pentathlon in 1997 & 1998)

1987	Anthony Brannen	5383
1988	David Bigham	5677
1989	Brian Taylor	5938
1990	David Bigham	6217
1991	Barry Thomas	5259
1992	Gavin Sunshine	5113
1993	Brett Heath	4557
1994	Brett Heath	4455
1995	Mark Bushell	4960
1996	Dean Macey	5026
1997	Erik Toemen	3234
1998	Ben Roberts	3254
1999	Jason McDade	4990
2000	Jamie Russell	4725
2001	Alex Zulewski	4700
2002	Edward Dunford	4758
2003	Edward Dunford	5343
2004	Kevin Sempers	5060
2005	Andrew Staniland	4984
2006	Daniel Awde	5069
2007	Daniel Awde	5123
2008	Michael Holden	5025
2009	David Guest	5372
2010	Jack Andrew	5295
2011	Liam Ramsay	5290

3000 METRES WALK

(Instituted in 1995)

1995	Stuart Monk	12:50.67
1996	Stuart Monk	12:43.33
1997	David Kidd IRL	12:40.17
	(2, Michael Kemp 12:54.70)	
1998	David Kidd IRL	12:45.85
	(2, Michael Kemp 12:49.55)	
1999	David Kidd IRL	13:24.41
	(2, Lloyd Finch 13:34.58)	

2000	Dominic King	12:44.51
2001	Lloyd Finch	12:30.97
2002	Dominic King	12:24.78
2003	Luke Finch	13:14.69
2004	Nick Ball	12:47.41
2005	Nick Ball	12:47.40
2006	Nick Ball	12:44.75

(discontinued after 2006)

UNDER-17

60 METRES

(Instituted in 1969)

1969	Tony Hadley	7.1
1970	Bob Munns	7.0
1971	Paul Evans	7.1
1972	Keith Rollins	7.2
1973	Alexander Gillies	7.1
1974	Ian Cooper	7.1
1975	David Baptiste	7.0
1976	Mike McFarlane	6.9
1977	Darren Bills	6.8
1978	Mike Powell	7.04
1979	Richard Haycock	7.0
1980	Mark Grzesiak	7.05
1981	Robert Brown	6.9
1982	Paul Keeble	7.13
1983	Elliot Bunney	7.02
1984	Robert Johnson	7.27
1985	Jamie Nixon	7.0
1986	David Cornthwaite	7.01
1987	Jason Livingston	7.06
1988	Andrew Mensah	7.03
1989	David Jackson	6.96
1990	Mark Walcott	6.95
1991	Michael Nartey	7.0
1992	Sam Omonua	7.01
1993	Kevin Mark	6.96
1994	Dwain Chambers	6.95
1995	Christian Malcolm	6.96
1996	James Davis	7.1
1997	Daniel Plummer	7.04
1998	Mark Lewis-Francis	6.79
1999	Mark Lewis-Francis	6.77
2000	Monu Miah	7.06
2001	Matthew Ouche	6.99
2002	James Ellington	6.93
2003	Craig Pickering	6.88

2004	Harry Aikines-Aryeetey	6.88
2005	Gerald Phiri	6.83
2006	Funmi Sobodu	7.04
2007	Andrew Robertson	6.87
2008	Kieran Showler-Davis	6.94
2009	Aaron Saunders	7.03
2010	David Bolarinwa	6.81
2011	Kelvin Tairou	7.00

200 METRES

(Instituted in 1968)

1968	Stewart Atkins	23.7
1969	Tony Hadley	23.7
1970	Stephen Ware	24.0
1971	not held	
1972	not held	
1973	not held	
1974	not held	
1975	Michael Garmston	23.4
1976	Michael Garmston	23.4
1977	Peter Little	23.0
1978	Roger Bennett	23.1
1979	Mark Fabes	23.3
1980	Lincoln Asquith	22.3
1981	Roger Hunter	22.9
1982	Martin Waldron	23.0
1983	Ade Mafe	21.95
1984	Mark Tyler	23.11
1985	Thomas Gibson	23.30
1986	Wayne McDonald	22.94
1987	Matthew Lampard	23.05
1988	Richard Howard	23.21
1989	Adrian Patrick	22.89
1990	Mark Walcott	22.48
1991	Guy Bullock	22.61
1992	Simon Bryant	22.48
1993	Kevin Mark	22.07
1994	Ross Baillie	22.51
1995	Christian Malcolm	22.25
1996	Luke Davis	22.45
1997	Tim Benjamin	22.43
1998	Tim Benjamin	21.51
1999	Paul Whitehouse	22.54
2000	Aaron Aplin	22.35
2001	Rikki Fifton	22.21
2002	James Ellington	21.80
2003	Julian Thomas	21.77
2004	Daniel Fagan	21.75
2005	Gerald Phiri	21.57

2006	Tony Corrigan	22.11
2007	Rhion Samuel	22.18
2008	Dan Putnam	21.94
2009	Jordan Arthur	22.26
2010	David Bolarinwa	21.59
2011	Josh Platt	22.30

400 METRES

(Instituted in 1969)

1969	Bob Munns	55.8
1970	Bob Munns	53.1
1971	Paul Sankey	52.8
1972	Phillip Grimshaw	51.0
1973	Wayne Tarquini	51.8
1974	Dale Bluemink	51.4
1975	Robert Bishopp	51.2
1976	Kenneth Worrall	51.9
1977	W Gibson	51.9
1978	Sidique Ahamed	50.9
1979	Philip Harvey	50.7
1980	John Weston	50.7
1981	Chris Thompson	51.0
1982	Ade Mafe	50.3
1983	Ade Mafe	49.8
1984	Mark Tyler	50.41
1985	Roger Henton	50.74
1986	Graham Fell	51.24
1987	Paul Wood	51.03
1988	Craig Winrow	50.28
1989	Robert Yates	51.70
1990	Simon McCullough	52.70
1991	Steve McHardy	49.79
1992	Guy Bullock	48.15
1993	Mark Hylton	49.62
1994	Dean Park	50.10
1995	Nizamul Hoque	50.88
1996	Kris Stewart	49.2
1997	John Shenava	50.17
1998	Gary Ankers	50.45
1999	Michael Snow	50.52
2000	Craig Erskine	50.24
2001	Richard Davenport	49.49
2002	Richard Davenport	48.58
2003	Ryan Thomas	49.45
2004	Bruce Tasker	48.85
2005	Christopher Smith	50.12
2006	Tom Miller	49.26
2007	Ross McDonald	48.78
2008	Thomas Hinton	49.94
2009	Paul Scanlan	49.17

| 2010 | Alex Boyce | 48.62 |
| 2011 | Clovis Asong | 48.39 |

800 METRES

(Instituted in 1968)

1968	Glenn Page	2:03.4
1969	not held	
1970	Kevin Williams	2:04.3
1971	Graham Side	2:00.9
1972	Tony Dyke	2:00.0
1973	John Ashton	1:58.1
1974	Malcolm Edwards	1:55.6
1975	K Rodgers	2:00.5
1976	Robert Berridge	2:00.9
1977	Julian Spooner	1:57.2
1978	Nigel Harper	1:57.9
1979	Paul Potter	1:58.7
1980	Colin Burton	1:59.6
1981	David Powell	1:59.7
1982	David Perks	1:59.7
1983	Daren Neale	1:58.40
1984	Gary Patterson	1:58.74
1985	Andrew Standen	1:59.61
1986	Paul Burgess	1:54.79
1987	Craig Winrow	1:54.65
1988	Craig Winrow	1:53.86
1989	Mark Sesay	1:54.01
1990	Alex Bowden	1:57.88
1991	Dan Park	1:58.47
1992	Eddie King	1:58.72
1993	Andrew Dale	2:00.59
1994	Bryan Hendry	2:02.39
1995	Matthew Dixon	1:58.43
1996	Matthew Crompton	2:01.89
1997	Barry Woodward	1:58.56
1998	Aaron McIndoe	2:00.08
1999	Ryan Preddy	1:57.77
2000	Adam Davies	1:58.86
2001	Richard Dowse	1:58.59
2002	Rhian Hastey	2:01.31
2003	Grant Prendergast	1:57.59
2004	Sam Bradley	1:58.95
2005	Andrew Gibson	1:57.40
2006	Nathan Woodward	1:55.83
2007	Charles Eastaugh	1:57.85
2008	James Senior	1:56.87
2009	Lloyd Hilton	1:58.91
2010	Robert Needham	1:56.43
2011	Matt McLaughlin	1:54.80

1500 METRES

(Instituted in 1969)

1969	Richard Findon	4:22.0
1970	David Miller	4:06.0
1971	Andy Barnett	4:10.6
1972	Barrie Moss	4:00.8
1973	Martin Wilson	4:00.0
1974	Sean Cahill	4:09.0
1975	Stephen Gilbey	4:03.7
1976	Chris Miller	4:07.7
1977	Steve Flint	4:07.3
1978	Richard Brightman	4:07.3
1979	Kelvin Newton	4:06.9
1980	Martin Maynard	4:08.9
1981	Alistair Currie	4:02.9
1982	Chris Damerell	4:04.8
1983	Darrell Smith	4:04.48
1984	Steve Halliday	4:06.7
1985	Davey Wilson	4:06.81
1986	D Morris IRL	4:11.20
	(2, Ben Mabon 4:12.21)	
1987	Wayne Dart	4:06.17
1988	Paul Darkins	4:06.76
1989	David Thompson	4:11.02
1990	not held	
1991	Richard Scholes	4:06.72
1992	Edward Bowen	4:06.41
1993	Paul Draper	4:11.00
1994	Paul Draper	4:10.38
1995	Matthew Dixon	4:04.62
1996	Ross Fittall	4:06.12
1997	Matthew Bailey	4:08.11
1998	Stephen Bates	4:05.40
1999	Ian Boneham	4:09.95
2000	Stephen Davies	4:06.02
2001	David Ward IRL	4:13.54
	(2, Tom Snow 4:16.36)	
2002	Colin Costello IRL	4:07.97
	(2, Sean Dirrane 4:09.57)	
2003	Matt Wood	3:59.71
2004	Brian Markham IRL	4:11.24
	(2, James Mills 4:12.98)	
2005	Simon Lawson	4:04.37
2006	Kenny Boyd	4:09.56
2007	Noel Collins IRL	4:09.52
	(2, Tom Bowerman 4:14.80)	
2008	Sean Bowden	4:10.07
2009	Stuart Ferguson	4:13.54
2010	Andrew Monaghan	3:57.65
2011	James Lamswood	4:01.79

3000 METRES

(Instituted in 1994)

1994	Richard Burke	9:27.72
1995	Gareth Turnbull	8:54.1
1996	Matthew Watson	9:03.77
1997	Matthew Bailey	9:11.85
1998	not held	
1999	Stephen Murphy	9:10.99
2000	Ahmed Ali	9:04.38
2001	Ahmed Ali	8:58.74
2002	Tom Snow	9:08.44
2003	David Bishop	9:06.83
2004	Brendan O'Neill IRL	9:01.27
	(2, Andy Nixon 9:12.12)	

(discontinued after 2004)

60 METRES HURDLES (3'0")

(Instituted in 1977)

1977	Peter Adams	8.2
1978	P Whelan IRL	8.57
	(3, A Desmond 8.99)	
1979	Kieran Moore	8.6
1980	Tom Leeson	8.3
1981	Paul Brice	8.6
1982	Ererton Harrison	8.34
1983	Jon Ridgeon	8.07
1984	Gary Lee	8.5
1985	Brett St Louis	7.92
1986	Glenn Davies	8.17
1987	David Bigham	8.42
1988	Mark Purser	8.34
1989	Carlton Haddock IRL	8.10
	(2, Berian Davies 8.18)	
1990	Neil Owen	8.17
1991	Richard Dunn	7.99
1992	Chris Pember	8.43
1993	Matthew Clements	8.13
1994	Damien Greaves	7.99
1995	Liam Collins	8.30
1996	Chris Baillie	8.33
1997	Chris Baillie	8.07
1998	Nathan Palmer	8.23
1999	Allan Scott	8.09
2000	Edward Dunford	8.10
2001	Edward Dunford	8.07
2002	Tom Stimson	8.27
2003	Richard Alexis-Smith	8.12
2004	Daniel Davis & Daniel Maynard	8.09

2005	Julian Adeniran	8.11
2006	Michael Baker	8.21
2007	James McLean	7.99
2008	Jack Meredith	7.89
2009	Themba Luhana	8.22
2010	Jake Porter	8.20
2011	James Taylor	8.17

HIGH JUMP

(Instituted in 1984)

1984	Nick Hay	1.97
1985	John Hopper	2.03
1986	Hopeton Lindo	2.00
1987	Tim Blakeway	2.01
1988	Brendan Reilly	2.02
1989	Brendan Reilly	2.13
1990	Andrew Lynch	1.94
1991	Antoine Burke IRL	1.97
	(2, Philip Diamond 1.94)	
1992	Stuart Ohrland	1.99
1993	Brad Knowles	1.96
1994	Robert Holton	1.90
1995	Edward Willers	1.96
1996	Colin McMaster	2.00
1997	Simon Bannister	1.93
1998	Ken McKeown	2.07
1999	Chuka Enih-Snell	2.02
2000	Chuka Enih-Snell	2.07
2001	Martyn Bernard	1.95
2002	Jamie Thomas	1.95
2003	Nick Stanisavljevic	1.95
2004	David Shields	2.02
2005	Darren Hammond	1.99
2006	Cameron Lake	2.03
2007	Mike Ehlen	1.95
2008	Sam Bailey	2.01
2009	Jordan Roach	1.89
2010	Patrick Jowett	1.95
2011	Chris Kandu	1.90

POLE VAULT

(Instituted in 1977)

1977	Tim Anstiss	3.60
1978	Tim Anstiss	4.21
1979	Billy Davey	3.90
1980	Billy Davey	4.30
1981	Jimmy Lewis	4.31
1982	Steve Fuller	4.00

1983	Alastair Graham	3.80
1984	Ian Lewis	4.10
1985	Ian Lewis	4.35
1986	Daniel Chalkley	4.20
1987	Justin Richards	4.10
1988	D Sheridan IRL	3.90
	(2, Patrick Daly 3.90)	
1989	Warren Siley	4.50
1990	Elton Hunt	4.20
1991	Peter Eyre	4.00
1992	Neil Turner	3.90
1993	Neil Young	4.40
1994	Martin Parley	4.00
1995	Christian Linskey	4.60
1996	Christian Linskey	4.70
1997	Richard Smith	4.20
1998	Chris Type	4.20
1999	Cameron Johnston	4.20
2000	Oliver Mahoney	4.20
2001	Chris Tremayne	4.40
2002	Keith Higham	4.60
2003	Michael Walker	3.80
2004	Michael Walker	4.40
2005	Andy Marsh	4.20
2006	Andy Marsh	4.65
2007	Ben Gregory	4.31
2008	Tim Parkin	4.30
2009	Lewis Newton	4.00
2010	Daniel Gardner	4.30
2011	Rowan May	4.80

LONG JUMP

(Instituted in 1970)

1970	Mike Ademola	6.02
1971	Martin Laker	6.13
1972	Stephen Kohut	6.44
1973	Stephen Pegler	6.65
1974	Andrew Taylor	6.38
1975	Gus Udo	6.37
1976	Gus Udo	6.66
1977	Trevor Sinclair	6.54
1978	Leroy White	6.37
1979	John Furnham	6.67
1980	Hugh Teape	6.85
1981	Mark Brooks	6.43
1982	Steve Folkard	6.58
1983	Barry Nevison	6.84
1984	David Roughley	6.68
1985	Tony McMurray	6.57

1986	Neil Wood	6.28
1987	Kevin Liddington	6.74
1988	Mark Gregory	6.49
1989	Oni Onuorah	6.90
1990	Oni Onuorah	7.07
1991	Darren Habberley	6.53
1992	Andrew Davies	6.17
1993	Matt Lethbridge	6.44
1994	Andrew Thornton	6.65
1995	David Butler	6.45
1996	James Morris	6.54
1997	Kevin Burke IRL	6.62
	(2, Robert Hollinger 6.40)	
1998	Chris Tomlinson	6.95
1999	Allan Scott	6.73
2000	Marlon Lewis	6.61
2001	Onen Eyong	6.78
2002	John Fletcher	6.57
2003	Danny Harris	6.77
2004	Luke Thomas	6.68
2005	Luke Thomas	6.78
2006	Nonso Okolo	6.76
2007	Kieran Showler-Davis	6.79
2008	David Guest	6.79
2009	James Lelliott	6.72
2010	Elliot Safo	7.00
2011	Oliver Newport	6.83

TRIPLE JUMP

(Instituted in 1977)

1977	Richard Garlick	13.39
1978	Nick Leech	13.71
1979	Anthony Bloomfield	14.10
1980	Hugh Teape	14.74
1981	Vernon Samuels	14.87
1982	Steve Folkard	13.78
1983	Lynton Boardman	13.74
1984	Lawrence Lynch	14.58
1985	Darren Gomersall	14.39
1986	Paul Farmer	13.62
1987	Mark Lawrence	13.75
1988	Philip Clarke	13.56
1989	Dave Reeve	13.74
1990	E Mahoney	12.81
1991	Ezra Clarke	13.08
1992	Adlan Woodhouse	13.31
1993	Marvin Bramble	14.13
1994	Matthew Thompson	13.63
1995	Michael McKernan	14.17

1996	Richard McDonald	13.66
1997	Leon Burnett	13.46
1998	Steven Shalders	14.42
1999	Allan Scott	13.74
2000	Kevin Thompson	13.82
2001	Gary White	13.72
2002	Graham Jackson	13.53
2003	Dexter Nicholls	13.26
2004	Jeremy Odametey	14.21
2005	Sean Wynter	13.68
2006	Stefan Tseng Ke Chen SIN	15.18
	(2, Nonso Okolo 13.70)	
2007	Kola Adedoyin	13.77
2008	Tunde Amosu	14.70
2009	Julien Allwood	14.12
2010	Bradley Pike	14.13
2011	Efe Uwaifo	14.24

SHOT (5kg)

(Instituted in 1971)

1971	Stephen Archer	15.27
1972	Andrew Monaghan	15.68
1973	Peter Cramer	14.34
1974	Shaun Hughes	14.05
1975	Andy Vince	16.03
1976	Alan Husk	16.67
1977	Tony Zaidman	14.69
1978	Tony Zaidman	17.87
1979	George Brocklebank	16.88
1980	Billy Cole	15.55
1981	Billy Cole	18.09
1982	Chris Ellis	18.37
1983	Mitchell Smith	14.72
1984	Simon Williams	15.84
1985	Guy Litherland	15.77
1986	Matt Simson	17.24
1987	Neal Brunning	17.45
1988	Jason Mulcahy	15.22
1989	Milo Kamu	16.63
1990	Malcolm Croad	13.96
1991	Simon Fricker	15.34
1992	David Burnett	15.51
1993	Matthew Bundock	14.96
1994	Emeka Udechuku	14.89
1995	Emeka Udechuku	18.14
1996	Carl Myerscough	18.40
1997	Adrian Cluskey	16.00
1998	Greg Beard	15.26
1999	Greg Beard	16.89

2000	Carl Saggers	16.21
2001	Eoin Leen IRL	18.25
	(2, Edward Dunford 15.50)	
2002	Andrae Davis	16.40
2003	Chris Gearing	18.09
2004	Shane Birch	15.97
2005	Jay Thomas	16.68
2006	Curtis Griffith-Parker	17.82
2007	Michael Wheeler	17.95
2008	Michael Wheeler	19.06
2009	Matthew Halton	15.55
2010	Chris Barnes	15.06
2011	Matthew Field	15.57

HEPTATHLON

(Instituted in 1997 as Pentathlon; Heptathlon since 2008)

1997	Robert Hollinger	3499
1998	James Anthony	3360
1999	Steven Green	3044
2000	Edward Dunford	3608
2001	Edward Dunford	3710
2002	Andrae Davis	3670
2003	Andrew Staniland	3306
2004	Oliver McNeillis	3556
2005	Nathan Woodward	3131
2006	Nathan Woodward	3314
2007	David Guest	3758
2008	Jack Andrew	4827
2009	Joseph Hutchinson	4560
2010	Blade Ashby	4612
2011	Tadgh Healy	4729

UNDER-15

60 METRES

(Instituted in 1991)

1991	Kevin Mark	7.29
1992	Jermaine Williams	7.17
1993	Ben Barnes	7.39
1994	Steven Wiggans	7.43
1995	Wayne Gray	7.34
1996	Tristan Anthony	7.38
1997	Tristan Anthony	7.23
1998	Darren Watson	7.50
1999	Kamil Tejan-Cole	7.42

2000	Alexander Coley	7.35
2001	Julian Thomas	7.37
2002	Andrew Watkins	7.06
2003	Danny Doyley	7.40
2004	Yusuf Aliu	7.29
2005	Deji Tobais	7.36
2006	Deji Tobais	7.25
2007	Laurence Owen	7.19
2008	Richard Hodgson	7.08
2009	Alex Kiwomya	7.28
2010	Alex Kiwomya	7.05
2011	Myles Richardson	7.13

200 METRES

(Instituted in 1991)

1991	Kevin Mark	24.45
1992	Michael Tietz	23.32
1993	Arif Shah	23.58
1994	Robert Allenby	23.74
1995	Wayne Gray	23.68
1996	Tristan Anthony	23.64
1997	Tristan Anthony	22.78
1998	Ryan Preddy	23.35
1999	Graham Blackman	23.79
2000	James Ellington	23.18
2001	Julian Thomas	22.74
2002	Andrew Watkins	22.57
2003	Craig Eaglesham	23.52
2004	Precious Ojighoro	23.15
2005	Tony Corrigan	22.77
2006	Deji Tobais	22.89
2007	Laurence Owen	22.76
2008	Joshua Hughes	23.52
2009	Feron Sayers	23.16
2010	Alex Kiwomya	22.19
2011	Myles Richardson	22.80

400 METRES

(Instituted in 1998)

1998	Ryan Preddy	50.72
1999	not held	
2000	not held	
2001	Craig Glanville	51.38
2002	Lewis Robson	52.67
2003	Precious Ojighoro	54.76
2004	Precious Ojighoro	53.71
2005	James Peden	53.24

2006	Dan Putnam	52.42
2007	Gerwyn Morgan	52.24
2008	Tom Holligan	52.86
2009	Matthew Hudson-Smith	52.78
2010	Aaron Pitt	51.01
2011	Ben Robbins	51.36

800 METRES

(Instituted in 1991)

1991	Jon Goodwin	2:12.04
1992	Paul Draper	2:04.77
1993	James Colclough	2:10.22
1994	Marc Newton	2:03.52
1995	Barry Woodward	2:05.26
1996	David Moulton	2:06.69
1997	Aaron Wilson	2:18.05
1998	Edward Bailey	2:08.79
1999	Richard Dowse	1:59.05
2000	Luke Hopson	2:11.08
2001	Alex Felce	2:03.88
2002	Martyn Gibbons	2:04.40
2003	Matthew Young	2:08.66
2004	Michael Cole	2:01.37
2005	Nicholas Johnson	2:06.40
2006	James Senior	2:03.13
2007	Paul Scanlan	2:07.68
2008	Daniel Chesworth	2:04.54
2009	Jack Gleave	2:04.92
2010	Joseph Lancaster	2:07.92
2011	Nikita Katende	2:01.95

60 METRES HURDLES (2'9")

(Instituted in 1991)

1991	Jon Snade	8.51
1992	Matthew Clements	8.30
1993	Christian Bird	9.12
1994	Patrick Brown	9.15
1995	Brian Pearce	8.80
1996	Jonathan Crawshaw	8.85
1997	Tim Greenwood	8.93
1998	Tim Sinclair	8.80
1999	Damien Munnelly IRL (2, Patrick Collins 8.99)	8.70
2000	Kevin Sempers	9.10
2001	Richard Alexis-Smith	8.28
2002	Daniel Davis	8.20
2003	Kieran Edward	8.95

2004	Matthew Tong	8.76
2005	James McLean	8.44
2006	Benjamin Cleary	8.69
2007	Ben Hopkins	8.99
2008	Cameron Goodall	8.61
2009	James Taylor	8.71
2010	Luke Jenkins	8.73
2011	Stanley Livingston	8.63

HIGH JUMP

(Instituted in 1991)

1991	Paul Smith	1.76
1992	not held	
1993	David Francis	1.71
1994	Kevin Drury	1.80
1995	Wayne Gray	1.88
1996	Ken McKeown	1.85
1997	Tim Greenwood	1.82
1998	Chuka Enih-Snell	1.91
1999	Mark Bidwell	1.80
2000	Mathew Chetwynd	1.69
2001	Alan Hassall	1.79
2002	Andrew Allan	1.78
2003	James Stokes	1.78
2004	Anthony Shurmer	1.71
2005	Nathan Williams	1.78
2006	John McCafferty	1.91
2007	Jack Jones	1.75
2008	Ross Walker-Stuart	1.92
2009	Feron Sayers	1.78
2010	Chris Alderman	1.75
2011	Scott McAnally	1.75

POLE VAULT

(Instituted in 1991)

1991	Neil Turner	2.85
1992	not held	
1993	Thomas Richards	3.50
1994	Christian Linskey	3.90
1995	Richard Smith	3.91
1996	Steven Brown	3.71
1997	Andrew MacDonald	3.50
1998	Michael Parker	3.00
1999	Chris Tremayne	3.20
2000	Steve Lewis	3.10
2001	Nathan Lawton	3.20
2002	Luke Cutts	3.30

2003	Andrew Marsh	3.00
2004	Andrew Marsh	3.30
2005	Tony Hillier	3.20
2006	Tim Parkin	3.20
2007	Tom Gibson	3.80
2008	Stephen Guest	3.60
2009	Nicholas Cole	3.00
2010	Harry Coppell	3.30
2011	Adam Hague	4.06

LONG JUMP

(Instituted in 1992)

1992	David Gilkes	6.15
1993	Nick Dowsett	5.82
1994	Marc Newton	6.04
1995	Kevin Hibbins	6.24
1996	Richard Phelan IRL	5.87
	(2, Christopher Jenkins 5.67)	
1997	Adam Wrench	5.48
1998	Alan Ruddock	5.70
1999	Paul Murphy IRL	5.78
	(2, Iain Hunt 5.58)	
2000	Alistair Hinze	5.91
2001	Paul Twidale	6.00
2002	Oliver McNeillis	5.89
2003	Luke Thomas	6.27
2004	Jamie Jones	5.98
2005	Deji Tobais	5.71
2006	Kieran Showler-Davis	6.23
2007	Matt Fletcher	6.17
2008	Robert Gayler	6.37
2009	Joel Grenfell	6.06
2010	Ross Maxwell	6.27
2011	Alex Law	5.85

SHOT (4kg)

(Instituted in 1992)

1992	Sudip Burman-Roy	13.14
1993	Ben Barnes	14.85
1994	Peter Waterman	13.54
1995	Adrian Cluskey	14.74
1996	Liam Walsh	13.84
1997	Christopher Wade	14.10
1998	Carl Saggers	15.74
1999	Eoin Leen IRL	15.05
	(2, Anthony Gallagher 13.90)	
2000	Simon Cooke	13.82

2001	Chris Gearing	14.73
2002	Shane Birch	14.98
2003	Jay Thomas	16.89
2004	Allan MacKay	12.83
2005	Michael Wheeler	14.76
2006	Michael Wheeler	17.46
2007	Tom Peacock	14.94
2008	Josh Newman	15.36
2009	Connor Guest	12.83
2010	John Kelly IRL	14.20
	(2, Daniel Preston-Routledge 12.40)	
2011	Kai Jones	14.47

PENTATHLON

(Instituted in 1992)

1992	Sam Allen	2404
1993	Sam Allen	2747
1994	Marc Newton	2800
1995	not held	
1996	not held	
1997	Tim Greenwood	2786
1998	Edward Dunford	2615
1999	James Dunford	2540
2000	Louis Moore	2865
2001	Ryan Shaw	2815
2002	Lewis Robson	2950
2003	Gregor Simey	2888
2004	Matthew Tong	2567
2005	James Harrison	2808
2006	David Guest	3087
2007	Cameron Irwin	2557
2008	Ross Walker-Smart	2680
2009	Jacob Paul	2932
2010	Aled Price	2708
2011	Sam Healy IRL	2796
	(2, Alex Law 2789)	

Index

Index

379

Index

Index

Index

Rowland, Mark 171, 173, 175, 199, 236
Rudd, Bevil 34, 37, 42–43
Rushmer, Alan 111
Rutherford, Greg 229–230, 232, 234, 236
Ryun, Jim 120, 141

Sage, Pat 183
Salazar, Alberto 143
Salvat, Frank 101
Sanderson, Tessa 153, 164, 220
Sando, Frank 80, 84
Savic, Milovan 137
Savidge, John 68, 78, 83
Scarsbrook, Stanley 56
Schmidt, József 110
Scott, Steve 30, 161
Searle, Vera 122
Segal, Dave 87, 100, 102
Segedin, Petar 76–78
Sharman, William 234
Sharp, Cameron 160
Sharpe, David 169
Shaw, Godfrey 18–19, 21, 88, 121, 145
Shearman, Montague 8–10, 13, 18, 34
Shenton, Brian 76
Sherwood, John 99, 110, 112, 114, 116, 124, 126
Shirley, Eric 85, 88, 100
Shrubb, Alf 23–25, 35, 59, 80, 99, 116, 131, 219
Silvester, Jay 103
Simmons, Tony 131, 134
Simpson, Joe 54
Simpson, Alan 108, 112, 117
Simson, Matt 191
Sinfield, Cyril 94
Singh, Milkha 100
Sir, Jozsef 57
Slykhuis, Wim 71
Smith, Alex 233
Smith, Calvin 163, 184
Smith, Chris 201
Smith, Colin 87–88, 90
Smith, Dave (English hammer thrower) 154, 166–67, 170, 233

Smith, Dave (Australian walker) 162
Smith, Geoff 162
Smith, Steve 188–89, 191–92, 194, 198–99, 236
Snell, Peter 43
Snook, William 11–13
Sollars, Lorretta 182
Solly, Jon 154, 170
Sotherton, Kelly 231
Sotomayor, Javier 165, 167
Spedding, Charlie 165
Stallard, Hyla 44, 47
Stamford Bridge 13, 15–17, 20–22, 24–26, 28–32, 34, 37, 40, 42–50, 52–53
Steele, Andrew 230
Steinle, Mark 226
Stevens, Gerry 117
Stevenson, David 109, 111
Stewart, Ian 99, 116–18, 124–26, 128–31, 135, 138
Stewart, Lachie 110, 125–26, 129
Stewart, Peter 128–29
Stinson, Robert 121, 145–46
Stock, Keith 155, 156, 158, 175
Stones, Dwight 14, 137
Storey, Stuart 113, 115
Strode-Jackson, Arnold 31, 35, 122
Sturgess, Bill 20
Sugioka, Kuniyoshi 104
Summers, Mike 216
Sunday Times 39, 153
Sutherland, Colin 140
Sweeney, Arthur 56–57, 61–62
Szabo, Gabriela 182

Taber, Norman 44
Tábori, László 83, 101
Tagg, Mike 114, 116, 126
Taipale, Armas 32
Taitt, Laurie 105
Tancred, Bill 115, 126, 130–31, 135, 143, 175
Tancred, Peter 115, 135
Tanui, William 184
Tarrant, John 95
Tayler, Dick 134
Taylor, Dick 116–17
Taylor, Graham 111

Index